# The **Media** in **Europe**

# The **Media** in **Europe**

## The Euromedia Research Group

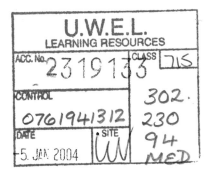
Edited by

## Mary Kelly

## Gianpietro Mazzoleni

## Denis McQuail

SAGE Publications
London • Thousand Oaks • New Delhi

First published 2004

SAGE Publications Ltd
6 Bonhill Street
London EC2A 4PU

SAGE Publications Inc.
2455 Teller Road
Thousand Oaks, California 91320

SAGE Publications India Pvt Ltd
B-42, Panchsheel Enclave
Post Box 4109
New Delhi 100 017

**British Library Cataloguing in Publication data**

A catalogue record for this book is available from the
British Library

ISBN 0 7619 4131 2
ISBN 0 7619 4132 0 (pbk)

**Library of Congress Control Number: 2003101546**

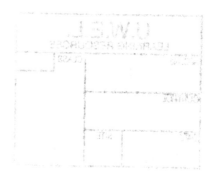

Typeset by C&M Digitals (P) Ltd., Chennai, India
Printed in Great Britain by The Cromwell Press Ltd, Trowbridge, Wiltshire

# Contents

# Notes on contributors

**Els De Bens** is Professor in the Department of Communication Science, University of Ghent, Belgium.

**Kees Brants** is Director of the M.A. in European Communication Studies at the University of Amsterdam and holds a Special Chair in Political Communication at the University of Leiden, the Netherlands.

**Jean-Marie Charon** is a sociologist and media specialist at the Centre national de la recherche scientifique (CNRS) and teaches at the Institut d'étude politique de Reunes.

**Jan Čulík**, Ph.D., is Lecturer in Czech studies at the University of Glasgow and editor of the Internet cultural and political daily *Britské*.

**Mario Hirsch** is a journalist, teacher and researcher on economic and policy aspects of the mass media, Luxembourg.

**Olof Hultén** is Head of Strategic Analysis, Corporate Development, Sveriges Television, Stockholm, Sweden.

**Karol Jakubowicz**, Ph.D., works for the National Broadcasting Council, Poland's regulatory authority.

**Mary Kelly** is Lecturer in the Department of Sociology, University College, Dublin.

**Bálazs Kiss** is Deputy Director of the Institute of Political Science of the Hungarian Academy of Sciences.

**Hans Kleinsteuber** is professor at the Institute of Political Science, University of Hamburg, Germany.

**Denis McQuil** is professor emeritus at the School of Communication Research, University of Amsterdam, and visiting professor at the University of Southampton, United Kingdom.

**Rosario de Mateo** is professor in the faculty of Communication Sciences at the Autonomous University of Barcelona, Spain.

**Gianpietro Mazzoleni** is Professor of the Sociology of Mass Communication and Political Communication, University of Milan, Italy.

**Werner A. Meier** is a media consultant and lecturer in the Department of Mass Communication, University of Zurich, Switzerland.

**Frands Mortensen** is Professor of Media Studies in the Department of Information and Media Studies, University of Arhus, Denmark.

**Helge Østbye** is Professor of Mass Communication at the University of Bergen, Norway.

**Marina Österlund-Karinkanta** is Senior Media Analyst at the European Union and Media Unit of the Finnish Broadcasting Company (YLE), Helsinki, Finland.

**Stylianos Papathanassopoulos** is Associate Professor of Media Organization and Policy in the Department of Communication and Media Studies, National University of Athens, Greece.

**Manuel Pinto** teaches in the Department of Communication Science, University of Minho, Portugal.

**Andrej Školkay** is lecturer in the Faculty of Mass Communication at the University of SS Cyril and Methodius in Trnava, Slovakia.

**Helena Sousa** teaches in the Department of Communication Science, University of Minho, Portugal.

**Josef Trappel** is head of media and communication research with Prognos, European Centre for Economic Research and Strategy Consulting, Basel, Switzerland.

**Wolfgang Truetzschler** is Senior Lecturer in Communication at the Dublin Institute of Technology, Ireland.

**Jeremy Tunstall** is Research Professor of Sociology, City University, London, United Kingdom.

**Elena Vartanova** teaches in the Faculty of Journalism at Moscow State University, Russia.

**Vida Zei** teaches communication studies at the University of Iowa and the University of Ljubljana, Slovenia.

# Acknowledgements

The Euromedia Research Group, primarily responsible for this book, belongs to a network of European reseachers that began life in 1982 as a workshop on media policy, convened by Dr Karen Siune of Arhus University, within the framework of the European Consortium for Political Research (ECPR). Since then it has continued on its own initiative, changing in membership over time, but with the same working methods and purposes. It aims to collect and exchange information and to develop and apply frameworks that help to describe and analyse developments in media structure and policy in the European region. The core activity of the group has been to meet regularly in each others' countries and to produce a sequence of books. One series (as in this case) is essentially informative, another analytical and devoted to the current media issues of the day. The most recent title in the latter series is *Media Policy: Convergence, Concentration, Commercialisation*. In the present case, the work of group members has been supplemented by a set of contributions from new colleagues and we are extremely grateful for this generous collaboration. We thank our very helpful publishers for encouragement and practical help and as editors we thank each other for our hard work and good co-operation in bringing disparate elements together successfully in the last few months.

**Denis McQuail**
**Mary Kelly**
**Gianpietro Mazzoleni**

# How to use this book

This book provides an accessible and informative account of European media systems.

Each chapter dealing with a single country follows the same structure and covers the same topics so that the reader should be able to find relevant information quickly and also make comparisons between countries on particular issues without difficulty. In place of an Index, we provide in advance a list of the section headings to be found in each chapter, as follows:

## NATIONAL PROFILE

### History, Structure and Ownership of the Media

*Print media:*

- The newspaper press
- The magazine press
- Book publishing

*Electronic (audio-visual) media*

- Television ▬
- Radia
- Film and video

*Internal and related on-line media*

### Politics, Policy, Law and Regulation

### Statistics

### References

# Introduction

DENIS McQUAIL

## THE BOOK

This is the fourth version of a handbook of European media systems produced by the Euromedia Research Group. It began in 1986 (as *Electronic Media Policy in Europe,* Berlin, Campus Verlag) and has since been published in two editions by Sage (1992 and 1997). On each occasion there has been extensive revision and updating and also a development of purpose. In the second edition, our scope was enlarged to cover the newspaper press as well as broadcasting and electronic media. For this new version we have enlarged the scope yet further to deal with all forms of a mass media, including the Internet. We have also, acccordingly, devised a new common structure for each 'national chapter'. Most importantly, this is no longer a book about 'Western Europe' (as in the title of the second edition), since we include chapters about Central and Eastern European countries, including Russia. Unfortunately, limitations of space (and even some uncertainties about what constitutes 'Europe') have prevented us from representing the whole European region, but we cover 85 per cent of its inhabitants, leaving Russia and the Ukraine aside. This enlargement has reflected the significant changes of the 1990s and also enriched the content for those who might use the book for comparative study of media systems.

The main aims of the book are to provide clear and informative accounts about the media system of each country, with reference to: media structure and audiences; ownership; new economic and technological developments; major policy issues and initiatives. The Euromedia Group began as a network for the study of media policy and media politics, with particular reference to changes caused by computerization, satellites and economic changes in the 1980s. As a result, the descriptions offered are informed by a deep understanding of the underlying social and political forces at work, and are not simply compilations of facts. Each chapter is also a chapter in the overall story of the national society concerned, told by an expert observer. In addition to description and analysis, a set of basic statistics about the media system of each country is appended, plus sources for further reading. The statistics are taken for the most part from secondary sources and are intended to support and illustrate the preceding analysis rather than to be used as primary sources in themselves for cross-national comparison.

## THE EUROPEAN CONTEXT

This book will be used for reference and is unlikely to be read as a whole, but anyone who does read it all, as the editors have done, is bound to be struck by the paradox of unity and dissimilarity of this set of national 'stories'. On the one hand, it supports the view that European media have much in common with each other and are quite distinct from those of the United States, Japan, Latin America, China, etc. A reading of the accounts from former communist countries also leaves the impression that these countries have rapidly rejoined the mainstream of European cultural and social traditions. On the other hand, the more one learns about each country the more different each story appears. For the most part, the homogeneity stems from economic and technological and political factors that are inevitably of much the same kind across a relatively small continent. The differences stem more from social, cultural and geographical factors. An intertwined history of the nations concerned makes a contribution to both similarity and difference.

Some of the more common features of the different systems include the: shared basic principles of law, human rights and democracy that have gradually been established since World War II; the existence of a mixed public and private broadcasting system in all countries; a tradition that permits (even if it discourages) some intervention in the media on grounds of public interest; competitive party political systems that still give shape to the outlook of the media and to their opinion-forming role; the role played by institutions of the European Union and the Council of Europe in regulating for access, diversity, harmonization of regulation and the pursuit of some cultural goals; the similar forces that everywhere make for linguistic and cultural identification, even if they then make for differentiation.

There are some evident dimensions of difference, with varying origins. One such is the variable grip of the mass newspaper on public attention and even of newspaper reading in general, some countries being avid readers, others not. A similar but not clearly related variable is the relative appeal of television and other audio-visual media, as measured by time spent. Another difference is the obvious one of size, with certain countries having a population or language hegemony and many small countries struggling somewhat with the consequences of this and the difficulties of viability and self-sufficiency in a global media environment. Thirdly, there are countries where public broadcasting is still well funded, secure and holding its own and others where it is none of those things. Fourthly there are differences in the extent to which party politics has a grip on the media in one way or another and others where the media keep more of a distance or devote themselves to non-political activities. Fifthly, there are still quite a few differences in the manner of distribution of electronic media, which change very slowly for reasons not easy to account for. This mainly concerns the varying rates at which cable television and satellite television have made inroads into terrestrial broadcasting. Finally we can note that the phenomenon of a 'digital divide' shows up very clearly in unequal rates of access and use, only partly explicable in economic terms.

## THE MAIN ISSUES

The different national cases reflect in different ways the response to a number of unresolved issues facing different media in different ways. At the most general level, four or five issues dominate the European media scene and have done so for some time. One of these relates to the long struggle for and against the deregulation and 'commercialization' of the electronic media in particular. For obvious reasons, this affected the former communist countries most intensively in the last few years, but it was already being experienced elsewhere. In most countries a new order has gradually emerged, without any public monopoly and with steadily increasing scope for commercial enterprise and private ownership. In some respects this might now seem to be an 'end-game' in which a cornered public broadcast sector fights a rearguard action against ultimate marginalization or worse. There is certainly a struggle over the alleged privileges and uncertain role of public service broadcasting but it is premature to forecast the conclusion.

The second main issue has to do with the development and application of new technologies that, over the course of the last two decades, have upset the reigning regulatory arrangements and ignited a smouldering conflict between public and private forces. The current phase of instability and uncertainty from this cause is linked with the digitalization of transmission and reception and also the growing role of the Internet in the overall media landscape. Thirdly, there is a long-running issue over the structure of ownership, affecting all media. There are commercial pressures towards long-term increases in the scale of media enterprises, involving transnational and cross-media developments of ownership. These trends are supported to some extent by the European Union, although they challenge principles of diversity and openness that are also valued at European level. Some countries have an interest in promoting the growth of dominant media firms, while others see it as threatening.

A fourth issue, with several dimensions, has to do with the whole process of Europeanization or integration at the level of Europe, in terms of media economic activity and policy. There are now a number of integrative elements in place and the idea of considering the wider context of Europe in making national policy has long been accepted. The debates about these matters used to focus on threats to national and European cultural identity and integrity arising from the globalization of media and the 'threat' of American cultural 'invasion'. This is no longer such an active issue, although in fact not fully resolved. The scope for cultural 'protectionism' is still under threat, although it is no longer open to a simple black-and-white formulation of options.

Finally, there are questions of overall control and accountability that have been raised by the expansion and (commercial) liberalization of media systems. There has been a reduction of supervisory capacity at the national level, without much compensation at the European level (although there is some capacity there). There are a number of media problems that have been diagnosed as increasing in the changed circumstances. These include the alleged declining cultural and informational standards of media across the board, under the influence of competitive pressures, lack of insulation from outside and weakening control. The arrival of the Internet promotes fears of accentuated 'old' problems of content harmful to the young and generally undesirable, or new problems in the form of cyber-crime and challenges to intellectual property relations. Essentially, the overall media scene is open to characterization as entering a state of 'ungovernability' or at best 'normlessness'. In practice there is little chance (or wish) of returning to stricter control, except where 'terrorism' or crime is at issue (and developments here offer little comfort). In many countries there is no practical means to combat the excesses of the media in respect of privacy, human rights or standards of decency. The goal of effective self-regulation is often emphasized but is largely still beyond reach.

These broad issues are only part of the story in each country and many of the following chapters give fascinating insights into local debates and conflicts, especially where competition between different media is involved and where politics gets involved, as it inevitably does.

# 1: Austria

JOSEF TRAPPEL

## NATIONAL PROFILE

Austria is located in the heart of Europe and is considered one of the 'bridges' between East and West because of its permanently neutral status since independence after the World War II. With its small home market of around 8 million inhabitants living in a surface area of 84,000 km², Austria is not one of the powerful economic forces in Europe. Its once important role in international diplomacy has declined over the years but, still, Austria hosts several departments of the United Nations in the International Centre in the capital, Vienna.

Austria shares borders with Germany, the Czech Republic and the Slovak Republic, Hungary, Slovenia, Italy, Switzerland and Liechtenstein. Deriving from the time when Vienna was the capital of the Austro-Hungarian monarchy, there are still some language minorities today living mainly in the southern and eastern parts of the country, but the large majority share the German language with its northern and western neighbours. Austria is an almost entirely Catholic country, with a small but growing Muslim community in and around the capital.

Since 1 January 1995 Austria has been a full member of the European Union and party to the Schengen agreement. In 2002 Austria replaced its former currency, the Schilling, with the euro.

Austria is a parliamentary democracy with a federal constitution. The President is head of state, with a primarily representative function. In parliament there are four parties, of whom the Social Democrats are the largest. In the general election of November 2002 the People's Party (ÖVP) gained a relative majority of 42 per cent over the Social Democrats (SPÖ), with 37 per cent, the right-wing nationalist Freedom Party (formerly the National Liberal Party, FPÖ), with 10 per cent, and the Green Party, with 9 per cent. After several months of talks, in March 2003 the ÖVP and the FPÖ formed a coalition government again. In 2000 the same coalition had provoked a harsh reaction from EU member states and the international diplomatic isolation of Austria for several months.

The new government concentrated its efforts on the critical issues of public deficits and implemented strict cost-cutting initiatives, with severe implications not only for the media sector.

## STRUCTURE AND OWNERSHIP

Austria's media landscape is characterized by high concentration, strong national media conglomerates and growing influence by international media actors. Since World War II the print media and electronic media have developed in a symbiotic relation, with a strong public service broadcaster on the one hand and equally strong local press barons on the other. The party-affiliated press declined over the 1980s and 1990s, leaving Austria with just three minor-party newspapers with diminishing public meaning. In contrast, press conglomerates became the driving economic forces of the 1990s with high ambitions in the newly opened area of private radio and television broadcasting. Public service broadcasting responded successfully with highly popular programming strategies.

## The print media

### The newspaper press

Austria's daily newspaper press restarted business after World War II and the full sovereignty of the republic (1955) with just thirty five newspapers. The following years were characterized by the rapid growth of the 'boulevard' press on the one hand and a first round of press concentration on the other. The circulation share of the party press declined from 50 per cent (1953) to 20 per cent (1971) (cf. Pürer, 1990) and reached a negligible share of 2.5 per cent in 2001.

The former flagships of the Social Democrat Party (*Arbeiter-Zeitung*) and the communist party (*Volksstimme*) were both shut down in 1991. The several newspapers of the Christian Democratic Party were dwarfed over the decades, only the *Neues Volksblatt* surviving with a minor circulation. In 2002 three partisan papers still existed.

This decline was paralleled by the unprecedented and spectacular growth of the *Neue Kronen-Zeitung*. This daily newspaper was founded in 1959, became the market leader in 1971 with a market share of 29 per cent and kept growing for thirty years thereafter. In 2001 the *Neue Kronen-Zeitung* represented some 43 per cent of the overall circulation of newspapers and is – in relative terms – considered one of the largest newspapers worldwide.

Market success as well as internal rivalry have driven the *Neue Kronen-Zeitung* into structural changes in the late 1980s. In 1988 the then two owners of the highly profitable *Neue Kronen-Zeitung* decided to dissolve their agreement and one of them took over the shares of the other. The remaining single owner had to pay for the shares of his former partner but was not able to find sufficient financial backing in Austria. Eventually, he sold 45 per cent of the company to the German *Westdeutsche Allgemeine Zeitung* (*WAZ*; 1 January 1988). Six months later, in June 1988, the *WAZ* landed its second *coup*. It acquired 45 per cent of the second largest newspaper, the *Kurier*. Subsequently, the two newspapers together formed the powerful company Mediaprint for joint operations in printing, advertising acquisition and distribution. In the following years the *WAZ* increased its stake to 50 per cent in the *Neue Kronen-Zeitung* and to 49 per cent in the *Kurier*. In 1996 Mediaprint controlled some 54 per cent of all newspaper printing and some 51 per cent of newspaper distribution in Austria (Melischek and Seethaler, 1999: 133). This interlinked conglomerate expanded its operations to the magazine sector, holding shares in all relevant weekly magazines.

The economic and editorial dominance of the *Neue Kronen-Zeitung* is to some extent balanced by the regional press. Most of the regional press barons face little or no regional competition in their home market, providing them with a quasi-monopolistic position. However, the *Neue Kronen-Zeitung* started to run regional editions, successfully challenging the regional press. This market configuration leaves little room for additional secondary newspapers. In April 2001 one such newspaper in Styria (the *Neue Zeit*) had to shut down its presses as a consequence of continued losses in the regional readership and advertising market. Just one such secondary newspaper each remains in Upper Austria, Salzburg, Vorarlberg and Carinthia; no such paper exists in Styria or Tyrol. There is no regional daily newspaper at all in Lower Austria or in Burgenland.

International media investment is less important in the regional press, although the German Axel Springer Verlag (which in Germany publishes among others the *Bild-Zeitung*) holds the majority share (65 per cent) of the regional daily *Tiroler Tageszeitung*, published in Innsbruck.

Only in the capital, Vienna, do newspaper owners provide the 1.6 million population with more diversity. Readers can choose between six daily local newspapers, with one being state-controlled (*Wiener Zeitung*). This highly competitive market is divided into a boulevard segment and a quality segment.

The monopolistic boulevard segment is dominated by the *Neue Kronen-Zeitung*, unchallenged since its rival newspaper *Täglich Alles* had to shut down its printed version in August 2000. Since then, *Täglich Alles* has been published only as a purely online newspaper. In March 2002 the *Neue Kronen-Zeitung* itself launched the free sheet *U-Express*, distributed in Underground (subway) stations in Vienna. By this step the management successfully thwarted the market entry of a competitor from abroad.

The quality segment is more competitive, with three main and two marginal newspapers. The *Kurier* is the second largest newspaper in circulation terms and is part of the *WAZ*/Mediaprint conglomerate. Even more quality-oriented, *Die Presse* competes with *Der Standard*. The former newspaper was controlled for decades by Austrian industrialists who first sold the majority of the shares (51 per cent in 1991) and later (December 1999) the remaining shares to Styria, the company publishing the largest daily in southern Austria (*Kleine Zeitung*) with strong affiliations to the conservative party.

In contrast, *Der Standard* is a 1988-launched liberal newspaper, financed with the initial support of the German Axel Springer Verlag, which pulled out its 50 per cent share in 1995. Since December 1998 the German Verlag *Sueddeutsche Zeitung* controls some 49 per cent of *Der Standard*. This newspaper has grown rapidly and reached a circulation level of some 120,000 copies daily (2000), about the same as its rival *Die Presse*.

Moreover, two smaller daily quality newspapers are published in Vienna. The *Wiener Zeitung* is state-owned and has the longest tradition of all newspapers in Austria. The *Wirtschaftsblatt* was launched with the assistance of the Swedish Bonnier group in October 1995, which still holds a 50 per cent stake in this slowly growing newspaper.

In general, the Austrian market for daily newspapers has reached an unprecedented degree of concentration. Of sixty six newspapers that have ever existed since World War II, fifty three have been shut down (Steinmaurer, 2002b). Among the remaining papers, some five are not economically viable. The size of the *Neue Kronen-Zeitung* with more than 1 million copies daily is out of all economic proportion and leaves very little room for the development of stimulating competition underneath.

### The periodical and magazine press

The rather limited diversity of the daily newspaper press is counteracted by a large number of weekly newspapers, magazines and other periodicals. All over Austria, weekly and monthly newspapers reflect regional and local events, some of them with remarkable economic success. Some 160 such newspapers are periodically published, with the *Niederösterreichische Nachrichten* (NÖN) and the *Oberösterreichische Rundschau* (OÖR) being the largest. Both publications are weekly newspapers with a strong local bias.

At the national level, the 1990s experienced a fierce competition between news and general interest magazines, ending with the conclusion of a co-operation agreement that unites the competitors under a shared entrepreneurial umbrella. In the 1970s the news and current affairs magazine *Profil* was launched. After several successful years the magazine was acquired by *Kurier* and integrated into the Mediaprint publishing group.

In 1992 the start-up company Verlagsgruppe *News* founded *News* as a popular weekly news, entertainment and lifestyle magazine. The German Axel Springer Verlag provided some 50 per cent of the funding, reduced its share later to 25 per cent and pulled out completely in 1998. This publication complemented *Profil* on the one hand and the existing weekly boulevard magazine *Die ganze Woche*, which was launched in 1985, on the other.

The overwhelming market success of *News* inspired the publishers to launch more entertainment-oriented magazines. In 1995 they launched *TV media*, an exhaustive television programme guide, in October 1998 *Format*, another news and current affairs magazine to compete with *Profil*, in 2000 *E-media*, a magazine addressing the Internet generation, and in November 2001 *Woman*, a fashion and lifestyle magazine for women. This rapid expansion was partly financed by the German Gruner & Jahr Verlag, part of the Bertelsmann group. Gruner & Jahr replaced the Axel Springer Verlag and took over 75 per cent of the Verlagsgruppe *News* in March 1998.

With the launch of *Format*, the Verlagsgruppe *News* attacked explicitly the market leader *Profil*. From the outset all actors were aware that the Austrian market was too small to support two news magazines addressing the same readership. It took less than two years of aggressive marketing before *Profil* had to capitulate and agree to far-reaching economic co-operation. Since September 2000 all magazines of the Verlagsgruppe *News* and *Profil* with its affiliated publications have been united under one editorial umbrella. The Austrian Federal Competition Court criticised this merger but finally accepted it on condition that *Profil* was guaranteed editorial independence for at least another four years (until 2006).

This merger of parts of the Verlagsgruppe *News* with parts of Mediaprint accelerated further the trend towards print media ownership concentration in Austria. In fact, there remain just two groups. The few small and medium-size regional newspapers are confronted with a highly integrated conglomerate comprising not only the first and second largest daily newspaper, all relevant news and entertainment magazines but also the financial power of the German Bertelsmann and *WAZ* groups.

### Book publishing

The latest survey (2001) counted 1,002 book publishers in Austria, of which the vast majority are not large enough to employ anyone else but the publisher. More than 800 of these publishers have a backlist of fewer than fifty titles. At the other end of the scale, only sixteen publishers have more than 500 titles to offer (source: Buchmarketing, 2001).

During the 1970s and 1980s some 3,000 new titles were released annually by Austrian publishers, a number that increased during the 1990s to some 5,000 on average. Compared with the 90,000 titles published in the German language every year, Austria contributes a fair share. However, a closer look reveals that the large majority of these newly published books have little or no market success. Measured by the percentage of titles that are reprinted at least once, only 10 per cent of all new books published in Austria are successful.

There are several reasons for this phenomenon. First, the German-language area appears as a quite homogeneous book market, much more so than the newspaper, television or radio markets. German-language books are equally available in Germany, Austria and Switzerland, with a strongly unbalanced trade structure. In 1998 Austria exported books to the value of €30.6 million to Germany, but imported books for €221.6 million, creating a substantial trade deficit. The much larger German market attracts young authors, who often leave their Austrian publisher after their successful first book and choose a German publisher thereafter. Second, the small size of the Austrian market does not allow for large structures as in Germany. Scheipl concludes that this disadvantage precludes economies of scale and prevents smaller actors from being profitable. Smaller publishers are confronted with much higher distribution costs and therefore lower profits. This mechanism disadvantages not only Austrian publishers but all publishers in the German language market below a critical sales volume (cf. Scheipl, 2002: 113).

In general, internationalization characterized the book publishing industry in Austria during the 1990s. In particular, larger and economically viable non-fiction publishers were acquired by international players. In 1995, Wolter Kluwers took over the Bohmann Verlag and acquired a 40 per cent stake in Manz two years later. Reed Elsevier entered the Austrian market in 1998 by acquiring the Orac Verlag, a publisher concentrating on legal and economic books. In 2000 the Sueddeutsche Verlag in Munich took over the majority of shares both in the Wirtschaftsverlag and in the Wirtschaftsverlag Ueberreuter. The conservative government announced furthermore its intention to sell the state-owned but economically successful Österreichischer Bundesverlag and its literary publishing companies (among them Residenz, Deuticke, Brandstätter) to private – possibly foreign – investors.

The state supports the publishing industry basically with three measures. First, the VAT rate for books amounts to 10 per cent, half the regular VAT rate. Second, direct subsidies are granted to publishers. In 2001 some €2.9 million was made available for this 'support for literature'. Third, Austria retained its system of fixed book prices. According to the respective law that entered into force in July 2000, publishers are entitled to fix the selling price of every book, and bookshops have to respect this price for at least twenty four months. A similar legal basis in Germany and Switzerland allows harmonized book prices in the entire German-language area.

## The electronic (audio-visual) media

Austria's broadcasting system is strongly dominated by the public service broadcaster, the ORF (Österreichischer Rundfunk), by any measure the largest media company in Austria. Until 1995 the ORF was the only legal broadcasting operator in Austria. Private broadcasters started operations after a long and painful process, repeatedly troubled by legal and administrative pitfalls.

By 2002 broadcasting in Austria was governed by the Federal Constitutional Law to safeguard the Independence of Broadcasting of 1974. The constitutional law defines broadcasting as a 'public service' to include both terrestrial and cable operations and prescribes the passing of legislation which will guarantee objectivity and impartiality of coverage, a range of viewpoints and the independence of the institutions and individuals concerned with broadcasting.

Furthermore, the legislation provides for separate laws for public and private broadcasting. The Federal Act on the Austrian Broadcasting Corporation of 1974, last amended in 2001, enables the ORF to broadcast public service-oriented programmes for radio, television and the Internet. The private sector is regulated by two federal laws, one on private radio broadcasters (Act on private radio broadcasting of 1993) and one on private television broadcasters (Act on private television of 2001).

Compared with most European countries, Austria has introduced a dual system of public and private operators with a considerable delay. While Austrian business and policy actors were unable to agree on a suitable agenda regarding how to proceed in broadcasting legislation during the 1990s, the level of international competition confronted the new private broadcasters in Austria with rather unfavourable economic starting conditions.

### Television

By 2002 more than 80 per cent of all Austrian households were either equipped with satellite receivers or linked to a broadband cable network. These households receive around forty television channels in the German language, one of which is an encrypted pay channel (Premiere World). Among these forty channels, only two are of Austrian origin, ORF-1 and ORF-2. Private local television programming is available on cable networks only in selected regions of Austria.

Despite this high number of available television programmes in the German language, the public service broadcaster ORF has managed to retain its leading position in the audience ratings. In 2001 the two public television channels reached a combined market share of 56 per cent, leaving 43 per cent to foreign competitors. Behind ORF-1 (23 per cent) and ORF-2 (32 per cent) followed the German channels RTL (6 per cent), Sat1 and ProSieben (5 per cent each). Even in cable and satellite households ORF held a stable 48 per cent of the viewing market between 1996 and 2001 (all data from Teletest 2001). This considerable market success of ORF is best explained as a consequence of its programme policy, which is oriented towards a mass audience.

The two channels are well received by the Austrian audience for different reasons. While ORF-1 is focused on entertainment – some 58 per cent of programming time is dedicated to entertainment genres and just 6 per cent to information – ORF-2 is highly successful with local content. In contrast, 64 per cent of the programming time is devoted to information and 35 per cent to entertainment. Between 18.00 hrs and 19.30 hrs from Monday to Friday, each regional studio presents local and regional news and current affairs programmes. These programme formats reach on average by far the highest audience, outpacing even the main news at 19.30 hrs. However, these local programming formats are the most expensive programme genres of the ORF.

This programming strategy reflects to some extent the economics of the Austrian public service broadcaster. Advertising and licence fee revenue contribute about the same amount to the global budget of the ORF. In the year 2000, 43 per cent of the total revenue of €853 million came from licence fees and 42 per cent from advertising sales (15 per cent comes from miscellaneous sources, among which the sale of broadcasting rights is the most important). Given this balanced revenue mix, programming has to satisfy the requirements of the advertising industry by attracting the fourteen to forty-nine age group and at the same time respect the public service remit that basically requires programming to cater for all citizens. ORF's response to this twofold challenge is the clear distinction between the entertainment-oriented concept of ORF-1 and the public service orientation of ORF-2.

Both channels are distributed by terrestrial means all over Austria as well as via digital satellite in encrypted format. Reception of ORF digital via satellite requires a smart card and the proprietory set-top box or D-box, which was designed for reception of the German digital pay-TV Premiere World. Moreover, the ORF contributes programmes to the German offering of ZDF digital as well as BR alpha from the Bavarian public service broadcaster.

ORF's television activities are complemented by its participation in the pan-European German-language channel 3SAT, which is managed by the four public service broadcasters ARD, ZDF (Germany), SRG SSR idée suisse (Switzerland) and the ORF. Furthermore, ORF runs together with a private partner TW1, a tourism and weather channel distributed free-to-air via digital satellite.

In early 2002 private television broadcasting virtually did not exist. The policy quagmire following the first law on private radio broadcasting in 1993 delayed the process of establishing a sound legal basis for private television until 2001. Only at the regional level, and then restricted to cable and satellite distribution, did some private broadcasters experiment. None of the private channels thus established any importance in terms of audience market share (all below 2 per cent).

However, after finally adopting the Law on Private Television in July 2001, the licensing process was completed by February 2002 and ATV was selected as operator for the one and only nationwide terrestrial frequency. Operations are expected to start in autumn 2002. ATV Privatfernseh-GmbH is owned by a mixed consortium of Austrian banks (Bawag, Erste), the pan-European holding company SBS, the cable operator UPC (which owns Austria's largest cable network, in Vienna) and, as largest shareholder, by the German Concorde Media, a Munich-based film rights company and television operator of Tele München, both controlled by Herbert Kloiber.

This first national private television operator is financed entirely by advertising revenue, limited only by the European restrictions as provided in the 'Television without frontiers' directive. Television advertising in Austria, which represented some 23 per cent of the whole national adverting market in 2001, is shared not only between the two channels ORF-1 and ORF-2 but also with so called 'advertising windows' used by the major private television channels originating in Germany and available on Austria's cable networks. By 2002 seven such 'advertising windows' were operational, selling advertising time on channels such as RTL, Sat1, ProSieben, RTL-2, etc. Technically, German advertising blocks are replaced by Austrian advertising spots mainly during prime time by Austrian cable operators. The Austrian advertising industry welcomed these additional slots as the former monopoly of television advertising held by the ORF vanished. Together these 'advertising windows' reached revenue totalling €87 million in 2001.

### Radio

Despite all policy efforts to encourage the development of a strong and vital private radio broadcasting industry in Austria, the ORF dominated the market in 2002. ORF's radio division produces four radio channels

serving distinct audiences. The local and regional channel Ö2 has the largest audience and reached an audience market share of some 39 per cent in 2001. Second is the rock and pop channel Ö3,which is distributed nationwide, reaching a market share of 38 per cent. The advertising-free classical music and information oriented channel Ö1 came third with some 5 per cent of the market and FM4, a new internationaly oriented channel, came last with just 2 per cent.

This market success leaves little room for the private sector. Since the early 1980s the Publishers' Association (Verband österreichischer Zeitungen) intended to develop private radio as a new business field but failed to propose a viable legal model to the government. In 1995, finally, the first private regional radio channels started operations in Salzburg and Styria, followed by a slew of forty three new channels all over Austria by April 1998. In each of the nine regions (*Länder*) one regional operator and a number of local operators were licensed, with the local press publishers running in almost all cases the largest radio station. The most successful of these channels reached some 15 per cent of the regional market, but the large majority was unable to survive despite a generous allowance of 172 minutes' advertising per day (since 2001).

Economic constraints and political pressure resulted in a revision of the private radio law in 2001, allowing private national radio chains on the one hand and more involvement of press publishers on the other. Consequently, the private radio landscape followed the well known Austrian pattern of media concentration. Two groups managed to integrate radio operators at a national level. First, the Antenne group operates the leading private radio stations in six *Länder*. These stations are each partly owned by the respective regional press baron but operate under the same brand heading. Second, Mediaprint started to build up a national chain branded as Krone Hitradio, referring to the dominant newspaper *Neue Kronen-Zeitung*. All these channels broadcast a rather similar mix of adult contemporary music formats and some information.

Besides these concentrated radio stations, a variety of smallish radio stations mainly at the local level complement Austria's radio landscape. Some of them consider themselves as 'third sector', non-commercial and not-for-profit radio operators.

## Film and video

Watching movies in cinemas is enjoying increasing popularity in Austria. After a slow but steady loss of interest in cinemagoing from the late 1950s until the late 1980s, the number of visits has grown strongly since 1992. That year marked the all-time low, with just 9.3 million visits. The figure doubled within a decade and in 2001 some 18.9 million cinema tickets were sold (source: AKM).

The resurgence of interest is paralleled by a fundamental structural change. The first multiplex cinema was opened in 1994 in Vienna and initiated a veritable boom. By the end of 2001 no fewer than twenty two multiplex cinemas were in operation all over Austria, eleven of them located in Vienna. Together these cinemas offered 225 screens and 49,000 seats (source: Fachverband der Lichtspieltheater der Wirtschaftskammer Österreich). Simultaneously most of the traditional cinemas had to close down. One of the last remaining cinema chains owned by Austrian investors (City Cinemas) went bankrupt in February 2002.

The growing number of cinema visits provides growing revenue. In 1999 an annual turnover of some €100 million was generated by Austrian cinemas, and in 2001 the turnover increased to €127 million (estimate; source: Fachverband).

The structural change triggered by the arrival of the multiplex cinemas influenced the market success of movies launched on the Austrian market. During the 1990s, each year some 250 new movies were released in Austria, some 120 of which were of US origin. While this relation is rather stable, the market share of US movies increased. In the year 2000 all top ten movies in Austria were of US origin, in 2001 nine out of ten. US movies held a box-office market share of 69.8 per cent in 1999 (source: *European Statistical Yearbook* 2001). The general trend suggests that a smaller and smaller number of movies capture a higher and higher market share (cf. Ungerböck, 2002: 102).

Austria's film output employs some 700 to 1,400 on a regular basis and generates some €135 million per year. Around one-third is contributed by the production of television advertising spots, 10 per cent by the production of cinema movies. The remaining shares come from television production, mainly commissioned by the ORF.

The number of cinema movies produced annually in Austria or in co-production with other countries varied between ten and twenty during the 1990s, reaching a peak in 1999 with twenty three movies. Around half of them managed to be released in Austrian cinemas. In 2001 some 2.5 per cent of box-office receipts were generated by Austrian films. The most successful genre of Austrian movies is light entertainment and local comedy with strong regional affiliations and having little prospect of international cinema release.

A second category of successful Austrian films during the late 1990s was linked with the Austrian director Michael Haneke, who co-produced several highly reputed movies, recognized at the European level (Prize of the Jury in Cannes, 2001).

The small national market and the sober export perspectives mean that public funds are needed to keep movie production up and running in Austria. In 2002 the national fund of the Österreichisches Film Institut provided some €7.5 million in subsidies for movies of Austrian origin. Severe cuts in the federal budget for culture in general have diminished this lifeline for Austrian film drastically since 2000. In 1998 the respective amount was almost twice the 2002 level at €12.9 million.

Besides the federal fund, several regional funds make subsidies available for movie production with regional affiliations (location, subject, etc.). The city of Vienna provided some €8 million in 2002, some other *Länder* such as Tyrol, Lower Austria and Salzburg offered some €1 million that year. Finally, the ORF committed itself in a mutual agreement with the Austrian film industry to invest a minimum of €4.5 million annually in Austrian film production. In turn, the ORF holds the national broadcasting rights after eighteen months of cinema release. In fact the ORF is the most important source of financing for the Austrian film industry as a whole.

The Austrian video market is characterized by the replacement of video by digital versatile disc (DVD). In 2001, some 80 per cent of the Austrian households were equipped with a video-cassette recorder (VCR) and 5.8 per cent with a DVD player. Revenue from the sale and hire of video-cassettes stagnated at the level of some €90 million, while sales of DVD software grew rapidly. In 1999 some €2.7 million was spent, ten times more than the year before.

In conclusion, film and video in Austria attract a growing audience. Cinema visits have returned as an attractive alternative to competing leisure activities. However, structural changes favour non-European consumption and force Austrian movies into a small and uneconomic market niche.

## The Internet and related on-line media

As in most other European countries, Internet access developed rapidly during the late 1990s and the beginning of the new decade. By the end of 2001 some 53 per cent of the Austrian population had access to the Internet, and 42 per cent of them had their homes connected. Over just four years, the Internet access rate had quadrupled.

Austria's media realized quickly that the Internet might develop as a fourth medium along with press, radio and television, and during the euphoric years of the 'new economy' most of the existing media launched their own Web site. In July 1997, the ORF launched its own Web portal, ORF ON, which was a separate business unit from the beginning, operating from its own location, with no intrinsic link with *ORF's* radio or television programming. Almost immediately, the Web site www.orf.at became the most successful Austrian Web site measured in hits and visits.

The latest revision of the television legislation in 2001 ruled for the first time on the activities of the ORF on the Internet. Against the former status of unregulated complementary activity, the new law restricts Internet activities by the ORF to 'programme related' services.

Even before the ORF's Web initiative, the daily newspaper *Der Standard* developed a distinct Web site, with the newspaper content being just one element among a number of different special interest channels. Subsequently, all major publishers launched Web sites with a clear reference to the respective print media, like www.krone.at or www.news.at. No successful Web-only media have been founded so far. However, one daily newspaper, *Täglich Alles*, shut down its presses in August 2000 but the Internet edition survived as a Web-only offering.

## POLITICS, POLICY, LAW AND REGULATION

Austria's media policy does not have a strong track record of effective intervention.

It took until April 1998 before a sizeable number of private radio operators started business and it took until autumn 2002 for the first private television operator to launch its programme. While the government was concentrating on the single issue of how to provide a sound legal basis for private broadcasters, other important and urgent issues escaped the attention of media policy.

The late 1990s saw another wave of media concentration, first and foremost affecting the press sector. After the arrival of the large German publisher *Westdeutsche Allgemeine Zeitung*, which took control of the two largest newspapers in the late 1980s, the arrival of the Bertelsmann group in 2000 linked those dominant daily newspapers with the dominant magazine publisher at the business level. No government action whatsoever has been taken to prevent such media conglomerates forming.

The two ruling parties – one conservative and one nationalist – took over government in February 2000 and added another issue to the media policy agenda. The overarching goal of budgetary discipline affected all media, but the press had to pay the highest price. First, the press subsidy scheme was drastically cut back. From its peak in 1990, when some €15 million was spent as a 'specific subsidy for the diversity of the press', the scheme was reduced to less than €7 million in 2001. Until early 2002 no support model to replace the old subsidy regime had been adopted, leaving the majority of Austrian newspapers in an unclear position. Indeed, one of them had to shut down its presses (*Neue Zeit*).

Second, the government decided without prior notice to suspend its financial support for postal delivery of newspapers in 2001, with severe consequences for smaller newspapers without access to any other home delivery service. Following loud protests by publishers the government eventually agreed a more appropriate step-by-step approach.

Reforms in the broadcasting sector yielded mixed results. The first private radio law was passed in 1993 and enabled the licensing of one radio broadcaster in each of the Austrian *Länder* (two in Vienna) to transmit radio programmes to a regional audience. The law distinguished between regional and local radio, the difference being that regional radio had the right to cover the entirety of a *Land*, while local stations were restricted to their local transmission area.

The legal quagmire began when unsuccessful contenders questioned the legality of the Regional Radio Law and the Austrian Constitutional Court upheld their complaint in 1995. It took another two years to adopt a new radio law which finally enabled more than forty private radio operators to start operations in April 1998.

In parallel, a new administrative structure to govern the new private broadcasting sector was prepared (KommAustria). The new government accelerated the process considerably and prepared in addition a private television Bill. In 2001, finally, KommAustria was launched as an administrative body to grant licences and frequencies to private radio and television operators. Furthermore, the Law on Private Television passed parliament together with a renewed law on the public service broadcaster ORF.

The Austrian Communications Authority KommAustria operates as administrative office for radio and television under the control of the Federal Chancellor (Prime Minister). The intended legal independence had not been achieved. Equally KommAustria administers the telecommunication sector under the supervision of the respective Minister and enables this body to profit from administrative synergies. However, KommAustria has no competence in the press, film and book sectors.

In 2001 parliament put an end to the frequent revision of the Regional Radio Law and adopted a new Law on Private Radio, replacing the former law. Whereas the former law took cognisance of the high level of media concentration in Austria and restricted press publishers and other media owners to a maximum holding of 26 per cent of the shares in any private radio operator, the new law lifted this restriction together with the strict regionalization. As of 2001, media owners may acquire up to 100 per cent of the shares of a private radio operator, as long as they hold less than 30 per cent of their own regional or national market. Moreover, private radio channels may combine their transmission area to establish a nationwide radio chain. These amendments enhance further cross-media ownership, resulting in a strong economic and entrepreneurial interest by the press in private radio. None of the leading private radio stations is fully independent of publishing companies.

The law on Private Television, adopted in July 2001, provides for one terrestrial nation wide frequency to be used by one private television operator. Remaining television frequencies are either used for local television or reserved for digital multiplexes that were intended to start operations in 2003. While the substance of the law was not disputed, many observers questioned whether the remaining national frequency should be granted to an analogue private television channel with mediocre economic prospects or be used rather to enhance digitalization, offering up to six competing channels to be distributed all over Austria by one multiplex. The government finally opted for the analogue channel, with little concern for the economic viability of the suggested business plan. In February 2002 the national licence was granted to ATV, which aimed to start operations in autumn 2002.

The law does not restrict private television further than the provisions of the EU directive 'Television without Frontiers'. There are no obligations as to content or the schedule. As regards ownership, the same rules apply as to private radio operators, excluding those media owners who control more than 30 per cent of their own market.

The guiding policy outcome regarding public service broadcasting is to retain the ORF as a strong national broadcaster with a clearly defined public service remit. During the public debate preceding the Public Service Broadcasting Law's revision, the question was raised whether the entire ORF or at least one of the two channels should be transferred to private ownership. The audience success of the ORF and the strong resistance by its management finally prevented the government from splitting the ORF into pieces. As a result, the ORF was transformed into a public foundation, the former board of trustees was renamed the Foundation Council (thirty five members) and the former General Superintendent became the Director General.

The public service remit is described in much detail, but none of the principles is clearly operational. For example, the law stipulates that 'the well balanced total programme must contain an equivalent proportion of sophisticated substantive elements. The annual and monthly programme schedules of television must be designed in such a way that, as a rule, there is a choice of high-quality programmes at prime time' (Broadcasting Law 2001, para. 4, art. 3). Such open wording is unlikely to have much impact on the ORF's attitude to programming.

Another intention of the government was to limit the influence of political parties and politicians on the ORF. The law therefore prohibits any politician at the national, regional or local level from becoming a member of the Foundation Council. Nonetheless, the modality of seconding these non-politicians remained the same as under the old law. Consequently, so-called 'independent experts', nominated by the political parties, became council members. The first major act of the council was the election of the new Director General in December 2001, and the political bargaining between 'experts' was no different from that between 'politicians' before.

The third innovation concerned the Audience Council, an institution with limited powers to advise on programming issues. Six out of the thirty five members were elected by fax and by the ORF's audience. Every licence fee payer was entitled to vote for the candidates. Because of the limited relevance of the Audience Council, the interest of the public in voting was disappointing. Less than 10 per cent of the electorate participated in the election.

Austria's media policy has been strongly focused on the attempt to encourage private broadcasting despite media trends that suggest the importance of concentrating on the development of such issues as digitalization and its various implications for the entire media system. Nor did the anachronistic attempt to implement a dual system of analogue public and private broadcasters take the specificities of a small state, sharing a language with a giant neighbour at the edge of the digital media revolution, sufficiently into account. The new Austrian government had a fair chance to redefine media policy as an enabling support to promote new media genres and innovative digital media services. The option chosen by the government is likely to enhance the virulent tendency to media concentration and does not offer an innovative way forward.

## STATISTICS

| | | |
|---|---|---:|
| | National population, 2001 | 8,075,000 |
| | Number of households, 2001 | 3,234,000 |
| | Movie admissions (ticket sales) | 18,980,000 |
| | Books published, 2001 | |
| | (titles) | approx. 5,000 |

| | | |
|---|---|---:|
| **Print media** | Circulation of daily newspapers, 2000 | |
| | *Neue Kronen-Zeitung* | 1,133,000 |
| | *Kurier* | 307,000 |
| | *Kleine Zeitung* | 294,000 |
| | *Oberösterreichische Nachrichten* | 127,000 |
| | *Die Presse* | 123,000 |
| | *Der Standard* | 119,000 |
| | *Tiroler Tageszeitung* | 118,000 |
| | *Salzburger Nachrichten* | 105,000 |
| | *Vorarlberger Nachrichten* | 73,000 |
| | *Wirtschaftsblatt* | 59,000 |

| | | |
|---|---|---:|
| **Broadcast media** | Audience share of television channels originating in Austria, 2001 (% all television households) | |
| | Public service | |
| | ORF-1 | 23 |
| | ORF-2 | 32 |

| | |
|---|---:|
| Private television broadcasters | 1 |
| Foreign channels | 43 |

Audience share of main radio channels, 2001 (%)

| | |
|---|---:|
| Public service | |
| OE-1 | 5 |
| OE-2 | 39 |
| OE-3 | 38 |
| FM-4 | 2 |
| All public service radio channels (ORF) | 85 |
| | |
| Private | |
| Antenne radio Private | 5 |
| Krone Hit Radio Private | 3 |
| All private radio channels | 15 |

| | |
|---|---:|
| Percentage of households with: | |
| Satellite (2000) | 45.1 |
| Cable (2001) | 39.5 |
| Terrestrial pay-television | n.a. |
| Video-cassette recorder (2001) | 78.2 |
| Satellite receiver (2000) | 45.1 |
| DVD player (2000) | 1.8 |

| | | |
|---|---|---:|
| **Electronic media** | Percentage of households with: | |
| | Digital television reception | 4 |
| | Internet access (2001) | 42 |
| | Personal computer (2001) | 61 |
| | Mobile phone ownership (2001) | 78.2 |

| | | € million | % |
|---|---|---:|---:|
| **Advertising spend, 2001** | Newspapers (daily) | 571,200,000 | 28.3 |
| | Magazines (including weekly newspapers) | 547,000,000 | 27.1 |
| | Television | 464,200,000 | 23.0 |
| | Radio | 163,500,000 | 8.1 |
| | Other (including cinema, outdoor, etc.) | 272,500,000 | 13.5 |
| | Total | 2,018.4 | 100 |

| | | |
|---|---|---:|
| **Ownership** | Main media companies, 2000: turnover (□ million) | |
| | ORF | 853.5 |
| | Mediaprint | n.a. |
| | Styria (estimated) | 300 |
| | Salzburger Nachrichten | n.a. |
| | Vorarlberger Nachrichten | n.a. |
| | News Verlag | n.a. |
| | Kurier | n.a. |

# 2: Belgium

ELS DE BENS

## NATIONAL PROFILE

Belgium became a unitary state as recently as 1830. After a feudal period the territory that is now Belgium was part of the Burgundian empire in the late Middle Ages. At the close of the fifteenth century it came under the rule of the Spanish line of the Hapsburgs, and subsequently, from 1713 onwards, under that of the Austrian House of Hapsburg. From 1794 till the fall of Napoleon Belgium was part of France. When the Congress of Vienna redrew the map of Europe in 1815 it made Belgium a part of the Kingdom of the Netherlands. This lasted no longer than fifteen years until, following a brief revolution, Belgium gained its independence.

Belgium is geographically very small (30,528 km²), but densely populated with some 10 million inhabitants (336.3 inhabitants per square kilometre). It has no fewer than three officially recognized languages: Dutch (58 per cent of the population), French (31 per cent) and German (11 per cent). About 1 million inhabitants are foreign: not only immigrants from the Maghreb countries, Turkey and Eastern Europe, but also a large number of Europeans and Americans who are employed by the European Union, NATO, and a wide range of multinationals and international organizations that have their administrative headquarters in Brussels. Over 1,000 journalists are accredited and work in Belgium; their strong presence is the natural consequence of the major role Brussels plays as the centre of EU policy making. These numerous foreign journalists, however, report very little to their home base about Belgium itself, except for juicy scandals, such as those around Dassault/Agusta (politial and administrative corruption), Dutroux (paedophile rings), and the poisoning of the food chain through the leakage of dioxin in animal feed. Consequently, it is usually the sensational reports about Belgium that attract attention abroad.

For 500 years of its history Belgium formed part of some foreign state and the country is divided culturally and politically by the differences between Flemings and Walloons. This may explain the apparent lack of a strong sense of nationality.

The dissension between Flemings and Walloons has had a decisive impact on political life. In the newly independent Belgium, French was the only official language. However, under the impulse of the Flemish Movement, the Flemings gradually acquired equal rights. This Flemish emancipatory movement often caused forceful conflicts, but the gradual formation of a federal state, in which Flemings and Walloons enjoy equal rights, has come about through parliamentary action, in a democratic way, and without bloodshed.

Through a number of constitutional reforms Belgium has been evolving towards a federal state. This has led to the devolution of power from the central government to the various regional governments. As a result Belgium today has an extremely complicated state structure, with a multitude of institutions, and a ubiquitous bureaucracy.

Belgium has a multi-party system, but as there are no clear majority parties, governments are formed by painfully drawn-out coalition building. Until recently the strongest positions were occupied by the Christelijke Volkspartij (Christian People's Party) in Flanders and by the Socialist Party in Wallonia. The rise of the Green parties, the progress of the liberal party, and the

# REFERENCES

Böck, Margit (1998) *Leseförderung als Kommunikationspolitik. Zum Mediennutzungs- und Leseverhalten sowie zur Situation der Bibliotheken in Österreich.* Vienna: Österreichischer Kunst-und Kulturverlag.

Fabris, Hans-Heinz Luge and Kurt (1986) 'Austria', in Hans J. Kleinsteuber, Denis McQuail and Karen Siune (eds) *Electronic Media and Politics in Western Europe.* Euromedia Research Group Handbook of National Systems. Frankfurt and New York: Campus.

Institut für Publizistik and Kommunikationswissenschaft der Universität Salzburg, eds (1977) *Massenmedien in Österreich – Medienbericht II.* Vienna: Internationale Publikationen/Buchkultur.

Institut für Publizistik and Kommunikationswissenschaft der Universität Salzburg eds (1983) *Massenmedien in Österreich – Medienbericht II.* Vienna: Internationale Publikationen/Buchkultur.

Institut für Publizistik and Kommunikationswissenschaft der Universität Salzburg eds (1986) *Massenmedien in Österreich – Medienbericht III.* Vienna: Internationale Publikationen/Buchkultur.

Institut für Publizistik and Kommunikationswissenschaft der Universität Salzburg eds (1993) *Massenmedien in Österreich – Medienbericht IV.* Vienna: Internationale Publikationen/Buchkultur.

Melischek, Gabriele and Seethaler Josef, eds (1999) (eds) *Die Wiener Tageszeitungen. Eine Dokumentation.* V, *1994–1955.* Frankfurt am Main: Lang.

ORF (2001) *Der ORF im Wettbewerb. Da and Zusammenhange zur Finanzierung* Vienna: ORF.

Panzer, Fritz Scheipl and Elfriede *Buchverlage in Österreich. Marktteil Buchproduktion – Umfeldbedingungen* Buchkultur.

Purer, Heinz (1990) *Presse in Österreich.*

Scheipl, Elfriede (2002) 'Buchve Umbruch' in Thomas Steinmau *Konzentriert und Verflochten.* Innsb Munich: Bozen.

Steinmaurer, Thomas (2002a) 'Das Med Österreichs' in Hans-Bredow-Inst *Internationales Medienhandbuch 2(* Baden-Baden: Nomos.

Steinmaurer, Thomas (2002b) *Konzentri flochten. Österreichs Mediensystem im* Innsbruck, Vienna and Munich: Boze

Trappel, Josef (1992) 'Austria', in Ber Ostergaard (ed.) *The Media in Western Euromedia Handbook.* London: Sage.

Trappel, Josef (1996) 'Austria', in Ber Ostergaard (ed.) *The Media in Western Euromedia Handbook.* London: Sage.

Trappel, Josef (2001) *Fernsehmarkt Prognos-Bericht.* Basel: Prognos.

Ungerböck, Andreas (2002) 'Film und Nahaufnahme' in Thomas Steinmau *Konzentriert and verflochten.* Innsb Munich: Bozen.

emergence of a party of the extreme right in Flanders (10 per cent in the national parliament and 15.5 per cent in the Flemish parliament) have affected the traditional balance of political power.

Officially, Catholicism remains the major religion (75 per cent of the population), although fewer and fewer people attend religious services. Today Belgium's Catholic character is still reflected in the daily press, which remains close to the Catholic socio-political group (or 'pillar') and its institutions.

Belgium is a highly industrialized country with a high standard of living and a well developed welfare system. In 2002, 7 per cent of the economically active population were unemployed. The population is ageing (20 per cent over sixty five years old), there are many families with no children, the number of single-person households is on the increase, and the working population is no more than 36 per cent of all Belgians.

Belgium is also a country of political scandals and sleaze. Pervasive politicization and the far-reaching system of political favours have greatly inhibited dynamic, creative socio-political development. In recent years there has been an accumulation of scandals that have forced several Ministers to resign. Journalists have been involved in the hype round these scandals and have often been accused by the politicians and the magistrates of indulging in muckraking rather than practising investigative journalism. The upshot of this contention has been a review of the codes of journalism and the founding of a Council of Journalism.

## STRUCTURE AND OWNERSHIP

### The print media

#### The newspaper press

At the founding of Belgium its constitution guaranteed complete freedom of the press. This meant that the country enjoyed one of the most liberal press regimes in Europe at the time. As a result, a large number of foreign journalists who were persecuted in their native country came to Belgium. They contributed to a flourishing migrants' press, but they also left their mark on Belgian journalism.

In the newly created Belgian state the political opinion press was foremost in the newspaper industry. Most of the newspapers that

are still being published today were founded during the late nineteenth-century newspaper boom which was the consequence of a multitude of factors: the abolition of the stamp duty (1848), the large-scale use of advertising as a source of revenue, the introduction of new technologies that lowered production costs and allowed faster composing and printing, growing urbanization, and the extension of the suffrage, which bolstered political emancipation and stimulated interest in a political opinion press.

World War I did not really hold back the further development of a flourishing newspaper press. Indeed, after the war all newspapers resumed publication. In the inter-war period the first tabloids appeared, alongside the political opinion newspapers. The Flemish press, which lagged far behind the French-speaking press in number of titles and circulation figures, expanded fast during that period.

The aftermath of World War II brought more of a break, or hiatus: the newspapers that had appeared during the war were banned from publication, and some newspapers that had been inactive during the war failed to resume publication. The newspaper press began to be characterized by growing concentration.

Belgium used to possess an outspoken political opinion press. Only the Rossel group published so-called 'neutral' dailies in the French-speaking part of the country. Today most newspapers lean towards one of the large political groups, but without any financial implications. The socialist papers that were once strongly financially linked with the socialist party relinquished that connection in the 1980s.

The ongoing concentration in the newspaper industry has acted as an impetus to the removal of all affiliations between the newspapers and more or less circumscribed religious, social or political groups (the so-called 'pillars'). Journalists can therefore express themselves much more independently and critically about politicians, but the question is whether they have come under pressure from the financial and business interests of their newspaper group's owners.

The debate is still open as to whether the newspapers are yielding to tabloidization as a consequence of the cut-throat competition for readers and advertisers. The results of available empirical research into this issue are often contradictory, but they do indicate a trend towards tabloidization: less political news, more personal political stories, less international news, more human interest articles, more story-telling, less investigative journalism, more service journalism, etc. Genuine editorials have disappeared from most dailies, and the front pages contain more sensational news.

Belgium still has a number of quality dailies, such as *De Standaard, De Financieel Economische Tijd* (FET), *De Morgen, Le Soir* and *La Libre Belgique*, but even these have been tempted by sensational reporting, mainly on the occasion of the scandals that constantly emerge.

Since 1958 the overall circulation figures of the newspaper press have not suffered any drastic (i.e. over 40 per cent) fluctuations, but they have been declining steadily, from 2,597,815 in 1958 to 1,917,152 in 2002. In 2002 the Flemish press accounted for 63.9 per cent, the French-language press for 36 per cent of total newspaper sales.

The public has no tradition of taking out subscriptions to their newspapers. Only recently have the publishers' more aggressive marketing strategies succeeded in raising the number of subscribers: in 2002 sales at the newsagent's accounted for 57.7 per cent and subscriptions for 42.5 per cent.

Belgians are no great readers of newspapers: 150 per 1,000 inhabitants (the Netherlands 310, Norway 600, Sweden and Finland 450), but they do read more newspapers compared with most Southern European countries (Italy 100, Greece 90 and Portugal 38). Market research shows that mainly young, adult, urbanized, single men fail to read newspapers, while young people in general appear to spend little time on newspapers.

To increase circulation figures all publishers have tried hard to make their papers more attractive. On the basis of extensive readership research, they have attempted to meet the needs of a changing reading culture. All dailies have had their layout altered in the last five years. Their new look now includes various columns and sections, inserts and supplements. Some dailies have increased their sales figures by going for tabloidization. Most newspapers, however, suffer from declining circulation figures, while production costs continue to rise. High distribution costs and rising labour costs, in particular, have made newspapers financially vulnerable and heavily dependent on advertising revenue.

As in the rest of Europe, newspapers are acutely dependent on advertising revenue: 'healthy' newspapers raise between 45 per cent and 60 per cent of their income from advertising. However, the numerous new players that have entered the field in recent years (commercial television and radio, new weekly magazines, a free newspaper, etc.) all depend largely on advertising. In the fierce battle for advertising the newspaper industry has been losing ground: while in 1988 newspapers received 24 per cent of all media advertising, by 2000 the figure had dropped to 15.7 per cent. During the economic boom of 1999 and 2000 the absolute figures of advertising revenue still rose, but the recession in 2001 caused the available advertising capital to shrink drastically, to decrease the amount of classified advertising (mainly job ads), which, together with brand advertising, forms a major source of revenue for newspapers.

Belgium used to be among those European countries (including the United Kingdom, Germany, the Netherlands, the Scandinavian countries) in which the newspaper and periodical press enjoyed more advertising income than any of the other media. Since 1998, however, television has been receiving the larger part: 42.8 per cent, versus 36.6 per cent for the printed media.

Since the 1950s mergers have drastically reduced the number of newspaper titles. No fewer than twenty seven dailies disappeared between 1950 and 2002. At the same time, the oligopolistic market structure made it impossible to launch new titles. Indeed, since World War II all new ventures in the sector have failed.

It is often said that the intensive mergers have weakened the plurality and the diversity of the press. This has been undeniably so when, as a result of the merger, editorial autonomy is entirely lost. However, when the merged newspaper succeeds in keeping its own ideological line and editorial autonomy, and when the merger makes more financial resources available for the editorial output, the process of concentration can be regarded as less negative. The Belgian newspaper industry offers examples both of 'negative' and of 'positive' concentration. Leaving aside *De Financieel Economische Tijd* and *L'Echo*, the two financial-economic dailies, as well as *Grenz Echo*, the small regional German-language newspaper, the newspaper industry is found to be controlled by no more than three media groups in Flanders and three groups in Wallonia.

### Press ownership in Flanders

The three most important press enterprises in Flanders are: VUM, De Persgroep and RUG.

VUM (Vlaamse Uitgevers Maatschappij) is the market leader with one quality

Table 2.1 *Decline in the number of newspapers and newspaper enterprises*

|  | 1950 | 1980 | 2002 |
|---|---|---|---|
| **Flanders** | | | |
| Titles | 19 | 12 | 10 |
| Enterprises | 14 | 7 | 4 |
| **Wallonia** | | | |
| Titles | 31 | 21 | 16 |
| Enterprises | 19 | 9 | 4 |
| **Belgium** | | | |
| Titles | 50 | 33 | 26 |
| Enterprises | 33 | 16 | 8 |

broadsheet (*De Standaard*) and three popular newspapers (*Het Nieuwsblad, De Gentenaar* and *Het Volk*). The publishing group employs about 300 full-time journalists and leans towards the Catholic socio-political 'pillar'. The group has recently been said to be on the verge of getting in the red as a result of high costs and heavy investment (including its purchase of the newspaper *Het Volk* in 1994, its participation in Mediabel, the Belgian French-language press group, as well as its investments in numerous digital activities). Its business plan includes a cut in the number of journalists.

De Persgroep is the second largest group. It publishes the two mass-oriented newspapers: *Het Laatste Nieuws* and its Antwerp edition, *De Nieuwe Gazet*. *Het Laatste Nieuws* is the tabloid with the largest readership in Flanders (circulation 265,000).

In 1989 De Persgroep acquired *De Morgen*, the socialist-oriented newspaper that had gone bankrupt, for the nominal amount of BFr 1 (€0.02). *De Morgen* itself was the result of a merger of *Vooruit* and *Volksgazet*, two socialist party newspapers. Under the ownership of De Persgroep *De Morgen* retained its editorial autonomy, and after recapturing a part of the market share it had before its difficulties, it is now creating a distinct profile of itself as a progressive quality newspaper. In contrast to VUM, whose core business remains publishing newspapers, De Persgroep has successfully launched a range of popular weekly magazines. It also owns 50 per cent of VTM, the popular Flemish commercial television station, and of Topradio, Mango and Q-Music, all of which are private radio stations.

RUG (Regionale Uitgeversgroep) emerged as a joint venture of two mainly regional newspaper groups, Concentra (*Het Belang van Limburg*) and De Vlijt (*Gazet van*

*Antwerpen*). Concentra is the dominant partner, with a participation of €15 million.

The only independent newspaper in Flanders that does not yet form part of a larger media group is *De Financieel Economische Tijd*, the financial-economic quality daily. Although it is financially sound, with a circulation of approximately 50,000, it is said to be looking for some form of co-operation with a Flemish or foreign press group.

These press groups have the following newspaper market shares in Flanders: VUM 43.3 per cent; De Persgroep 28.1 per cent; RUG 23.4 per cent; *FET* 5.2 per cent. Most large newspaper groups are controlled by holding companies, with the exception of De Persgroep and Concentra (RUG), whose majority shareholders are the Van Thillo family and the Theelen family respectively.

### Press ownership in Wallonia

In Wallonia Rossel is the newspaper market leader, with its broadsheet *Le Soir* and its tabloids, *La Meuse* (Liège) and *La Lanterne* (Brussels). These are so-called 'neutral' newspapers: they do not lean towards any specific political, social or religious 'pillar'. In 1968 Rossel also gained control of *La Nouvelle Gazette*, the liberal daily. Taking advantage of family feuds within the company, the French media tycoon Robert Hersant (Socpresse) succeeded in acquiring 40 per cent of Rossel. Until 1997 Rossel also incorporated the loss-making socialist dailies *Le Peuple, Le Journal de Charleroi* and *La Wallonie*, but when the readership kept declining (to under 7,500, the limit below which government support is withdrawn in Wallonia) the three newspapers merged into *Le Matin* but Rossel ended the collaboration.

In 1999 the Rossel group acquired a 48 per cent share in *La Voix du Nord*, the main French regional newspaper (Mediabel is also allied with La Voix du Nord, see below).

Société Anonyme d'Information et de Productions Média (IPM) publishes the Catholic newspaper *La Libre Belgique* and the liberal *La Dernière Heure*. The merger of these titles into one press group in 1973 did not prevent them from losing market share, and the original owners were replaced with a new media holding company in which the Le Hodey family has a major share. Mediabel, the third most important Walloon media group, took a 51 per cent participation in IPM in 1995. The main newspaper published by Mediabel is *Vers l'Avenir*, a leading Catholic Walloon newspaper which used to be owned by the diocese of Namur. In recent years Vers l'Avenir has bought virtually all regional Walloon Catholic dailies and now publishes one national edition with different regional or local editions (*Le Jour/Le Courrier, Le Courrier de l'Escaut, L'Avenir de Luxembourg*). The majority share Mediabel was holding in IPM apparently created a duopoly in Wallonia: Rossel versus Mediabel/IPM. Mediabel, however, has strengthened its position by entering into an alliance with La Voix du Nord, the French group that owns 49 per cent of Vers l'Avenir. An interesting detail in this context is that in 1999 market leader Rossel also acquired a share in La Voix du Nord, as a result of which both the Rossel group and Mediabel/IPM are now allied with the French Voix du Nord.

When, in 2000, Mediabel wanted to readjust its bloc of shares with a view to reducing the diocese's share to 25 per cent, it chose a new partner company, in which Flemish VUM held over 50 per cent of the shares. To IPM, and particularly to the Le Hodey family, this transaction was unacceptable for various reasons, and they were backed up by an arbitration committee. Today Mediabel still participates in IPM.

It is clear that the six prominent media groups make it virtually impossible for independent small newspapers to survive. *FET*, the Flemish independent financial and business quality paper, has made it known it is looking for a partner. *L'Echo*, the Walloon financial and business daily, is already allied with Rossel (14.5 per cent), IPM (9 per cent) and Vers l'Avenir (4.5 per cent). *Grenz Echo*, Belgium's only German-language newspaper, has always found it hard to survive. In 1996 Rossel acquired 50 per cent of *Grenz Echo*.

As in the rest of Europe, it has been the socialist newspaper press in particular that has found it hard to cope with the conditions of the new media landscape. When the Flemish *De Morgen*, the daily with socialist leanings, found refuge with De Persgroep, it went through some troubled years, but it now appears to be holding its own as a left-oriented quality paper.

In Wallonia the socialist newspaper press has failed to survive. After its departure from Rossel and a short stay with Mediabel, *Le Matin* entered a joint venture with *France Soir* until it was finally forced to close in 2001, in spite of continuing government support. This implies that Wallonia no longer has any progressive, left-oriented newspaper, in spite of the socialist party's historical prominence in this part of Belgium.

Most newspaper groups have also developed activities in the periodical press, commercial radio and television. This has resulted in conflicts of interests: De Persgroep, which has a 50 per cent share in the major Flemish commercial television company (VTM), has often been criticized for being too partial towards this commercial station in its newspapers and weekly magazines. Belgium, unlike the United Kingdom and Germany, has no Sunday papers.

### The periodical and magazine press

The periodical press is highly concentrated: in each of the two communities it is dominated by two periodical groups and one newspaper group. The largest group is Sanoma, the Finnish media giant that also took over VNU, the Dutch periodical concern, in 2001. Through Mediaxis, its Belgian branch, this group publishes all women's magazines as well as the majority of television magazines in Belgium. Roularta, a periodical publisher, holds the monopoly of the news weeklies (*Knack*), after having ousted all competitors from the market. Roularta is also active in the lifestyle magazine and family magazine sectors.

Next to these two leading magazine publishing groups there are two smaller publishers, the Dutch Audax, which has taken over the periodicals of *Het Volk* newspaper, and a newcomer, Think Media, which focuses on men's magazines.

Two newspaper publishing groups, De Persgroep and Rossel, are also active in the weekly magazine market. De Persgroep, whose titles include *Dag Allemaal*, the most widely read television weekly in Flanders, takes up a particularly strong position next to Sanoma and Roularta.

As in the newspaper sector, the market for periodicals is saturated, and newcomers stand little chance of success. In 2001 three newly launched weeklies disappeared after a brief life. The television weeklies make up the largest segment of the periodical market. Like the newspapers, the periodicals have to compete fiercely for advertising revenue among themselves, because of the appeal of commercial television.

## The electronic (audio-visual) media

After the *World War II* public broadcasting was given a complete monopoly. Television was introduced fairly late (1953) because television sets had to be compatible with both the French 819 line system and the European 625 line standard.

In May 1960 a law was enacted creating two broadcasting corporations: one for Flanders (BRT) and one for the French-speaking community (RTBF). In 1997 the Belgisches Fernsehen und Rundfunk was created for the German-speaking community. As these three broadcasting corporations gradually gained more autonomy and their own individual legal frameworks, we shall discuss them separately.

The setting up of cable networks in 1960 turned out to be an important factor in the audiovisual landscape. By the mid-1970s half of all households had been connected to a cable network. Today Belgium is the most densely cabled country in the world (98 per cent of all television households). At first the cable companies were confined to distributing the national channels, but quite soon they started distributing the output of foreign television broadcasters as well. Among the latter, only the public service channels were at first allowed access to cable, but after some time selected commercial stations were admitted as well.

As a result the public has for many years been exposed to a plethora of national and foreign television channels; television households receive thirty to forty television stations. This has made Belgium an interesting testing ground for investigating whether, and to what degree, a large and varied supply of channels undermines viewers' loyalty to their own national station.

In the 1980s there was a favourable climate for launching new commercial stations. When the general monopoly of the public broadcasting corporations was broken by the legalization of the numerous private radio stations that had been operating illegally, the first commercial television stations were licensed in 1987 in Wallonia (RTL-TVI) and in 1989 in Flanders (VTM).

### Television and radio in the Flemish community

In the 1970s the public broadcasting corporation increasingly became the target of criticism: it was deemed to be too paternalistic, too little innovative, too bureaucratic, and above all too heavily politicized. Not only its board of directors and its management but also its high-level broadcasting staff were appointed according to political criteria (which were themselves the reflection of the political party representatives in

parliament). It followed that it was the politically best placed rather than the best qualified individuals who tended to get appointed and promoted. Naturally, such a system inevitably made dynamic and creative operation of the stations virtually impossible. Moreover, the public broadcaster received only 50 per cent of the total proceeds from the radio and television licence fees, and had to make do with a rather low budget. The fact that the public broadcaster's annual government grant had to be agreed on by the Flemish parliament placed the political parties in a position to put the public broadcasting corporation under continuous pressure.

The malaise that pervaded the corporation helped create a favourable climate for introducing a Flemish commercial television station. VTM (Vlaamse Televisie Maatschappij – Flemish Television Company) was launched in 1989 with great success: the targeted audience share of 20 per cent was easily exceeded and in 1995 it rose as high as 44 per cent, while the public television broadcaster's share dropped to 29 per cent.

After the substantial loss of viewers and unabated discontent, all the public broadcaster's top people were dismissed. A new manager (Bert De Graeve) was headhunted. He initiated fresh profiles for the two public television networks and laid off no fewer than sixty top staff. The general idea was to do away with politicized appointments and crippling bureaucracy. In 1997 the public broadcasting corporation was turned into a limited company governed by public law. Its name was changed to VRT (Vlaamse Radio Televisie – Flemish Radio and Television), its staff lost their civil servant status and its overall budget was augmented. Its new profile proved to be a success and the public television broadcaster today has about the same share of Flemish viewers as VTM, the main commercial station: approximately 32 per cent for the VRT and 37 per cent for VTM.

Initially, the government gave VTM a monopoly of commercial television and required newspaper and periodical publishers to become the company's majority shareholders (which was exactly the opposite of what is provided by any cross-ownership law!). This legal construction, with the monopoly and the obligatory participation of Flemish publishers, was rejected by the European Commission. VNU, the Dutch magazine publisher, had taken a 44 per cent participation, but sold it to De Persgroep and Roularta, the two

Belgian publishing groups that now hold 100 per cent of the shares in VTM.

In 1994 VTM's monopoly position was undermined by the controversial launch of VT-4, a new commercial SBS-TV station. As VT-4 was officially based in London, as a UK company it was in a position to circumvent VTM's eighteen-year-old monopoly. VT-4 was a typical U-turn construction, as it was exclusively directed at Flanders, with Dutch-language programmes only. The Flemish cable companies were found willing to distribute VT-4's programmes through their networks, in spite of the resistance put up by the Minister in charge of media policy. However, the station turned out to be only moderately successful (it never exceeded an 8 per cent audience share). Eventually it officially became a Flemish station in 2002. Whether this move will save VT-4 from insolvency remains an open question.

VTM's answer to the threat posed by VT-4 was to launch a second channel (K-2) even before VT-4 had actually started broadcasting. K-2 has a small audience share (about 7 per cent).

Under pressure from the European Commission, VTM's monopoly was terminated in 1998.

Meanwhile, a range of thematic television channels have been launched: Vitaya (lifestyle), TMF and JIM-TV (music), Kanaal Z (business and finance), Libert.com (travel) as well as some shopping channels. These appear to find it hard to attract sufficient advertising to survive. Indeed, the excessive fragmentation of the television market in Flanders today leads to ruinous competition among the stations.

At the launch of VTM, and following its huge success, the public television broadcaster was panic-stricken and responded by adopting an imitation strategy, i.e. by offering more popular entertainment during prime time. The programme profile of the second channel in particular was frequently altered, until the corporation finally settled for two different, fully fledged channels that are equal and complementary. The first channel (TV-1) aims at as wide an audience as possible with more popular programmes, while the second channel (Canvas) is devoted to high-quality programmes for viewers who want some sort of added value.

Several studies have shown that the prime-time programming of TV-1 is very similar to that of VTM. Also the profiles of K-2 (VTM's second channel) and of VT-4 resemble each other strongly: entertainment only and a lot of American series and formats.

In Flanders foreign-language programmes are subtitled in Dutch.

As far as radio broadcasting is concerned the public corporation finds itself in a comfortable position. Until 2001, it held the monopoly on nationwide radio broadcasting, with a total of five channels. The private radio channels in Flanders form no real competition as they were prohibited from networking and from extending their transmission ranges beyond the local. In 2002 the authorities yielded to the growing pressure to grant nationwide licences to commercial radio stations. After competitive tendering nationwide radio licences were granted to two commercial stations. Q-Music (owned by the Flemish commercial television channel VTM) and 4FM (owned by Think Media, publisher of periodicals). These, however, have found it hard to compete with the five successful public radio stations.

The public broadcaster has a strikingly high share of the radio audience (84.2 per cent). This success is the result of two factors. Until 2002 only the public broadcasting corporation had access to frequencies that allowed it to cover the whole of Flanders. This gave the corporation the edge over the numerous private radio stations, which were confined to a strictly local transmission range. Moreover, the public broadcaster's five radio stations have been smartly tailored to exert a strong appeal to segmented audiences. Radio 1 is the general current affairs and service station; Radio 2 offers entertainment and is regionally oriented; Klara is the culture station; Studio Brussel broadcasts light music for a young audience; Radio Donna is given over to pop music. Q-Music (VTM) and 4FM (Think Media), the two private radio stations that received a nationwide licence in 2002, have fallen short of expectations and appear to be unable to challenge the strong VRT-radio loyalty among the Flemish audience.

Public broadcasting is mainly funded with public means. As in the United Kingdom and in Sweden, public television is not allowed to carry advertising, though sponsoring is permitted. Public radio stations may have advertising revenue up to a €50 million limit. The government grant in 2002 was €206,197 million (comparable broadcasters in Norway or Finland, with about the same number of inhabitants, enjoy higher budgets). This government grant is laid down in a management contract at a fixed amount, which is increased yearly by 4 per cent. Moreover, the VRT receives a supplementary subvention of €10 million that is earmarked for the development of digital television.

In 2002 the radio and television licence fee was abolished in Flanders. The broadcasting corporation had been receiving only 50 per cent of the total proceeds anyway, the number of licence dodgers had been increasing, and the authorities wanted to make it clear that the funding of a public broadcasting corporation is part of a public service.

VTM made a profit from the very start. In 1997 its profits amounted to €15.6 million. Although in 1999/2000 profits declined following the economic recession, the company remains financially healthy.

*Regional television.* In Flanders regional television started in 1992. The regional stations were meant to complement the national channels. Their distribution was limited to the respective regions, they had to offer mainly regional information, and their broadcasting time was limited to 200 hours per year, though non-stop repeats were allowed. The eleven regional stations have semi-public status, they are funded with advertising as well as with public means. They have been successful in attracting viewers, but advertisers and local authorities have been less eager to finance them and, as a result, several of them now find themselves in difficulties. TV Brussel, which receives sufficient funding from the authorities, does not have these financial problems. RUG and De Persgroep, the newspaper groups, and Roularta, the magazine publisher, participate in a number of regional stations. A recent change in the regional television decree allows the broadcasting time to be extended, but it does not offer any prospects of government support.

*Pay-television.* Pay-television has never got off the ground in Flanders. Via the cable networks, Flemish viewers can already receive a wide range of free stations with a large film offering. The presence of numerous and easily accessible video shops is thwarting the development of any pay-per-view film channel. In 1985 Filmnet (Richmond – Rupert) was the first pay-per-view film channel to be started up, but it never managed to reach break-even point. Canal Plus acquired Filmnet in September 1996, and now offers an analogue and a digital range with Canal Plus Televisie. Although it possesses contracts for football rights Canal Plus Televisie still finds it hard to attract a viable number of subscribers. In 2001

it had 128,000 and 42,000 subscribers for its analogue and its digital range respectively.

## Television and radio in the French-speaking community

Like its Flemish counterpart the French-language public service broadcaster was threatened by far-reaching politicization, deadening bureaucracy, and an endemic shortage of financial means. As its annual grant was dependent on government approval, it was exposed to political pressure. The corporation was suffering from a deep malaise. In October 1997 it was decided to restructure the corporation, to increase its autonomy, to guarantee a fixed annual government grant, to reduce the number of staff with the status of tenured civil servants, and to hire staff on a temporary basis.

The 1997 decree turned the RTBF into an autonomous state enterprise, similar to the VRT. Parallel with the VRT in Flanders, the RTBF was run on a 'management contract' (October 1997) with the government of the French community. This contract regulated its funding and programming. The 1997 management contract was found to be ill defined, and it was replaced with a new one in July 2001, which requires 75 per cent of all RTBF broadcasts to be produced in one of the regional production centres, thereby indicating clearly that the RTBF attaches greater importance to decentralization than does its Flemish counterpart.

In contrast with Flanders, politicization continues, as the power of the RTBF's heavily politicized board of directors has not been cut back. In 1997 Chr. Druitte, the Director General, was appointed on the basis of his political background. Because problems continued to affect the corporation, he was replaced by J. P. Philippot, solely as a result of yet another political intervention.

The RTBF decree emphasizes the importance of producing programmes of its own, reflecting the cultural heritage and identity of the French-speaking community in Belgium.

As in Flanders, public television was faced with a commercial competitor in the late 1980s. RTL-TVI was started up in 1987. It is 66 per cent owned by the RTL group (a combination of CLT, Bertelsmann and Pearson) and 34 per cent by French-language newspaper publishers. The alliance with RTL, which was a powerful European player, promised a rosy future for RTL-TVI, but the new station found itself heavily challenged by TF-1, the French commercial station, and by FR-2 and FR-3, the French public stations. It appeared that over 40 per cent of Belgian French-speaking viewers watched these French stations. Although RTL-TVI's viewing figures were somewhat better (between 23 per cent and 26 per cent) than those of the RTBF, they fell short of expectations. When, in 1989, the RTBF was given permission to carry advertising, some degree of co-operation with RTL-TVI was established. This co-operation, however, did not result in a strong increase in advertising revenue for the RTBF, which remained as 'poor' as ever. The advertising revenue was distributed as follows: 24 per cent for the RTBF and 76 per cent for RTL-TVI. In 1997 the collaboration between RTBF and RTL-TVI came to an end, the RTBF running its own advertising service, with a government-imposed volume ceiling. It follows that, in Belgium, a public television broadcaster carries advertising in the French-speaking community, but not in Flanders.

In 1995 RTL-TVI made an attempt at further expanding its audience share by launching RTL Club, a second channel, which broadcasts mainly films.

In more recent years new commercial thematic stations have been added: AB-3, Canal Z, Event-tv, a shopping channel.

As a consequence of a strict economy drive and frequent labour unrest, including strikes, public television programming strategy has been the subject of numerous changes. In 1993 the difficulties culminated in the abolition of Télé 21, the second channel. In March 1994 a new second channel, La Deux, was started up. Like the VRT's second channel (Canvas), La Deux broadcasts cultural programmes, targets minority audiences and covers events, including sport.

The first channel, La Une, offers more general programmes and it competes directly with RTL-TVI during prime time. The RTBF offers more and longer newscasts than RTL-TVI, and it invests heavily in producing its own programmes, as it has always striven to promote its cultural identity throughout its programming. As we have indicated above, the RTBF cherishes its decentralization policy: it is run in regional, autonomous production centres.

RTL-TVI offers popular programmes, including a strikingly high number of American series and films. RTL Club targets a younger audience with mainly American series and films. As a regulatory principle,

however, RTL-TVI is obliged to allocate one-third of its programming to French-language programmes.

The television landscape in the French-speaking community is much more fragmented than in Flanders, where competition from foreign stations is relatively feeble.

In contrast with Flanders, where the five public radio stations have held on to their prime position, in Wallonia they have been heavily challenged by private stations, mainly because the latter are allowed to set up networks that effectively extend their transmission ranges. The private radio stations were legalized as early as 1981. Since 1985, when they were given permission to carry advertising and to network, they have been developing fast: Radio Contact (35 per cent RTL), BE-RTL (RTL-TVI and Rossel), Nostalgie and Fun are very popular and constitute serious competition for the five public radio channels.

As in Flanders, the public broadcaster has profiled its radio channels very sharply: La Première is a general channel; Fréquence Wallonie broadcasts popular and regional programmes; Musique 3 is the culture channel; *21 Radio* is the youth channel; Bruxelles Capitale offers popular programmes for a slightly older audience. In recent years the public radio stations have become more successful, but Radio Contact and BEL-RTL, the two private radio networks, still cover 38 per cent of the radio market.

*Regional television.* Since 1972, when a pilot project for regional television was started by the government in Wallonia, twelve regional stations have been granted a licence. As in Flanders, their transmission ranges and broadcasting time were limited and their programming had to include regional information and entertainment. Although, from March 1990 onwards, regional stations in Wallonia have been allowed to carry advertising, the authorities have made great efforts to support the regional stations financially: the governmental decree provides for an annual grant for operating costs, and the stations receive half of €3.7 per cable subscriber per year. Also, local authorities have been prepared to invest in regional television. Thus regional television maintains its semi-public status. Just as its Flemish counterpart in Brussels is supported by the Flemish authorities, the French-speaking Brussels regional station, Télé Bruxelles, is entirely funded by the French-speaking community.

*Pay television.* Canal Plus Belgique, a subsidiary of Canal Plus France, has been active in the French-speaking part of Belgium since 1989. The RTBF owned 26 per cent of the shares, Canal Plus France 42 per cent and the rest were owned by Deficom, a company that consists of mainly Belgian enterprises. In 2000 the RTBF and Deficom sold their shares to Canal Plus France for €20.6 million.

The government required Canal Plus Belgique to invest €2 million annually in French-language audio-visual productions. In 1990 Canal Plus Belgique concluded a contract with the Royal Belgian Football Association, a move that undoubtedly contributed to raising the number of subscribers to Canal Plus to some 190,000 and getting it out of the red in 2000.

Unlike in Flanders, in Wallonia the obligatory radio and television licence fees have not been abolished. The proceeds from the fees are divided equally between the public broadcasters and other public services (mainly education). In 2001 the government direct grant to the RTBF amounted to €167,425 million.

Financial difficulties are endemic in the RTBF: in 1996 it showed a deficit of €6.4 million. To rectify this situation, a draconian financial reconstruction scheme was set up, under the name 'Horizon 97'. Under this scheme, the government grant to the RTBF is rising by 6 per cent over a five-year period (in contrast, the VRT's government grant is increasing by 4 per cent annually). With the proceeds of the sale of its shares in Canal Plus Belgique (€20.6 million) to Canal Plus France, the RTBF wanted to pay off its debts and invest in digital technology and educational progammes. In 2002 the RTBF still showed a €10 million deficit.

Both public radio and public television are allowed to broadcast advertising, but the advertising revenue cannot exceed 25 per cent of total RTBF income. The new management contract imposes a five-minute advertisement-free period before and after children's broadcasts on the public television broadcaster (as in Flanders), but not on commercial RTL-TVI! This is a paradox in such a small country: in the French-speaking community commercial television has no five-minute rule, while in Flanders it does.

As we have indicated, RTL-TVI finds it difficult to compete with the French TF-1, which also targets the Belgian advertising market. Since 2000 RTL-TVI has stopped making a loss.

### Television and radio in the German-speaking community

In 1977 the Belgischer Rundfunk und Fernsehen BRF was founded. This German-language public broadcasting corporation, which has its head office in Eupen, broadcasts radio programmes from 6.00 a.m. to 10.00 p.m. daily. After 10.00 p.m. it relays RTBF radio broadcasts. Since 1993 it has also had a weekly current affairs television programme. The BRF has been allowed to collaborate with private partners and it has plans to offer a daily television newscast.

Apart from its public broadcasting service, German-speaking Belgium also boasts a dozen local radio stations that have the same legal status as those in the French-speaking community.

## The Internet and related on-line media

Owing to the liberalization of the telecommunication sector, Belgacom, the leading Belgian operator, has been faced with competition both in its fixed and in its mobile telephone services.

Its fixed telephone services were challenged by the Flemish cable networks. The latter have been quick to convert their cable network into a switched network that is capable of operating a telephone service. Telenet started in 1996. Belgacom's mobile telephone service, Proximus (3,981,000 subscribers), has two strong competitors: Mobistar (2,547,000 subscribers) and KPN Orange, which changed its name to Base (1,000,000 subscribers).

The proceeds from the auctioning of UMTS licences fell short of expectations. The operators who were awarded a licence, Proximus, Mobistar and Base (KPN), have postponed introducing their UMTS services.

Belgacom and Telenet also compete fiercely in offering fast ISDN connections: Telenet's Pandora and Belgacom's ADSL system. Telenet tried to attract subscribers to its fast Internet service with low pricing, but subsequently it quietly doubled its rates. In 2002 the American-British group Callahan took a €940 million controlling interest in Telenet and the Flemish cable networks, but in the same year the coalition asked for a delay in payment.

While Belgacom has 5,060,000 subscribers to its fixed telephone network, Telenet had only 207,000 subscribers in 2001. This shows that competing with the leading national operator is far from easy. Thanks to its clever marketing strategy Telenet was able to attract more users for its broadband service, Pandora, than Belgacom was able to for ADSL. It should also be observed that in Belgium broadband connections were implemented faster than had been planned (from 54,652 lines in 1996 to 389,979 lines in 2000).

Approximately 50 per cent of all Belgians own a mobile phone, and about the same percentage have a fixed telephone line.

According to the National Institute of Statistics (2000) 42 per cent of the population have access to a personal computer and 38 per cent make use of the Internet. Further expansion of the Internet is hampered by the fact that telephone services are relatively expensive. As in most European countries, Internet users mainly use e-mail, discussion lists, chat lines and data consulting. E-commerce and new e-zines have had less success and have faced financial problems.

All newspaper and weekly magazine publishers have developed digital activities. Most of their services, which complement the printed versions of their publications, are free. Newly created e-newspapers and e-magazines were not as successful as anticipated, and came to a premature end.

Canal Plus offers a digital cable package: its interactive services are transmitted through a set-top box that is connected to the cable network.

The VRT started a digital television pilot project in 2002. To general amazement, the management opted for terrestrial digital television, even though the entire country is densely cabled. Rather than make use of cable, which is ideal for two-way exchange, they preferred to use telephone lines for their interactive services. Moreover, the set-top boxes for terrestrial digital television are incompatible with those for digital television through the cable network. At the moment 100 television households are involved in a pilot project. The results of this pilot project will determine whether terrestrial digital distribution was the correct decision.

## POLITICS, POLICY, LAW AND REGULATION

### The press

Belgium's constitution guarantees complete freedom of the press. Articles 14 and 18 prohibit any form of preventive censorship and allow repressive measures only if the freedom of speech is proved to have been abused.

As far as offences against the press code are concerned, a special safeguard is provided in Article 98 of the constitution, which states that such offences do not fall within the competence of an ordinary criminal court, but must be referred to the Court of Assizes, the so-called 'People's Court', where judgement is passed by a jury. This procedure obviously protects journalists, as public opinion is likely to side with the press.

Belgian legislation does contain a number of restrictions on the freedom of the press. These are derived from fundamental constitutional rights, such as the individual's right to privacy and to protection against defamation. Further restrictions are based on the need to protect the public interest (national security, moral standards, the monarchy, etc).

There is no legislation on media concentration or cross-ownership. As there is no specific EU legislation concerning media concentration either, the general regulations on the concentration of companies apply. To safeguard pluralism, the European Commission permits member states to impose specific anti-trust regulation within their national territories. In contrast to a number of other countries, Belgium has made no use of this so far. When a concentration appears to be in the making, Belgian legislation stipulates a duty to report to the Competition Council. So far this council has never intervened.

With a view to promoting pluralism in the printed media, the Belgian government has always adhered to a system of indirect support (reduced postal and telephone rates, subsidized newsprint supply, zero VAT rate, interest-free loans, etc). Following a political compromise in 1973 all newspapers started to receive financial support from the government in the form of direct grants. This gave rise to a wave of criticism as it did not really help insolvent newspapers. Subsequently the direct support system was made more selective, with more financial support for the insolvent papers, but the total amount that was allocated kept decreasing. Eventually the Flemish government decided to stop direct grants to the press altogether and replace them with governmental advertising, and financial support for journalist training and the development of digital activities.

The government of the French-speaking community still hands out direct financial aid to the newspapers, but only as long as a paper's sales figures remain above 7,500 copies. Part of the funds derives from the proceeds from the sale of radio and television advertising (€2.48 million): 75 per cent from RTBF advertising, 25 per cent from RTL advertising.

## The electronic media

The Flemish and French communities are fully autonomous in constructing a regulatory framework for their respective public broadcasting corporations. It is practically impossible to give a complete and detailed survey of this legal framework, as it is constantly being reviewed. It must be noted, however, that the Flemish government has often taken measures that run counter to EU regulations, e.g. when awarding a monopoly to one single commercial broadcaster, requiring newspaper and periodical publishers to participate in that commercial station, trying to keep VT-4 off the cable network, etc.

Before they can apply for a licence, all broadcasting companies need to be recognized by a broadcasting commission: in Flanders by the Vlaams Commissariaat voor de Media (VCM), and in the French-speaking community by the Conseil Supérieur de l'Audiovisuel (CSA). It is the duty of these bodies to establish whether the legislation is being observed and to impose sanctions if necessary.

The French-speaking community permits all audio-visual media to carry advertising, but it puts a ceiling on the public radio and television broadcaster's advertising revenue. In Flanders, public television is prohibited from showing advertising, though sponsorship is permitted. Flemish public radio is allowed to have advertising revenue, but with a financial ceiling (€50 million in 2002).

European Union rules apply to audio-visual advertising in Belgium. Under these rules the member states retain the right to be more restrictive for their own national stations. Flanders used this right when it imposed the rule that prohibits advertising five minutes before and after children's programmes. The French-speaking community has adopted the restriction for public television, from 2003 on, though not for commercial television.

The advisory body for the media in Flanders is the Mediaraad (Media Council), which advises the Minister for the media as well as the Flemish parliament. In the French-speaking community the Conseil Supérieur de l'Audiovisuel is qualified to do this, while, at the same time, it functions as a controlling body and decides on the allocation of radio and television licences. In Flanders the latter is the responsibility of the VCM (Vlaams Commissariaat voor de Media, the Flemish Broadcasting Commission).

## STATISTICS

| | |
|---|---|
| National population | 10,000,000 |
| Number of households | 4,609,000 |
| Overall cinema admissions | 23,500,000 |

**Print media**    Circulation of main daily newspapers, 2002. We use the English concepts: *broadsheet*, quality newspaper; *tabloid*, popular newspaper; *broadloid*, between the two (borrowed from B. Franklin)

| Group | Circulation | Copies sold | Ideology | Type |
|---|---|---|---|---|
| **Flanders VUM (43%)** | **501,937** | **408,773** | | |
| De Standaard | 98,169 | 78,995 | Catholic | Broadsheet |
| Het Nieuwsblad/De Gentenaar | 266,069 | 217,960 | Catholic/ Catholic | Broadloid |
| Het Volk | 137,699 | 111,818 | Catholic | Tabloid |
| **De Persgroep (28.1%)** | **380,665** | **265,480** | | |
| Het LaatsteNieuws/ De Nieuwe Gazet | 316,267 | 217,221 | Liberal/ Liberal | Tabloid |
| De Morgen | 64,398 | 48,259 | Progressive | Broadsheet |

| | | | | |
|---|---|---|---|---|
| **RUG (23.4%)** | **380,665** | **221,009** | | |
| *Gazet van Antwerpen* | 146,350 | 121,097 | Catholic | Broadloid |
| *Belang van Limburg* | 112,601 | 99,912 | Catholic | Broadloid |
| **FET (5.2%)** | | | | |
| *Financieel Economische Tijd* | 63,815 | 49,687 | Independent | Broadsheet |

## Wallonia

| | | | | |
|---|---|---|---|---|
| **Rossel (51%)** | **346,042** | **279,481** | | |
| *Le Soir* | 164,581 | 133,502 | Independent | Broadsheet |
| Sud Presse: | 181,461 | 145,979 | | |
| *La Meuse* | | | Independent | Tabloid |
| *La Lanterne* | | | Independent | Tabloid |
| *La Nouvelle Gazette* | | | Liberal | Broadloid |
| **Mediabel (41%)** | **304,324** | **224,504** | | |
| IPM: | | | | |
| *La Libre Belgique* | 68,212 | 53,884 | Catholic | Broadsheet |
| *La Dernière Heure* | 98,237 | 70,507 | Liberal | Tabloid |
| Editions Vers l'Avenir: | 119,875 | 100,113 | | |
| *Vers l'Avenir* | | | Catholic | Broadloid |
| *Le Jour/Le Courrier* | | | Catholic | Broadloid |
| *Le Courrier de l'Escaut* | | | Catholic | Broadloid |
| *Le Matin* (closed 2001) **(1.5%)** | 18,000 | 8,500 | Socialist | Broadloid |
| *L'Echo* **(4.7%)** | 34,476 | 26,296 | Independent | Broadsheet |
| *Grenz-Echo* **(1.8%)** | 12,342 | 10,082 | Independent | Broadloid |

Source: CIM.

Total circulation, Belgian press, 1,917,152; 63.5 per cent Flemish press; 36.0 per cent French-language press; 0.5 per cent German-language press.

| | |
|---|---|
| **Broadcast media** | *Audience share of main television channels, 2000 (%)* |

*Flanders*

| | |
|---|---|
| Public | |
| VRT TV-1 | 23.4 |
| TV-2/Canvas | 8.2 |
| Private | |
| VTM | 30.1 |
| KA-2 | 7.7 |
| VT-4 | 7.8 |

*French-speaking community, 2000 (%)*

| | |
|---|---|
| Public | |
| RTBF La Une | 17.7 |
| RTBF La deux | 3.4 |
| Private | |
| RTL-TVI | 18.1 |
| Club RTL | 5.6 |
| French | |
| TF-1 | 16.9 |
| FR-2 | 10.1 |
| FR-3 | 6.3 |

Source: CIM.

*Audience share of radio channels, 2000 (%)*

*Flanders*

VRT

| | |
|---|---|
| Radio 1 | 7.7 |
| Radio 2 | 32.3 |
| Radio 3 | 1.5 |
| Studio Brussel | 7.5 |
| Donna | 35.2 |

| | |
|---|---|
| Private | |
| Radio Contact | 6.9 |
| Top Radio | 3.3 |
| Radio Mango | 1.7 |
| Energy | 0.3 |

*French-speaking community*

RTBF

| | |
|---|---|
| Fréquence Wallonne | 9.8 |
| Radio 21 | 5.6 |
| La Première | 5.4 |
| Bruxelles-Capitale | 2.1 |
| Musique 3 | 2.0 |

| | |
|---|---|
| Private | |
| Contact Radio | 18.8 |
| Bel RTL | 18.8 |
| Nostalgie | 8.9 |
| NRJ/Energie | 5.3 |
| Fun | 5.2 |
| Contact 2 | 1.5 |

Source: Radio Metrie.

| | |
|---|---|
| Percentage of households reached by all forms of satellite, cable or terrestrial pay-television: | 98 |

| | |
|---|---|
| Percentage of households with: | |
| VCR | 76 |
| Satellite receiver | 1 |
| DVD | 4.4 |

| **Electronic media (% of population** | | |
|---|---|---|
| | Internet users | 38 |
| | Mobile phone subscribers | 65 |

| **Advertising Spend (%)** | | |
|---|---|---|
| | Newspapers | 17.2 |
| | Magazines | 13.6 |
| | Free papers | 5.3 |
| | Television | 43.2 |
| | Radio | 10.4 |
| | Film | 1.4 |
| | Outdoors | 8.9 |

# REFERENCES

Antoine, F. (1995) *La Belgique*. Les Télévisions du monde. Paris: Corlet-Télérama-Centre national du cinéma-Procirep.

Antoine, F., d'Haenens, L., and Saeys, F. (2001) 'Belgium' in L. d'Haenens and F. Saeys (eds) *Western Broadcasting at the Dawn of the Twenty-first Century*. Berlin: Mouton De Gruyter.

Biltereyst, D. and Van Gompel, R. (1997) 'Crisis and renewal of the fourth estate: on the post-war development of the Flemish newspaper press', *Communications: the European Journal of Communication Research* 22 (3): 275–300.

Biltereyst, D., and Burgelman, J.C. (1995) 'Belgium' in Bertelsmann Foundation and European Institute for the Media (eds) *Television requires Responsibility* II, *International Studies*. Gütersloh: Bertelsmann.

Burgelman, J. (1989) 'Political parties and their impact on public service in Belgium: elements from a political-sociological approach', *Media Culture and Society* 2: 167–93.

De Bens, E. (1991) 'Flanders in the spell of commercial television', *European Journal of Communication* 6 (2): 235–45.

De Bens, E. (2001) *De pers in België. Het verhaal van de Belgische dagbladpers. Gisteren, vandaag en morgen*. Tielt: Lannoo.

De Bens, E. and Ostbye, H. (1998) 'The European newspaper market: structural changes', in D. McQuail and K. Siune (eds) *Media Policy: Convergence, Concentration and Commerce*. London: Sage.

De Bens, E. and De Smaele, H. (2001) 'The inflow of American fiction television on European broadcasting channels revisited'. *European Journal of Communication* 16: 51–76.

Lentzen, E. (1996a) 'La presse quotidienne francophone' *CRISP* 1515–16.

Lentzen, E. (1996b) 'La presse hebdomadaire francophone' *CRISP* 1519.

Verstraeten, H. (1980) *Pers en macht: een dossier over de geschreven pers in België*. Leuven: Kritak.

Voorhoof, D. (1995) 'Openbare Omroep', *Kluwer Mediarecht* 4 (35): 1–14.

# 3: The Czech Republic

JAN ČULÍK

## NATIONAL PROFILE

The Czech Republic came into being in January 1993, when Czechoslovakia, a federal state, split into two independent countries, the Czech Republic and Slovakia, as a result of irreconcilable differences between the Czech and Slovak governments. Czechoslovakia was founded in 1918 after the disintegration of Austria-Hungary at the end of the First World War. In the inter-war period it was a plural democracy with an advanced media infrastructure (Czechoslovak Radio began broadcasting in May 1923) and a vibrant, indigenous film industry (due to a sophisticated system of import duties, levied on foreign films, which financed local film production).

Between 1938 and 1939 Czechoslovakia succumbed to Nazi Germany and after a semi-democratic interregnum in 1945–8 it became a part of the totalitarian, communist Soviet Bloc in February 1948. Approximately from the mid-1960s the communist regime found itself on the defensive: reformers within the system initiated a sustained push for freedom, using contemporary literature and culture as an instrument of democratization. This campaign for democratic reform culminated in the so-called Prague Spring of 1968, a period of several months when Czechoslovakia enjoyed almost absolute freedom of expression and engaged upon an intensive debate about the totalitarian excesses of its immediate past and the alternatives for its political future. This was a remarkable period in the history of the Czech media: newspapers, radio and television provided professional and highly sophisticated coverage of the issues under debate. A number of leading broadcasters emerged as figures of national importance. Equally remarkable was the work of the Czechoslovak media during the first week of Soviet occupation, following the Warsaw Pact military invasion of 21 August 1968 which put a stop to the Prague Spring. From the early hours of the invasion the media went underground, defying the invading forces, and provided a round-the-clock, independent news service, calling for sensible, peaceful resistance and preventing chaos and bloodshed. A network of regional studios was quickly set up and the 'Free Czechoslovak Radio' was never silenced by the invading armies.

In the 1970s and 1980s Czechoslovakia suffered a revenge for the liberalising 1960s and their culmination, the Prague Spring. The Soviet Union threw the country into a harsh, neostalinist mode and instigated a direct assault on the intelligentsia. The media system was purged of all reformists and was turned into a machine which spouted emotional, ideological propaganda whose intensity remained practically unchanged until the fall of communism in 1989. Oppression in the 1970s and 1980s was much stronger than in the other Central European communist countries. As a result, journalism was practically destroyed as a profession. It was particularly destructive that journalists in this period were expected systematically to publish lies in support of the occupying regime and that the population knew that journalists were lying to them.

Under communism all the media were state-owned. From 1990 onwards the state-owned newspapers came into private hands. The privatization of newspapers was often questionable. For many, the pattern used was that of the *Mladá fronta (Young Front)* daily.

The old state-owned newspaper was technically closed down, so that there would be no legal continuity. A new paper was founded by private owners with a very similar name, *Mladá fronta Dnes (Young Front Today)* (later shortened to *MF Dnes, YF Today*). Thus the new private owners could take over the trade mark of the old newspaper, its subscribers and its share of the market without paying any compensation to the state. For instance, the former Communist Party daily *Rudé právo (Red Rights)* became a privately owned, centre-left newspaper *Právo ([Our] Rights)*, *Zemědělské noviny (Farmers' Daily)* became *Zemské noviny (Country Daily)*, *Večerní Praha (Evening Prague)* became *Večerník Praha (Prague Evening Paper)*. Most of these privatized newspapers were eventually sold by the new Czech owners to foreign media companies.

The destruction of the professional media in the Czechoslovakia of the 1970s and 1980s cast a shadow over the development of the media in the 1990s. The most discredited communist propagandists had to leave but many rank-and-file journalists simply switched sides. These individuals rarely found in themselves the courage to produce independent and critical writing because they could at any time be accused of behaving questionably in the past. Until approximately 1996–7 most of the media uncritically supported the centre-right government of Václav Klaus and various anti-communist campaigns. Many young people without a political past and without journalistic experience were taken on by the media in the 1990s: a typical journalist was usually much younger than thirty. The lack of a continuous tradition of professional and/or investigative journalism meant that most of the journalistic output of the 1990s was timid, unenterprising, superficial and conventional. Most of the print media ended up in foreign hands, and there was little funding of systematic, in-depth investigative journalism. Foreign newspaper owners were interested in quick profits and were not bound by the obligations of public service journalistic work.

## STRUCTURE AND OWNERSHIP

### The print media

#### The newspaper press

There are three major '*serious*' daily political newspapers (their average daily print runs in December 2001 are given in brackets[1]): *Mladá fronta Dnes (The Young Front Today)* (309,226), *Právo (Our Rights)* (213,964) and *Lidové noviny (The People's Paper)* (88,835). *Mladá fronta Dnes* and *Právo* have gone through a questionable privatization process (see above) and have developed from state-owned dailies published in the communist era into privately owned newspapers. *Lidové noviny* was created by dissidents as a photocopied monthly with a print run of 400 copies, two years before the fall of communism. A newspaper called *Lidové noviny* used to be a leading daily in Czechoslovakia before the Second World War and several unsuccessful attempts have been made since 1989 to emulate the pre-war example.

*Mladá fronta Dnes (MFD)* is a middlebrow daily with a centre-right orientation. It caters for the intellectually undemanding general reader, whom it addresses not only with news and comment but also with various advertising, marketing, regional and special interest supplements. The political views of *MFD* are close to the views of the centre-right Freedom Union party, a small political organization with considerable influence on the media, especially those which are based in Prague. *Právo* is a centre-left daily whose commentary and analysis tend to be of slightly higher quality than those of *MFD*. The political views of *Právo* are close to the views of the ruling Social Democratic Party. *Právo* also supports indigenous capital against international competition, for instance the chief executive of commercial Nova Television in his dispute with the US company Central European Media Enterprises (see below). Some people refuse to read *Právo* because they associate it with its predecessor, the Communist Party propaganda mouthpiece *Rudé právo*, from the years before 1989. After the fall of communism, *Lidové noviny* was an attempt to create an authoritative intellectual newspaper, along the lines of the London *Times*. This attempt has not been successful. After several radical changes of staff, direction and ownership, *Lidové noviny* is now struggling to increase its readership by introducing tabloid themes while trying to retain its reputation as a newspaper read by the 'cultural elite'. *Lidové noviny* is moderately centre-right.

*Hospodářské noviny (Economic Daily;* December 2001 daily average print run 74,968[2]) specializes in economic and business issues; some critics accuse this newspaper of being a haven of inflexible, bureaucratic practice, surviving from the communist past. *Sport* (59,254) is a daily newspaper devoted to sporting events. The Czech Republic has two major nationwide tabloid newspapers, *Blesk (Flash*; average daily print run 320,913) and *Super* (132,946). *Super* supports Václav Klaus´s Civic Democratic Party and Vladimír Železný's Nova Television.

With the exception of *Právo*, which is owned by Borgis, and controlled by the newspaper's editor-in-chief, a communist era *Rudé právo* journalist Zdeněk Porybný, the other daily newspapers are in foreign hands. *Mladá fronta Dnes* and *Lidové noviny* are owned by Rheinisch-Bergische Druckerei-und Verlagsgesellschaft, a company based in Düsseldorf. *Blesk* and *Sport* (as well as a number of weekly publications) are owned by the Swiss publishing firm Ringier. (Its Czech subsidiary is registered as the property of Ringier-Springer, based in Amsterdam.) *Super* is owned by E-media, which is the property of the Austrian firm Epic Holding. *Hospodářské noviny* is owned by Economia, over which the German newspaper *Handelsblatt* and the US daily *Wall Street Journal* jointly exercise majority ownership. With the exception of some small variations, the printruns of the Czech national newspapers have been in decline since 2000.

The daily regional press is wholly owned by a single company, Vltava Labe Press (PNP) which is the property of Pol-Print. Medien, a company based in Passau, Germany. The Vltava Labe Press (PNP) group has bought out all the Czech regional newspapers, sacked most of the journalists and replaced the papers with a centrally produced publication with local variations on one or two pages only. Even in the two national newspapers it owns, *Zemské noviny* and *Slovo*, several pages are almost identical. This practice seems to have destroyed these two national newspapers: the average daily printrun of *Zemské noviny (Country Newspaper)* dropped from 342,000 copies in January 2000 to 39,000 in September 2001; the daily printrun of *Slovo (The Word)* decreased from 53,000 in January 2000 to 8,400 copies in December 2001.

Vltava Labe Press (PNP) controls Czech regional daily publishing through its network of regional newspapers *Deníky Bohemia (Bohemia Daily Newspapers)*. This company has acquired all the remaining regional daily newspapers in Moravia, the eastern part of the Czech Republic. *Deníky Bohemia* have now in total the highest daily printrun of all the Czech newspapers. If the printruns of all their regional variations are added together, *Deníky Bohemia* tops the league, with a daily printrun of 442,290 copies.[3] However, some observers point out that these are local newspapers and probably do not strongly influence the political views of the readers.

In January 2002 the regional newspapers owned by Vltava Labe Press (PNP) attracted in total the highest volume of advertising, Kcs 104.3 million.[4] *Mladá fronta Dnes* was in second place with Kcs 102 million. The amounts of advertising, attracted by other daily newspapers in January 2002 are given in millions of Czech crowns in brackets after their titles: *Blesk* (Kcs 32.8 million) *Právo* (Kcs 23.3 million) *Hospodářské noviny* (Kcs 23.2 million), *Lidové noviny* (Kcs 22.9 million), *Sport* (Kcs 7.2 million), *Super* (Kcs 5.8 million). Since the turn of the century *MFD* has increased its advertising income by more than 25 per cent, but the increase has not been steady; the movements in advertising income at other newspapers have been variable.

### The periodical and magazine press

The most influential weekly news magazines are possibly *Týden (The Week)* (published by the Swiss citizen Sebastian Pawlowski; 50,000 copies sold weekly), *Respekt* (a centre-right political weekly, close to the Freedom Union political party, which is published by Prince Karl Schwarzenberg, a former Chancellor of President Václav Havel, 30,000 copies), and the economic magazines *Ekonom (Economist)* (28,000 copies), published by Economia, and its competitor *Euro* (23,500 copies), brought out by the Czech company Euronews.[5]

*Reflex* (one of the magazines published by Ringier, 60,000 copies sold weekly) is on the borderline between a current affairs periodical and a 'society' glossy. The magazine market is otherwise dominated by tabloid and lifestyle periodicals. The most widely circulated lifestyle magazine is *Rytmus Života (Rhythm of Life)*, published by Europress (240,000 copies), the Sunday edition of the tabloid *Blesk*, brought out by Ringier, sells 206,000 copies; Mona Prague, owned by VNU Magazine Group International, of Haarlem, in the Netherlands, publishes a number of other widely read lifestyle magazines, such as *Týdeník Květy (Blossoms Weekly)* (160,000 copies) and *Story* (135,000 copies); similar tabloid glossies are also produced by Stratosféra, a company co-owned by the Dutch firm VNU Hearst Prague of Haarlem. The most successful of these is *Spy* (132,000 copies).[6] The most widely read glossies feature celebrity gossip and soft porn, including advice on readers sexual problems.

In January 2002 *Týden* acquired advertising worth Kcs 4.1 million, *Respekt* Kcs 1.1 million, *Reflex* Kcs 3.7 million, *Týdeník Květy* Kcs 6.4 million, and *Spy* Kcs 6.9 million.[7]

### Book publishing

After the fall of communism in 1989 the book publishing market was liberalized. While there were some fifty state-owned publishing houses in Czechoslovakia under the communist regime, there are more than 2,700 registered book publishers in the Czech Republic alone. When censorship was abolished a wave of hitherto banned publications flooded the market, but the public soon tired of them. The average printruns, which used to reach tens of thousands of copies under communism, stabilized at about 3,000 copies. Currently, only some 150 publishers bring out more than twenty titles annually. In 1999 1,270 publishers produced at least one title. Some 200 publishing houses produce 80 per cent of the overall book production of the country. Five per cent VAT is levied on book production.

It is estimated that some 12,500 book titles were brought out annually by the end of the 1990s. While the average printrun has been decreasing throughout the decade, the number of published titles has been increasing. Approximately 90 per cent of all published books are in Czech; English is the most frequently used foreign language. Unusually, some 30 per cent of all published books are fiction: this is due to the fact that many works of literature were banned for half a century and there is much catching up to be done: the proportion of fiction is slowly decreasing. Many fiction titles published nowadays, belong to the category of escapist, 'romantic', sentimental literature. Translations from thirty two languages formed a third of all published books in 1999. Only 12.3 per cent of all published books were textbooks.

Throughout the 1990s there were serious problems with book distribution. The state distribution system was broken up after the fall of communism and was gradually replaced by some seventy private distribution firms which are trying to compete against each other, often with a very limited range of titles and technological and professional back-up. After the fall of communism many bookshops were liquidated, but the situation improved and there are some 800 permanent specialist bookshops – more than there were prior to the fall of communism. Books are sold at approximately 2,000 places now.

Prices are not fixed nationally as in France or Germany, but most booksellers respect the prices recommended by publishers. However, books are often sold at remaindered prices, even quite soon after publication, due to publishers or distributors's financial problems, thus destabilizing the market. *Nové knihy (New Books)* a nationwide weekly bibliographical list of newly published titles, collapsed and no up-to-date comprehensive information is now available. The Union of Czech Booksellers started publishing the annual *Books in Print* in 1996.

There are no marketing analyses dealing with the functioning of the book market in the Czech Republic. Booksellers are being offered ever more titles and so they order ever fewer copies. They constantly look for more titles and rarely restock the older ones. Only 5–7 per cent of booksellers use computer technology for distribution, sales and ordering.[8]

## The electronic (audio-visual) media

### Television

Czechoslovak state television began broadcasting on 1 May 1953, while its second programme went on the air in May 1970; from 1983 Czechoslovakia also broadcast on its territory the first programme of Russian television for the occupying Soviet troops. After the fall of communism, state-owned Czechoslovak Television was turned into a public service system. From 1992 there was a federal, Czechoslovak channel and a Czech and a Slovak television station. After the division of Czechoslovakia in 1993, Czech Television retained two nationwide terrestrial channels: the mainstream programme ČT-1 and the cultural programme ČT-2.

In 1993 the regulatory authority, the Council for Radio and Television Broadcasting, awarded for free a television licence for a commercial, culturally oriented nationwide terrestrial television station to a consortium of six Czech and Slovak individuals, headed by Vladimír Železný, and Ronald Lauder's company, the Central European Development Corporation, which later became Central European Media Enterprises (CME). The new commercial television station, Nova TV (the Czech Independent Television Station, ČNTS) started broadcasting on 4 February 1994. From its inception, it dropped the cultural remit and went aggressively for down-market, tabloid broadcasting, including pornography. The financial success of the station was phenomenal. According to estimates, in the first years of its existence it was watched by some 70 per cent of Czech audiences. In the third year of broadcasting, Nova TV recorded an operating profit of US $45 million on the basis of turnover of US $109 million. In 1995 a dividend of US $12 million was paid out by the television company.[9]

The American company CME, trying to strengthen its hold on the television station, bought out the participation interest in ČNTS from the original Czech and Slovak founders of the station, achieving 99 per cent ownership. At the same time CME made it possible for Vladimír Železný to acquire a 60 per cent majority in CET-21, the licence holder, hoping that he would always represent CME's interests. But from 1998 Železný began, in secret, to act against the interests of CME, so in April 1999 he was sacked from the post of chief executive of ČNTS. Železný then found indigenous financial backers in the Czech Republic, and in August 1999 he switched the American-backed Nova TV (ČNTS) off the air, replacing it with his own Nova TV Mark 2, funded by Czech money. CME sued Železný and the Czech Republic at the international chamber of commerce in Amsterdam and the Czech side lost. Železný has to re-pay CME US $28 million and the Czech Republic has to pay CME US $500 million in damages. Information about who are the current owners of Nova TV is not available: their identities are covered by a number of front organizations.

Although attempts have been made since the fall of communism to turn the former Czechoslovak Television, a communist propaganda tool, into a public service station, these attempts have not been completely successful. Czech Television has remained a large, untransparent, post-communist colossus of some 4,000 employees with its own internal ethos. In 1993–8, Czech Television's chief executive, Ivo Mathé, continued to place emphasis on entertainment. Mathé was a good technical manager and provided the television station with up-to-date technology. News and current affairs remained relatively undeveloped in his era. After Mathé's departure, several attempts have been made, since 1998, to professionalise Czech Television, in particular its news and current affairs department, and to open up its finances to public scrutiny. (Czech television is financed by a compulsory licence fee, amounting to some Kcs 5 billion annually, which is levied from all television viewers.) A fourth attempt at reform failed spectacularly in December 2000–January 2001, when the Council for Czech Television appointed a former BBC journalist, Jiří Hodač, as Czech Television's chief executive. This appointment resulted in an open rebellion by Czech Television employees, led by the news and current affairs department, whose members, fearing a professional audit, turned, in order to protect their position of unaccountability, an internal labour dispute into a public political struggle.

In December 2000, on hearing about the appointment of Jiří Hodač, the rebels began to transmit highly emotional broadcasts, hijacking the output of the station for their own ends. They aligned themselves with an opposition political party (the Freedom Union) and used popular discontent with the government of the day to bring out some 80,000 people to demonstrate in the streets of Prague against an alleged government attempt to stifle the independence of Czech Television. The new chief executive with BBC experience was deposed within a matter of days and things reverted to the status quo ante. The Council for Radio and Television Broadcasting has characterized the Czech Television rebellion as 'probably the most serious crisis since the fall of communism in 1989'[10] and imposed the highest possible fine, Kcs 2 million, on Czech Television for the behaviour of its employees during the Television rebellion.

After the rebellion, parliament changed the Czech Television Act, stipulating that the selection process leading to the appointment of a new Czech Television chief executive must be transparent and fully open to public scrutiny at all its stages. But in autumn 2001 a new Council for Czech Television appointed a new permanent chief executive in secret, in direct contradiction of the new law, thus opening itself to possible accusations that political pressure was at work. The appointee, Jiří Balvín, was a

Czech Television insider, representing the internal ethos of this unreconstructed, large post-communist institution.

A number of well known Prague cultural figures supported the rebellion, fearing with some justification that the opening up of the finances of Czech Television might compromise the often informal subcontractors' infrastructure on which many film makers and other cultural workers were financially dependent. They were afraid that the role of Czech Television as the only major surviving source of cultural subsidy for the support of the work of Prague artists and intellectuals might end.

There is another commercial television broadcaster, TV Prima, which has developed from a regional broadcaster and was temporarily owned by the Czech Investment and Postal Bank (IPB). This had succumbed to corruption and had to be renationalized by the Czech government. The true identity of the owners of the station is not known, but in spring 2001 there arose problems between the bank which currently controls IPB and Domeana, the firm which represents the current owners of *TV Prima*.

The Czech Internet daily *Britské listy* is suing the council for Radio and Television Broadcasting in order to force it to reveal the real owners of *Nova TV* and *Prima TV*. The council argues that the law prevents it from revealing the identities of the true owners.

More regulatory problems arose in the autumn of 2001 in connection with a regional televison station TV Galaxy, which broadcasts to Prague and Hradec Králové and on satellite and cable. The television station, whose licence holder is Martin Kindernay, also transmits programming made by a satellite and cable televison station, TV-3, owned by the Luxembourg-based company European Media Ventures. The Luxembourg company tried to seize Martin Kindernay's licence and thereby to gain control over the terrestrial broadcasting of TV Galaxy in the cities of Prague and Hradec Králové; the Council for Radio and Televison Broadcasting took steps to prevent this operation.[11]

The audience shares of all main Czech television stations are relatively stable, except that the popularity of *ČT-1* dropped from 28 per cent in 1998 to 21 per cent in 2001 and the viewing figures for *TV Prima* rose during the same period from 9 per cent to 17.5 per cent. The viewing figures for *Nova TV* have remained around 50 per cent over the past few years and the viewing figures for the cultural public service channel

*ČT-2* have stayed at about 8 per cent. The viewing figures for the rest of the television sector, i.e. for cable and satellite channels, do not exceed 5 per cent.[12] There are fifteen satellite television broadcasters, registered in the Czech Republic[13] and ninty four cable television broadcasters.[14] The three most influential cable consortia are headed by foreign companies: UPC Czech Holding, of the Netherlands, owned by United Pan-Europe Communications, the Netherlands; Intercable CZ – Vision Networks Tsjechie Holding, the Netherlands; and TES Media – Central Europe Cable Holdings (ING Baring, USA).

### Radio

Czech Republic has a public service Czech Radio, which is financed by a compulsorily levied licence fee. Czech Radio operates the following nationwide stations: Radiožurnál (on FM and AM), a mixture of news and current affairs and popular music, ČRo-2 Prague (on FM and AM), a programme for older listeners ČRo-3 Vltava (on FM only), a cultural programme and ČRo-6 RSE (on AM only) a current affairs programme, formerly put out by the Czech service of the American station Radio Free Europe/Radio Liberty, which was hived off from the US broadcaster in 1994, turned into a separate, privately owned station and later incorporated into public service Czech Radio. Czech Radio also operates eight regional studios which contribute some of their output to the nationwide stations and also run their own regional programming. There are only two commercial nationwide radio stations (Frekvence 1 and Radio Impuls) and more than sixty independent regional stations, some of which broadcast to several regions or larger towns. These include the BBC (which broadcasts the output of its Czech Service and some programmes of the BBC World Service in English) and the French-owned radio station Evropa-2. ČRo-1 Radiožurnál has a 12.2 per cent share of the listening public, ČRo-2 Praha has 6.6 per cent, Radio Impuls has 13.4 per cent, Frekvence 1 has 9.5 per cent.

### Film and video

Unlike Czech literature, which does not seem to have produced any major work since the fall of communism, Czech cinema seems to have quickly overcome the crisis of the early 1990s and is now producing major and important new work. In 1990–2 the government gradually abolished the state monopoly of film making which had existed from 1945. In 1992 the government created a State Fund for the Support of Czech Film Making, which is controlled by the Culture Ministry. Since 1994 the Czech Republic has been a member of the Council of Europe's Eurimage Fund for the support of film co-production and distribution and of the Europe-wide institution Eureka Audiovisuel. In 2000 the Eurimage programme supported the distrubution of twenty European feature films in the Czech Republic to the tune of Kcs 5 million.[15]

While under communism thirty to forty feature films were made in Czechoslovakia annually, in the second half of the 1990s between fifteen and twenty features were made in the Czech Republic, most of them with financial support by Czech public service television. According to some observers feature film making in the Czech Republic would collapse without the support of Czech Television. In 1990, shortly after the fall of communism, 51.4 million cinema tickets were sold; in 1995–2000, only some 9 million tickets were sold annually. Systematic state support for film making is still lacking, owing to unsolved legislative problems. The Fund for the Support of Czech Film Making provides grants for film makers to the tune of some Kcs 60–70 million annually. In 2000 the Czech state supported various cinematographic activities to the tune of Kcs 123 million; in 1999 it was Kcs 77 million.[16] The four most successful films in 2000 were *Princezna ze mlejna (Princess from the Mill)* (Czech Republic, Bontonfilm) 481,000 tickets sold, *Samotáři (Loners)* (Czech Republic, Cinemart) 442,000 tickets sold, Gladiator (USA) 379,000 tickets sold and *The Sixth Sense* (USA) 332,000 tickets sold. Feature films are also released on video and on DVD: the video distributors' income reached Kcs 1 billion in 2000: Kcs 390 million was income from hiring films out, Kcs 460 million was income from videocassette sales and Kcs 110 million was income from DVD sales. Bonton Home Video controlled 36 per cent of the video market in 2000; Warner Home Video controlled 26 per cent of the market.

## The Internet and related on-line media

The first computer in Czechoslovakia, owned by the Prague Technological University (ČVUT), was connected to the Internet in November 1991. Officially, Czechoslovakia was connected to the Internet in February 1992. Initially the Internet was developed in Czechoslovakia/Czech Republic by lecturers from technological universities. Since 1995 it has been possible to use the Internet commercially. In 1999, under considerable public pressure, the Czech Telecom introduced lower dial-up charges, which are still considered too high and a barrier to wider access to the Internet.[17]

Most government and civil service departments have Internet pages. The Czech Register of Companies is freely accessible on the net. The government has a programme of introduction of the Internet in schools, although its realization lags behind the countries of Western Europe. All major newspapers in the Czech Republic have their Internet pages. The broadcasting of public service radio and a number of commercial stations is available on the Internet. Czech public service television and commercial *Nova TV* make their news and current affairs programmes available on-line. A number of Czech Internet providers operate portals which offer a basic news and information service, as well as a search engine (www.seznam.cz, www.atlas.cz, www.centrum.cz). While the Internet versions of established newspapers have the strongest commercial impact, there are some Internet-only daily publications (e.g. *Britské listy*, www.blisty.cz) which attempt to do investigative journalism and challenge the conventional interpretation of events as presented by the domestic mainstream media.

In December 2000, 14 per cent of Czech households had access to the Internet. In 2000 almost 80 per cent of the users of the Internet in the Czech Republic were men. Women usually did not have access to their own computer and used the Internet once a week, while men used the Internet daily. By 2001 the number of women users had grown to 25 per cent. Students represent one-third of users. More than 50 per cent of users are under the age of twenty five. Eighty per cent of all users are under the age of thirty five. Many of the youngest users share a computer when accessing the Net; up to five young users often share the same machine. People over the age of twenty five usually have a computer of their own. Twenty six per cent of users are university-educated, 62 per cent of users have secondary education. Most users of the Internet still come from the information technology sector. Most live in large towns or their vicinity. Sixty per cent of Czech Internet users use the Net daily.

## POLITICS, POLICY, LAW AND REGULATION

The media system in the Czech Republic is primarily regulated by the Press Act (No. 46/2000 of the Collection of Laws, promulgated in February 2001) and by the Act on Radio and Television Broadcasting (latest update in May 2001). It is also governed by the Czech Bill of Fundamental Rights and Freedoms (Act No. 23/1991 of the Collection of Laws, promulgated on 9 January 1991). The Czech Syndicate of Journalists published a Journalists' Code of Ethics on 18 June 1998.

According to the Czech Press Act, the publisher of a periodical is responsible for the truthfulness of published information. Individuals who consider themselves harmed by information published by a periodical or in the electronic media have a legal right to demand the publication of their reply. The Czech Press Act gives journalists the right to protect their sources of information, unless the sources are involved in a criminal act. Periodicals which are not properly registered with the Culture Ministry may be fined.

The main regulatory organs for the media are the Council for Radio and Television Broadcasting, the Council for Czech (public service) Television, the Council for Czech (public service) Radio and the Advertising Council. As can be seen from the above, especially from the recent history of Czech Television and Nova Television, the regulatory institutions in the Czech Republic are weak and are often accused of political bias.

The future of the media in the Czech Republic depends on the future developments in the political arena. At the moment, the main political parties exercise influence over the main media outlets, especially the principal television stations, through informal behind-the-scenes contacts with top management. It seems unlikely that the situation will change in the future: politicians in the Czech Republic find it convenient to have docile and emasculated media. Foreign owners do not seem to interfere in politics in the Czech Republic, since most political developments in the country are too abstruse for outsiders and are locked in the 'inaccessible' Czech langage. Foreign media owners seem to be keen to exploit the Czech market for profit, flooding it with lowbrow entertainment material. This influence of the down-market international media sector is likely to grow stronger in future.

## STATISTICS

| | |
|---|---:|
| Population (2001) | 10,294,822 |
| Number of households as economic units (1991) | 3,983,900 |
| | |
| Overall movie admissions (2000) | 8,719,000 |
| Books published (titles, by 1999) | approx. 12,500 |

**Print media** Circulation of main daily newspapers (December 2001)

| | |
|---|---:|
| *Mladá fronta Dnes* | 309,226 |
| *Právo* | 213,964 |
| *Lidové noviny* | 88,835 |
| *Hospodářské noviny* | 74,968 |
| | |
| Tabloid newspapers | |
| *Blesk* | 320,913 |
| *Super* | 132,646 |
| | |
| Sporting daily | |
| *Sport* | 59,254 |
| Regional newspaper, produced centrally | |
| *Deníky Bohemia* | 442,290 |

**Broadcast media**

Audience share of main (50 per cent + national reach) terrestrial, cable and satellite television channels (%)

Terrestrial
Public
| | |
|---|---|
| ČT-1 | 20.6 |
| ČT-2 | 11.5 |

Private
| | |
|---|---|
| TV Nova: | 45.6 |
| Prima TV: (data from January–February 2002) | 17.4 |

Main cable television providers
UPC ČR
Intercable CZ

Satellite television providers
HBO ČR (film channel)
EastBox Digital (eighteen thematic programmes)

Main radio channels, with audience reach and share (data from the second half of 2001)

| Public service | Audience | Share(%) |
|---|---|---|
| ČRo-1 Radiožurnál | 1,012,000 | 12.2 |
| ČRo-2 Praha: | 456,000 | 6.6 |
| ČRo Brno: | 142,000 | 2.0 |
| ČRo České Budějovice: | 107,000 | 1.4 |
| ČRo Plzeň: | 68,000 | 0.8 |
| ČRo-3 Vltava: | 67,000 | 0.7 |
| ČRo Hradec Králové: | 62,000 | 0.9 |
| ČRo-6 RSE: | 52,000 | 0.4 |
| ČRo-Regina 1: | 39,000 | 0.4 |
| ČRo Ústí nad Labem: | 36,000 | 0.4 |
| ČRo Olomouc: | 28,000 | 0.3 |
| ČRo Ostrava: | 28,000 | 0.4 |

Private

Nationwide
| | | |
|---|---|---|
| Radio Impuls | 979,000 | 13.4 |
| Frekvence-1 | 749,000 | 9.5 |

Regional/local

| | | |
|---|---|---|
| Radio Blaník | 347,000 | 5.0 |
| Country Radio | 152,000 | 2.0 |
| Kiss Hády | 130,000 | 1.7 |
| Radio Orion | 129,000 | 1.6 |
| Radio Vysočina | 114,000 | 1.7 |
| Radio Čas | 108,000 | 1.4 |

Audience reach of all main forms of satellite, cable or terrestrial pay-television

Main cable television providers

UPC ČR: operates 372,000 sockets, reaches 700,000 households.
Intercable CZ: operates 200,000 sockets, reaches 350,000 households.
TES Media: operates 85,000 sockets.

Main satellite television providers

EastBox Digital
FTV Prima
CET 21
HBO Česká republika
Česká programová spolecnost

There are no terrestrial pay-television stations in the Czech Republic.

Percentage of households with video-cassette recorders, satellite receivers, DVDs, 2000.

| | |
|---|---|
| Video | 48 |
| Satellite receivers | 8.8 |
| Cable television | 25.4 |
| DVD | n.a. |

**Electronic media**

No digital reception in the Czech Republic.

| | |
|---|---|
| Households with access to the Internet, December 2000 | 14.0 |
| Inhabitants with a mobile phone, end of 2001 | 68.9 |

**Advertising spend (%)**

| | |
|---|---|
| Television | 46 |
| Print | 37 |
| Radio | 7 |
| Street/billboards | 7 |
| Internet | 1 |
| Other | 2 |

**Ownership**

The largest daily newspaper publishers

*Blesk*, Ringier ČR
*Mladá frouta* Dnes, Mafra
*Právo*, Borgis
*Super*, E-media
*Lidové noviny*, Lidové noviny
*Hospodářské noviny*, Economia

Mafra and Lidové noviny are owned by Rheinisch-Bergische Druckerei- und Verlaggesellschaft, Germany. E-media is owned by Epic Holding, Austria. Economia is controlled jointly by the *Wall Street Journal* and Handelsblatt.

The following major companies also publish magazines:

Ringier ČR: *ABC mladých techniků a přírodovědců, Blesk, Blesk magazín, Nedělní Blesk, Reflex, Týdeník Televize.*

MAFRA (owned by Rheinisch-Bergische Druckerei- und Verlaggesellschaft, Germany): *Magazín Dnes+TV,* the Internet news portal *iDnes, Mladá fronta Dnes.*

Axel Springer Praha: *Auto Exclusive, F1 Racing, Playboy, Auto Tip, Autoprofi, Svět motorů, Hokej, Popcorn.*

Bertelsmann Springer Cz: *Technický týdeník, Doprava a silnice, Istav – Informace ve stavebnictví, Stavba, Můj dům, Stavební příručka, Stavebniny pro můj dům, Mozaika, Katalog užitkových vozidel, Trucker, Materiály pro stavbu, Katalog rodinných domů. Truck Katalog – Katalog užitkových vozidel, Doprava a cesty, Spotřebiče pro domácnost, Koupelna a její vybavení, Okna, dveře, zimní zahrady, Vytápění, Podlahy, Panel Story.*

Borgis: *Magazín Dům a bydlení, Magazín Právo, Právo, TV, Televizní týden:*

Burda Praha: *Anna, Křížovky, Katka, Speciál Cinema, Autohit, Betynka, Byrda, Náš útulný byt, Nejlepší recepty, Naše krásná zahrada, Bydlíme s květinami, Svět ženy.*

Československý sport (owned by Ringier): *Sport, Volno.*

E-media (owned by Epic Holding, Austria): *Super, Super Magazín, Super neděle.*

Economia (controlled by the *Wall Street Journal* and Handelsblatt): *Hospodářské noviny, Marketing & Media, Právní rádce, Moderní obec, Bankovnictví, Ekonom, Listy, Logistika, Moderní řízení, Obchodní věstník, Odpady, Ovel, Stavitel, Technik, iHned.cz, mam.cz, Víkend HN.*

Europress: *Bravo, Bravo Girl! Bydlení, Chvilka pro tebe, Napsáno životem, Praktik, Rytmus Života, Tina, Žena a Život, Dívka, Čas na lásku.*

Lidové noviny (owned by Rheinisch-Bergische Druckerei- und Verlaggesellschaft, Germany): *Lidové noviny, Pátek Lidových novin.*

Mona (owned by VNU Magazine Group International, Netherlands): *Puls, Praktická žena, Ring, Story, Týdeník Květy, Vlasta, Beau Monde – Báječný svět, Překvapení, Střecha nad hlavou, Kuchyně pro labužníky, Půdní byt, Nové byty a pozemky, Koupelka, Men's Health, Postgraduální medicína, Sestra, Zdravotnické noviny, zdn.cz, Singmaking, Strategie, istrategie.cz.*

Vltava-Labe Press: *Deníky Moravia, SD, Severočeské deníky Bohemia, Jihočeské Deníky Bohemia, Západočeské Deníky Bohemia, Večerník Praha, Východočeské Deníky Bohemia, Středočeské Deníky Bohemia, Slovácko, Naše Opavsko, Týden u nás, Vyškovské noviny, Břeclavsko, Prostějovský týden, Nové Přerovsko, Hranický týden, Moravský sever, Slovácké noviny, Naše Valašsko, Nový život.*

The largest private radio stations:

Frekvence-1. Largest owners: Europe Développement International, 63.8% Evropa 2, 25.5%.

Radio Impuls. Owners: Ing. Ivan Baťka, 34%; Eurocast Rundfunk Beteiligungs 66%.

The main commercial television broadcasters:

CET-21/television Nova. Owners: PhDr. Vl. Železný, 11.8%; Vilja, 21.5%; Mgr P. Kršák, 16.6%; CEDC Management. Services, 1.4%; Česká spořitelna, 0.2%; MEF Media, 24.0%; Edikon, 24.5%.

FTV Premiéra, Prima television. Owners: Domeana, 29.3% (100% owned by GES Holding); GES Real Investment, 70.7%.

The largest cable television providers UPC Česká republika (UPC Czech Holding, Nizozemsko, owned by United Pan-Europe Communications, Nizozemsko). Owners: ICT, Los Angeles, 0.03%; UPC Czech Holding, 99.97%.

Intercable CZ, Vision Networks Tsjechie Holding, Nizozemsko. Owner: Vision Networks Tsjechie Holding, 100%.

TES Media, Central Europe Cable Holdings (ING Baring, USA). Owner: Central Europe Cable Holdings, 100%.

Satellite TV providers

EastBox Digital. Owner: New Media Investment, Švýcarsko, 100%.

HBO Česká republika. Owner: Ceska Holdings, USA 100%.

# NOTES

[1] Source: ABC CR, the details published by M&M (Media &Marketing), www.mam.cz.

[2] ditto.

[3] ditto.

[4] Source: A.C. Nielsen, the details published by M&M (Media &Marketing), www.mam.cz.

[5] Source: http://www.istrategie.cz/data/ov_nak_per_tisk/casopisy/2001_07_01.htm

[6] Source: ABC CR, the details published by M&M (Media &Marketing), www.mam.cz

[7] Source: A.C. Nielsen, the details published by M&M (Media &Marketing), www.mam.cz

[8] See the Internet pages of the Union of Czech Booksellers and the analysis by its Chairperson, Dr. Jaroslav Císar, at http://www.sckn.cz/ckt/ index.html.

[9] See the relevant quarterly and annual reports, submitted by CME to the US capital markets regulator Securities and Exchange Commission, http://www.sec.gov.

[10] See the 2001 Annual Report of the Council for Radio and Television Broadcasting, Section 3.2.1, http://www.rrtv.cz/zprava2001/321.html

[11] See the 2001 Annual Report of the Council for Radio and Television Broadcasting, Section 3.2.4, http://www.rrtv.cz/zprava2001/324.html .

[12] See the report (in Czech) at http://www.arbomedia.cz/uploads/updoc/odhady_vydaju_20010830.pdf

[13] See the 2001 Annual Report of the Council for Radio and Television Broadcasting, Section 3.3, http://www.rrtv.cz/zprava2001/33.html .

[14] See the 2001 Annual Report of the Council for Radio and Television Broadcasting, Section 3.4, http://www.rrtv.cz/zprava2001/34.html .

[15] See the information of the Czech Culture Ministry (in Czech) http://www.mkcr.cz/?menu=5&department=10

[16] *Report on the current state of the Czech Cinematography*, 2000, the Czech Culture Ministry, Prague.

[17] See the *Report on Internet in the Czech Republic (Výzkum Internetu)* Network media service and the Czech Culture ministry, , 2000, http://www.vyzkumInternetu.cz/zav_zprava/v_inter_C.pdf

# REFERENCES

Kroupa, Vladimír, and Šmíd, Milan, "The Limitations of a Free Market: Czech Republic" pp. 61–110, in *The Development of the Audiovisual Landscape in Central Europe since 1989*, ULP/John Libbey Media, Luton, 1998.

Šmíd, Milan, Média, internet, Nova a já, (The media, the internet, Nova TV and myself), ISV Publishers, Prague, 2000.

Šmíd, Milan, Kaplan, Frank, L. and Trager, Robert, 'The Czech Republic's Broadcasting Law: Provisions, Problems and Expectations.' http://www.grady.uga.edu/coxcenter/MonoCzech2.htm.

Culík, Jan and Pecina, Tomáš, V hlavních zprávách: Televize (On the Main News: Television), ISV Publishers, Prague, 2001.

Culík, Jan, articles on the Czech media in Central Europe Review, see http://www.ce-review.org/authorarchieves/culik_archieve/culik_main.html, passim.

Culík, Jan an entry on Czech Republic, in Censorship: *World Encyclopedia*, vol. 1., edited by Derek Jones, Fitzroy Dearborne Publishers, London – Chicago, 2001, pp. 621–631.

Quarterly and annual reports, submitted to the US Securities and Exchange Commission, see http://www.sec.gov.

Reports of the Czech Council for Radio and Television Broadcasting, see http://www.rrtv.cz/ en/.

*Radio and Television Systems in Central and Eastern Europe*, Council of Europe Publishing 1998.

Kaid, Lynda Lee, *Television and Politics in Evolving Democracies*, Nova Science Publishers Inc., 1999.

Osvaldová, Barbora, Zpravodajství v médiích (News reporting in the media), Prague, Karolinum 2001.

Jirák, Jan and Köpplová, Barbora, Média a spolecnost (Media and society), Prague, Portál, 2003.

# 4: Denmark

FRANDS MORTENSEN

## NATIONAL PROFILE

Denmark has a population of 5.3 million spread over 43,069 km². The country is as flat as a pancake, and therefore easy to cable and cheap to provide with terrestrial broadcasting. Urbanization is uneven, with 1.5 million living in the capital Copenhagen, 1.4 million in provincial towns with more than 10,000 inhabitants, 1.2 million in towns with more than 1,000 and 1.2 million in the rural areas. The number of households is 2.44 million. Danish is the language spoken by everybody except a limited number of refugees and guest workers (immigrants make up 7 per cent of the population). Denmark is, compared with many other countries, a relatively homogeneous society with respect to culture and values.

Denmark has been a member of NATO since 1949 and of the European Union since 1973, but there is an old tradition of cultural and political affiliation with the Nordic countries, and Scandinavia is often considered as one unit (but it should not be in relation to media markets).

The political system is a multi-party system with more than ten political parties standing at elections and eight to ten parties elected to the parliament (Folketinget). No single party has a majority and the political system has for decades made compromise decisions. The government has nearly always been a coalition, and for the last thirty years always a minority one. The Social Democratic Party has for more than half a century been the largest party, but that came to an end in 2001, when Venstre (a liberal party) overtook the Social Democrats. For ten years from 1983 Denmark had a centre government under the leadership of the Conservative Party, then in 1993 a centre-left government

with Social Democratic leadership ruled until 2001, when Venstre formed a centre-right government and its leader became Prime Minister.

Denmark is a capitalist society with a large public sector, but the state has very limited involvement in industrial production. The standard of living is high, as is the distribution of consumer goods. Most Danes think Denmark is one of the leading examples of a welfare state. Media policy is an issue for debate in Danish society, but it has never been close to becoming the main election issue.

## STRUCTURE AND OWNERSHIP

### The print media

#### The newspaper press

A close relationship between newspapers and political parties existed as the press developed over the last century, reaching a peak at the time of the First World War when 150 newspapers were published. But competition and commercialization of the press began a process of concentration. In 1945 there were 123 newspapers, in 1982 forty seven, while in 2002 the number was twenty nine. The circulation was, in 1945, 1.7 million copies (with 4 million Danes), in 1982 1.8 million copies (and 5.1 million Danes) and in 2002 1.4 million copies (and 5.3 million Danes). Despite an increase in population (and even more so in the number of households, as one-third of Danes now live alone) the total circulation has decreased, especially in the last fifteen years. Most of the closures took place in the provinces, resulting in a monopoly for city newspapers. In the capital the number of papers decreased from thirteen in 1945 to ten in 1982, and seven in 2002. Furthermore, newspapers are no longer affiliated to political parties. After the closure of the last Social Democratic paper in 2001, it is commonly acknowledged that all Danish newspapers are to be found at the centre/right of the political spectrum. The most left-wing paper (*Ekstra Bladet*) has a former Conservative Minister of Justice as editor-in-chief!

Only three Danish papers can be characterized as national papers, two of them are tabloids (*B.T.* and *Ekstra Bladet*), while the biggest one is the broadsheet *Morgenavisen Jyllands-Posten*, which is not, like the tabloids, published in Copenhagen, but in the biggest town of the provinces, Århus. The rest of the papers published in the capital circulate mostly in Copenhagen, while papers in the provinces also tend to circulate in the town of publication. Only four have regional distribution. Besides the two tabloids and three special papers, all the papers are broadsheets of the omnibus type (written for everyone on everything), with the provincial papers increasingly concentrating on local material.

Denmark has Sunday papers, which are Sunday editions of the weekday papers, and the circulation has been quite constant. In 2001 there were ten Sunday papers with 1.3 million copies distributed. The figures for 1982 were eleven titles and 1.2 million copies.

The biggest structural change in the last fifteen years has been the decline of the tabloids. Their circulation has halved since the break-up of the television monopoly in 1988 and the start of satellite television in Danish in 1990. Since then, sex, violence and royal gossip are no longer a monopoly of the tabloids. The three biggest broadsheets (so-called quality papers) have together had quite a success, both in absolute figures and relative to other papers.

The Danish press is entirely privately owned, mostly in the form of limited companies, and often organized as foundations in order to prevent hostile take-overs. Concentration of ownership was moderate until the 1980s. Then Det berlingske Officin started to buy some weak papers in the provinces. In 2001 the company was taken over by the Norwegian industrial conglomerate Orkla. The latter now controls one-third of the total circulation of daily newspapers. Foreign ownership had not existed until then, except the ownership by the Swedish company, Bonnier, of the financial paper *Børsen*.

Until the arrival of Orkla the owners of the Danish press regarded themselves as publishers, not as capitalists. The object was high circulation figures, not net profit. Orkla demands 15 per cent return on invested capital, a figure that no Danish paper has shown for the last twenty years. It is, however, generally recognized that the financing of the press will increasingly have to rely on the more efficient use of existing resources. The number of pages rose by thirteen in the non-local broadsheet papers between 1985 and 2000 and by five in the local papers, but in 2001 the three biggest broadsheet papers reduced the number of pages and announced further reductions in both editorial pages and special supplements.

The Danish press is dependent on advertising to a varying degree. For the big broadsheets and tabloids, 55 per cent of income comes from newspaper sales, 42 per cent from advertising, and only 3 per cent from other activities. The regional papers get 42 per cent of their income from sales, 48 per cent from advertising and 10 per cent from other things, while the local provincial papers get 36 per cent from sales, 28 per cent from advertising and 35 per cent from other activities, especially printing. Two different trends have appeared in relation to press advertising. Denmark had a boom in the 1990s, and advertising expenditure grew 50 per cent between 1994 and 2000. In 2001 a recession started, and it has not stopped yet. Second, there has been some shifting in the placement of advertisements. Newspapers have seen their share of the total advertising spend decline from 32 per cent to 29 per cent, while electronic media increased their share from 19 per cent to 21 per cent. But not all print media suffered in this way. The advertising spend in the free local weeklies and free consumer magazines has increased from 20 per cent to 23 per cent.

Readership patterns, however, show danger signals for the print media, and especially for newspapers. In the 1970s it was common knowledge that 90 per cent of Danes had read a weekday paper yesterday. In 2001 the figure was just below 75 per cent, while in terms of age, 85 per cent of those over fifty years had read a paper yesterday, but only 65 per cent of those under thirty.

### The periodical and magazine press

The weekly magazine press has for twenty years been totally controlled by two Danish media companies, Egmont (a third of the circulation) and Aller (two-thirds). The total circulation was 1.7 million in 2001, a fall from 2 million in 1982. Women's magazines, only three in number, made up 14 per cent of the circulation in 2001, compared with 21 per cent in 1982. The biggest group is family magazines, with four titles and 45 per cent of circulation in 1982 and 42 per cent in 2001. The one with the biggest circulation is *Familie Journalen*, a very traditional family magazine (1.2 million Danes still live in rural areas). The gossip and television magazines (with a lot of stuff on the royal family) is the only growing group: four titles and 0.5 million copies in 1982 and 0.7 million in 2001. The magazine press was a gold mine in the 1990s, although advertising income (which contributes only 15 per cent of the total income of weekly magazines) stagnated. Of total advertising expenditure, only 3 per cent goes to magazines. Readership figures show that 75 per cent read at least one weekly magazine in 1982; in 2001 this figure grew to 80 per cent, despite the fall in total circulation!

### Book publishing

In 1990 there were about 11,000 book titles published and sales revenue was DKr 1.8 billion. The figures grew slowly but steadily to 14,500 titles and DKr 2.6 billion in 1999. Profit was low, about 4 per cent of turnover. Three publishing groups became dominant in the 1990s with the Danish Gyldendahl group as the leading one, from both an economic and a cultural point of view. The other ones are Bonnier Forlagene (owned by Bonnier) and Egmont group (owned by Egmont). Together they have about 50 per cent of total turnover. In 1999 3,300 titles were translations, 70 per cent from English, 13 per cent from Scandinavian languages, 7 per cent from German and 4 per cent from French. The rest of the world together took 5 per cent. Non-fiction dominates with 11,000 titles in 1999, fiction 3,300. Also published were about 2,000 titles for children and young people, a slow growth from 1,200 in 1990. The old system of fixed book prices was given up in 2001.

## The electronic (audio-visual) media

### Television

The broadcasting of television started on a regular basis in 1953 as part of the radio monopoly Statsradiofonien, later Danmarks Radio, now DR. (On the establishment of Statsradiofonien see under 'Radio'). The studios and management were based in Copenhagen. In the 1970s DR established only one studio outside the capital, namely in Århus. DR produced all the Danish material itself, except some popular drama, and bought about 50 per cent abroad, especially from the United Kingdom and United States.

Cable television started in the 1960s, when the Danes formed communal aerial installations and so gained access to broadcasting from Sweden, and from West and East Germany. By the beginning of the 1980s two-thirds of the population had access to foreign television, either by cable or, along the border, by terrestrial reception. A third of viewing time was spent on foreign television.

Digitalization of television began in 1998 in cable and satellite. In 2001 there were 46,000 digital cable households and 150,000 DTH households on two platforms: ViaSat, owned by MTG, and Canal Digital, owned by Telenor, but development is slow. Terrestrial digital television has been legislated for by the parliament four times, but nothing has happened yet.

The appearance of satellite television in 1982, when EUTELSAT Council allowed Satellite Television (later bought by Rupert Murdoch and renamed Sky Television), was a shock, also for Danish politicians. As part of a national cultural self-defence they decided to break up the monopoly of DR and create a new national television station. It was named TV-2, started broadcasting in October 1988 and had five purposes.

First, it should protect Danes from foreign cultural influence. Second, it should create competition regarding news broadcasting; DR had been accused of a left-wing reporting bias. Third, it should move outside the capital, and accordingly the headquarters were located in Odense, and eight regional television stations were built. Fourth the heavy bureaucracy of DR should be avoided by placing most of the programme production outside the station with independent producers (following the model of Channel 4 in the United Kingdom). And finally advertising should be allowed (but only between programmes, and no advertising for alcohol), but should not be the only income. TV-2, which like DR is an independent public institution with public service obligations, also draws on licence fee income. In 1990 this constituted 36 per cent of the total income, in 2000, 27 per cent.

*DR* and *TV-2* are the only national terrestrial television channels. In 1983 local channels were allowed, being transmitted terrestrially and by cable, and thirty four stations tried to survive. At the start there was no state support, and advertising was allowed in 1988, so survival for the local stations was hard. They did not play any significant role, apart from the local station in Copenhagen, Kanal 2, until networking was introduced in April 1997. Eleven of them then formed the network TvDanmark, controlled by SBS, a US company located in Luxembourg.

Satellite television in Danish started in 1990, when the MTG-owned Scandinavian channel ScanSat split into three national channels and created TV-3 Danmark. The station was located in the United Kingdom, on the grounds of UK advertising rules that allowed programme breaks and advertising for alcohol. In 1995 MTG launched two channels, ZTV for youth and TV-6 for women, but their success was limited, and in 1996 they were united and renamed TV3+. TV-3 and TV3+ are based on advertising, but in the late 1990s they started to collect low pay-television charges. Sport and US series and films dominate the programming. News broadcasting stopped in 1999.

In 1996 DR started a satellite channel, DR-2, a public service channel, which reaches only three-quarters of all households. Programming is very serious (nickname 'Channel Clever'), financing is by licence fee. TV-2 also has a satellite channel which started in October 2000 named TV-2 Zulu, a youth channel, financed by advertising and the licence fee. And in January 2000 TvDanmark created a new satellite channel, TvDanmark 1, located in London, while the terrestrial network was renamed TvDanmark 2. Programming is as for TV-3.

In March 1997 DR, TV-2 and the national telecom, TDC, started a sports pay channel in cable, but it closed in December, after losses of more than DKr 200 million.

So since October 2000 Denmark has had eight national TV channels and two pay-TV film channels with Danish subtitles (TV 1000 and Canal+ Danmark), while there are still only 5.3 million Danes. Foreign television can be received in 80 per cent of the households, Three-quarters have access to at least twenty four channels, but the Danes prefer their national television. Eighty-eight per cent of all viewing time is spent on the Danish television stations.

DR and TV-2 are public service institutions with an obligation to broadcast a diversity of programmes, and they have been quite a success. TV-2, after only a year, was the most frequently viewed channel in Denmark, and still is. Together with DR, TV-2 had more than two-thirds of all viewing time in 2001. But the public service channels have a problem attracting younger viewers. Those between the ages of twelve and twenty years spend only 56 per cent of their viewing time on the channels of DR and TV-2, those between twenty one and thirty four 60 per cent, and those over fifty five 76 per cent.

The finance available in the Danish television system has developed tremendously. In 1990 it was DKr 2.1 billion; by 2000 it had more than doubled to DKr 4.9 billion. Licence fee income for television increased from DKr 1.3 billion in 1990 to 2.2 billion in 2000. However, in percentage terms this represented a reduction from 62 per cent to 45 per cent of total income. Advertising increased from DKr 0.6 million to DKr 1.8 billion and pay-television grew from DKr 0.2 billion in 1990 to Dkr 0.9 billion in 2000. But even with this increase, there is not enough money in the system for eight national channels.

### Radio

In 1926 the monopoly of radio broadcasting was given to Statsradiofonien, following the model of the BBC in the United Kingdom. From the very beginning, it was to be financed by licence fees, and thus the cost of broadcasting should not burden the state budget as such. No commercials were allowed. Statsradiofonien (since 1964 Danmarks Radio, now DR) has the status of an independent public institution, and therefore is neither a private business nor part of the state apparatus. The responsibility for broadcasting matters has been placed with a variety of Ministers over the years. At present it belongs to the Ministry of Culture.

The first AM radio channel, P-1, was in 1951 joined by a second, P-2, both of them national channels. The international frequency conference in Stockholm in 1961 assigned Denmark four national FM channels, and in 1963 DR started a third music channel, as a counter-move to a very popular commercial Danish pirate radio channel, broadcasting from a ship in the Øresund and closed down by the police in 1962. In the 1970s DR slowly developed regional radio channels as part of the second channel. The regional system was completed in 1982 when the ninth station opened.

The fourth channel was assigned to Denmark in 1984 in connection with the international expansion of the FM band from 100 MHz to 108 MHz, but was not brought into service at once. This surplus frequency became part of an intensified debate in the 1980s and 1990s on how to break the monopoly of DR in national and regional radio broadcasting.

The problem played a central role in the negotiations about the Media Agreement 2001–4, when a majority of the parties decided to invite tenders for both a fourth and a fifth nationwide radio channel, the latter reaching only around 80 per cent of the population. The presupposed content of the channels was described in a way that made the fourth channel most attractive to DR (classical and modern music, speech, news and current affairs), while the fifth channel was supposed to be purely commercial, but having an obligation to offer news – 'comparable to the level of DR'. Even though eight private companies took part in the tender, the new Radio and Television Board decided to allocate the fourth channel to DR. The channel was launched during spring and summer 2001. Whether the fifth channel or even more nationwide radio channels will be put up to an auction will depend on the revision of the Media Agreement, announced by the new government to take place during 2002.

Local radio is organized in two layers. The first consists of a commercial layer of around 100 local radio stations. Here three major network company stations have developed through proxies in spite of the legislation against networks. A few independent local stations dominate this group. The non-commercial layer consists of approximately 120 stations, covering a wide range of community interests, run by non-profit local organizations and associations. The non-commercial stations can apply for public subsidies from the Ministry of Culture for basic costs and financing of special programme productions. The amount of this public fund is DKr 50 million per year.

DR, which since 2001 has had four channels, had a high and stable share of the radio market during most of the 1990s, i.e. 80 per cent in 1994. But in later years its market share has declined, to 65 per cent in 2000. Weekly reach among the young audience during the same period has fallen to 31 per cent for the age group twelve to nineteen years, and this indicates that DR has developed a serious generation problem. The younger audience groups (twelve to forty years) seem to prefer local commercial radio.

Before the channel reform of 2001 DR P-1 (culture, art, current affairs, news) had a 6 per cent share; P-2 Music (a shared channel with P-4, broadcasting nights and weekends) had a share of 4 per cent; P-3 (the popular music channel) 23 per cent and P-4 (a regional channel shared with P-4) had a share of 33 per cent.

The answer from DR to the generation problem has been to build up a more aggressive strategy. P-3 and P-4 are now more distinctively both age and music-formatted – P-3 aiming primarily at thirteen to thirty and P-4 at twenty-five and over. Computer-aided select systems for music have been developed along the same lines as for the commercial local radio stations, only with more Danish music. In order to keep a public service profile and to serve the youth audience needs for quality news, P-3 in 2001 launched formatted news during peak hours (noon to 6.00 p.m. on weekdays). This has been a controversial initiative, offending the traditional advocates of public service news as news for all citizens, setting a common agenda. On the Web site you will find all DR channels streaming and in addition three music style formatted Web channels for the young audience (twelve to twenty): SKUM 1, SKUM 2 and SKUM 3.

The commercial local radio sector is still not allowed to network except for short news programmes and during night-time. Radio commercials have a share of the total advertising market which is less than 2 per cent, and a considerable number of the commercial stations are running on the edge of bankruptcy or acting in a grey area between information and commercials.

### Film and video

In 1988, when the television monopoly was broken, there was already a process of concentration occurring among Danish cinemas. In nearly all the towns of the provinces, there was a cinema monopoly, if there was a cinema at all. Fifty per cent of municipalities had no cinema in the 1980s. Only in Copenhagen was there real competition between two chains, Nordisk Film (now owned by Egmont, the biggest media company in Denmark), and Metronome (now Sandrew Metronome). This situation has not changed much; some twenty cinemas have closed since then, and in 2001 there were 164 cinemas with 350 screens. There is only one national chain, Nordisk Film. Cinecity, a German company which tried to build up a national chain, collapsed and their cinemas were put up for sale.

The number of screened films has declined tremendously, from 1,216 in 1988 to 621 in 2000. Most of them (315) are American. Of the new releases (in total 192), 108 are from the United States, seventeen are Danish and fifty one from other European countries. Admissions in 1988 were nearly 10 million, and this figure is rather constant: in 2000, 10.6 million. In terms of films watched, 7.5 million watched US films, 2 million watched Danish productions, with just 1 million watching European and other films.

The distributor market is dominated by four companies: Nordisk Film with 29 per cent of titles, UIP with 26 per cent, Sandrew Metronome with 18 per cent and Disney/Buena Vista with 12 per cent. Their share of admissions is nearly the same.

Gross box office including VAT was DKr 330 million in 1988; in 2000 it had gone up to DKr 554 million. Of the top twenty feature films, there were fourteen from the United States in 2000, and six from Denmark.

The production of Danish film went up in the late 1990s, encouraged by state subsidies. The Danish Film Institute, established in 1972, has a total budget of DKr 349 million, with DKr 196 million used to subsidize production and development, and DKr 44 million for distribution and marketing. The number of feature films produced has gone up from approximately ten per year in the 1980s to seventeen in 2000, while the official target is 24 per year.

The Danish video market is the double of the cinema market. In 1999 turnover was DKr 1.1 billion, a figure that has been almost the same since 1996. Selling and rental take nearly 50 per cent each. Titles are the same as in the cinemas, but with one-year delay.

## The Internet and related on-line media

In 2001 every other household (54 per cent) had access to the Internet, compared with 1997, when the figure was as low as 8 per cent. Forty-seven per cent of families had a personal computer in their home in 1997 – in 2001, 69 per cent. Of the entire population, 73 per cent had access to the Internet, either at home or at work. These figures place Denmark among the top five of Internet-literate nations. Behind these figures will be found considerable demographic differences regarding use. Students are the most frequent users of the Internet (96 per cent). Among people not included in the work force only 23 per cent have access to the Internet at home. Age, education and gender are also major factors, e.g. 41 per cent of men access the Internet every day, compared with 30 per cent of women. The most frequent use is reported to be e-mailing – 39 per cent use the Internet frequently for that purpose, and the same goes for searching out specific information. Net banking is used frequently by 25 per cent of users. In 2001, 21 per cent of the population had purchased goods or commodities on the Internet during the last year, most frequently tickets for cinemas, concerts or theatres.

The Internet as a medium for advertising has not proved its efficacy compared with the print and electronic media, but none the less there has been a rapid growth in advertising expenditure, from DKr 85 million in 1999 to DKr 316 million in 2000.

Among the fifteen most popular Danish Web sites are the Internet versions of three of the major daily newspapers. The two public service broadcasting companies – DR and TV-2 – are among the top ten, indicating the use of the Internet as part of the 'multiple platform strategy' of the traditional media. Especially in youth programming, you will find examples of interactivity between audience and programmes, involving radio, television, mobile phones (SMS), e-mail and chat, but most of the programme-related material is additional information. A growing number of radio and television programmes from the public service providers are stored and accessible to the public for a period of time after broadcasting.

Broadband Internet has not been a success yet. Nearly 90 per cent of households have a possibility to get ADSL, but only 152,000 had subscribed by the end of 2001. The price is also high: approximately DKr 10,000 for 2 Mbit/s per year.

# POLITICS, POLICY, LAW AND REGULATION

No general principle guides overall media policy. The electronic media have been regulated carefully and in detail, and a market economy has only slowly been introduced. The print media on the other hand have had very limited regulation and by and large have lived according to that logic.

Until 1980 there was no explicit media policy. Then the government established the

Royal Media Commission with the assignment to create a coherent national media policy. This resulted in six reports in the mid-1980s, but in parliament there was no majority to transform the recommendations into law. The same happened when a media committee was at work in the mid-1990s. So the media system remains a patchwork with no dominant principle, to the despair of every systematist.

The system has always been considered as a national one, and foreign players have been rare, for which reason Orklas's takeover of Det berlingske Officin was a real shock. For years there was a tendency to ignore the media policy of the European Union, but that changed in the late 1990s.

Until 2001 the electronic media system was regulated directly by the Ministry of Culture, and most decisions were open to political debate. Now the situation has changed. A new and totally independent Radio and Television Board has been set up. The major tasks of the Board are to issue final permits to two new territorially based analogue radio channels, and to the future digital radio and television channels. In addition the board must carry out tasks previously handled by the old ministerial committee on Local Radio and Television, the Board for Radio and Television Commercials, and the Satellite and Cable Board, which have all been abolished. Apart from the above-mentioned tasks the Radio and Television Board issues satellite and cable permits, handles cases of illegal advertising and subsidies, hidden advertising, the supervision of advertising directed towards children, and cases concerning the local radio and television area as second instance. It also appears that the new Radio and Television Board will analyse and comment on the public service remit of DR and TV-2.

Another interesting, and more and more powerful, regulatory agency is the Danish Competition Authority, which from 1998, according to the competition law of the European Union, has started examining the media system and made important decisions on, for instance, sports rights and the dominant position of TV-2 in the electronic advertising market.

## The press

Freedom of the press goes back more than 150 years, to the constitution of 1849. It gives everybody the right to impart information, and it prohibits censorship. Other laws specify and set limitations on this freedom, notably the press law, the penal code and procedural law. The legal framework of the press does not encompass monopoly regulation (as does the general EU system), but it does provide for a state subsidy scheme.

The laws deal with editorial responsibility, the right of reply, the right to privacy, libel, defamation, incitement to crime, and the right of journalists to protect their sources. In addition to the legal regulations the press has created a set of voluntary ethical rules which were incorporated in law in 1991. At this point the press law's system of editorial responsibility was expanded to include broadcasters.

Unlike the other Nordic countries, Denmark does not have a tradition of active political intervention in the newspaper business, as for instance through direct subsidy. The existing subsidy – exemption from VAT and cheap postal rates – is difficult to evaluate precisely. But in 2001 the value of the cheap postal rates was DKr 0.25 billion, while exemption from VAT was about DKr 0.75 billion. But although this form of subsidy helps the industry by enabling it to sell its product relatively cheaply, it does nothing to change structural problems. On the contrary, it supports the biggest papers most.

Despite the fact that many newspapers are in crisis, it is not expected that the parliament will establish a system of direct subsidy. And newspaper owners and editors have consistently argued that direct subsidy would make the press dependent on the state in an unacceptable manner.

## The electronic media

All national broadcasting is regulated by the Broadcasting Act (Bekendtgørelse No. 701, 2001). In the same law the community antenna network and other types of cable networks are regulated, as well as satellite broadcasting. Included also are rules on advertising and sponsorship.

The general aims and scope of public broadcasting (news, information, education, entertainment and art) are based on the main objectives: quality, diversity and plurality. Fairness and impartiality are mentioned as objectives in relation to the transmission of information. Special consideration must be given to the Danish language and Danish culture, including the diversity of cultural interests in Danish society as a whole. Also the on-line activities, including Web services, of DR and TV-2 (http://www.dr.dk and http://tv2.dk) are made part of the public service obligations and as such subject to its rules (Broadcasting Act para. 6).

Independent boards, appointed by the Ministry of Culture and the parliament, govern the public service broadcasting institutions. The Board of Governors for DR consists of thirteen members, three appointed by the Minister of Culture, including the chairman, eight by parliament and two by and among the staff. The Board of Governors of TV-2 consists of twelve members. Eight of them, including the chairman, are appointed by the Minister. Two members are selected by the staff, and two by the eight regional stations. As a whole the governors of the two boards must have knowledge of the media, business management and culture. Each of the eight regional TV-2 stations has a locally appointed board, based on county and municipal representatives and local associations. All appointments are for four years. DR and TV-2 each had its own Programme Advisory Board, with no real political influence, and they were closed down in 2002.

DR is financed exclusively by licence fees, TV-2 partly by advertising and licence fees. Since 1990 the public service institutions have been given four-year budgets with an annual increase, recent years mainly following the trend of prices and salaries. The licence fees are jointly collected by DR and distributed by the Minister to the national broadcasters and – since 1997 – to other media, i.e. support of local radio and television programming (DKr 25 million, less than 1 per cent of the total licence fee income – Dkr 3.2 billion in 2001).

The regulation of the first three radio channels of DR and the television channels of DR and TV-2 are handled by the Ministry of Culture. Other things, including the fourth radio channel of DR, are under the Radio and Television Board.

Parts of the regulation of local and community radio and television are decentralized. Each municipality, or a group of neighbouring municipalities, has an obligation to form a Local Radio and Television Board, appointed by the town council. Appointments are for four years.

One of the major tasks of the local board is to issue licences for local stations – local radio for a maximum of five years, local television for seven years. Only local associations, established with the purpose of producing and broadcasting local programmes, are entitled to a non-commercial licence and in most municipalities several stations share a transmitter and one frequency, sharing the programme hours. Local business companies, including local newspapers, are allowed to be part of the association. However, if a local newspaper has a majority position it is required that the station serves as a forum for a diverse local debate. A commercial licence can be issued to an association whose members represent a diversity of local business and cultural interests. In that case such a station will have a frequency of its own, an accepted prerequisite for commercial income.

In 1997 networking was allowed for local television. However, the stations were required to allow one hour for daily local news programming and three hours of so-called windows for non-commercial local television stations. One of the first acts of the new centre-right government was to abolish this requirement of commercial television stations (DKr 25 million per year).

The Local Radio and Television Boards furthermore have to monitor local programmes in order to ensure that the regulations concerning advertising, sponsorship and sales of programme hours are not violated. They have to prioritize among the applications for programme support to the central fund and make sure that the funding is used as specified. In cases of disagreement between a station and the Local Radio and Television Board, any decision can be appealed to, to the central Radio and Television Board, which makes the final decision.

Major reform of this area has been on the agenda of the right-wing parties in recent years, allowing deregulation, i.e. increased access for commercial radio and television, both at a local and at a nationwide level. Included in that reform is the privatization of TV-2, leaving DR alone as a public service institution, maybe even with a reduced range of programming possibilities, concentrated on 'serious programming'.

The problem for the centre-right government is that public service programming is quite popular with viewers. *TV-2* caters for popular tastes, and among liberal and conservative parties in the *TV-2* regions there is quite strong resistance to any plans to 'deregulate' *TV-2*.

The new government has not yet announced its plans for a reform of the media policy, and it is uncertain what will be proposed. Will Denmark have a true liberal media policy reform or will the centre and right-wing parties still be closet Social Democrats as they have been in media politics for the last twenty years?

## The Internet and related on-line media

As for the Internet-based media, there is no specific policy.

# STATISTICS

Figures are from 2001, unless otherwise indicated.

| | |
|---|---|
| National population | 5,349,212 |
| Number of households | 2,444,000 |
| Movie admissions (ticket sales) | |
| Overall admissions | 11,920,000 |
| Danish films | 3,714,000 |

| | |
|---|---|
| Books published, 1999 (titles) | |
| For adults | 14,455 |
| of which: | |
| Fiction | 3,285 |
| Non-fiction | 11,170 |
| For children and young people | 1,916 |

**Print media**  Circulation of main daily newspapers

| National | |
|---|---|
| Morgenavisen Jyllands-Posten | 179,243 |
| Berlingske Tidende | 147,849 |
| Politiken | 140,983 |
| BT | 128,660 |
| Ekstra Bladet | 127,853 |

| Regional | |
|---|---|
| Jydske Vestkysten | 87,123 |
| Nordjyske Stiftstidende | 81,693 |
| Århus Stiftstidende | 59,563 |

**Broadcast media**  Main terrestrial, cable and satellite television channels (with approximate audience share):

| | Distribution | Reach(%) | Audience share(%) |
|---|---|---|---|
| Public | | | |
| TV-2 | Terrestrial | 99.7 | 35 |
| DR 1 | Terrestrial | 99.8 | 28 |
| DR 2 | Satellite | 78.1 | 3 |
| TV 2 Zulu | Satellite | 65.3 | 2 |
| | | | |
| Private | | | |
| TV-3 | Satellite | 70.9 | 8 |
| TV-3+ | Satellite | 65.9 | 4 |
| TvDanmark 2 | Terrestrial | 74.5 | 6 |
| TvDanmark 1 | Satellite | 49.6 | 2 |

Main radio channels, public and private, with approximate audience share, 2000 (%)
Public

| | |
|---|---|
| P1 | 6 |
| P2 | 4 |
| P3 | 23 |
| P4 | 33 |

Private

| | |
|---|---|
| Local radio/other radio | 35 |

Percentage of households reached by all main forms of satellite, cable or terrestrial pay-television:

| | |
|---|---|
| Canal + Danmark | 4.8 |
| TV 1000 | 4.6 |

Percentage of households with video-cassette recorder, satellite receiver, DVD player:

| | |
|---|---|
| Video-cassette recorder | 81.1 |
| Satellite receiver | 17.3 |
| DVD player | 7.2 |

**Electronic media**

Percentage of households with digital television reception, by whatever means:

| | |
|---|---|
| Satellite | 6.3 |
| Cable | 1.9 |
| Total | 8.2 |

Internet household penetration and use (%)

| | |
|---|---|
| Home | 60 |
| Work | 53 |
| Total | 73 |

Mobile phone ownership and use

| | |
|---|---|
| Mobile GSM subscriptions, end 2001 | 3,935,797 |
| Outgoing mobile traffic, July–December 2001 (minutes) | 1,624,814,000 |
| SMS sent, July–December 2001(number of messages) | 730,912,000 |

**Advertising spend, 2000 (%)**

| | |
|---|---|
| Newspapers | 30 |
| Magazines | 3 |
| Television | 16 |
| Radio | 2 |
| Other | 49 |

**Ownership**

Main media companies, 2000

| | Turnover ¤ million | Share of market |
|---|---|---|
| Egmont | 1,069 | No holding in press/television |
| Orkla Media | 799 | 36% of daily newspapers |
| DR | 362 | 31.8% of television viewing |
| TV-2/Danmark | 203 | 36.3% of television viewing |
| Politiken | 199 | 18.7 % of daily newspapers |
| Morgenavisen Jyllands-Posten | 146 | 13.6% of daily newspapers |

# REFERENCES

Carlsson, Ulla and Eva Harrie (eds.) *Media Trends in Denmark, Finland, Iceland, Norway and Sweden.* Goteborg: Noricom, 2001.

Nikoltchev, Suzanne, *Legal Guide to Audiovisual Media in Europe. Recent Legal Developments in Broadcasting, Film, Telecommunications and the Global Information Society in Europe.*

Ministry of culture home page: http://www.Kum.dk/sw832.asp

# 5: Finland

MARINA ÖSTERLUND-KARINKANTA

## NATIONAL PROFILE

Finland has 5.2 million people but it is sparsely populated. It has a total area of 338,145 km² and a population density of seventeen persons per square-kilometres. Almost 70 per cent of its inhabitants live in cities. Vast areas of the country are only thinly populated. Finland has two official languages, Finnish and Swedish. The Swedish-speaking minority amounts to 291,000 people, that is, 5.6 per cent of the population. Most of them live in the coastal areas of western and southern Finland. Sámi is spoken by small groups, mainly in Lapland. Foreign languages are spoken by 109,000 people as their mother language. Half-way between Finland and Sweden are the autonomous Åland Islands with a population of 26,000, almost all Swedish-speakers.

The parliament is unicameral and its 200 seats are divided as follows (2002): the Social Democratic Party with fifty two, the Centre Party with forty seven, the National Coalition Party with forty six, the Left Wing Alliance with twenty, the Swedish People's Party with eleven, the Green Party with eleven, the Christian Democrats with ten, the True Finns Party with one, the Alkio Center Group with one and the Åland Islands with one seat. Of the 200 representatives seventy four are women.

The present government is an exceptionally large coalition government (as was the previous one). The government includes the Social Democratic Party (which holds the Prime Minister's post), the National Coalition Party (conservatives), the Left Wing Alliance and the Swedish People's Party. The Green Party left the government in May 2002.

For centuries Finland was part of Sweden. For 100 years (1809–1917) it was part of Russia as an autonomous grand duchy under the Russian czar. Swedish remained the administrative and cultural language and the laws of the Swedish period remained in force. Finnish became the majority language of Finland, but it was not until the 1860s that it was standardized (Alho, 1997) and began to be used, when needed, in official contexts. A legal statute gave both languages equal status in 1902. Through a parliamentary reform in 1906 the unicameral parliament was established as a parliament elected by universal suffrage. Finland was then the first country in the world to give women the right both to vote and to stand for parliament. On 6 December 1917 Finland declared its independence. In 1918 there was a civil war, after which Finland became a republic. The Constitutional Act of 1919 included a paragraph on freedom of speech which gave everybody the right to publish printed or picture products. It also affirmed Finnish and Swedish as the official languages of Finland. This was also stated in the new constitution which came into force on 1 March 2000. On 1 January 1995 Finland joined the European Union.

The economic recession at the beginning of the 1990s hit Finland quite hard and led to high unemployment. Even after the economic recovery and the resulting slow decrease in unemployment, it was as high as 9.1 per cent in 2001. The effects of the recession were seen in the media, too, especially within the newspaper sector and in media advertising. In many ways Finland has been in the forefront of the new technologies during the 1990s. One spectacular phenomenon was its long-held leading position in world statistics both in the number of Internet hosts per thousand inhabitants and in mobile phone penetration. Another was the great success of the electronics company Nokia in becoming the world leader in mobile communications.

## STRUCTURE AND OWNERSHIP

The newspaper business is the biggest media sector, with over 70 per cent of media turnover. Relative to size of population, only Norway and Japan have a higher newspaper circulation. In the broadcasting sector, the public service broadcaster YLE is strong, with a television audience share of 43 per cent and a radio audience share of 56 per cent. Ever since the advent of television, Finland has also had a private television company, *MTV*, which is financed through advertising.

### The print media

#### The newspaper press

Finland's first newspaper appeared on 15 January 1771, when the country was still part of Sweden. The oldest newspaper that still appears is the Swedish-language newspaper *Åbo Underrättelser*, established in 1824. In fact, twenty six of the present newspapers were established in the nineteenth century. The biggest paper today is *Helsingin Sanomat*, the first issue of which appeared in 1889. In 1900 there were eighty five newspapers, in 1930 176 and in 1960 199. In 1970 there were 237 newspapers, in 1980 247, and a record figure was reached in 1990 with 252 newspapers. In 2001 there were 199 newspapers, forty nine of which are dailies (four to seven times a week) and fourteen are Swedish-language papers.

The total circulation of newspapers was slightly more than 4 million in 1991, but the economic recession of the early 1990s resulted in a decline which continued until the late 1990s, although it evened out in the end. The decline has finally ceased and circulation now stands at 3.2 million in both 2000 and 2001.

The biggest newspaper, *Helsingin Sanomat*, is published by Sanoma Corporation within the SanomaWSOY group. It is by far the most dominant newspaper in Finland. In fact, it is the biggest daily in the Nordic countries. Its circulation is 446,380, which is

14 per cent of the total newspaper circulation in Finland, and it is one of nine national dailies. Besides the two evening tabloids and some special interest (thematic) and political newspapers, mostly non-dailies, the other newspapers are really more regional than national. The biggest Swedish-language newspaper, *Hufvudstadsbladet*, founded in 1864, had a circulation of 53,000 in 2001.

The three largest morning newspapers, *Helsingin Sanomat*, *Aamulehti* (published by the Alma Media Group) and *Turun Sanomat* (published by the TS group), together make up more than 20 per cent of the total circulation. The circulation figures of the main newspapers are given in the statistics at the end of the chapter. Since 1980 the biggest three have increased their market share slightly, the evening tabloids have increased their share quite substantially from 3.6 per cent, but the second newspapers' share (i.e. newspapers in towns with at least two papers) has declined drastically.

The biggest newspaper publishers are the SanomaWSOY group and the Alma Media Group. They are now also the biggest media companies in Finland. Both are listed on the Helsinki Stock Exchange and were formed through mergers, Alma Media on 1 April 1998 and SanomaWSOY on 1 May 1999. In 2000 SanomaWSOY published eleven newspapers (six of which were dailies) with a circulation of 813,000 copies, which was 25 per cent of the total circulation. In the same year Alma Media published twenty five newspapers (ten of which were dailies) with a circulation of 585,000 copies, which was 18 per cent of the total circulation.

Following its acquisition of the Dutch VNU's Consumer Information Group (CIG), which was completed on 1 October 2001, SanomaWSOY is now the largest media group in the Nordic region with pro-forma net sales in 2000 of €2.26 billion, and is Europe's fifth largest magazine publisher. The biggest owners are members of the Erkko family, the original founder of the Sanoma Corporation. Aatos Erkko owns 29 per cent and other Erkko family members 19 per cent. Other major owners are insurance companies and cultural foundations, etc.

According to a sample survey in 2000 by the Finnish Newspapers Association (FNA) the income structure of newspapers was as follows: advertising 62 per cent, subscriptions 32 per cent and sales of individual copies only 6 per cent.

The economic recession of the early 1990s hit the newspapers very hard when, on top of the fall in circulation, media advertising revenue started decreasing. It was not until 1999 that it regained this revenue level. In 2001 newspapers had 56 per cent of the total media advertising. Likewise the total revenue of newspapers and free papers fell in the 1990s and then started growing in 2000 (Sauri, 2001: 14–15).

People usually read the dailies in the morning before going to work, and the majority of newspapers are delivered to people's homes based on annual subscriptions. Finns spend about forty minutes a day reading newspapers and read three newspapers on average during a week.

### The periodical and magazine press

In contrast with newspapers, the circulation of consumer magazines showed an increasing trend all through the 1990s. The circulation amounted to 5.4 million copies in 1990 and to 6.2 million copies in 1999 (Sauri et al., 2000). In addition, the circulation of trade and business magazines stood at 3.8 million copies in 1999 and customer magazines at 5.5 million copies. The circulation figures of these two latter groups have declined since 1990. In economic terms this sector also coped with the recession of the early 1990s more easily than the newspapers.

In contrast to what happens with newspapers, subscriptions form the main part of the income of magazines even though the share fell from approximately 74 per cent in 1992 to 64 per cent in 2000. Single-copy sales account for 8 per cent and advertising accounts for 28 per cent of magazine revenue (up from 16 per cent in 1992) (Sauri et al., 2001).

There were 2,819 magazine titles in 2001 (magazines published at least four times a year) (Finnish Periodical Publishers' Association).

The biggest magazine publisher, Sanoma Magazines, is part of the SanomaWSOY group. It publishes 270 magazines in ten countries. The Otava-Kuvalehdet group was formed in 1998 and is the second largest publisher of magazines and books in Finland. The magazine publishing division, Yhtyneet Kuvalehdet, publishes thirty three consumer magazines in Finland and four in Estonia. Its subsidiary, *Kynämies*, publishes thirty seven magazines.

The biggest family and general magazines have a circulation of more than 200,000 and are weekly magazines: *Seura* (Yhtyneet Kuvalehdet, circulation 257,121), *ET-lehti* (Sanoma Magazines), *7 päivää* (Aller Julkaisut) and *Apu* (A-lehdet). The biggest comic magazine is *Aku Ankka* (*Donald Duck*, with a circulation of 287,685, publisher Sanoma Magazines). The biggest customer magazine is *Pirkka*, a retailers' (Kesko group) magazine for loyalty card customers in Finland. Its circulation amounted to 1.4 million in 2001 with ten issues annually, including a Swedish-language version.

Finns spend about forty two minutes a day reading magazines. The average Finn reads ten different magazines when calculated as follows: if a person has read one of the four issues of the magazine, the person is counted as a reader of that magazine.

### Book publishing

The total number of book titles published in Finland has grown during the last twenty years from 6,500 titles in 1980 to 13,200 titles in 1999 (Minkkinen, 2001). Of the total number 84 per cent were non-fiction and 16 per cent fiction. About 85 per cent of the titles published in Finland are domestic. In 1999, of the number of total titles published, 59 per cent were domestic in Finnish, 4 per cent in Swedish, 19 per cent domestic in other languages and 17 per cent were translated books.

Some twenty years ago there were seven main publishers. Now, mostly through mergers, there are four major publishers and many small ones. The biggest, WSOY, is part of the SanomaWSOY group, Otava is part of the Otava-Kuvalehdet group, and Tammi was bought by the Swedish company Bonnier in 1996 (see statistics at end of chapter). The fourth major publisher is Gummerus Publishers.

## The electronic (audio-visual) media

### Television

Television began as a private project, TES-TV. The public service company YLE began test transmissions in 1957 and regular transmission on 1 January 1958. A second public television channel was established in 1964 by YLE as it took over TES-TV. The private television company, which is financed by advertising and is nowadays known as MTV (MTV-3 Finland), had already been established in 1957, originally to assist YLE. Until the end of 1992 it operated in windows on YLE's television channels. In 1987 a third television channel started. It was originally jointly owned by YLE (50 per cent), MTV (35 per cent) and Nokia (15 per cent). It became MTV's subsidiary in 1990 and was wholly owned by MTV in 1997. In 1993 all commercial television operations moved to the third channel, MTV-3 Finland received its own operating licence and the Act on Yleisradio (the Finnish Broadcasting Company, YLE) was passed. On 1 June 1997 a second private television channel, Channel Four Finland, started. It is now owned by SWelcom within the SanomaWSOY group (91 per cent) and the TS group (9 per cent).

The four national terrestrial television channels together had a 94 per cent share of television viewing in 2001. Cable television channels had 1 per cent and satellite channels 3 per cent of television viewing by the whole population. In cable television households, the cable television channels had a share of 3 per cent and the satellite channels 7 per cent. National television is thus quite strong. Some 42 per cent of all households are connected to cable television networks. The must-carry regulation covers all national free-to-air channels and all YLE's services. The cable networks also carry a substantial number of satellite channels. In addition, about 11 per cent of all households enjoy satellite channels by means of the DTH and SMATV systems.

Digital terrestrial transmissions were launched on 27 August 2001, with three multiplexes. Since three of the licensees dropped out, there are now (as of May 2002) nine digital television channels on air, four of which are simulcasts of the four analogue national channels. The new channels are YLE-24 (news), YLE Teema (culture, education, science), FST (Swedish-language programming by YLE), Subtv (Alma Media's cable television channel with regional programming obligations in the digital terrestrial operating licence), Urheilukanava (sport, jointly owned by the commercial television companies) and Wellnet (lifestyle channel; so far only demos). At the end of 2001 the network covered 72 per cent of the population. Three new programme licences will be granted in autumn 2002.

In addition, there are three minor regional television operations over the air: television Tampere (commercial television covering Finland's third largest city) and *När-TV* and *KRS-TV*, two non-commercial small-scale Swedish-language stations on the west coast.

Sweden's television channel SVT Europa is retransmitted over the air in the south of Finland and, on the west coast, the two national public service channels of Sweden's SVT are also retransmitted (two separate stations).

Until the mid-1990s television advertising revenue increased nicely both in Fmk millions and as a percentage of media advertising as a whole. Even in the difficult years of the economic recession in the early 1990s, television advertising grew, not taking inflation into account. In absolute terms, television advertising revenues declined in the early 1990s. With the appearance of Channel Four Finland, a restructuring of the market came about. The advertising revenue of MTV-3 Finland (including sponsorship, etc.) started decreasing, while the growth of television advertising as a whole also slowed down.

YLE's public service remit is to provide full service programming for all citizens on equal terms, and to discharge certain special duties defined by law. This is reflected in the programme structure which covers different programme types more evenly than that of the commercial companies. YLE has more factual and children's programmes than the commercial companies. YLE shows education and culture, which is almost absent from the commercial channels. They, on the other hand, carry more foreign fiction, feature films and entertainment; it is quite clear that Channel Four Finland does this more than the MTV-3 channel.

In 2001 YLE's television programming amounted to 10,654 hours of which 9 per cent were by FST, YLE's Swedish-language division. Of YLE's programme hours 57 per cent were domestic. YLE's own new production amounted to 41 per cent.

In 2001 the television programming hours of the MTV-3 channel amounted to 5,073 hours. Of this amount 32 per cent was its own production, 24 per cent other domestic production and 44 per cent foreign production. The programme hours of Channel Four Finland amounted to 3,900 hours, of which 24 per cent were domestic programming.

As regards the origin of foreign programmes, there are also big differences between the television companies. YLE is the company with the most varied imports. Of YLE's total programme hours in 2001 (the analogue channels) 9 per cent originated from the United States, 13 per cent from the United Kingdom, 6 per cent from the other Nordic countries, 10 per cent from other European countries and 5 per cent from other parts of the world. Of MTV-3 programmes 29 per cent originated from the United States, and for Channel Four Finland the figure was as high as 50 per cent.

With the increasing number of television channels on air, the average daily time spent viewing grew slowly from ninety nine minutes in 1989 to 167 minutes in 2001. YLE's share of viewing has declined to 43 per cent while MTV-3 has a 39 per cent share, and Channel Four Finland has come to a stop at a 12 per cent share.

Pay-television has not gained many subscribers in Finland. The total subscriber figures have not been released, however.

### Radio

Radio broadcasting began with trials by radio amateurs in 1921. Regular transmissions began in 1923, and in 1926 the Finnish Broadcasting Company, YLE, was established; at that time it was privately owned. In 1930 YLE became the sole broadcaster in Finland and in 1934 its shares were acquired by the state. For fifty years the public service company YLE was the only radio broadcaster to be given an operating licence. 1985 was the first year that operating licences were given to private companies for local radio operations.

At present, Finland has five national radio channels, one of which is the private Radio Nova. It is owned by Alma Media (74 per cent) and a company jointly owned by the Swedish MTG Radio and the Norwegian P4 Radio Hele Norge (26 per cent). YLE has three national Finnish-language radio channels and one national full service Swedish-language channel (Radio Vega). In addition, YLE has a fourth channel, a Swedish-language youth channel (Radio Extrem), with a network coverage of 48 per cent of the population. YLE's Radio Ylen Ykkönen broadcasts arts and culture, Radiomafia popular culture and Radio Suomi news and regional programmes (in windows). YLE also has a network in Lapland that broadcasts Sámi-language programmes. Digital Audio Broadcasting (DAB) was introduced as an operative pilot project in October 1998 and YLE now has three new digital channels in Finnish, one regular additional service in Swedish and additional services occasionally. The network covers 50 per cent of the population.

Private radio operations have increased over the years from, initially, local stations with local content to larger networks and greater commercial orientation. There are about seventy local radio operating licence holders and about ten semi-national radio networks or chains of local stations. Foreign companies are well represented as owners of the biggest networks: Kiss FM (SBS/Luxembourg), Classic FM (GRW/UK), NRJ (NRJ/France) and SuomiPOP (Metromedia International, USA).

The private stations brought about an increase in radio listening as a whole from an average of 122 minutes a day in 1985 to the record figure of 223 minutes in 1994. In 2001 the average time spent listening was 208 minutes. YLE's share of listening has declined to 56 per cent. Among Swedish-speakers YLE's share of listening totals 69 per cent, with YLE's Swedish-language channels scoring 61 per cent.

In contrast with the other media sectors, the advertising revenue of private radio companies increased in 2001 by 6 per cent.

### Film and video

After a period of decline in gross box-office revenues ending in 1987 with a bottom figure of Fmk 136 million, the film business grew for two years, stagnated in the early 1990s, again started to climb and has been growing very well since 1995. The number of cinemas has decreased from 312 in 1981 to 225 in 2001. The number of screens is 343 and has been about the same for fifteen years. Most films are imported. The number of domestic film releases has, in the main, varied between eight and thirteen for the last twenty years. Finns do not go to the cinema very often, on average 1.4 times per person in 1999.

Finnkino (owned by Rautakirja since 1994, which has been a SanomaWSOY subsidiary since 1999) is Finland's biggest cinema-owner with fifteen cinemas offering sixty nine screens. In 2001 Finnkino's turnover was €47.6 million.

Finnkino is also one of the big video distributors in Finland, the others being Buena Vista, the Danish Egmont Entertainment and the Norwegian-Swedish Sandrew Metronome. Together they account for 80 per cent of the video market (Sauri, 2001: 74–5).

Most videos are of American origin. After a long period when video rentals dominated the market, the turnover of video rentals started decreasing in 1990 while sell-through videos increased in value and took a definite lead in 1994. In 2001 sell-through videos accounted for FmK 250 million and video rentals for Fmk 143 million and the video market declined owing to DVD records taking market share. The turnover of DVD records was Fmk 178 million in 2001.

The average daily video viewing is quite low, only nine minutes per day. Most of it is viewing of recorded television programmes.

## The Internet and related on-line media

The first Internet service provider in Finland – *EUnet Finland* – was founded in 1993. Later the telecom companies Sonera (a 53 per cent state-owned listed company) and Elisa Communications (previously the Helsinki Telephone Company) grew quickly in this field and became the biggest ISPs. Fast Internet connections are available. Cable modems are supplied primarily by Helsinki Televisio (the cable television network in Helsinki, owned by the SanomaWSOY group). Of the network's 219,000 households (2001), 19,000 have cable modems. ADSL connections are supplied by, inter alia, Elisa Communications and for enterprises by KPNQwest, but the price to households is relatively high.

Internet penetration by the end of 2001 was 36 per cent, while the penetration of personal computers was 51 per cent. The most popular sites are owned by Sonera, Microsoft and the Jippii group, followed by the two broadcasting channel sites MTV-3 and YLE, and the site of the largest newspaper, *Helsingin Sanomat*.

According to information gathered at the end of 2001, 2.1 million Finns (52 per cent) used the Internet at least once a week and 2.5 million (62 per cent) had used the Internet during the previous three months. E-mail and the www services are the most popular applications; 58 per cent had used e-mail and 53 per cent the www services during the previous three months (Gallup Web). However, according to another study, only 8 per cent had purchased goods for their own use through the Net. Most purchases were from domestic companies; the most popular products were books and magazines and music and videos (Statistics Finland).

# POLITICS, POLICY, LAW AND REGULATION

## Media concentration and vertical integration

One can say that, except for television, over-all vertical and horizontal concentration has been growing lately. Contrary to the situation in many other countries there are no special regulations limiting cross-ownership or concentration of the media. This has not been seen as a problem and has not been the subject of any big political debates or any committee work initiated by the authorities. A trend towards concentration/convergence/vertical integration has occurred mainly through the mergers forming the biggest media companies, the SanomaWSOY group and the Alma Media group. They now operate in most of the media sectors. In addition, a trend to reuse media products on different platforms is evolving.

The SanomaWSOY group had a turnover of €1,730 million in 2001. It consists of Sanoma Magazines (magazine publishing and distribution, movie distribution, interactive services), SWelcom (television, broadband and cable television, mobile and Internet services, audiovisual production services), Sanoma (newspaper publishing and printing, business information services), Rautakirja (kiosk operations, press distribution, bookstores, entertainment and leisure, including cinema, e-business) and *WSOY* (publishing books, etc., printing, calendar operations). It has some minority shares in radio companies, but no national radio involvement.

Alma Media was formed on 1 April 1998 as a merger of the second biggest newspaper company in Finland, the Aamulehti group, and the commercial television company MTV (MTV-3 Finland). Alma Media owns 23 per cent of Sweden's TV-4. The other major owner, the Swedish company Bonnier, owns 33 per cent of Alma Media. Other major shareholders of Alma Media are insurance companies.

Alma Media's turnover in 2001 was €478 million. It consists of the following divisions: Alpress (regional newspapers, local and free papers), the Business Information Group, Broadcasting (television, cable television, radio), Alma Media Interactive (R&D projects) and Alprint (printing services). Its activities are not as widespread as those of SanomaWSOY. Alma Media has only a minority share in magazine publishing and no book printing or cinema activities.

The third biggest newspaper publisher is the TS group. Its turnover was €276 million in 2001, making it the fourth largest media company. The printing business forms the biggest part of the turnover. It is also involved in radio and has a minority share in television.

The public service company YLE (the Finnish Broadcasting Company, Yleisradio), broadcasts national and regional full service radio and television programming. It has no interests in the press sector but seeks to make its services available on different electronic platforms (the Internet, mobile phones, etc.). Its subsidiary Digita owns the national radio and television transmission networks. In due course YLE will sell its shares to the current other shareholder, Télédiffusion de France (TDF), which now owns 49 per cent.

A few years back, in 1996, YLE was the biggest media company in Finland. It is now the third biggest. Through mergers and take-overs the newspaper media market has moved towards greater concentration. In radio the number of private stations has increased ever since 1985, but during the last few years an increasing number of stations have been incorporated in chains dominated by foreign ownership.

## Regulation

In regulation, too, there is a trend towards convergence. The regulator strives to make the same framework of regulations suitably applicable to different sectors.

On 19 April 2002 a government Bill was introduced by the Minister of Justice on changes in the exercise of freedom of speech. It would bring the press, broad-casting and even the on-line media within the same framework with respect to respon-sibility and the use of freedom of speech.

The Council of State grants operating licences for radio and television over the air, with the exception of YLE, which operates on the basis of the Act on Yleisradio. The Council of State also determines the tele-vision (licence) fee.

In June 2002 a number of changes to the communications market legislation prepared by the Ministry of Transport and Communi-cations were ratified. A government Bill intro-ducing new changes to the Communications Market Act is being prepared and it will also implement the EU regulatory framework for all electronic communication.

The Finnish Communications Regulatory Authority (FICORA) supervises compliance with the Act on Television and Radio Opera-tions, with the exception of the ethical prin-ciples of advertising, tele-shopping spots and the protection of children. These are supervised by the Consumer Ombudsman. FICORA's duties are regulated by the Act on Communications Administration (625/2001), which came into effect on 1 September 2001.

A self-regulating Council for the Mass Media (Julkisen sanan neuvosto) was estab-lished in 1968 for publishers and journalists in the field of mass communications. Its task is to interpret good professional practice and defend freedom of speech and publication in newspapers, magazines, radio and television. It regularly makes decisions on the basis of complaints, and the decisions are published.

## The press

The press is regulated through the Act on the Freedom of the Press (1/1919), under which everybody has the right to publish printed products. In spite of amendments over the years the Act is now considered to be quite outdated.

The number of newspapers with ties to political parties has decreased considerably. In 1966 half the newspapers were officially politically linked. In 1989 political newspa-pers formed only a fourth. At the beginning of 2001 there were only eighteen, including some that appeared only once a week (Nordenstreng et al., 2001: 71). State subsi-dies were introduced in 1967. Distribution subsidies were introduced in 1982. During the 1990s the subsidies decreased but have remained at Fmk 75 million (€12.6 million) since 1997. A press subsidy board (lehdistö-tukilautakunta) makes a proposal concerning the granting of the selective subsidies (€5 million) and the Ministry of Transport and Communications presents it to the govern-ment for decision. Subsidies to political newspapers (€7.6 million) are given in pro-portion to the number of each party's seats in parliament.

## The electronic media

*Television and radio.* From 1 January 1994 the Act on Yleisradio (the Finnish Broad-casting Company, YLE) came into effect. This act defines YLE's public service remit and authorizes YLE to operate by right of that law without an operating licence.

As of 1 January 1994 the television direc-tive of the European Union also came into force in Finland. Since 1995 Finland has been a member of the European Union which, in the field of communications, has resulted in legislative changes at a more rapid pace through the need to implement EU directives.

A revision of broadcasting legislation came into effect on 1 January 1999 with the Act on Television and Radio Operations, the Act on the State Television and Radio Fund and Acts amending other relating Acts. This legislation replaced the Radio Equipment Act and the Cable Transmission Act. The (technical) Radio Act was replaced with a new Radio Act from 1 January 2002.

The highest decision-making body of the public service broadcaster YLE is the Administrative Council, elected by parliament. YLE is financed through the State Television and Radio Fund, the assets of which consist of television fees paid by households and operating licence fees paid by the commercial television companies. Increases in the television fee are proposed by the Administrative Council of YLE and decided upon by the Council of State (the government). The latest increase came into effect on 1 July 2000 when the fee rose to €165.15. Compared with other Western European countries it is not high. Calculation of the operating licence fee is defined in the Act on the State Television and Radio Fund and is tied to the turnover of the commercial television companies. Of YLE's total revenue in 2001, €364.5 million, 83 per cent originated from television fees, 12 per cent from operating licence fees and 5 per cent from other revenues. YLE has no advertising or sponsorship income.

Changes to the communications market legislation came into effect on 1 July 2002 through which the regulations on telecommunications, digital radio and television transmission networks were made uniform, digital radio and television transmission networks were opened up for information society services, digital programme and digital network licences will be granted and the regulation of digital radio and television transmission networks were moved to the Telecommunications Market Act, renamed the Communications Market Act.

Another change that came into effect was that the operating licence fee paid by the operating licence holders (television companies) was cut by 50 per cent. These fees are paid to the State Television and Radio Fund, the aim of which is to finance the operations of YLE. The aim is that there should be television fee increases every year from 2004 on. Until then the gap in YLE financing will be covered by the income acquired when YLE sold 49 per cent of its subsidiary Digita to TDF and by selling off the rest of the shares.

The self-governing Åland Islands have a different broadcasting arrangement of their own. The Autonomy Act for Åland (1991) gave the Åland Islands the right to grant operating licences for broadcasting on the Åland Islands. The Provincial Act on broadcasting on the Åland Islands was passed at the end of 1993 and gave Åland the right to levy its own licence fees. The public service broadcaster is Ålands Radio och TV. Three television channels are retransmitted: SVT-1 and SVT-2 from Sweden's and Finland's TV, which is a mix of YLE TV-1 and YLE TV-2 (mainly Swedish-language programming).

*Film and video* Regarding films, the distribution of films and videos used to be subject to censorship. This changed on 1 January 2001 through a number of Acts. As of 1 January 2001 only films for minors (i.e. under the age of eighteen) are censored. The television companies have also agreed on a joint national framework of self-regulation where programmes are divided into suitable or unsuitable programmes for children under sixteen.

State subsidies are given to support national film production. They increased from only Fmk 21 million in 1989 to Fmk 65 million in 1999 and up to Fmk 70 million in the state budget for 2002. Most of the subsidies go to the Finnish Film Foundation (Suomen Elokuvasäätiö) which allocates it to production.

## The Internet and related on-line media

The Penal Code regulations also apply to Internet content and allow opportunities for the authorities to intervene where there are cases of criminal offences. However, the present legislation is not suitable for regulating Internet content. The Bill introduced in February 2002 on the use of freedom of speech includes, as a new feature, regulations on the responsibility for communication through on-line media. A new Act implementing the EU directive on e-commerce came into effect on 1 July 2002. Proposals concerning self-regulation measures have been on the agenda. Different aspects of the Internet are monitored by various Ministries. In the Ministry of Transport and Communications this is done in the Unit for E-commerce and Data Security. FICORA supervises the use of the Finnish Internet domain names and grants the domain names.

# STATISTICS

| | |
|---|---|
| Population, 2001 | 5,194,901 |
| Households[1] | approx. 2,380,000 |
| Movie admissions, 2001[2] | 6,500,000 |
| Books published, 1999 (titles) | 13,000 |

Source: Minkkinen (2001: 6).

**Print media**

Circulation of main daily newspapers, 2001[3]

| | |
|---|---|
| *Helsingin Sanomat* (national, seven days a week) | 446,380 |
| *Ilta-Sanomat* (national evening tabloid, six days a week) | 218,829 |
| *Aamulehti* (regional, seven days) | 135,478 |
| *Iltalehti* (national evening tabloid, six days) | 134,777 |
| *Turun Sanomat* (regional, seven days) | 115,142 |
| *Maaseudun Tulevaisuus* (national rural, three days) | 89,197 |
| *Kauppalehti* (national financial, five days) | 85,292 |
| *Kaleva* (regional, seven days) | 83,151 |
| *Keskisuomalainen* (regional, seven days) | 77,135 |
| *Savon Sanomat* (regional, seven days) | 67,219 |

**Broadcast media**

Audience share of main terrestrial, cable and satellite television channels, 2001 (%)[4]

Public

| | |
|---|---|
| YLE TV-1 | 22.8 |
| YLE TV-2 | 20.5 |
| Total | 43.2 |
| SVT Europa, SVT-1, SVT-2 | 1.2 |

(retransmission and over-spill of Swedish public service television)

Private

| | |
|---|---|
| MTV-3 | 39.1 |
| Channel Four Finland | 11.6 |
| Satellite channels | 3.1 |
| Cable channels | 1.2 |
| Other | 0.5 |

Main radio channels: audience share , 2001 (%)[5]

Public YLE

| | |
|---|---|
| Radio Ylen Ykkönen | 8 |
| Radiomafia | 6 |
| Radio Suomi | 41 |
| FSR (YLE's Swedish-language channels) | 1 |
| Total | 56 |

Private

| | |
|---|---|
| Radio Nova | 14 |
| Kiss FM | 6 |
| NRJ | 3 |

| | |
|---|---|
| SuomiPOP | 2 |
| Sävelradio | 2 |
| Other private stations | 17 |
| Total | 44 |

Households with satellite, cable and terrestrial pay-television (%)[6]

| | Total penetration | Pay-TV |
|---|---|---|
| Satellite (DTH and SMATV) | 13 | approx. 4 |
| Cable | 42 | approx. 2 |
| Terrestrial | 100 | 0 |

Households with a video-cassette recorder, satellite receiver or DVD player (%)[7]

| | |
|---|---|
| VCR | 78 |
| DTH households | 6 |
| DVD player | 9 |

| | | |
|---|---|---|
| **Electronic media** | Digital television households (any means)[8] | approx. 6 |
| | Internet access (%)[9] | 37 |
| | Internet use (once a week)[10] | 2,100,000 |
| | Mobile phone (%)[11] | 90 |
| | Number of mobile phone subscriptions per 100 inhabitants[12] | 75 |

| | | |
|---|---|---|
| **Advertising spend, 2001**[13] | Newspapers | 51.3 |
| | Free papers | 4.8 |
| | Magazines | 17.4 |
| | Television | 18.2 |
| | Radio | 3.8 |
| | Internet | 1.0 |
| | Cinema | 0.2 |
| | Outdoor | 3.3 |
| | Total (€1,066 million) | 100 |

**Ownership**  Main media companies[14]

| | Turnover, 2001 (€ million) | % of total newspaper circulation, 2000 | % of TV viewing, 2001[15] |
|---|---|---|---|
| Sanoma group | 1,730 | 25 | 11.6[a] |
| Alma Media group | 478 | 18 | 39.9 |
| YLE (total revenue) | 365 | – | 43.2 |
| TS group | 276 | 5 | –[a] |

a The Sanoma Group owns 90.55% and the TS Group 9.45% of Channel Four Finland, whose share of television viewing is 11.6%.

# REFERENCES

Alho, Olli (ed.) (1997) *Finland: a Cultural Encyclopedia*. Helsinki: Finnish Literature Society.

Gallup Media (2002) *Mainonnan maara Suomessa 2001*. Helsinki: Suomen Gallup Media.

Minkkinen, Virpi (2001) *Books in the 1980s and 1990s: the Publishing, Distribution and Reading of Literature*. Culture and the Media 2001: 3. Helsinki: Statistics Finland.

Nordenstreng, K. Wiio, O. A., eds (2001) *Suomen mediamaisema*. Vantaa: WSOY.

Sauri, Tuomo (2001) *Mass Media in Finland: Structure and Economy*. Culture and the Media 2001: 1. Helsinki: Statistics Finland.

Sauri, T., Kohvakka, R. Minkkinen V., eds (2000) *Finnish Mass Media 2000*. Culture and the Media 2000: 1. Helsinki: Statistics Finland.

Soramaki, Martti (2001) 'The arrangement of public service broadcasting in Finland', memorandum, 10 September. Brussels: Corporate Affairs, Yleisradio, the Finnish Broadcasting Company (YLE).

Osterlund-Karinkanta, Marina (2001) 'Media policy issues in Finland', memorandum. Helsinki: EU and Media Unit, Yleisradio, the Finnish Broadcasting Company (YLE).

Osterlund-Karinkanta, Marina (2002) 'Medien in Finnland' in Hans-Bredow-Institut für Medienforschung (ed.) *Internationales Handbuch Medien*. Baden-Baden: Nomos.

## Internet references

Legislation: http://www.finlex.fi

Legislation on radio and television in English at: http://www.mintc.fi/www/sivut/english/tele/statutes/index.html

Ministry of Education: http://www.minedu.fi

Ministry of Justice: http://www.om.fi

Ministry of Transport and Communications: http://www .mintc.fi

Council for Mass Media: http://www.jsn.fi

Finnish Book Publishers' Association: http://www.skyry.net

Finnish Film Foundation: http://www.ses.fi

Finnish Newspapers Association (FNA): http://www.sanomalehdet.fi

Finnish Periodical Publishers' Association: http://www.aikakaus.fi

Alma Media: http://www.almamedia.fi, annual reports

Channel Four Finland: http://www.nelonen.fi

MTV-3 Finland: http://www.mtv3.fi

Sanoma: http://www.sanomawsoy.fi, annual reports

Statistics Finland: http://www.stat.fi

Suomen Gallup Media: http://www.mdc.fi

YLE: http://www.yle.fi/fbc, annual reports

## Statistics sources

[1]Households approximately 2,373,000 (2000). Source: Statistics Finland/Income Distribution Statistics. (Approximation 2001 made by the author: 2,380,000).

[2]Source: Finnish Chamber of Films, www.filmikamari.fi.

[3]Source: Web site of the Finnish Audit Bureau of Circulation, www.levikintarkastus.fi.

[4]Source: television-meter survey, Finnpanel – YLE/Audience research.

[5]Source: KRT (National Radio Survey covering Finnish speakers aged nine and over).

[6]Finnish Satellite Association SANT, Finnish Cable Television Association, YLE.

[7]VCR, November 2001, Statistics Finland/Consumer Survey; DTH, Finnish Satellite Association SANT; DVD, November 2001, Statistics Finland/Consumer Survey.

[8]YLE.

[9]November 2001, Statistics Finland/Consumer Survey.

[10]Suomen Gallup Web.

[11]November 2001, Statistics Finland/Consumer Survey.

[12]August 2001, Ministry of Transport and Communications, press release 17 September 2001.

[13]Source: Suomen Gallup Media. Net advertising revenue including classified advertising.

[14]Suomen Lehdistö 6/01. FNA publication.

[15]Television-meter survey, Finnpanel – YLE/Audience research.

# 6: France

JEAN-MARIE CHARON
Translated by Denis Mcquail

## NATIONAL PROFILE

With 60 million inhabitants, France is a very centralized country, with the over-development of its capital Paris and of the Paris region. This structure explains why most media, apart from the local press, concentrate their activities and their resources in this region. A significant indicator of this, at the present time (2000) is that out of the total of 31,900 French journalists, more than 60 per cent practise their profession in the Paris region (Devillard et al., 2001: 67).

France is also at a pivotal point between the north and south of Europe, a fact that is expressed in the differences in reading behaviour and in press structures according to whether one is in the north-east of France, where they are close to those of Germany or Switzerland, or south of the Loire, where they are close to those prevailing in Italy or Spain. Despite the fact that religious practice has notably declined, France was for long essentially Catholic, torn apart by religious warfare until the seventeenth century, with Protestantism at issue. Its Jewish community, today one of the most important in Europe, is of long standing, although the share of Islam is growing, now the third religion.[1] This diversity is also witnessed in the existence of community media (a Catholic daily, periodicals of different faiths, radio and television stations representing the principal religions).

The state has historically played a particularly important role in economic, social, cultural and political matters. With respect to the media, the first newspapers saw the light of day with the support and control of the state. The latter still plays an important role

in the press by means of a very substantial system of aid, at the same time guaranteeing co-operative or collective structures, whether it concerns support for the AFP (Agence France Presse) or the support given to the distribution system. Audio-visual media for their part were under monopoly public control until the beginning of the 1980s, with public service radio and television[2] comprising numerous stations and chains, representing a considerable audience. The particular role of the state in the media is expressed in the existence of a Minister charged with these matters, under the title of 'communication', currently linked with responsibility for 'culture'. It is also manifested by a tendency to multiply legislative texts. The most recent law concerning audio-visual media dates from 2000, while the printed press is governed by a law of 1986.

France has always been innovative in respect of the media. It was among the first countries to see the birth of a periodical publication, la Gazette, in 1631. The revolution of 1798 offered for the first time the image of a country where several hundred newspapers were published. In 1832 Charles Louis Havas founded the first news agency. In 1863 Moise Millaud was the first in Europe to succeed in launching a popular newspaper, very cheap (one sou), Le Petit Journal, sold by single copies. In 1865 this was printed on the first rotary press, invented by the engineer Marinoni. Broadcast radio made its appearance in the 1920s, developing at first in the form of private regional stations. The first demonstrations of television took place on the eve of the Second World War. Following the war, radio

Table 6.1   *Circulation of national quality and popular dailies over the long term ('000)*

|  | 1960 | 1975 | 1994 | 2000 |
|---|---|---|---|---|
| Le Figaro | 384 | 382 | 386 | 358 |
| Le Monde | 166 | 425 | 354 | 3,348 |
| Libération | – | 17 | 169 | 160 |
| Le Parisien[a] | 756 | 310 | 423 | 485 |
| France Soir | 1,115 | 633 | 203 | 120[b] |

[a]The figures for 2000 add together *le Parisien* and *Aujourd' hui*, which is a national version produced by the Paris region title.
[b]Figure not checked by the Diffusion Conseil, the body empowered to validate circulation.

and television stations, now principally national in range, would be developed within the framework of a public monopoly that lasted until the law of 1982, affirming the principle of freedom of communication. The same year a plan was launched for the development of cable television. In the following year began the massive diffusion of Minitel, a small electronic on-line information terminal, under the control of the Direction Générale des Télécommunication,[3] which has since become France Télécom.

## STRUCTURE AND OWNERSHIP

The landscape of the French media is characterized by relative weakness in the daily sector, even though, in contrast, magazines are numerous and generally prosperous. Radio is much listened to and also very diverse, following liberalization in the 1980s. As for television, it has also achieved diversification by way of cable (in a modest degree), satellite and (soon) by digital terrestrial transmission. The most recent years have been good, on the whole, both for book and cinema. After an initial delay the diffusion of the Internet is proceeding rapidly, even if the majority of French people still have no experience of this medium. The economy of the media taken together is suffering from the relative weakness of the French advertising market, which is insufficiently reactive to innovation, such that two-thirds of advertising expenditure is directed towards media other than the press, radio and television.

### The print media

#### The newspaper press
The written press achieves a turnover of €11 billion, of which nearly 40 per cent accrues to the daily press. The number of dailies has not changed much during the last decade, with a total of eighty one titles, of which ten are national dailies of political and general information (amongst which are three quality dailies – *le Monde, le Figaro* and *Libération* – and three dailies of opinion), ten specialist dailies (business, sport, etc.) and sixty one local and regional dailies (the highest circulation is achieved by one of these, *Ouest France*, with nearly 800,000 copies sold). This relative stability has been little disturbed by the arrival of the free dailies *Metro* and *Vingt-Minutes* in Paris, but also in Marseilles, then Lyons, with the launch of *Marseilles Plus*.

The daily press experienced a powerful movement towards concentration in the 1970s and 1980s, which still leaves its mark today. It was principally led by Robert Hersant (Socpresse and France Antilles groups) and affected the regional press (with titles such as *Paris Normandie, le Progrès de Lyon, le Dauphiné Libéré*, etc.) just as much as the national press (*le Figaro, France Soir, l'Aurore*), these subject to reorientation of strategy following the death of their founder. They have, moreover, experienced a reorganization of their capital, with the entry of the aviation firm Dassault. On the other hand, several regional groups expanded their portfolio of titles around a principal title (*Sud-Ouest, la Dépêche du Midi, la Voix du Nord, la Montagne*). Finally, the Hachette Filipacchi Médias group (HFM), a leader in the magazine publishing sector, succeeded in acquiring the Provencal group, which became *la Provence*, in Marseilles, at the same time progressively adding other titles from the south-east region, principally *Nice Matin*. International groups, aside from Pearson in the financial daily *les Echos*, are little represented in the daily French press, because of legal provisions that slow down or block their entry.

The daily press suffers from a fairly general lack of profitability, apart from the case of the *Echos* and the sporting daily *l'Equipe*. Several titles are chronically loss-making (the opinion dailies *la Croix*, *l'Humanité* and *Présent* as well as the popular *France Soir*). This stems partly from production costs that remain excessive, partly from the often inadequate advertising resources, not to mention often stagnant or declining circulation.

The reading of daily newspapers is now at a rather low level. There is clear evidence of a tendency towards occasional reading, with regular reading by no more than 36 per cent of the population and non-reading ('never read a daily') settling at 27 per cent, with particular reference to the younger age groups (up to forty five years of age) (Donnat, 1998: 178). Consistent with this, the percentage of buyers of dailies is also rather low, with France having a rate of 149 copies sold per 1,000 inhabitants.

### The magazine and periodical press

In contrast to the daily press, the mass public magazine sector has a large audience, since, according to a 2001 study, French people read an average of 6.9 titles. Women are ahead in this, with an average of 7.3. Ninety-six per cent of French women are readers of magazines[4]. During the last twenty years, overall circulation has increased by some 65 per cent[5]. The main sectors are the television press (weekly), the age-related press (young and old) and, still growing, the category called 'special interest' which translates into a constant tendency towards greater specialization in this form of publishing (leisure, discovery, activities, hobbies, etc.). The vitality of this kind of publishing is reflected in an exceptional figure for new start-ups each year (400 in the year 2000 alone).

Such dynamism cannot help but be translated into a strong trend towards concentration, the parallel phenomenon to the constant appearance of newcomers, independent titles or small groups. This concentration of the market is marked by the position of the leader, the Hachette Filipacchi Média group, followed by two European groups, Bertelsmann (by way of its affiliate Prisma press) and Emap. The share taken by German and British groups well indicates the international dimension of this form of publication, with HFM realizing more than half its turnover outside France, one of its leading titles, *Elle*, being published

in thirty countries. The weight of the leaders does not hold back the great vitality of other groups, more national, of average size, often performing well in certain segments of the market, such as Bayard (press for young and old), Excelsior (popular science), Marie Claire (women), Perdriel (news, business, etc.) (Charon, 1999).

The profitability of the magazine publishing groups is often good (above 10 per cent for groups such as Marie Claire or Excelsior), without being exceptional relative to global or European groups in the same sector. We should note that there also, while still being competition vis-à-vis the audio-visual sector, the ratio of advertising to sales income is 40/60, which is lower than can be observed in neighbouring countries, notably Great Britain.

The technical and professional press was for long the smallest sector, with two national groups operating in it, CEP (Havas)[6] and Editions sociales. The second was re-acquired during the 1990s by the Dutch group Wolters Kluwer, while the first has been refounded within Vivendi Universal Publishing (VUP) and is in the process of transfer. This is to say that at the moment this form of publishing is developing and increasing in professionalism, but it finds itself essentially controlled by groups with their headquarters outside France.

### Book publishing

After the relatively disappointing decade of the 1990s for book publishing, the situation has noticeably improved since 2000, with significant increases in sales. On the other hand, studies of reading behaviour[7] show that when the book-buying public grows, the marginal category of 'heavy readers' tends to decline, constituting a worrying development, notably affecting general literature. In effect, although during the course of the last decade the number of people who have bought books has been maintained (exceeding about 62 per cent or 63 per cent), the share of those that have read at least twenty five books each year has declined from 66 per cent to 58 per cent. The reversal affects all social categories, but is greatest for workers, artisans and heads of enterprise (Donnat, 1998: 98).

As for publication structures, these are dominated by a strong degree of concentration around two poles, Hachette[8] on the one hand and Vivendi Universal Publishing on the other. Both are to some degree engaged in international strategies.[9] Hachette is very active in the distribution, circulation and sale of books (Relais H, Relay, etc.) in France[10] but also internationally. Within the two groups, the experience of centralized administration and maximum synergy in relation to the book pole has come to nothing, emerging finally as a trend towards great autonomy between their different sectors and types of book publishers. The weight of the two leaders of the sector has not held back the rise of houses of medium weight, essentially national, such as Gallimard or le Seuil, exhibiting considerable vitality, with the constant arrival of newcomers.

## The electronic (audio-visual) media

### Television

Television, with its turnover of €5.5 billion, remains dominated by the analogue form of transmission that offers seven networks on six channels, almost exclusively national. It was during the 1980s that the analogue offer was increased from three to six networks. One of these networks, France 3, offers national programming for most of its output time, but also transmits "regional news" programmes every day, thanks to a decentralized structure, mainly devoted to news.[11] Two networks are transmitted on the fifth channel: France 5, with an educational remit, during the day, and ARTE (cultural, franco-German) during the evening and night. On the fourth channel Canal + is transmitted, a thematic network (cinema and sport), in return for subscription. Local analogue channels occupy a totally marginal place, as a result of cable or production problems (Toulouse, Lyons, Alpes), but are experiencing a modest rebound, with authorizations given in Clermont-Ferrand and Bordeaux[12] to affiliates of the regional press. A number of holders of a community television licence, connected with a social movement, hope that digital terrestrial television will provide a new opportunity for this form of television.

Alongside analogue television, there has been a programme of development of cable television since the end of 1982, which has experienced difficulties of commercial development, resulting in a very modest degree of subscription. Because of this, satellite distribution has been more or less inevitable, with two concurrent commercial offers – Canal Satellite and TPS – distributing several dozen networks,[13] with a steady rate of growth. It should also be noted that an offer of "digital terrestrial television" (TNT) is being gradually introduced, with thirty two networks, for which the Conseil Supérieur de l'Audiovisual (CSA), the regulatory organ for audiovisual media, evaluated applicants in spring 2002.

The creation of Canal + in 1984 constituted the first appearance of pay and thematic television, since which date the thematization of television has accelerated, with dozens of networks proposed for cable and satellite,[14] amongst which news channels and those for children, sport, film and music, etc., continue to predominate.[15] In 2001 pay-television attracted 10.78 million subscribers.

Public television today comprises four analogue networks, of which three (France 2, France 3 and France 5) are grouped in a common holding company,[16] France Télévision. The agreements signed between France and Germany that have led to the creation of ARTE have resulted in this being a separate company, even though the French authorities had wished, since a vote on the law in December 2000, to integrate it into France Télévision. The holding company is also at the head of the thematic networks, with participation in some of these (history, etc.). France Télévision was also one of the original instigators of the *bouquet satellite*, TPS. France Télévision should also to be at the head of eight channels, distributed from terrestrial digital television. For completeness, it should be noted that the overseas territories and departments are served by a specific company, RFO, while in the international arena France is a partner in TV-5, which takes a number of its programmes from the public service branch (including the television news of France 2).

Private television is dominated by large industrial groups or international concerns: TF-1, the network leader, is controlled by the Bouygues group (BTP and local public utilities), which is the principal shareholder in TPS, also the thematic networks, principally LCI (the main continuous news channel). M6, a generalist network which is developing a time-shift form of programming, is controlled by the RTL group (an affiliate of Bertelsmann), also Suez-Lyonnaise (which is involved in cable by way of the Noos company). Canal +, which also exploits the Canal Satellite package, belongs to the Vivendi Universal group. Its activities are extensively internationalized in Europe (Spain, Belgium, Italy, Poland). Other operators are involved in thematic networks, amongst them Hachette (Lagardère), in Canal Satellite especially, also in production, AB (RTL-9, also a 'mini-package' proposed as an option in the offer of Canal Satellite).

### Radio

Radio is an important medium, in terms of the size of its audience, the time spent listening and the diversity of programming. Its turnover is increasing moderately, being of the order of €1 billion. The sector comprises four large, distinct segments: three general national radio services (for long transmitted on long wave, but gradually going over to FM); national thematic networks (music, information, cultural, religious and community affairs); private independent radio; several hundred local radio associations. Since the second half of the 1990s thematic and local radio has overtaken the generalist national radio services.

Public radio is divided into three distinct groups: the most important – Radio France – offers six main networks[17] aimed at the metropolitan territory. The second is RFO, which transmits radio and television programmes to overseas departments and territories. Finally, Radio France Internationale (RFI) transmits a continuous news channel in French and in local languages to the whole world (on short and medium wave, or FM). The programming of Radio France taken as a whole has the lead position in the radio market, with a cumulative audience of the order of 28 per cent. Disposing of the 'historic' public generalist programme, with France Inter, which has second place in respect of audience size, Radio France established a new continuous news programme, France Info, in 1987, which reaches a very significant audience. In 2001 Radio France reorganized its network of forty local stations, under the label France Bleue, proposing instead a national programme refreshed by local content and by specific programmes and news produced by each station.

The private generalist radio stations, as well as a number of the thematic networks with which they are associated, belong to two communication groups that are largely internationalized, being Lagardère[18] and the RTL group (Bertelsmann).[19] Besides smaller operators (independents), we should note the case of the NRJ group, born with the radio libres at the start of the 1980s, which is the third group of private radio stations, although it has directed its internationalism towards several European countries. Today it has four national networks,[20] each corresponding to a musical style, defined in terms of a target age group.

Several hundred radio associations are regularly given frequencies by the CSA, which has the task of guaranteeing a substantial share of wavebands to this form of radiophonic expression. A 'Fund for Support of Radiophonic Expression', supplemented by a 1 per cent tax on radio and television advertising receipts, contributes to the financing of radio associations.

### Film and video

French cinematographic production constitutes a dynamic sector by comparison with other European countries, since it represents a little more than €900 million. The sector relating to cinema exhibition (620 enterprises) generates turnover of the order of €700 million. Video production (more than 450 enterprises) has progressed very rapidly to more than €800 million.

The dynamism of the cinematographic sector has been greatly stimulated by the habit of cinemagoing, which has been growing even since 2001 with the introduction of subscription tickets allowing more films to be seen at a lower price. These cards have been particularly effective in stimulating cinemagoing among the young, who are in any case the most frequent cinemagoers. Research into cultural habits (Donnat, 1998: 235–9) shows that half the French public (49 per cent) go to the cinema at least once a year. Among these a little more than half go at least once every two months. Among the high attenders (more than twenty times a year) are found especially those aged twenty to twenty-four, the professional and intellectual occupations, students and Parisians. In respect of video use, the 1990s were marked by a reversal of the relation between renting and purchase. In 1989 14 per cent rented cassettes and only 7 per cent bought them, while in 1997 the purchasers accounted for 37 per cent, the renters 28 per cent (Donnat, 1998: 149–52).

## The Internet and related on-line media

In respect of the Internet and on-line media, France presents a paradoxical spectacle. On the one hand, the availability of personal computers and the level of access to the Internet is low in European terms, but on the other hand, the number of applications of new media (especially ordering, consulting bank data, electronic directories, etc.) is very high and widespread in society, because of the level of diffusion of 1980s equipment, namely the Minitel.[21] The more this familiarized people with information searching and transactions on-line, the more it acted as a brake on the acquisition of personal computers or of a modem. In understanding the responsibility of Minitel for the slow growth of the Internet, it should also be recalled that the French public has always shown itself to be conservative in relation to technological innovations, as in respect of television, first in relation to colour television, then the video-recorder, not to mention the telephone. In all these, France was much slower than its European neighbours. The deficit can be rapidly made up, bearing in mind that in 2000 a quarter of the population owned a personal computer and one in seven benefited from Internet access at home.

As for the operators, the large communications groups, Lagardère (Hachette)[22] and Vivendi Universal, considered playing a major role in providing access, alongside AOL, before the latter merged with its rival Time Warner. Today these groups cannot help but recognize the modesty of their achievement in this activity, sometimes accompanied by heavy losses, while France Telécom presents itself as the main challenger to the large world operators, along with Wanadoo. From the point of view of the offer of services, this looks, as everywhere, a little like the bursting of the 'speculative bubble'. Numerous providers have had to abandon their services.[23] Amongst the large information providers, notably the media (written press: le Monde, Libération, les Echos, l'Equipe, etc.;[24] television: TF-1, Canal plus, M6, France 2; radio: NRJ, RTL, Radio France, etc.), the trend is now towards regrouping and rationalization of investments and of research into strategies for finding new recipes, such as subscription (Bayard Web). The phenomenon is all the more clear since the losses are often considerable, while the advertising receipts do not follow.

A new phase opens with the question of the still slow development of the high-capacity Internet, the commercialization of WAP, which marks the opening of UMTS before which each of the large telecommunication operators appeared to hesitate, renegotiating its schedules and tariffs with the regulatory body – the Agency for the Regulation of Telecommunications (ART) – and the state. For the content providers, the delays come as a respite and a chance to rationalize their strategies, knowing that no one can depend on the emergence of an economic model which will deliver, as by a miracle, all the unknowns of a medium based on a free service without getting sufficient returns from advertising or related resources.

## POLITICS, POLICY, LAW AND REGULATION

Officially, convergence holds a central place in media policies. Since 1997 there has been no let-up in the wish to make good the backwardness of France in relation to the offer and use of services on the Internet or in relation to multimedia content. Spectacular initiatives have been launched to give a popular dimension to this campaign, such as the 'Internet Fair' which is held each year in early spring.[25] Ministries are expected to develop information and services in relation to this issue. Some of them, such as that of Education, have put significant resources into the equipment of educational establishments and teaching provision.

The Commissariat Général au Plan has taken the initiative with studies reviewing future prospects centred on the theme of convergence.[26] It is still the case that policies and structures have remained largely sectoral, such as those relating to the written press, the audiovisual, cinema or the Internet.

### The press

The policies relating to the press have for long concentrated on questions of the modernization of technology and the support for the development of the general and political news and opinion press, with daily newspapers having priority. Concretely, this orientation is manifested in the existence of a particular service attached to the office of the Prime Minister and the Minister of Culture and Communication, one of whose principal tasks is to deal with and realize support for the press. It is also demonstrated by the fact that, each year, parliament votes, in the state budget, a sum dedicated to 'direct support' for the press. The amount is far from negligible, at around €150 million. However, it is relatively modest compared with the 'indirect support' that is in the form not of budgetary donations to newspapers, but of exemptions or reductions in taxes (VAT, local tax, etc.) or postal tariffs. The global figure for such direct and indirect support comes to nearly €2 billion.[27]

The priority in favour of the general and political news press and especially daily newspapers does not prevent aid from benefiting all forms of the press (especially VAT and the remission of local tax). On the other hand, there have been gradual adjustments in the postal subsidy, with a policy called 'targeting', that gives precedence to dailies and to periodicals of general and political news.[28] There is also a new form of support for the *portage* of daily newspapers, similar to the contribution given to financing the Agence France Presse,[29] of which the principal beneficiaries are also the informational and political titles. During the 1970s a subsidy was introduced for 'dailies with weak advertising income', which benefitted only journals of opinion.[30] Finally, in 1997, parliament decided on the creation of a new subsidy intended for the 'modernization of the daily press', paid for by a 1 per cent tax on extra-media advertising receipts.

Beyond these general orientations, the state stands as a guarantor of pluralism, or at least the limitation of concentration.

In respect of pluralism, the state guarantees mutual or co-operative structures in favour of press titles, with reference to the supply of newsprint, the distribution of information, by means of a French international news agency. On these two last points the state is today confronted with the obsolescence and inflexibility of structures which date respectively from the 1947 law on press distribution and the 1957 law on the statutes of the AFP. It is a question of necessary, but delicate, reforms that will need to be introduced during the decade. On the matter of concentration, the law of 1986 fixes a threshold of concentration of the press (less than 30 per cent of circulation for the same publisher, in the case of the daily press). This legal text turns out to be virtually inapplicable, for lack of an adequate jurisprudence. It does not seem, however, that the legislature is likely to pass any new law on this point. One option is to wait for a possible European law, the other is to treat the press in the same way as any other economic sector and to submit it to the same competition requirements.

## The Electronic media

As for television, France has been characterized by a propensity to modify its legal basis. Since 1982 and the law liberalizing audiovisual communication, there seems to have been almost a cycle of two or three reforms of the law a decade. The most recent dates from 2000 and is particularly directed at encouraging the public audiovisual system towards a more competitive and diversified form in terms of both programming and distribution. In concrete terms, a holding body has been created for regrouping public television channels, with the post of chairperson set for a period of five years. The new law has changed the arrangements under which the regulatory structure – the High Council for Audiovisual Media (CSA) was able to intervene in the face of a proliferation of cable and satellite programmes. Finally, it defines the framework that would apply to digital terrestrial television and the prerogatives of the CSA with regard to it.

Since the law of November 1986 the state no longer intervenes directly in the main body of television, which is the private sector and which is subject exclusively to regulation by the CSA, established by the law of 1989.[31] The CSA decides upon licences to transmit (on the basis of candidate applications). It examines the obligations laid on operators. It grants frequencies. It holds operators accountable for keeping to laws and regulations as well as other commitments. Finally it is the CSA that discusses and decides on the renewal of licences. Beyond these "structural" interventions, the CSA guarantees the monitoring of audiovisual media in such a way as to verify accordance with the diversity principle in respect of news; to protect "vulnerable audiences", especially children and young people, or to limit violence. It has also instituted, along with operators, a designation of programmes that enables the public to be warned about the degree of violence or their pornographic character. The CSA has a range of sanctions at its disposal that go as far as provisional or even definitive revocation of the right to transmit (never yet applied). The authority of the CSA, its docility in respect of the wishes of governments, or its understanding in relation to the pressures of operators, remain a matter of constant debate, something that is doubtless connected with the manner of appointment of its members by the political authorities.[32] This does not prevent, like it or not, the steady reinforcement of its legitimacy over the course of time. Until, perhaps, a new law arrives to change its composition or its powers.

In relation to the public sector, the state adopts, by contrast, the role of shareholder or guardian, which is sometimes shared by the CSA, leading to situations that can be rather paradoxical. Thus it approaches parliament to vote funds for the public radio and television networks, on a proposal made by the Minister of Culture and Communication. The representatives of the state entrust the use of this budget to the administrative councils. On the other hand, it is the CSA that nominates the chairpersons of the public bodies,[33] assesses their observance of their obligations, examines their balance sheets and projections and publishes a report on their performance in all these matters.

The direction given to audiovisual policy for public broadcasting during the 1990s evolved little, being marked by declarations of attachment to the public sector, without any corresponding clarification or updating of its mission and without providing the means to fulfil it. The state has instead shown a tendency to adapt to new situations by a policy of following the current trend. It has thus pre-empted the fifth channel that became free after the failure of a private network – France 5 – before installing Arte there during the evening, then an educational television programme, France 5. Rather than having an ambitious policy for quality television it has been more a matter of a general drift, including public programming, towards a commercial model, very much oriented to a mass public. Faced with the development of satellite distribution, the state has pushed France Television to integrate one of the satellite packages, TPS, in the direction, paradoxically, of the currently most commercial operators, TF-1 and M6. As with radio in 1987, the state has allowed Radio France to become a niche in the thematic networks, with a programme of current news (France Info), just as it allowed this same public organization to react to the quasi-exclusivity of the new networks for the youth public (Fun, Skyrock, NRJ) by the creation of a youth theme programme, le Mouv', in 1998.

None of this has gone beyond a minimalist definition of public service broadcasting: to inform; to educate; to entertain. This comes from never having any policy initiative that could constitute a platform for a more ambitious and coherent policy. The state could have found itself faced with a request to clarify these matters from the European Commission, but it would have been a question of doing so in the face of arguments concerning competition which would be based on the mixed financing of the public networks. In respect of finance, the general tendency of the state is at one and the same time opportunist and devious. At times, it makes up financial shortages with subventions from the state budget, at others it increases the level of the licence fee but less so than in neighbouring countries. It allows the level of advertising receipts to grow, to challenge the limits set by the law of 2000. This does not prevent top policy makers and government spokespersons from regularly announcing that they would not be opposed to the abolition of the licence fee. The main consequence of such persistence in lack of ambition and perspective is to be found in a level of audiovisual production that suffers all round from lack of resources.

The same ambiguities affect terrestrial digital television. Public television is to have eight of the thirty three channels, although the financing is unclear, beyond an initial budgetary allocation.

## The Internet and related on-line media

At the legislative level, a major law on the information society announced in 2000 is supposed to constitute an important step in a policy of encouragement and support for the Internet and on-line media. Initiatives were taken to encourage the diffusion of personal computers (VAT reductions, etc.) but in reality they were limited to efforts on the part of the public services. The law finally adopted in 2001 appears to be much less innovatory and ambitious than expected. It bears on the freedom of encryption, the electronic contract and responsibility (especially of the technical providers). It includes a number of European provisions and new texts, especially relating to the rights of authors.[34]

A "Forum for Rights on the Internet" was established on 31 May 2001 – a structure for dialogue and arbitration, styled an organ of co-regulation – with reference to problems posed by the use of the primary contents and services. It should help the adaptation of the law in the domains of activity covered by the Internet. It is charged with making recommendations to public authorities and also to Internet agencies and actors.

In the absence of specific legislation the Internet has on several occasions been the object of passionate debates and of controversial judicial decisions in the application of French law. One example concerned the application of the law relating to the dissemination of racist or 'denial' material (the so-called Loi Gayssot) on the Yahoo site, with reference to the auctioning of Nazi artefacts. The judge[35] in effect ordered the American provider to deny French users access to the site. This was accepted, although it has only relative efficacy and is liable to be contested in an international jurisdiction.

## Some major cross-cutting issues

Several large topics that cut across the preceding headings have been or will become a target of policy initiatives and debates. In the first place come matters concerning relations between news and the functioning of the judicial system. The multiplication of 'politico-financial' scandals, extensively 'mediatized', with the rise of so-called investigative journalism has led to the appearance in several statutes, relating to penal procedure, of the phrase 'respect for the presumption of innocence', as well as provisions concerning media coverage of the justice system. If one of the provisions of the 1993 law seemed to give comfort to the freedom of information (by recognizing the right to confidentiality of sources for journalists), on the other hand there are provisions that limit the possibilities for the media to publish and disseminate images.[36]

The same debate opposing restriction of liberties and the protection of the person could well start up again for television in respect of audiences, children and young persons. In fact it goes beyond the category of information and encompasses fictions, shows, debates, games, even documentaries aimed at young people, but also the whole offer of television in so far as it is accessible to a young audience. Some proposals go in the direction of adapting to television measures contained in the 1949 law (cf. Charon, 2002: 26–34), concerning the press and publication and designed for the protection of youth, with the aid of a committee charged with handling problems which might arise not only with programmes aimed at young people, but also with adult programmes to which young people have access. The debate is just beginning, unless it is merely a rerun for the *n*th time of a more general debate between supporters of freedom and those who put more weight on the protection of sensitive or vulnerable audiences.

Beyond this is another debate that has recurred since the end of the 1980s with reference to the professional ethics of journalism. Voices are regularly raised to demand a strengthening of the legal provisions, when they are invoked. Others support the intervention of some authority, whether established by journalists, by the media (a press council) or by the public power (an ethical committee), or alternatively an extension of the powers of existing regulatory authorities (like the CSA). Media professionals (journalists and editors) are largely united in opposition to such a move. Others strive for voluntary and pro-active measures such as the clarification of codes, setting up mediators (ombudsmen) or developing arenas for public debate on public informational practices. More or less connected with this matter, it is of note that the 'Education Nationale' has in recent years developed programmes that lead progressively towards the decoding of news and better understanding of the media.

We should note, in conclusion, amongst the novelties and the constants of policies followed in relation to the media, those measures in favour of 'difference' or 'cultural diversity', which lean towards adapting the rules of the market so as to prioritize the creation and expression of the national culture. Amongst these proposals are several relating to books, for instance the 'unique book price' designed to preserve a network of bookshops sufficient to make a large range of titles and genres of books commercially viable. The alternative is reducing prices and extensive promotion, by way of supermarket sales, leading to a narrowing down of supply to titles and genres that are very attractive. In respect of television or cinematic works and music, measures tend both towards national and European quotas and towards support in the form of advance financing (advance receipts, subsidies, etc.[37]). We must return to the vital question of authors' rights, with the part played by the societies for the administration of rights, that have re-emerged as a result of convergence and especially because of the development of the Internet and on-line media. In all these matters, we can clearly discern a division between the fairly consensual national preferences on the part of professionals and also public authorities on the one hand and, on the other, the ideas cherished by the large international commercial media groups (including those with their headquarters in France) which incline heavily towards conceptions that are much more Anglo-Saxon and globalist.[38]

# NOTES

[1]Under the pressure of immigration from the Maghreb and Africa which has taken over as the main feature of immigration into southern Europe during the second half of the twentieth century.

[2]Public broadcasters comprise Radio France, Radio France Outre-mer, France Télévision and ARTE, whose budgets (partly from licence fees and partly from the state budget) are voted each year by the parliament.

[3]At first freely available to all telephone subscribers who gave up their annual printed telephone directory in favour of an 'electronic directory'.

[4]AEPM study of the magazine audience, 2001.

[5]Data from the Diffusion Conseil show growth between 1981 and 2001 from 1,294,000 to 2,135,000 copies.

[6]Of which the Editions du Moniteur, l'Usine Nouvelle, the Test group (informatic press), etc.

[7]Principally *Les Pratiques culturelles de Français* carried out every seven years, the latest being in 1997 (Donnat, 1998).

[8]The turnover of Hachette books in 2000 rose to €830 million.

[9]For instance, VUP acquired the North American educational publisher Houghton Mifflin in 2001.

[10]In fact this is a matter of the historical role of Hachette, whose activities began with bookshops, then with the distribution of books and later the press, a sector in which the group occupied a monopoly position before the Second World War.

[11]The regional structures of France 3 are also active in production, but this has notably decreased during recent years.

[12]This relates to the Centre France-Montagne and Sud Ouest groups.

[13]In 2000, 133 networks were available on cable or satellite.

[14]Which does not prevent cable and satellite from distributing generalist programmes such as RTL-9, TMC or Paris Premiere, without counting the large generalist European network.

[15]Thematic channels are more diverse than this, since one can find channels for history, discovery, weather, television series, cooking and comedy not to mention the showing of foreign channels from Germany, Spain, Italy, North America and Arab countries.

[16]Of which the capital is held by the state, with mixed finance derived from licences, a budgetary contribution and advertising.

[17]France Inter, France Info, France Culture, France Musique, France Bleue Régions, le Mouv.

[18]Europe 1, Europe 2, RFM.

[19]RTL, RTL-2, Fun.

[20]NRJ, Chérie FM, Rire et Chansons, Nostalgie.

[21]A small terminal with a modem, screen and keyboard for accessing a videotext network, since 1983, by way of the telephone. The leading application, which justified free distribution of this apparatus to all telephone subscribers, was the electronic directory which replaced the printed directory in all households wishing it.

[22]Lagardère group ceded Club-Internet in 2000 to Deutsche Telekom.

[23]Canal Web once proposed several dozen television networks on the Internet.

[24]The written press has benefited from public support for multimedia investment, in the form of returnable advances, in reality only partially returnable, for sums amounting to a little over €2 million a year since 1998.

[25]This follows the lead of the very popular 'Music Fair' created by the Ministry of Culture during the 1980s.

[26]To be precise, entitled "The evolution of tasks of state faced with technological changes in the media". Their conclusions are contained in two reports, Dagnaud (2000) and (2000).

[27]If the calculation is made at a VAT rate of 19.6 per cent, bearing in mind that newspapers pay a tax of 2.1 per cent.

[28]It remains so even to globally favourable magazines that are sold by postal subscription, whereas the sale of daily newspapers in France depends less on postal subscription than on sales at kiosks or home delivery.

[29]Under the form of state subscriptions representing something of the order of 40 per cent of the turnover of the agency, being a little more than €90 million.

[30]Not wishing to define what was a daily of opinion, the legislature preferred to apply 'technical' criteria, assuming that the opinion press receives little advertising (the threshold was fixed at 20 per cent of turnover), has a low rate of circulation (threshold fixed at 200,000 copies), with a price making it accessible to a large number (less than €1.5). In practice, this identified two national dailies, *la Croix* and *l'Humanité*, plus one regional, the *Populaire du Centre*.

[31]The 1989 law in fact mainly reformed the public audiovisual sector, with reference to the precedent of the 1986 law. It established the High Council for the Audiovisual which replaced the National Commission for Communication and

Freedoms (CNCL), which itself had taken over from the High Authority for the Audiovisual Media, established by the law of 1982. At each of these legislative steps, the prerogatives of the structure of regulation are found, reaffirmed and made more precise, at the same time as developing over the course of the years a form of jurisprudence for these "administrative authorities".

[32]Its nine members are appointed by the presidents of the National Assembly and Senate, also by the President of the Republic. The president of the CSA is nominated by the President of the Republic, amongst the three members that he appoints.

[33]This mode of appointment seems to have led to the very frequent, if not systematic, nomination of presidents from the professional milieus (France Télévision, Radio France), rather than from the 'state commissions' (Radio France International).

[34]The subject of numerous lawsuits between journalists and publishers, both in the written and in the audiovisual press, which have given rise to a series of judgements on the part of the courts, leading to the enlargement of the classic right of authorship on the Internet, which may in due course weigh heavily on the conditions for retrieving information from the Net, the publishers attempting to establish the notion of "collective work" for journalistic work, believing themselves disadvantaged by comparison with their Anglo-Saxon colleagues in the matter of copyright.

[35]The Court of Final Appeal in Paris ordered Yahoo, in May 2001, to deny access to French Internet users of the relevant part of the site.

[36]Forbidding, for instance, the publication or diffusion of pictures of persons wearing handcuffs or pictures deemed to be 'degrading' to the individuals concerned.

[37]In which the Centre National de la Cinématographie (CNC) plays an important role.

[38]Exemplified by the polemical declarations of Jean-Marie Messier, president of Vivendi Universal, concerning the "cultural clause".

# STATISTICS

| | |
|---|---|
| Population | 60,000,000 |
| Number of households | 24,430,000 |
| Movie admissions, 2001 | 166,000,000 |
| Books sold, 2001 | 405,000,000 |

**Print media**  Circulation of main daily newspapers, 2000

| | |
|---|---|
| L'Equipe | 2,619,000 |
| Le Monde | 1,993,000 |
| Le Parisien | 1,716,000 |
| Le Figaro | 1,386,000 |
| Libération | 886,000 |
| Les Echos | 728,000 |
| France Soir | 587,000 |
| La Tribune | 531,000 |
| La Croix | 303,000 |
| L'Humanité | 291,000 |

Source: Circulation Council.

Circulation of main daily regional newspapers, 2000

| | |
|---|---|
| Ouest France | 767,000 |
| Sud Ouest | 336,000 |
| Voix du Nord | 320,000 |
| Le Progrès | 263,000 |
| Le Dauphiné | 255,000 |
| La NRCO | 247,000 |
| Est Républicain | 210,000 |
| La Montagne | 209,000 |

| | |
|---|---|
| *La Dépêche* | 205,000 |
| *Les DNA* | 201,000 |

Source: Circulation Council.

Circulation of main magazines, 2000

| | |
|---|---|
| *TV magazine* | 4,489,000 |
| *Télé 7 jours* | 2,371,000 |
| *Télé Z* | 2,291,000 |
| *Télé loisirs* | 1,956,000 |
| *TV hebdo* | 1,826,000 |
| *Télé star* | 1,682,000 |
| *Femme Actuelle* | 1,538,000 |

**Broadcast media**

Audience share of main television channels, average, 2000 (%)

| | |
|---|---|
| TF-1 | 33.4 |
| France-2 | 22.1 |
| France-3 | 16.8 |
| M6 | 12.7 |
| Canal plus | 7.5 |
| Cinquième/Arte | 3.4 |
| Average daily viewing time, 2001 | 209 minutes |

Audience share of main radio channels, 2001 (%)

| | |
|---|---|
| Radio France | 28 |
| RTL-1 | 13.3 |
| France Inter | 9.0 |
| Europe | 8.7 |

| | |
|---|---|
| Number of households reached by satellite, cable or terrestrial pay-television | 10,780,000 |

Percentage of households with:

| | |
|---|---|
| VCR | 90 |
| Satellite receiver | (2,900,000) |
| DVD player | 14.1 |

**Electronic media**

Percentage of households with:

| | |
|---|---|
| Internet access | 14 |
| Mobile phone ownership | 63 |

**Advertising spend, 2000 (%)**

| | |
|---|---|
| Press | 45.2 |
| Television | 30.1 |
| Radio | 7.1 |
| Outdoor | 11.6 |
| Cinema | 0.8 |

# REFERENCES

Baptiste, Eric (2000) *Convergence of Media and Industrial Strategies*. Paris: Documentation française.

Charon, Jean-Marie (1999) *La Presse magazine*. Paris: Découverte.

Charon, Jean-Marie (2002) *La Presse des jeunes*. Paris: Découverte.

Dagnaud, Monique (2002) *The promotion of Cultural Diversity*. Paris: Documention française.

Devillard, V., et al. (2001) *Les Journalistes français à l'aube de l'an 2000: profils et parcours*. Paris: Panthéon Assas.

Donnat, Olivier (1998) *Les pratiques culturelles des Français*. Paris: Documentation française.

# 7: Germany

HANS J. KLEINSTEUBER

## NATIONAL PROFILE

Describing the national characteristics of Germany is far from easy. Modern Germany was founded as a latecomer in Europe in 1871 as the Deutsches Reich. But the territories that make up today's Germany look back at a long history of developing a common identity and a common culture, based on historical events that were experienced together and of course the German language. But it is not just the national language of the more than 80 million inhabitants of Germany, but a language which is also spoken in Austria and parts of Switzerland. Altogether this constitutes a common language space – and therefore a media market – of about 100 million people.

The old Germany followed an expansionist policy, initiated disastrous wars in Europe and lost them. So the borders of the German Empire – that once included people of Polish, French or Danish identity – were changed and limited to the German-speaking core; modern Germany declared that all borders are final and maintains friendly relations with its neighbours. As a consequence there are very few historical minorities living inside the country's borders, the largest being Danes south of the Danish border and Sorbes (Slavic-speaking people in Eastern Germany).

But modern Germany is not just a nation state today, it has changed into a multicultural society. Located in the middle of Europe, it historically offered a home to millions of people that came from neighbouring countries and settled down on German territory. Also, at times, parts of Germany were controlled by Austrian, French, Danish, Swedish and other rulers. As

a consequence, German history was always strongly shaped by non-German influences. Again, starting in the 1950s, foreigners moved in large numbers to Germany, most of them as migrant labourers ('guest workers'), others as political refugees or for economic reasons. About 10 per cent of the population are today what is called 'foreign', meaning that they came from another country and are not German citizens. Many others have been naturalized and are counted as Germans. In large metropolises like Berlin or Hamburg up to a quarter of the population are non-German.

The turbulent history of the part of Europe that is called Germany today was shaped by the existence of relatively small states that only loosely co-operated in the old German Empire under a weak Hapsburg crown that disappeared altogether in 1806. As a result, the country looks back at a very long tradition of extreme political and economic decentralization. The political system during times of democracy has always been federal and even today – after the capital moved from tiny Bonn to the largest city, Berlin – there is no clear centre in the country. When the present Federal Republic was founded in 1949, it was established out of the individual *Länder* (the regional states) that already existed at that time. According to the constitution, they still have the final say on all matters of culture. The flexibility of the federal system was again demonstrated when the former communist regime of the centralistic German Democratic Republic (GDR) crumbled and finally disappeared in 1989/90. The eastern territories established themselves as five new *Länder* and joined the existing eleven *Länder* of the Federation (East Berlin merged with West Berlin). Both elements, the federal system and the consequences of (re)unification are very much reflected in the media system and give it some unique features.

Today Germany is home to about 82.1 million people who live in a territory of 356,954 km$^2$, the population density is about 232 per km$^2$, one of the highest in Europe. The number of households is about 35 million. Relatively high incomes and economic wealth ensure high expenditure on advertising and media consumption. The figure for total advertising expenditure in 2000 was €33 billion, up 61 per cent from 1990, €23 billion of which went to the media. Compared with other parts of Europe, Germany enjoys a comfortable lifestyle but also shows signs of continuing stagnation. The rate of economic growth is among the lowest on the continent.

# STRUCTURE AND OWNERSHIP

The generally decentralized structure is reflected in many ways in the media. The typical newspaper is a local product and public service broadcasting is based on regional *Länder* organizations. On the other hand, commercial media actors – print or television – often consider Austria and German-speaking Switzerland as a legitimate part of their activities and provide their markets for magazines and television programmes with content that is generated in Germany. Another aspect of decentralization is the fact that there is no clear media centre in the country: news media tend to centre around the political decision makers in Berlin, the news agency dpa (Deutsche Presse Agentur) and the weekly prestige press are located in Hamburg, public service broadcasting is present in many regional cities and commercial television has its centres in Munich and Cologne. This structural decentralization does not contradict another element, the relatively high concentration of ownership, as some of the leading European media players are located in Germany. The largest media company in Europe, Bertelsmann, still has its headquarters in the sleepy provincial town of Gütersloh; today it controls the RTL group, the most successful commercial television venture in Europe, and enjoys a higher turnover in the US market than in Germany. Another powerful actor was Leo Kirch and

his Kirch group, controlling a large share of the commercial television market and being the sole provider of pay-television. Kirch's empire fell apart and entered insolvency in April 2002. Kirch also held a share in the Springer company, the largest publishing house in Europe, now under the controlling influence of Frieda Springer, the widow of founder Axel Caesar Springer.

## The print media

### The newspaper press

The general characteristics of the German press include these features: (1) a large number of titles; (2) strong local papers, often as a monopoly; (3) only a few national papers; (4) a large number of magazines. Over recent years the structure of the press has seen few changes. In the year 2001 the number of 'independent editorial units' (meaning full publishing entities that produce all parts of a paper) for daily newspapers was 136 (in 1954: 225); among these were 129 subscription newspapers and seven tabloids. It is very common to publish (sub)local versions of a paper, and thus the number of different editions was much higher, the total being 1,584. This gives the impression that the press is highly diversified and centred around localities; in fact many papers are part of chain businesses and most information is contributed by the national news agency, dpa (in Hamburg). Figures for the size of the newspaper market were as follows: 23.8 million newspapers per day, 4.5 million on Sundays and 1.9 million weekly newspapers (year 2000). The circulation figures show that, among the dailies, 16.4 million copies are reported as local or regional papers; 1.7 million copies are national, most of them being sold by subscription. Another 5.7 million papers are 'sold on the street', another word for the tabloid press, often referred to in Germany as the 'boulevard press'. The leading tabloid paper is *Bild-Zeitung* with national distribution by regionalized editions; other tabloids have only local or regional significance.

As pointed out, national distribution of a paper is the exception. Prominent among the exceptions are the *Frankfurter Allgemeine Zeitung* (*FAZ*, political position: moderate conservative), the *Süddeutsche Zeitung* (moderately left), *Frankfurter Rundschau* (social democrat) and *Die Welt* (definitely conservative). Some also count the much smaller *tageszeitung* (*taz*) as national, which started in 1979 as an 'alternative' paper and is owned as a co-operative venture by its readers (and follows a somewhat 'Green' line). The phenomenon *Bild-Zeitung* (i.e. picture paper) deserves special mention in describing the German press. This daily paper (on Sundays: *Bild am Sonntag*) published by the Springer company has the extraordinarily high circulation of more than 4 million copies (in 2001: 4.4 million) per weekday. It uses a tabloid format, follows questionable reporting standards and traditionally shows a strong right-wing orientation.

The daily newspaper industry had a turnover of €10.8 billion in 2000, of which €6.9 billion came from advertisements. It still gets the largest share of all advertisement money (28 per cent), but – as in other countries – faces problems of decline. Seventy-eight per cent of the population (age fourteen or over) regularly read a newspaper; most readers are to be found in the forty to sixty-nine age group, with more than 80 per cent active readers. Press readership is lower among young people aged twenty to twenty-nine, which reaches only 66 per cent. Sales of newspapers are stagnating, but definite differences between West and East have to be recognized. The generally depressed situation in east Germany is reflected in declining sales figures and serious loss of advertisement revenue. The situation is more stable in the west.

It should be mentioned that the larger migrant communities in the country are served by newspapers from their respective countries that are printed in Germany (sometimes edited in Germany as well). About one-third of this population is Turkish-German, and the leading Turkish paper *Hürriyet* sells more than 100,000 copies per issue. There are two more Turkish papers and others from the former Yugoslavia, Greece and Spain. Turkish satellite television is prominent as well, and there are debates as to whether the consumption of media content from one's home country makes integration more difficult. The tiny ethnic minorities are served as well: roughly 30,000 Danes read their paper, *Flensborg Avis*, radio and television offer programming in the Sorb language.

The German market for daily newspapers shows definite signs of concentration. The largest market share (23.6 per cent) goes to the Axel Springer company, the largest publishing house in Europe, with dailies like *Bild, Welt, Hamburger Abendblatt, Berliner Morgenpost*, etc. Springer also has a dominant

position in the market for Sunday papers. Second position is taken by the regional publisher WAZ group with a share of 6 per cent; third place is occupied by the Stuttgarter Zeitung group with 5 per cent, followed by the Cologne-based DuMont Schauberg with 4.4 per cent. The Bertelsmann company is still weak in dailies and ranks eighth through its majority-owned Gruner & Jahr subsidiary (2.8 per cent). Newspaper companies have reacted to the reduction in earnings from advertising and the stagnation of sales by streamlining internal operations. The Springer company, for example, merged the newspaper offices of *Die Welt* and *Berliner Morgenpost* in Berlin.

The norm in the smaller newspaper markets is one local monopoly paper, while in the big cities a few competing newspapers usually share the market. In Berlin, the new capital of the country, the market is highly competitive, with seven subscription papers, whereas Hamburg, the second largest city, has only three subscription papers and suffers from the market dominance of Springer, which accounts for more than 80 per cent of all newspapers (subscription and tabloid sold).

### The periodical and magazine press

All in all, 2,040 general magazines (with 124 million copies) and 3,590 specialized magazines (with 17 million copies) were published in 2000. About half the general magazines are sold by subscription (48 per cent), the rest on the street (52 per cent). About 10 per cent of all advertising money goes into general magazines and another 5 per cent supports specialized periodicals.

Some of the weekly magazines have gained special prominence. The Hamburg weekly *Der Spiegel*, originally designed to copy the American *Time Magazine*, for long enjoyed a virtual monopoly of the market for political news. With its investigative style of journalism, it has made quite a number of scandals public and is reckoned the most influential political publication. During the last few years *Focus* (a Burda publication) has challenged this position with a politically more conservative line and flashier design. The market for general interest magazines is still quite active, *Der Stern* by Gruner & Jahr (controlled by Bertelsmann) being the most successful and best known, with a liberal and investigative format. Quite influential as a 'highbrow' weekly is *Die Zeit*, a politically independent paper that still follows a newspaper format (now part of the Holtzbrinck group).

The magazine market shows a somewhat different structure from that of newspapers. It is dominated by four large companies. The biggest market share is held by the Bauer company, a relatively unknown publisher that is mostly active in the 'yellow' segment (in German: 'rainbow magazines'). Its market share is 22.3 per cent with thirty six titles. The other three publishing houses are Springer (twenty nine titles), Burda (twenty four) and Gruner & Jahr (thirty one), which is controlled by the Bertelsmann conglomerate. Together they account for a market share of 58.6 per cent (2000). The rest of the market is distributed between smaller actors, among whom Holtzbrinck is another important actor.

### Book publishing

The book markets of the German-speaking countries of Europe are highly integrated, meaning that books published in Austria or Switzerland are freely available on the German market and vice versa. Many of the leading book publishers have been acquired during the last decades by the large media companies, for example Ullstein by Springer and Rowohlt by Holtzbrinck. A special case is Bertelsmann, which has bought up the largest book publisher in the world, Random House in New York, and also controls dozens of German book publishers in many different markets, including paperbacks (Goldmann, etc.), hard-cover (C. Bertelsmann, etc.) and academic books (Springer – not related to the Springer company) and many others.

In the year 2000 about 83,000 book titles were published in Germany (1990: 61,000), among them 63,000 as first editions. Twenty-five per cent of these are categorized as social science books and 16 per cent as literature, language, fiction and poetry. About 10 per cent of the titles are published as paperbacks. The annual turnover of the industry was DM 18.4 billion. According to studies, 59 per cent of the general population pick up a book to read at least once a month. A special feature of the German book market is a system of fixed prices (retail price maintenance), an age-old principle that is under increasing attack from the European Union.

## The electronic (audio-visual) media

Radio transmissions started in 1923. The only channel was financed by a monthly fee and production responsibility rested with the state postal service, with strong political control, mainly by the Ministry of the Interior. Programming was quite plural, though; one of the authors of radio plays was Bertolt Brecht (*Nachtflug*). The seizure of power by the Nazi regime on 30 January 1933 brought an immediate change (on the same day) as the old directorate of the radio organization was forced to resign. Radio was immediately seized and became the central propaganda tool of the Third Reich. In 1945 what remained of the radio infrastructure fell into the hands of the Allied occupation forces, who built up a new radio network from scratch.

The radio system before 1945 was centralized. Its structural development after 1945 reflected the fact that Germany had been divided into different occupation zones and the occupation forces created regional broadcasters (more or less) along *Länder* borders that still exist today. The British forces established one unified organization, the NWDR, that covered the north and west of Germany. The NWDR reflected some of the centralism of the BBC. In the 1950s this organization was split by party rivalries into NDR for the north (Lower Saxony, Hamburg and Schleswig-Holstein) while the WDR took over in the west (North Rhine-Westphalia). The Americans established regional, that is, *Länder*-wide, broadcasting organizations, as in Hesse (HR) and Bavaria (BR) that are still in existence today. More broadcasters were added as a result of the unification process. The resulting structure makes up today's public service system, responsible for radio and television services.

### Television

Television transmission started in 1954 with one TV channel. It was based on the co-operation of all *Länder* -organizations that established for the purpose the Arbeitsgemeinschaft der Rundfunkanstalten Deutschlands (ARD). The different ARD-broadcasters share the responsibility for the programmes among themselves according to size (for example, the large west German WDR accounts for 21.3 per cent of programming, the small Radio Bremen for 2.5 per cent), while some activities are provided centrally. The news of ARD Aktuell comes from Hamburg.

An attempt by the federal government to introduce a second channel was stopped by the Federal Constitutional Court in 1961 in a decision that has pointed the way to this day. All national broadcasting activities were to take place at the level of the *Länder* rather than at federal level. *Länder* swiftly moved to prepare for a second channel. It started in 1963 as Zweites Deutsches Fernsehen (ZDF), based on the common agreement of all *Länder* to jointly establish a new public service broadcaster independent from ARD with its centre in the city of Mainz. At the same time the existing (ARD) broadcasters introduced regional third channels (NDR III, etc.), jointly called ARD-3. The first two channels offered a general programme, the third channel started with a high content of regional and cultural programming. The third programmes, some of them sub-regionalized at times, together with the regional radio programmes, concentrate on providing all regions of the country with a well developed service. In addition ARD-1 shows programming that is generated in different parts of the country, so that public service broadcasting is a strong factor in supporting regional identities.

Already in the 1970s there were attempts to break the public monopoly and introduce commercial broadcasting. These actors, mainly in the newspaper industry, actually succeeded in 1984/5 when a dual system was established. After some years of inactivity, the public broadcasters began to react to the challenge and started to offer on the one hand more entertainment content on their general channels, on the other they established a number of new specialized channels, among them a joint offering with Austria and Switzerland in the German-language region (3sat), a German–French cultural channel (ARTE), a documentary channel (Phoenix), a children's channel (Kika). Also the ARD-3 programmes are being distributed via satellite and cable and therefore available in most households. This adds up to a situation where most Germans have ten or more public service channels available. Deutsche Welle (DW-tv) is the foremost broadcaster in the country, again based on a public service format, financed by the federal budget and transmitting twenty four hours worldwide in three languages.

The first commercial competitors to the public broadcasters were RTL (originally transmitting from Luxembourg as RTLplus across the border) and Sat-1 (originally distributed via satellite). During the following years new general channels were introduced (Pro-7, Vox, RTL-2, Kabel 1) as well as specialized channels for music (Viva 1 + 2), sport (DSF), news (ntv, N-24), etc. Also in big cities (Berlin, Hamburg, Munich) and some regions (Franconia, Rhein-Neckar, Saarland, etc.) sub-regional and metropolitan television was introduced. After a rather diversified beginning in the television business most channels were bought up and merged into two groups that are often called 'sender families'. One is part of the Kirch group, consisting of (among others) Sat-1, Pro-7 and DSF, the other is the RTL family, controlled by Bertelsmann and including RTL, RTL-2, Vox and others. Only a few minor channels remain independent, among them Viva and ntv.

Over 90 per cent of all households receive television programmes via cable or satellite (2000: 91.4 per cent); less then 10 per cent is terrestrial. This puts Germany in a unique situation among Europe's large countries, as a very large share of all households receive around thirty German-language programmes 'free', that is, outside pay-television. Besides this offering, some foreign channels are generally fed into the cable systems (and of course are available via satellite) like CNN, MTV (both with German-language options).

This situation makes any attempt to start pay-television quite complicated. Analogue pay-television was first introduced by the Premiere company in 1991 (then jointly owned by Bertelsmann, Kirch and Canal Plus). In 1996 Leo Kirch started his own pay venture (DF-1) with packaged digital television. After several years of in-fighting Bertelsmann sold out and Premiere plus DF-1 were merged into the Kirch empire as Premiere World, offering about thirty channels of the usual pay diet, mainly out of Kirch's huge film library. Pay-television met an especially difficult market situation in Germany, as a freely available multi-channel environment already existed. Also the Kirch company used a set-top box (d-box) with a proprietary architecture, forcing competitors who wanted to join digital television to work under Kirch's supervision. Premiere World never reached more than 2.4 million households (2001/2) and produced heavy deficits, amounting to several billion euros. Rupert Murdoch's News Corporation acquired a share of 22 per cent in the deficit-ridden company and carries an option to take more. In April 2002 parts of Kirch's conglomerate company moved into insolvency, mainly because of the huge deficit in pay-televison. ARD and ZDF each offer a package of free digital television via Kirch´s d-box, but the audience is minimal. The public broadcasters joined ranks with RTL, the consumer electronics industry and others to introduce the Multimedia Home Platform (MHP) for future digital television, and in 2001 even Kirch reluctantly supported MHP.

For the last few years RTL has enjoyed the highest audience ratings, followed by ARD, ZDF, Sat1 and Pro 7. Over this period the combined ratings of the third channels (ARD-3) have slightly increased. In the year 2000 television received about €4.7 billion or 20 per cent of all advertising money. A special aspect is that viewers of public television are much older than those of their commercial competitors. The former attempt to attract younger viewers but have to do so with the existing programme scheme as they are at present barred from introducing any new channels. Media consumption between the east and west of the country still differs considerably: Germans in the former GDR watch more television and read fewer newspapers. They prefer commercial to public television and have a special liking for the regional third channels (ARD-3) that regularly show material from the old GDR archives.

### Radio

As is to be expected, nearly all radio is either regional or local. Besides two nationally distributed public service programmes (DeutschlandRadio), a remnant of the unification process, all other programmes are limited to a regional or local range. The *Länder* organizations of the ARD also run the regional radio networks, typically offering five to six channels, including a popular format ('adult contemporary', usually with some commercial spots), one with classical music, often one with news only, sometimes a channel catering for older people (German *Schlager* music) and/or for youngsters. In the more densly populated parts of Germany sub-regional and to some extent local programming is offered.

Radio is available on cable and to some extent on satellite (Astra Digital Radio), but most of the reception is terrestrial, because much of the actual consumption is in a mobile environment (car radio, etc.). Radio programmes distributed by cable and satellite are of little importance; digital radio as Digital Satellite Radio (DSR) was offered via

cable for several years, but was cut off for lack of interest. After years of research and trial projects a new digital version of radio, called Digital Audio Broadcasting (DAB), was introduced in 1999 and most of the country is covered by a network of DAB transmitters, partially paid for out of the public broadcasting fee. But interest in DAB is minimal.

The public service monopoly in radio existed until 1985 when the first commercial radio stations were licensed. As the licences are handed out by *Länder*-based broadcasting authorities, the situation is diverse as quite different policies are pursued. As a rule, the *Länder* of the south offer licences for local radio stations whereas in the north regional networks are the rule. The most populous *Land*, North Rhine-Westphalia, decided to introduce a unique two-columns model in which local commercial broadcasters are legally required to offer some radio time to local non-commercial citizen groups. On the whole, commercial broadcasting is rather diversified in terms of ownership, but the large media conglomerates are often involved and own shares in the most popular stations, as do the local newspapers. The larger regional networks and the leading metropolitan stations tend to be profitable, whereas the small local stations often struggle for survival.

In the larger markets (like Berlin or Hamburg) quite a number of commercial radio stations are active, the most successful usually following the leading format of 'adult contemporary' or variations of this (*Deutsch-AC*). Others offer less popular formats, but common to all is strictly commercial management, following the American models. A commercial station, Klassik Radio (managed by the Bertelsmann company) owns licences in a number of German cities. The leading newspaper *FAZ* established a business news station in 2001 (first in Frankfurt, than extended to Munich and elsewhere). About €732 million or 3 per cent of all advertising money goes into radio (2000).

Local radio of the community type had a difficult start in Germany. Media developments usually take place in an atmosphere of strong governmental influence and attempts to establish pirate radio were heavily prosecuted. Understanding of a non-profit, community-based type of radio was nearly non-existent, enjoyed little political support and is still relatively underdeveloped.

The first station of this type, Radio Dreyeckland, is still active. It started in the border region between France and Switzerland and can be seen as a German version of a French *radio libre*. In the year 2000 about fourty non-commercial stations were on the air, most of them in the south west *Land* of Baden-Württemberg (fourteen), in the south (Bavaria ten), in Hesse (seven) and Lower Saxony (six). The city of Hamburg has one such station, one (Freies Sendekombinat, FSK) is organized like a federation, offering radio time to different groups (politics, women, city quarters, university). Besides these regular community stations, some are organized as public access channels and offer service on a 'first come, first served' basis.

### Film and video

The film and video industry of Germany is quite typical for Europe. All in all there are about 4,600 cinemas (2000) in Germany which account for about 10.6 seats per thousand inhabitants. The film market is heavily dominated by American productions. About fifty (1998) to seventy five films (2000) that have been made in Germany make it into the cinemas each year. This accounts for a market share for German-produced films of between 16.7 (1997) and 9.4 (2000) per cent. Compared to this, American dominance is impressive. In the year 2000, 165 American films reached a market share of 81.8 per cent. Among all other countries, only imports from Britain have any siginificance (2000: 5.1 per cent). The video industry has shown some increase in turnover (1991: DM 1.641 billion, 2000: DM 1.827 billion). This is distributed between leasing videos (666 million), video sales (828 million) and DVD sales (333 million) for the year 2000.

Because of the long-lasting crisis in the film production industry, a system of cultural subsidies and economic stimuli on several levels has been built up. The federal government introduced a small levy that has to be paid on every cinema ticket bought that goes into a pool for film support. Also, a number of the *Länder* run their own scheme for support, mainly those that have a base in film production (like *NRW*, Bavaria, Berlin, Hamburg). Further public service broadcasters agreed to aid the industry by financing selected film projects that in return are shown on television after they have finished in the movie theatres. The system of subsidies is – typically for Germany – rather decentralized and a film-maker may have to appeal to several institutions before enough financing is secured.

## The Internet and related on-line media

Concerning the Internet, the share of Germans that use this new service is – according to an ARD-Online study of 2001 – 38.8 per cent (figures for 2001), including 48.3 per cent of all males and 30.1 per cent of all females. The two main providers of online services are *T-Online*, a daughter company of Deutsche Telekom, and AOL-Online. All major media established online presentations of their respective service; the most successful among the broadcasters are: rtl.de (1.48 million hits in February 2002), sat1.de (800,000), sport1.de (510,000) and wdr.de (500,000) – WDR is the public broadcaster of North-Rhine Westphalia. The public service broadcasters have invested heavily in online services and all of them established portals that concentrate on news (tageschau.de), regional matters and material to accompany their programmes. Their commercial competitors emphasize entertainment, games and interactive chats. Also all major newspapers are active in online services; some like that of the FAZ paper (faz.de) have started to charge for extensive use. The central news agency, dpa, does not offer its rich information service to end users, instead it provides online news that is presented by newspapers under their own names. So far the consequences for the traditional media are not threatening; most endangered are the newspapers that have already lost some of their business in classified advertisements.

## POLITICS, POLICY, LAW AND REGULATION

### The press

Because of Germany's catastrophic history, 1945 was a virtual 'hour zero', with the collapse of the Nazi dictatorship and its propagandist media system. First steps were taken by the occupation authorities to introduce a new structure of (licensed) German newspapers and magazines; virtually all famous names stem from these years (except *Bild*). Rather similarly, broadcasting started under the control of the allies and was only gradually placed in German hands. This regime ended in 1949 with the founding of the Federal Republic, on the basis of the new Basic Law as its constitution. Article 5 of the constitution (Basic Law of 1949) says:

> Everybody has the right to free expression and publication of his opinion in word, writing and picture and the right to obtain information without hindrance from sources generally accessible. The freedom of the press and of reporting by broadcasting and film is guaranteed. There must be no censorship. (Article 5(1))

Besides these general guidelines that are part of the human rights section of the constitution, not much reference to the media is to be found. Article 70 stipulates that lawmaking for the press rests with the *Länder*, but the federal government may specify a common frame of regulation (article 75), which it never did. All *Länder* passed press laws that contain similar regulations (about publishers' information, journalists' rights and other matters), as such making sure that newspaper companies are treated equally everywhere. Besides these laws, a system of self-regulation has emerged: a Press Council (Deutscher Presserat), that includes representatives of publishers and journalists, handles complaints and makes reprimands public. An Advertisement Council serves a similar function.

A special regulation for the press was included in the Federal Cartel Law in 1976. The critical definition of market dominance was more strictly specified for the press than for other branches. But enforcement of these rules was not hard-line, also the publishers have attempted to revoke the legislation.

## The electronic media

In the crucial year 1949 much of the broadcasting infrastructure had already been established on a regional basis. The constitution reflects this fact by offering the *Länder* final responsibility over all questions of broadcasting, which is still the case today. This position was upheld many times (some say: created) by the Federal Constitutional Court in leading decisions, the first one dating back to 1961. This leads to a unique situation worldwide: public service broadcasting rests on *Länder* broadcasting laws, while commercial broadcasting is regulated by state media authorities (fifteen altogether).

The markets for radio programming are regulated by the *Länder*, therefore national radio is nearly non-existent.

Public service broadcasting today is based on organizations, created by the *Länder*, of a very peculiar legal construction (called *Anstalt*), with a Director General (*Intendant*) at the head. When several *Länder* co-operate, they jointly sign an agreement that constitutes the legal basis; for example, NDR (Norddeutscher Rundfunk) provides radio and television for four northern *Länder*, ZDF was jointly established by all sixteen *Länder*. These broadcasting organizations are financed mainly by a monthly fee, also some advertising money is earned. At the beginning of 2001 the combined fee for radio and television was €16.15 per month. Control of the *Anstalt* is by a Broadcasting Council (Rundfunkrat) that includes representatives of politics (members of parliament and government) and 'socially relevant groups' to guarantee pluralism (Churches, chambers of commerce and trade unions, sports, women, culture, the environment, etc.). In fact the most powerful groups in this system are the two main political parties (the Christian Democrats and Social Democrats). They are usually strong enough to decide among themselves about the appointment of leading personnel in the organization. Often they apply a policy of 'black and red' proportional representation, the party in government selects the *Intendant*, the opposition party the Vice *Intendant,* and so on.

Commercial broadcasting too is regulated entirely by the *Länder*. Problems that concern more than one state are addressed in an agreement, negotiated between all *Länder* (*Rundfunkstaatsvertrag*), that is regularly updated. The latest (the fifth) started at the beginning of 2001. Licensing and the general monitoring of programmes are done by fifteen state media authorities (*Landesmedienanstalten*; Berlin and Brandenburg run a joint organization). Their responsibility also includes television programmes with national distribution; supervision is then done by one of the authorities. The *Länder* jointly established two more organizations to handle problems of concentration (KEK) and public service finances (KEF). Germany has by far the most complex structure for broadcast regulation in the world, not least because the authorities are too small to handle large media conglomerates and a licensee may change to another *Land* if it is not satisfied.

Under the constitution, telecommunications matters are the final responsibility of the federal government. After abolishing the Postal Ministry, a Regulatory Authority for Telecommunications and Post (Regulierungsbehörde für Telekommunikation und Post) was established in 1998 that handles all matters of telephony, etc. The resulting separation between broadcasting regulation at the *Länder* level and telecommunications regulation at the federal level results in a highly fragmented structure, which clearly collides with the tendency towards convergence and digitalization. Politicians are well aware of the problem, but so far they have proved unable to change anything. The results are sometimes odd. To handle the new information and communication technologies the federal government passed a law in 1997 for new communication services, while all *Länder* joined together to agree a policy for media services on the Internet in the same year; some of the wording of both documents was identical.

Because of the federal basis of West Germany it was relatively easy to incorporate additional territories into the Federal Republic. This happened with the Saarland, which returned from France in 1956. It established the small SR organization with an emphasis on German–French border themes. The federal logic also made it easy to integrate the former German Democratic Republic into the existing system. When it collapsed in 1989/90 the eastern state split up into five *Länder*. Each either established its own broadcasters (MDR, ORB) or joined western organizations (NDR).

## The Internet and related on-line media

It is certainly not easy to separate the new media from traditional media, in fact in many cases we find situations of transition and convergence. Generally speaking, in most fields Germany is not a leader in the new media in Europe for a number of reasons. Concerning the digitalization of television it lags behind other countries like Britain, mainly because of the critical situation in pay-TV. The break-up of the Kirch empire will probably mark another phase of uncertainty. In the field of radio digitalization, Germany was keen to introduce DAB technology and invested several hundred million euros, but the take-up is minimal. The introduction of broadband infrastructures

with interactive capacity is demanded by state actors, but limited by uncertainty about the future of the cable networks. In general the penetration of the Internet is below the northern part of Europe but above that of the south.

Starting about 1995, the federal governments of the then liberal-conservative spectrum (until 1998) and later the 'red – green' government (since 1998) were equally keen to introduce what was mostly called the 'information society', meaning a society in which information technologies and information jobs play a leading role. Plans were realized to have all schools wired, to introduce special support for research in information and communication technologies and the study of informatics. State authorities promised to go ahead in introducing e-government wherever possible and work on the introduction of e-voting. But none of this differed much from the plans of other European countries and similar measures by the European Union. In general, opinion polls demonstrate that Germans are relatively sceptical about new technologies, and interest in new media is low.

In terms of technology policy heavy emphasis was put on the EU project of introducing digital radio, based on the technology of digital audio broadcasting (DAB). Much of the development was done in Germany and it was established as a regular service in 1999. But sales of receivers are minimal and DAB could well turn out to be a total failure – at least for the immediate future. Also Digital Video Broadcasting in its terrestrial version (DVB-T) has been introduced in pilot projects, and plans are under way to introduce a regular service in the year 2002. Switching to DVB-T will not have much impact, as most households receive the television signal via cable or satellite. A general digital initative of the federal government seeks to end analogue television by 2010 and analogue radio by 2015. It seems doubtful that these goals will be reached.

Broadband networks for high-speed Internet and interactive television services are seen as the 'information highways' of the next generation. In Germany they are still in their infancy. This has to do with the stagnation that has taken place with regard to the huge cable networks that reach more than 60 per cent of all households and are still mostly under the control of Deutsche Telekom. This telecoms company has been ordered by the European Union to sell its cable networks, but has done so in only a few *Länder*. Most of the cable systems were scheduled to go to John Malone's Liberty company but the sale was stopped by the anti-cartel authority. So Deutsche Telekom is still looking for an interested investor, but the value of the network is going down. In the meantime Telekom is selling its own high-speed Internet service via DSL lines (called T-DSL) and has provided more than 2 million households (2002) with the new technology. This gives Telekom an advantage and makes it even more difficult to sell the remaining cable networks to anybody who is prepared to risk money and establish a hybrid network with broadband capacity for more television channels, video on demand and telephony. Whereas Germany was – among Europe's large countries, at least – a front-runner in cabling in the 1980s, the country has, with regard to broadband networks, been in a state of stagnation for a number of years.

## Transnational and European aspects

As was pointed out above, Bertelsmann is a classic transnational player which today earns higher returns on the American than on the German market. The company's strategy is to concentrate on content and it therefore has become the largest book publisher in the world (controlling Random House and many other publishers in different countries). It is also active in the global music business (BMG) and the strongest actor in European commercial television (RTL group). The Bertelsmann company traditionally follows a decentralized structure of profit centres which implies that some of the top management is located in the United States.

Typically for a transnational company, its scope is global; the capital is still German, though, controlled by the Mohn family and company workers of Bertelsmann.

Other German media actors have developed much less of a global perspective. Some companies like Burda have at least moved some of their activities out of Europe, for example running printing plants in North America. But most of the investment of larger actors is in neighbouring countries. Very much to the dislike of Austrians, much of the newspaper industry in that country is controlled by German companies, especially the WAZ group which owns the two largest newspapers. The WAZ group has, like other publishing houses, also moved into Eastern European markets, bought up existing newspapers and issued new magazines that usually copy successful publications of the west.

On the other hand, most global companies are active one way or an other in the German market. CNN (AOL Time Warner) holds a share in the German news channel ntv, Disney in Super-RTL, Murdoch in Premiere World. Some of the cable systems are controlled by non-German actors, satellite television is controlled mostly by the Luxembourg Astra company (in which Deutsche Telekom is a shareholder). The financial troubles of the Kirch group in 2002 will certainly lead to some rearrangements that could include more foreign investors: Murdoch of News International. But, in general, non-German control of the media is still weak. This reflects the fact that the market with its decentralized structure and strong political involvement is difficult for foreigners to cope with. But this will change, of course, with the further withdrawal of politics from the media and the Europeanization of media politics.

# STATISTICS

| | |
|---|---:|
| Population | 82,100,000 |
| Number of households | 34,700,000 |
| Movie admissions (ticket sales) | |
| 1999 | 149,000,000 |
| 1992 | 106,000,000 |
| Books published, 2001 (new titles) | 82,936 |

**Print media**

National
| | |
|---|---:|
| *Bild-Zeitung*, Hamburg (Springer) | 4,396,000 |
| *Süddeutsche Zeitung*, Munich | 436,000 |
| *Frankfurter Allgemeine Zeitung*, Frankfurt | 408,000 |
| *Die Welt*, Berlin (Springer) | 255,000 |
| *Die Tageszeitung*, Berlin | 59,000 |

Regional
| | |
|---|---:|
| *Westdeutsche Allgemeine*, Essen (WAZ group) | 558,000 |
| *Freie Presse*, Chemnitz (*Stuttgarter Zeitung*) | 386,000 |
| *Rheinische Post*, Düsseldorf | 341,000 |
| *Mitteldeutsche Zeitung*, Halle (duMont) | 351,000 |
| *Hamburger Abendblatt*, Hamburg (Springer) | 288,000 |
| *Kölner Stadtanzeiger*, Cologne (duMont) | 276,000 |
| *Magdeburger Volksstimme*, Magdeburg | 263,000 |
| *BZ*, Berlin (Springer) | 259,000 |

Circulation of newspapers, 2001
| | |
|---|---:|
| Daily (per day) | 28,400,000 |
| Weekly (per week) | 1,900,000 |
| Magazines (per issue) | 129,700,000 |

Market shares of major newspaper publishers, 2000 (%)
| | |
|---|---:|
| Axel Springer | 23.6 |
| WAZ | 6.0 |
| *Stuttgarter Zeitung* | 5.0 |
| DuMont Schauberg | 4.4 |
| *Süddeutscher Verlag* | 3.3 |
| *Frankfurter Allgemeine Zeitung* (*FAZ*) | 3.0 |
| Ippen Group | 2.9 |
| Gruner & Jahr | 2.8 |
| Holtzbrinck | 2.5 |
| Madsack | 2.4 |

**Broadcast media**

Audience share per television channel, 2001 (%). All are on cable and satellite; all public service channels are also terrestrial, private commercial ones are sometimes terrestrial.

| | 18:00–20:00 | 20:00–01:00 |
|---|---:|---:|
| ARD-1 | 13.3 | 14.3 |
| ZDF | 16.2 | 13.5 |
| ARD-3 | 15.9 | 14.4 |
| SAT-1 | 10.6 | 10.0 |
| RTL | 14.8 | 15.7 |
| Pro-7 | 6.1 | 8.3 |
| Other | 23.0 | 23.9 |

Radio
It is not possible to give figures on radio channels, as no national programming of significance exists.

Percentage of households with:
| | |
|---|---|
| Satellite (2001) | 56.3 |
| Cable (2001) | 33.2 |
| Pay-television subscriptions (2001) | 10.4 |
| VCR (2001) | 67.8 |
| Satellite receiver (2001) | 35.9 |
| DVD player | 8.0 |

**Electronic media**

Percentage of households with:
| | |
|---|---|
| Digital television reception (2001) | 5.1 |
| Internet access, 2001: | |
| Internet users | 24,800,000 |
| Share of total (%) | 38.8 |
| | |
| Mobile phone subscription (2001) | 56,240,000 |
| Share of total (%) | 69 |

**Advertising spend, 2000 (%)**

| | |
|---|---|
| Newspapers | 22.9 |
| Magazines | 25.6 |
| Television | 42.8 |
| Radio | 6.0 |
| Posters | 2.7 |

**Ownership**

Main media companies, 2001

| | Turnover (€) | Employees |
|---|---|---|
| Bertelsmann (worldwide activities) | 20,036,000,000 | 82,162 |
| Gruner & Jahr (mostly owned by Bertelsmann) | 3,042,000,000 | 12,964 |
| Axel Springer | 2,864,000,000 | 14,000 |
| Georg von Holtzbrinck | 2,365,000,000 | 12,500 |
| Pro-7 Sat-1Media (formerly owned by Kirch group) | 2,028,000,000 | 10,729 |
| Westdeutsche Allgemeine (WAZ group) | 2,000,000,000 | n.a. |
| Heinrich Bauer | 1,655,000,000 | 5,742 |
| RTL Television (mostly owned by Bertelsmann) | 1,475,000,000 | 950 |
| Hubert Burda | 1,396,000,000 | 6,717 |

# REFERENCES

Altendorfer, O. (2001) *Das Mediensystem der Bundesrepublik Deutschland*. Wiesbaden: Westdeutscher Verlag.

ARD, ed. (annual since 1969) *ARD-Jahrbuch* (ARD Yearbook). Cologne: ARD.

Bausch, H., ed. (1980) *Rundfunk in Deutschland*, 5 vols. Munich. dtv.

BDZV, ed. (annual) *Zeitungen* (Yearbook of the Publisher's Organization). Bonn: BDZV.

Deutscher Presserat (annual) *Jahrbuch* (Yearbook of the Press Council). Konstanz: UVK.

DLM Yearbook (biennial, since 1988) *Jahrbuch der Landesmedienanstalten* (Yearbook of the *Länder* Supervisory Organizations). Munich: Fischer.

Hans-Bredow-Institut, ed. (biennial) *Internationales Handbuch für Hörfunk und Fernsehen*. Baden-Baden: Nomos.

Hickethier, K. (1998) *Geschichte des deutschen Fernsehens*. Stuttgart: Metzler.

Humphreys, P.J. (1994) *Media and Media Policy in West Germany: the Press and Broadcasting since 1945*. London: Berg.

Kleinsteuber, H.J. and Thomass Barbara (1999) 'Germany: continuity of the *Länder* system and the rise of urban television' in M. de Moragas Spá et al. (eds) *Television on your Doorstep. Decentralization Experiences in the EU*. Luton: University of Luton Press.*Media Perspektiven* (annual) *Daten zur Mediensituation in Deutschland*. Frankfurt: ARD.

Meyn, H. (1999) *Massenmedien in der Bundesrepublik Deutschland*. Berlin: Colloquium.

Pürer, H. and Raabe J. (1994) *Medien in Deutschland: Presse*. Munich: Ölschläger.

Schwarzkopf, D., ed. (1999) *Rundfunkpolitik in Deutschland. Wettbewerb und Öffentlichkeit* (2 vols). Munich: dtv.

Stuiber, H. (1998) *Medien in Deutschland: Rundfunk* (2 vols). Constance: UVK Medien.

ZAW, ed. (annual) *Werbung in Deutschland* (Yearbook of the German Advertisement Association). Bonn: ZAW.

Periodicals: *Media Perspektiven, Rundfunk und Fernsehen, Publizistik, message*.

# 8: Greece

STYLIANOS PAPATHANASSOPOULOS

## NATIONAL PROFILE

Greece is a small European country, located on the southern part of the Balkan peninsula in the south-eastern part of Europe. By the middle of the nineteenth century, Greece had just emerged from over four centuries of Ottoman rule. Thus for many decades Greece was confronted with the tasks involved in the process of nation building, which has had consequences in terms of the formation of the over-extended character of the state.

The total area of the country is 132,000 km$^2$, while its population is of 11.5 million inhabitants. Most of the population, about 4 million, are concentrated in the wider metropolitan area of the capital, Athens. This extreme concentration is one of the side effects of the centralized character of the modern Greek state and the unplanned urbanization caused by the industrialization of the country since the 1960s. Unlike other European countries, almost all Greeks, about 98 per cent of the population, speak the same language, Greek, as a mother tongue, and share the same religion, Greek Orthodox.

Regardless of this homogeneity, political life in the past was dominated by a profound cleavage: modernists versus traditionalists, left versus right, while the Church has always played a role in influencing the attitudes of society. Furthermore, this situation has largely arisen from the tensions in society since the Second World War. These tensions, combined with the absence of a strong civil society, have made the state an autonomous and dominant factor in Greek society. The state is not only relatively autonomous but also has an 'over-extended' character. This situation has been associated with a weak and atrophied civil society where the state has to take on additional politico-ideological functions (Mouzelis, 1980). This makes the system less self-regulatory than under developed capitalism such as exists in Britain or in the United States. Moreover, the lack of self-regulation is also noticeable at the level of politico-ideological superstructure, because in a weak civil society even the economically dominant classes do not manage to form well organized and cohesive pressure groups. Owing to the persistence of patronage politics, even bourgeois parties and interest groups are articulated within the state machinery in a clientist/personalistic manner (Charalambis, 1996; Mouzelis, 1995). This has led the state to promote the interests of particular types of capital rather than the interests of capital as a whole. A further consequence of the lack of self-regulation and weak civil society has been to allow the state to intervene strongly in the politico-ideological sphere. This is also seen in its strict control over the broadcasting media.

## STRUCTURE AND OWNERSHIP

The mass media have been characterized by an excess of supply over demand since the foundation of the modern state. In effect, it appears to be a kind of tradition in Greece, since there are more newspapers, more television channels, more magazines and more radio stations than such a small market can support (Papathanassopoulos, 1999).

Looking at Greek media history, one observes various explosions in the sector. The last ones took place in the mid-1980s and especially in the late 1980s with the deregulation and privatization of the broadcasting system. During the 1990s one chronologically observes a first explosion in the mid-1980s in the newspaper market. A second one took place in the broadcasting sector in the late 1980s owing to the deregulation of the state monopoly of broadcasting frequencies, resulting in a plethora of private, national and local, television channels and radio stations. There are, in 2002, 160 private television channels and 1,200 private radio stations. In the mid-1990s one also observed a new explosion in the magazine sector, which resulted in a new proliferation of magazines (from 400 to 900) (Papathanassopoulos, 2001b).

In addition, Greece has undergone commercialization of the broadcasting sector, adopting a market-led approach, resulting in more channels, more advertising, more programme imports and more politics. As in other countries, publishers and other business-oriented interests have entered the broadcasting scene in large numbers. Since the mid-1990s one notes various efforts by the state to regulate the sector (regarding radio and television licences, advertising time, programme quotas, protection of minors and media ownership).

Although developments in the media sector may not entirely respond to the needs of the industry, it has been surprisingly adaptable and flexible in the face of new political developments. To understand this, one must remember that the system has worked under Western democratic rule for only twenty five years now, and it has had suddenly to face all the upheavals that other Western media systems have taken years to deal with (Papathanassopoulos, 1997a).

On the other hand, since 1989, the media sector has mostly been monopolized by businessmen, shipowners, construction and related interests. Regardless of the plethora of media outlets, the media sector is dominated by a handful of companies, such as Dimosiographicos Organismos Lambraki, Pegasus Group, Kathimerini, Tegopoulos A.E., Alpha Group, Altec High-tech Group, the Vardinogiannis family (see list of main media companies at end of chapter). Most of them initially entered the press sector, and owing to the haphazard deregulation of the end of 1980s they have also entered smoothly the radio and then the television sectors. These companies nowadays have an interest not only in every aspect of the Greek media sector, but they also control approximately 90 per cent of the total media market in terms of audiences and advertising revenues. Dimosiographicos Organismos Lambraki is the publisher of the most popular daily newspaper *NEA* and Sunday *VIMA* (it has also a daily morning edition). It also owns a good number of magazines (lifestyle, family, economy, high-tech, etc), 11 per cent of Teletypos (owner of market leader Mega Channel), television production studios, as well as interests in the Greek Internet through its company DOL Digital, and in book publishing (Ellinika Gramata). Similarly, Pegasus Group (owned by the Bobolas family with interests in construction) has interests in the press (daily newspapers *Ethnos* and *Imerisia)*, magazines, and television (10 per cent of Teletypos, Mega Channel) and television production studios, and in the Greek Internet (e-one.gr). Kathimerini (owned by the Alafouzos family with interests in shipping) owns the respected daily morning newspaper *Kathimerini*, and its English-language edition, radio stations (Medodia, Sky) and has interests in the Greek Internet (e-go.gr) and printing. Tegopoulos A.E. (owned by Christos Tegopoulos) owns the second most popular Greek daily *Eleftherotypia* and its Sunday edition as well as 8 per cent of Teletypos (Mega Channel) and a television production studio. Alpha Group owns the analogue channel Alpha TV and digital platform Alpha Digital as well as radio stations (Alpha News, Alpha Sport, Polis). The Vardinogiannis family, with interests in shipping and oil refining, controls many Greek media through offshore companies, including television (Star Channel, Teletypos), television production (Audiovisual), magazines (*Attikes Ekdoseis*), etc. Labrakis, Bobolas, Tegopoulos and Vardinogiannis have also interests through Teletypos in the pay-television and digital satellite television of Multichoice Hellas/Nova.

## The print media

### The newspaper press

Traditionally, the press used to watch all the developments of political life and to play an important role in the political scene. However, since the fall of the Dictatorship (1974), the press has been going through a process of modernization. The development of advertising as one of its main sources of revenue in the 1960s has worked as a catalyst concerning the newspapers' political choices, and especially neutralized party political partisanship.

Moreover, the advent of new printing technologies in the 1980s (Leandros, 1992), the entry of entrepreneurs and businessmen into the media sector, as well as strong competition from television, have changed the field since the 1980s (Psychogios, 1992; Zaoussis and Stratos, 1992; Paraschos, 1995). As a result, the content of the press has become more objective and the traditional close association with particular parties or individuals has been superseded by a tendency to identify more with a political camp, right, left or centre. Partly this has arisen out of the need to attract a broader spectrum of readers to increase circulation in a time of economic difficulties and partly it has reflected a drift within the political community itself towards larger bloc parties. However, the political stance of the newspapers is always present, especially in periods characterized by a politically intense climate and of course during elections (Komninou, 1996).

Regardless of the fact that the level of literacy in the population is high, newspaper readership is very low (sixty three out of 1,000 bought a daily paper in 2000). Since the arrival of private television and radio and with the plethora of magazines, newspaper advertising and readership have come under pressure. By 2001 there were about 280 local, regional and national daily newspapers. However, the biggest twenty two nationally circulated daily titles in 2001 were located in Athens (Papathanassopoulos, 2001a).

Another characteristic is that there is a strong Sunday press, again mainly originating in Athens, since almost all dailies have their Sunday edition. Most of the Sunday papers offer a supplement or they increase the number of pages in order to cater for the interests of a wider readership. By and large, due to the competition of the electronic media, the Greek press has tried to cope with the new conditions by redesigning its titles and/or publishing new ones. In 1989 there were thirteen dailies with a total average circulation of 1.27 million copies, while in 2001 there were twenty three titles with a total average daily circulation of 50,000 copies (Papathanassopoulos, 2001a). On the other hand, the press share of advertising revenue has decreased, from 18 per cent in 1988 to 15 per cent in 2002, according to the annual reports of the advertising

monitoring agency Media Services (1988–2001). Additionally, the newspapers present two additional paradoxes (Papathanassopoulos, 2001a). Firstly, while the average circulation of newspapers in Greece is falling, the same cannot be said of the number of daily titles. Though a number of established newspapers suspended or ceased publication in the 1990s, new titles, or old ones under new ownership, seem to spring up all the time. Examining the annual data of the Association of Athens Daily Newspaper Owners, one sees that in 1979 there were twelve morning and afternoon dailies published in Athens with an average daily combined circulation of 713,000 copies. In 1989, the best year for the dailies in the last twenty years, there were twenty two titles with an average daily combined circulation of 1,128,589 copies. However, in 1999, with circulation declining by half to 500,893, the number of papers increased only marginally to twenty three. Secondly, since 1993, when the publishers saw that the sales of their newspapers were declining rapidly, all newspapers started offering gifts to their readers ranging from books, cars, houses, etc. But, as relevant data reveal, the constant 'priming' of printed media with 'offers' or gifts only temporarily halts the decline of circulation. It seems that gifts and special offers have become a constituent part of newspaper publication, resulting in a significant drop in sales if the practice is abandoned.

### The periodical and magazine press

The Greek market is a very rich market in magazine titles, with more than 900 popular and special interest titles. However, there are about fifty consumer magazines – mostly monthlies – of real importance. While the circulation of the general interest weekly magazines has declined, the special interest monthlies are gaining the upper hand. The television listings market has expanded as well to reflect the increase in programming and now comprises nine titles. The highest-circulation magazines are linked with television game shows and offer cash prizes. During the 1995–6 period, one witnessed a new explosion of the magazine sector with new titles entering the field. This growth was also reflected in their advertising revenue. However, the magazine sector has entered a period of reshaping in terms of titles and publishers in order to cope with the new and highly competitive media environment.

By and large, developments in the magazine sector during the last five years are the following: first, the 'old' weekly information-oriented magazines have perished. Some years ago this category represented the bulk of magazine sales. This has also to do with the entry in recent years of the Sunday newspapers into the magazine market, through supplements that may be considered magazines in their own right. Second, there has been an increase since 1992 in the volume of specialized magazines, which have tried to attract the interest of younger readers. Thus one notes new titles in women's and men's interest magazines, music, computer magazines, sports, business and financial magazines, motor car and motor cycle magazines, technology, history, home furnishing and decoration magazines, etc. Third, television guide magazines still attract the highest sales in the magazine sector but whether the market can support new titles is questionable. Fourth, there has been an increase in 'light entertainment' magazines which cover gossip regarding celebrities and their personal lives. Fifth, in the period 1995–9, there was a major increase in monthly general and specialist magazines, which combine the lifestyle of younger people with politics and societal issues.

In terms of sales, the television-guide magazines come first and are followed by monthly women's magazines, and monthly consumer and lifestyle magazines. However, total sales in the magazine sector have increased.

### Book publishing

Book production has been steadily increasing since 1990. In fact more people are employed in the sector than ever before and the reading population appears to be more open to new ideas. The market increased considerably during the 1990s owing to unprecedented growth, which is still way behind that in other EU countries (as a percentage of total expenditure, new titles, etc.). Still, the Greek market has come a long way from the stagnant state that existed until the mid-1980s. In fact, there has been a general increase in book publishing in the last two decades. In 1970, 2,027 new titles were published; in 1994 the number had risen to 4,197. According to the specialist magazine *Ichneftis*, the number of titles published in 1996 was 5,058 and 6,804 in 2000. The increase was mainly an outcome

of the growth in literature for children, in history and in Greek and foreign literature (Leandros, 2000).

While the sector's growth rate is high, it is still way down compared with percentage increases in other EU countries. Yet competition is high among publishing houses, which are more numerous in Greece than elsewhere in Europe. However, half the publishers issue only ten titles annually. Only 2 per cent publish more than 100 books a year. In fact, book production remains unevenly distributed. The twelve most productive publishers between 1998 and 2000 produced 35 per cent of the publications during that period, according to the National Book Centre (*www.book.culture.gr*). This shows that the book publishing sector is gradually becoming concentrated in fewer publishing houses, at least in relation to their publishing productivity.

According to the National Book Centre, Greek publishing activity is typically labour-intensive, without great capital investment, and heavily concentrated in the country's two larger cities: in 1996, 84 per cent of the country's publishing companies were located in Athens and 11 per cent in Thessaloniki. The unit price of books was fixed during the winter of 1998. VAT on books amounts to 4 per cent on the retail price and varies from 4 per cent to 18 per cent on production. It is estimated that the gross value of book sales, including considerable state subsidies, varies from Dr 55 billion to Dr 60 billion (US$195 million to US$215 million) per annum. Consumer demand varies according to the category of books.

## The electronic (audio-visual) media

### Television

Greek television and radio were born and established under dictatorships. Broadcasting was established, as in most European countries, as a state monopoly, and this remained after the restoration of parliament in 1974. In fact, the state was the sole controller of the broadcast media and government manipulation of state television news output was common practice.

The deregulation of broadcasting, as in other European countries, represented more than the removal of certain rules and regulations. As in most countries, it was rather the outcome of the internationalization of broadcasting in addition to pressure from domestic economic forces. As in most European countries, broadcasting deregulation commenced with the radio frequencies (in 1987) and then moved on to television (1989). The entry of private television channels was led by Mega Channel, owned by Teletypos, a group of the most powerful publishers in Greece (see above). It was quickly followed by Antenna TV, owned by a shipowner and owner of Antenna Radio. In effect, transmitters sprang up all over Greece, most of them operating on a de facto but technically speaking illegal basis.

However, imported television programmes and domestic production have both soared, thanks to massive increases in television advertising revenue. While the regulatory structure has remained cloudy, the dominance of two of the private networks – Mega Channel and Antenna TV – has been clear from very early on. Challenges from other private channels, including Alpha (previously Sky) TV and Star Channel, have made some dent in Mega and Antenna's audiences. In the 1996/7 television season, for the first time since deregulation, the cumulative monthly shares of the two leading private television channels (Mega and Antenna) did not exceed 45 per cent. In 2001 they attracted 44 per cent of the television market while Alpha and Star attracted 29 per cent.

Mega, Antenna, Alpha and Star are pitched at a mass-market audience. Sitcoms, satire shows, television games, soap operas, movies and television films as well as tabloid-style news and informational programmes dominate their output. As the private channels' entertainment-dominated schedules have waxed stronger there has been a parallel decrease in educational and documentary programmes.

Private television channels, though they initially relied to a high degree on cheap imports, swiftly built up the level of local and in-house production. The share of Greek-originated production is now larger than that of imports and is mostly transmitted in prime time, while imported programmes dominate the rest of the broadcasting time.

A major element in the broadcasting scene is the decline in viewership of the public service broadcasting services. Few other public broadcasters in Europe have suffered as badly from the introduction of private television. The Greek public broadcaster, Hellenic Broadcasting Corporation

(ERT) has sharply declined in ratings and advertising expenditure. As regards television, ERT's channels' viewership has declined to 10 per cent (ET-1 6 per cent and NET 4 per cent ) in 2001, which resulted in large advertising losses (ERT's advertising market share in the first seven months of 2001 was 4 per cent of total television advertising). In effect, all ERT's three channels have witnessed a steady erosion of market share since private commercial television was launched in late 1989. ERT had also accumulated debts of Dr 45 billion. However, by 1999 ERT managed to pay off the bulk of its debt. In fact the 1999 and 2000 budgets were the first ones that found ERT profitable and in 2001, for the first time for a long period, ERT had no debts.

Moreover, many argue that ERT is too bureaucratic and overstaffed. It has 3,500 permanent staff, plus 1,500 occasional or external employees/collaborators. For years politicians had been unable to approve any of the numerous plans for its salvation. ERT's problems stem from the public broadcaster's one-time role as a mouthpiece of government propaganda. This led to the erosion of its credibility in the eyes of the public and was in effect, the entry ticket for private television and the total deregulation of the television sector. In effect, ERT had to pay for the democratization and increased number of television channels, since it was unprepared to meet competition from private broadcasters.

Public broadcasting (after the 1987 law) consists of:

1   Two national coverage channels (Elliniki Teleorasi 1 (ET-1) and NEA Elliniki Teleorasi (NET), previously ET-2) which are based in Athens.
2   A third channel, ET-3. This is based in Thessaloniki and has stronger coverage in northern Greece but also can be seen in other parts of Greece. In effect, it is the regional channel of ERT and its profile emphasis is given to northern Greece, arts and culture.
3   Hellenic radio (ERA) which broadcasts four national radio channels (ERA-1 to ERA-4) originates from Athens through seventeen relay stations. There is also a fifth channel, the Voice of Greece, which is aimed at

Greeks abroad and includes regional programmes. *ERA-1* is mainly the information radio station of the public broadcaster, *ERA-2* mostly entertainment, *ERA-3* is a quality and classical music station and *ERA-4/Sports* is a sports and music radio station.

4   It also publishes its weekly television/radio listing magazine *Radioteleorasis*.

However, since 2000 the public broadcaster has implemented a long overdue reorganization and the results have started to appear, although there is still a long way to go. *ERT*'s management has aimed to turn a new page in the public broadcaster's troubled history. In October 1997 the first channel *ET-1* became a general channel with more emphasis on entertainment. The second channel with the previous name *ET-2* does not exist any longer. In fact, it has been relaunched under a new name, NET (Nea Elliniki Teleorasi – New Hellenic Television) and is mainly a round-the-clock information channel with news bulletins, information programmes, talk shows and documentaries. It remains to be seen whether the ambitions of the *ERT* management will be realized. On the other hand, *ERT* has to reduce labour costs by voluntary retirement of some of its personnel. In effect, through a new law and a redundancy plan, *ERT*'s management aims to retire 1,062 of its personnel by 2002.

In terms of financing, *ERT* appears to be in better condition. All households have to pay Dr 12,000 to Dr 14,000 (€39 to €42) per annum for public broadcasting, which is collected through domestic electricity bills. In 1999 *ERT* collected Dr 62 billion through the licence fee plus Dr 3.7 billion through television advertising and sponsorship. Its programming costs in 1997 were Dr 16 billion, while in 1998/9 this went up to Dr 27 billion. Moreover, labour costs accounted for Dr 31 billion.

*ERT* looks to the future with ambition. Its first aim is to re-attract viewers, but it also has plans for the digital era. In effect, its public image seems to be better nowadays than some years ago. In the digital era *ERT* wants, in collaboration with other private interests, to create a digital satellite platform. Under law 2644 of 1998 *ERT* already holds a licence for a digital platform. *ERT*

has formed a daughter company called Nea Syndromitiki Tileorasi (New Subscription Television). However, most of *ERT*'s plans are on paper – its digital future has not yet materialized.

While cable television is virtually non-existent in Greece, pay-television has found a niche on analogue terrestrial television. Multichoice Hellas dominates pay-television. It buys premium programming from sister company NetMed Hellas, which operates the channels FilmNet, K-TV and Supersport. These remain the first and only analogue pay-television services in the country. The monthly subscription fee for FilmNet is Dr 7,500, for Supersport Dr 9,100 and for the three pay channels Dr 11,200.

FilmNet was launched in October of 1994, offering a diet of blockbuster movies and live league soccer games. In 2001 it pulled in 290,000 subscribers. In 1996 the network acquired the exclusive soccer rights to the Greek championship for the period 1997–2001 at Dr 15 billion. In August 1996 NetMed Hellas launched two more pay-television services, Supersport and K-TV, using a frequency leased from the state broadcaster, *ERT*. In summer 1998 Supersport won a new battle for the exclusive rights to televize the Greek Basketball League games from 1998 to 2002, offering an unprecedented Dr 11.6 billion for the rights for the first two years. In 2001–2 NetMed Hellas dealt with individual basketball teams. In effect, by 2001 Supersport dominated television sports games in the Greek market, since it had the exclusive rights to cover soccer and basketball, the most popular games in Greece. Currently, the company is negotiating the renewal of the contracts, while it has lost the most attractive soccer games to its competitor in digital television, Alpha Digital. NetMed Hellas has signed exclusive rights with all major Hollywood studios to broadcast new releases to Greek subscribers.

The Greeks have not paid much attention to satellite television, although the deregulation of the television system started with the retransmission of satellite channels via UHF frequencies. But, at the beginning of the new century, digital satellite television seems to be the new 'love affair' of the Greek television universe. In fact, since the beginning of 2000, there is already a digital satellite platform (Nova), a second one (Alpha Digital) has started operation (October 2001), and a third (Interactive) holds an official licence to broadcast. At the end of 2001 two digital satellite platforms, Nova of Multichoice Hellas and Alpha Digital are operating. In fact the story, if not the development, of Greek digital satellite television started in March 1998, when Multichoice Hellas announced plans to go ahead with its digital satellite project Nova, initiating Greece into the digital age.

However, the development of digital and pay-television will depend on the right moves of their players, such as the decision to use compatible decoding technology. This is because the Greek broadcasting market is small and it would hardly sustain competing digital platforms operating incompatible decoding technologies. On the other hand, regardless of the fact that the penetration of analogue pay-television is high – approximately 10 per cent due to Multichoice Hellas – a major obstacle for the development of digital and pay-television is the plethora of free-to-air terrestrial channels. The average viewer has access to a large number of free television services, and is not used to a 'pay-TV culture'. Moreover, viewers will have to buy new reception equipment and to pay a monthly subscription fee, when, owing to the austerity measures, their spending power remains low. Then, the satellite operators have to offer to their prospective subscribers attractive television and interactive services at a reasonable price. Greek people have proved that they are very attracted by new technologies. The high penetration of cellular phones is an indication.

The Nova platform belongs to Multichoice Hellas. The latter's ownership status is made up of Myriad Development with a 40 per cent stake, and Greece's Teletypos (owner of the private television station Mega Channel) with 40 per cent. The Cypriot television company LTV holds 18 per cent and Sun Spot Leisure 2 per cent. The second digital satellite platform, Alpha Digital, is a joint venture of Mr Efstathios Tsotsoros (45 per cent), who is also the chairman of private station Alpha TV, Greek businessman George Kontominas (40 per cent) and the Onassis Foundation (15 per cent). The chairman and managing director of the new company is Efstathios Tsotsoros and, so for, the company has invested €89.6 million.

### Radio

As was noted above, the radio sector was deregulated with the entry of municipal and private local stations. Nowadays, private stations dominate the radio sector (see statistics at end of chapter). Around 1,200 radio stations broadcast regularly throughout Greece; the most important ones are located in Athens and have networking arrangements with local stations. Generally, each of Greece's fifty two administrative regions has two or three local commercial radio stations, with more in the largest cities. However, most of them are without an official licence to broadcast. The government in 1997 invited radio stations which operate in the Athens and Thessaloniki region to apply for a licence. In March 2001 the government announced the twenty eight most desired radio licences for the Attica region, causing anger among those stations not granted a licence. The issue still remains open for seven more licences in the Attica regions, while a similar situation is expected when the new licences are granted in the other major cities, especially in Thessaloniki, which is the second largest city in the country.

There are three categories of radio stations in Greece: state-owned, municipal and private. The vast majority are privately owned and of a local character (transmitting via the FM frequencies). State-owned and municipal radio stations exhibited a sharply declining trend in audience figures and advertising revenue. As regards the use of radio, Greeks listen to the radio for approximately four hours daily, while those between the ages of twenty five and fifty four are the most loyal to radio.

### Film and video

While the rise of Greek cinema in the post-war period is closely connected with the establishment of the Finos Films production company, which was launched in 1943, Greek cinema, after many years of decline, has shown a rise in the last few years. Cinemagoing was a regular feature until the advent of television. In effect, since the mid-1970s, the film industry has suffered under the impact of television and the commercial success of US films. In 1982 the Minister of Culture, Melina Mercouri, adopted a policy aimed at the promotion of Greek films, and especially independent Greek producers, through the support of the Greek Film Centre, which that was inaugurated in 1970. By 2001 many Greek film makers had benefited from the Centre's co-production programme and funding. In effect, the Greek Film Centre remains the primary producer of new films.

Since 1999 some Greek films have been particularly popular, especially commercial productions such as *Safe Sex* (2000), a kaleidoscopic comedy about Athenians' amorous pursuits which topped the country's ticket sales – the first time a Greek film has done so in thirty years. However, US films dominate the box office. This is also due to the fact that only a few new Greek films are produced each year (about twenty) and fewer have a commercial success. On the other hand, *Safe Sex*'s success demonstrates that cinemagoers are interested in Greek films that are fast-paced and scripted according to the grammar of television.

## The Internet and related on-line media

Greece has the lowest proportion of Internet users in the European Union. According to the EU, the PC penetration rate in Greece was 11 per cent at the end of 2001, compared with an EU average of 36 per cent. Not surprisingly, Greece lags behind other European countries on a wide range of Internet indicators. In 2001, according to a national survey conducted by the V-PRC Institute (2001), 10 per cent of the population were reported as having an Internet connection. By comparison, the average Internet connection rate throughout the European Union was 18 per cent in 2000. Moreover, the number of Web sites originating in Greece is roughly one-tenth the number of German Web sites and one-fifteenth the number of UK sites. The number of secure servers is a rough indication of a country's e-commerce readiness. With only one-fifth the number of secure servers per capita of the entire European Union, Greece remains relatively unequipped for on-line transactions. Corporate use of the Internet also trails behind the rest of Europe. Only 32 per cent of all companies surveyed in Greece by the European Union reported having Internet access by the end of 1999, compared with an EU average of 63 per cent. A smaller percentage of Greeks report that they use banking on-line (17 per cent) than citizens throughout the Union (25 per cent) (Eurobarometer, 2000).

# POLITICS, POLICY, LAW AND REGULATION

Greece has a rather strict, – to some, tight – regulatory framework on almost all aspects of the media. The problem is that most of the regulations are either too strict or out of date and are not easily implemented. For example, Article 40 of law 1086 of 1988 allows the courts to scrutinize the finances of the press and broadcast companies, but no action has been taken. Moreover, law 2328 of 1995 envisages television companies paying a fee for the use of their frequency. Up to now, no free private channel has paid the state a drachma. Additionally, the laws of 1989 and 1995 (2328) speak about the allocation of terrestrial television licences. But no such licences have been awarded yet. Well, not exactly, since law 2644 of 1988 on pay-television and digital television in a clause notes that those television companies which have applied for a terrestrial licence operate legally until the licences are allocated! Moreover, law 2325 does not allow publishers to own more than two daily political newspapers – one morning and one evening daily, published in Athens, Piraeus or Thessaloniki – but again it depends. In August 1998, with presidential decree 214, the government announced a regulation to oversee the 'transparency of media ownership', and in 2002 the government voted a regulation for the 'basic shareholder', meaning that a person/company that has been involved in public works cannot own more that 5 per cent of the shares of a media company. Well, again, up to the time this chapter went to press, nothing had yet been done.

These are a few examples of what I call a 'policy of non-action'. The reason seems to be simple: successive governments since 1989, the year of television deregulation, appear to continue playing an 'on and off' game with the television owners, who also have other interests in the Greek economy. In fact, hopes of bringing order to the unregulated broadcasting environment come and go on a periodic basis. Hopes were raised in July 1993, when the 1990–3 Conservative government announced its decisions. The Socialist administration of the late Andreas Papandreou (1993–6) in its first days announced that it would re-examine the whole regulatory environment and the licences. But the licences were never awarded. Papandreou's successor in the Socialist Party and in government, Kostas Simitis, after winning the 1996 general election decided to 'bring order' to the allocation of frequencies. According to a 'map of the frequencies', the government announced it would grant six national television licences, fifty eight regional licences and fifty three local licences to private channels. Up to the time of writing the official licences have yet to be awarded. The result is that market forces have created an over-crowded broadcasting environment – 160 national and local television broadcasters operating alongside the state broadcaster *ERT*'s three national television channels.

The National Broadcasting Council (NBC) was formed in 1989 to oversee the audio-visual sector and to act as a 'buffer' between the government and the broadcasters. In effect, during its first administration the NBC remained inactive, if not virtually absent from the broadcasting affairs of the country. But one has to admit that the role of the NBC was only to advise the govern-ment. On the other hand, the NBC during its first administration (1990–3) produced three codes on the operating conditions of radio and television stations: one on adver-tising, the second on journalistic ethics and the third on programming. During its second administration, a new law was intro-duced by the Socialists in 1993, whereby the NBC's board members were reduced from nineteen to nine. However, the nomination procedure for the election of NBC board members is a contentious issue. The rules stipulate that four members should be nominated by the party in power, four by the opposition parties and the chairman by the president of the National Assembly, giving the government a controlling vote. In its second administration (1993–7), the NBC adopted a more active role on a number of broadcasting related issues. It imposed fines on national and local channels for various reasons. On national channels for some of their 'reality' and news programmes, and on the local channels because they failed to pay copyright fees for broadcast programmes. In its third administration (1997–2001) it had to examine the files of radio and television stations who had applied to get an official licence to broadcast. The proposed licences for the radio stations in the Attica region provoked the anger of the excluded stations. However, it is the Minister of the Press and the Mass Media who grants the licences to private stations.

What is equally interesting about the history of broadcasting deregulation in Greece is the entry of publishers and other entrepreneurs on to the broadcasting scene, as in most cases in Europe. As we have already seen, the media sector is dominated by a handful of companies. Needless to say, most of them have other interests in the wider business sector. This raises a question over the new media magnates' motives. Some politi-cians, among them the Chairman of the Hellenic Parliament and media analysts, are concerned about how easily and quickly the media sector could be concentrated in the hands of a few influential magnates. To a certain extent, the new television environ-ment gives the impression that it has largely copied the situation in the printed press and there is a clear indication that there are too many stations for such a small market.

In effect, all television stations face severe financial problems – in fact most of the media are in the red. This has made analysts wonder about the real intentions of their owners. It seems that Greece has entered a new era of 'interplay' between media owners and politicians. In this new game each party tries to gain tactical advantages because each needs the other. The entry of business-men and shipping owners and other busi-ness interests on to the media scene is an important way in which these interests try to influence public opinion and to exert pressure in the political arena for their business interests.

# STATISTICS

| | |
|---|---:|
| Population | 11,500,000 |
| Number of television households | 3,710,000 |
| Movie admissions, 2000 | 13,500,000 |
| Books published, 2000 | 6,804 |

**Print media**

Circulation of daily newspapers, 2001

| | |
|---|---:|
| *Ta Nea* | 84,586 |
| *Eleftherotypia* | 79,296 |
| *Ethnos* | 53,644 |
| *To Vima* | 50,357 |
| *Kathimerini* | 40,431 |
| *Eleftheros Typos* | 36,948 |
| *Espresso* | 31,707 |
| *Apogeymatini* | 23,254 |

**Broadcast media**

Audience share of national terrestrial television channels in prime time slot, 1 September 2000 – 31 August 2001 (%)

| | |
|---|---:|
| Private | |
| Mega Channel | 22.1 |
| Antenna TV | 21.9 |
| Alpha TV | 15.3 |
| Star channel | 13.4 |
| Alter | 2.2 |
| Tempo | 2.2 |
| Public | |
| ET-1 | 6.1 |
| NET | 4.2 |
| ET-3 | 1.0 |

Source: AGB Hellas.

Audience share of main radio channels, December 2001 – January 2002

| | |
|---|---:|
| Private | |
| Sky | 13.5 |
| Antenna | 12.4 |
| Sfera | 12.1 |
| Melodia | 11.2 |
| Village | 9.4 |
| Supersport | 9.0 |
| Love | 8.6 |
| Flash | 8.6 |
| Ciao | 7.5 |
| Public | |
| ERA Sport | 3.5 |
| NET | 2.1 |
| ERA | 1 |

Source: Alco.

| Electronic media | Percentage of households with: | |
|---|---|---|
| | Terrestrial television | 98 |
| | Terrestrial pay-television | 10 |
| | Satellite digital television | 3 |
| | Cable | Negligible |
| | VCR | 47 |
| | Satellite receiver | 4 |
| | DVD player | 3 |
| | | |
| | Percentage of households with: | |
| | | |
| | Digital TV reception | None |
| | Internet access | 10 |
| | Mobile phone ownership | 72 |

| Advertising spend, 2001 (%) | Television | 43.50 |
|---|---|---|
| | Magazines | 35.03 |
| | Newspapers | 16.81 |
| | Radio | 4.66 |

**Ownership**

Main media companies and main activities
*Dimosiographicos Organismos Lambraki:*
Press (newspapers *VIMA, NEA*)
Magazines (*Eidikes Ekdoseis*)
Television (11% of Teletypos (Mega Channel) television production studio)
Internet (DOL Digital, portal: in.gr)
Printing, book publishing, travel, education
*Pegasus Group:*
Press (*Ethnos, Imerisia*)
Magazines (*Eikones*)
Television (10% of Teletypos (Mega Channel) television production studio)
Internet (e-one.gr)
Printing
*Kathimerini:*
Press (*Kathimerini, Kathimerini* English edition)
Radio (Medodia, affiliation with Sky)
Internet (25% of portal e-go.gr)
Printing
*Tegopoulos A E:*
Press (*Eleftherotypia*)
Television (8% of Teletypos (Mega Channel) television production studio)
Printing
*Alpha:*
Television (Alpha TV and Alpha Digital)
Radio (Alpha News, Alpha Sport, Polis).
*Altec (high-tech):*
Television (Alter)
Information technology (Altec)
*Vardinogiannis family:*
According to the press this shipowning and oil refining family has interests in many Greek media through offshore companies in television (Star Channel, Teletypos-Mega Channel), television production (Audiovisual), magazines (*Attikes Ekdoseis*), etc.

# REFERENCES

Association of Athens Daily Newspapers Owners (1998) *Circulation and Advertising Statistics*. Athens (in Greek).

Charalambis, Dimitris (1996) 'Irrational contents of a formal rational system' in Christos Lyrintzis, Elias Nicolacopoulos and Dimitris Sotiropoulos (eds) *Society and Politics: Facets of the Third Hellenic Democracy 1974–1994*. Athens: Themelio (in Greek).

Karakostas, Ioannis and Tsevas Athanassios (2000) *Media Regulation*. Athens: Sakkoulas (in Greek).

Kolovos, Nicos (2000) *Cinema: the Art of the Picture Industry*. Athens: Kastaniotis (in Greek).

Komninou, Maria (1996) 'The role of the media in the Third Hellenic Republic' in Christos Lyrintzis, Elias Nicolacopoulos and Dimitris Sotiropoulos (eds) *Society and Politics: Facets of the Third Hellenic Democracy 1974–1994*. Athens: Themelio (in Greek).

Leandros, Nicos (1992) *The Mass Print Press in Greece*. Athens: Delfini (in Greek).

Leandros, Nicos (2000) *The Political Economy of the Media: Industry Restructuring in the Era of Information Technology Revolution*. Athens: Kastaniotis (in Greek).

Media Services (1998–2001) *Annual Reports of Advertising Expenditure*. Athens: Media Services (in Greek).

Mouzelis, Nicos (1980) 'Capitalism and the development of the Greek state', in Ray Scase (ed.) *The State in Western Europe*. London: Croom Helm.

Mouzelis, Nicos (1995) 'Greece in the twenty-first century: institutions and political culture', in Dimitris Constas and Theofanis, G. Stavrou (eds) *Greece prepares for the Twenty-first Century*. Baltimore MD and London: Johns Hopkins University Press.

Papathanassopoulos, Stylianos (1997a) 'The politics and the effects of the deregulation of Greek television', *European Journal of Communication* 12 (3): 351–68.

Papathanassopoulos, Stylianos (1997b) *The Power of Television*. Athens: Kastaniotis (in Greek).

Papathanassopoulos, Stylianos (1999) 'The effects of media commercialization on journalism and politics in Greece', *Communication Review* 3 (4): 379–402.

Papathanassopoulos, Stylianos (2000) *Television and its Audience*. Athens: Kastaniotis (in Greek).

Papathanassopoulos, Stylianos (2001a) 'The decline of the Greek press', *Journalism Studies* 2 (1): 109–23.

Papathanassopoulos, Stylianos (2001b) 'Media commercialization and journalism in Greece', *European Journal of Communication* 16 (4): 505–21.

Paraschos, Manolis (1995) 'The Greek media face the twenty-first century: will the Adam Smith complex replace the Oedipus complex?' in Dimitris Konstas and Theofanis G. Stavrou (eds) *Greece prepares for the Twenty-first Century*. Baltimore MD and London: Johns Hopkins University Press.

Psychogios, Dimitrios, K. (1992) *The Uncertain Future of the Athenian Press*. Athens: Diaulos (in Greek).

V-PRC Institute (2001) *The Profile of Greek Internet Users*. Athens: V-PRC (in Greek).

Zaoussis, Alexis and Stratos, Konstantinos (1995) *The Newspapers 1974–1992*. Athens: Themelio (in Greek).

# 9: Hungary

BÁLAZS KISS

## NATIONAL PROFILE

Hungary had a very lively press sector from the creation of the Austro-Hungarian monarchy in 1867 until the First World War and again in the inter-war period. The greatest writers and poets wrote for the papers, which created an important tradition of journalism with a strong tendency to morality and with a close cultural integration of the political and journalist with literary elites. After the Second World War, and particularly with the communists coming to power in 1949, the press became very reduced because of three main reasons. The first was the liquidation of the private press: only state-owned media were permitted to exist. The second was heavy censorship, which mopped up opinions differing from those of the single party. The third reason was the preference given to literature, instead of journalism, in political education and propaganda.

After 1956 the Kádár regime can be claimed modern because it used the much quicker and more popular press as a channel of propaganda. It even had the press imitate the public sphere by launching discussions on public issues and problems. The period also saw the birth of several special periodical titles for the different strata of Hungarian society; through them, the messages of the regime were able to reach social groups in different ways and forms.

In sum, on the one hand the media were under very thorough control in the state socialist period, on the other, however, gradually they provided an opportunity to the reformist forces to publish their views, particularly in the latter years. Thus the media reflected, though in a very careful and opaque way, the different trends and efforts in the political elite.

The media played an even more important role during the transitional period, since they made it possible for the new democratic political forces to make themselves known to the public and journalists wrote extensively about the Western ideas and democratic institutions. This process, with the media, the journalists and the intelligentsia preparing both the public generally and the communist elite in particular for the transition, concluded with the fairly benign political system change between 1988 and 1990.

This experience, with the media playing a large part in making the political transition relatively simple, convinced politicians, particularly the newcomers, that the media should not be left alone, but should be kept under control. That conviction has had its consequences ever since and the media have certainly been the longest-standing unsettled question in Hungarian politics since 1990.

The first, rightist, majority (1990–4) considered the whole sphere of the mass media overwhelmed by hostile socialist (ex- or post-communist) and liberal political forces, and every criticism by the journalists was felt to confirm that suspicion. The government tried to counterbalance the leftist biases by buying and supporting rightist newspapers. That was not very effective, the circulation of the pro-government newspapers lagged far behind that of the other side. Thus the government made much effort to dominate the electronic media, which were exclusively public until as late as 1997. The socialist–liberal coalition government (1994–8) also tried to dominate the media. They had no problem with the print media, since most of the former pro-government press soon went bankrupt. Conditions in the electronic media changed quite quickly. For example, the new president of Hungarian Television fired more staff on his first day in office than the previous presidents during the years before. The tensions have also been eased remarkably in consequence of the law on radio and television passed at the end of 1995, and the consequent birth of the commercial media. In 1998 the new rightist administration, which exhausted its mandate in April 2002, soon resumed the fight to counterbalance the alleged leftist preponderance in the media. It strengthened its position in the press by uniting two rightist newspapers, and that was where the government advertisements were published and where members of the government preferred to give interviews, etc. Because of the popularity of the private electronic media, public television and radio ceased to be so important politically. Anyway, the government did its best to put them under progovernment control: it put loyal persons into the posts of the media presidencies, who, in turn, changed the editors of the news and political programmes and made it impossible for critical journalists to keep their jobs.

The present media situation is said to be unacceptable by all of the main players in Hungarian politics. Both sides speak about unbalanced media, but mean two different things: the right thinks that most of the whole sphere is still biased against conservative values, while the other side complains of the rightist and nationalist propaganda of the public media. Each of them would like to change the law on the electronic media, but, since such legislation needs a two-thirds majority in the parliament, the situation does not seem likely to change at all soon.

## STRUCTURE AND OWNERSHIP

### The print media

#### The newspaper press

There are thirty six daily newspapers if all the paid-for ones are counted. The country has twelve national daily newspapers and twenty-four regional and smaller urban ones. As for the regional papers with considerable circulation, there is a daily newspaper in each of the nineteen counties except the one around Budapest. Of the twelve national daily titles, four are quality political papers, three are economic ones, four are tabloids, and one is about sports. The greater part of the newspapers is published in the morning, most of the evening dailies are free, but the circulation of the latter is rather low. The Sunday papers are not too popular; the national and regional papers have six issues per week with thicker Saturday issues.

There are several free daily papers, most of them published outside the capital. One of them is *Metro*, the Hungarian version of the Scandinavian paper. It has a circulation of 327,000, which is not much less than the circulation of all the national quality newspapers. Its publication used to be concentrated on Budapest and the area around the capital, but since April 2001 it can be found in the county centres as well.

The share of tabloid titles in the daily newspaper market has been rising; in the first half of 2002, two old titles (*Mai Nap* and *Tözsdei Kurir*) re-entered the market after a long pause. Another sign is that the leading tabloid paper has caught up with the most important quality one after years of competition. Two of the other national quality papers are declining faster and have fallen behind most of the country dailies in circulation.

*Népszabadság* is the leading quality paper, with a circulation of about 211,000. The second most important daily is *Magyar Nemzet* with a bit less than half the former. These two papers are clearly profiled politically. The former is close to the socialists, the latter to the conservatives. The two other national dailies are considered to be leftist.

The ownership of the newspapers is very concentrated. About half the circulation belongs to the papers published by the Ringier group. The company has half the *Népszabadság*, it owns *Magyar Hírlap*, another quality daily paper, *Blikk*, which is the tabloid with the highest circulation, and it also has *Nemzeti Sport*, the national sports newspaper.

Foreign companies own the larger part of the regional papers: Axel Springer, Westdeutsche Allgemeine Zeitung (WAZ), Funk Verlag und Druckerei (FVD) and Associated Press (AP), that is, two German companies, an Austrian and a US company. Axel Springer is the strongest, with nine county dailies. WAZ with five, then FVD with three, and AP with three follow it.

Sometimes it is almost impossible to know which foreign firms are behind certain Hungarian publishing companies. *Magyar Nemzet* is published by AAB Marketing Services, which is registered in Delaware. Central European Media Investment with 'Anglo-Saxon financial investors in the background' owns the new tabloid.

*Népszabadság* is the only national quality newspaper that makes a profit for the owners. The leading county papers are also profitable. For long, *Magyar Nemzet* has survived only with huge support from the state. After the 2002 elections, its sales and subscription increased considerably. Although *Magyar Hírlap* is one of the worst-selling titles, it has considerable revenue from advertising because its readership consists of managers to a considerable extent. Despite this, the newspaper shows a deficit. The financial situation of *Népszava*, the fourth national newspaper, is even less stable.

The prospects for newspapers are not very rosy. The television companies increase their share of the advertising market. The situation of the national papers is even worse than the regional ones, because while the latter can keep their readers or not lose them too quickly, the former have to meet the challenge of a shrinking readership, that is, shrinking advertisement earnings. In 2001 the share of the terrestrial television channels in advertising spend was 57.5 per cent, that of the daily papers reached 14 per cent only, the periodical press 13.5 per cent.

### The periodical and magazine press

As far as circulation is concerned, the free *Budapesti Piac* shows the highest figures with more than 800,000 copies. This title is an advertising weekly with little information or Budapest news. Among the non-free titles with a large circulation, *Story*, a weekly about the stars and celebrities, is first with 479,000 copies. Then come the three main television programme magazines with more than 970,000 in all. The main women's weeklies reach circulations of between 300,000 and 360,000. *Szabad Föld*, a weekly mainly for the non-urban population, has a circulation of 200,000. None of the political and economic titles reaches more than 50,000 per week, except for the most prestigious and influential – *HVG* – with about 134,000. *Szabad Föld* and *HVG* are the closest to a typical general interest weekly but, in point of fact, there is no such weekly title in Hungary.

The Hungarian version of *Reader's Digest* has the highest circulation (235,000) among the monthly titles. The magazines for youth are mostly Hungarian versions of German originals sometimes with the same title (for example, *Bravo*, *Bravo Girl*), sometimes with Hungarian ones (for example, *100 × Szép* instead of *Mädchen*). They reach circulations of about 70,000. Women's and men's magazines sell about the same amount (for example, less of *Cosmopolitan* and more of *Playboy* and *FHM*). The magazine market seems to be fairly stable, even growing, as is shown by the fact that new titles have been launched.

Although there are more than 100 publishers, as with the newspaper industry, ownership is concentrated in relatively few hands.

### Book publishing

About 9,000 titles are published per year. In 2001 the number of copies reached 35.7 million, which meant a 24 per cent decrease from the previous year, mainly because of the decline of professional publications. Half the titles are scientific and professional and approximately 25 per cent are fiction. About one-third of the fiction is light reading.

There are more than 100 publishing houses, mostly very small ones with a couple of titles yearly. The big companies publish some hundreds of titles and, for example, one single publisher dominates half the market in school books and textbooks. Although the greater part of the publishing houses deal with classical publishing only, some have established networks of bookshops and clubs as well to increase sales. With Hungarian being a relatively small language, translation is a very important activity, and all the outstanding foreign authors are published in Hungarian very quickly. The population traditionally buys many books; consequently the sphere has a fairly stable financial situation in spite of the low state subsidies.

## The electronic (audio-visual) media

### Television

For geographical and other reasons, there are four terrestrial television frequencies. With one of them belonging to the military, three can be distributed among the broadcasters. One of them is used by the first channel of the public television (m1), another one by the 2001 market leader TV-2, owned mainly by the Scandinavian Broadcasting and the third by RTL Klub, the Hungarian affiliate of the German RTL group. The latter two are commercial companies. All three channels are of general interest.

Beyond m1, public television has two more channels (m2, Duna TV) which broadcast via satellite. The latter is supposed to shape its programming, taking into account Hungarians living outside Hungary. The first channel broadcasts programmes for domestic minorities and also religious programmes, while the second replays several programmes of the first. The law compels cable companies to put the public television programmes into their packages. Without that regulation, two of the three public channels could not be seen by most of the Hungarian audience because only a few households have a satellite receiver.

Although predominantly a public service organization, which raises revenue from a universal licensing system, public television is entitled to broadcast advertisements as well, although they are supposed not to break into programmes. Since these two sources of revenue have never been enough for the company to survive, Hungarian Television has had to lean on massive state subsidies, which has always inevitably led to sometimes cruder, sometimes more refined, pro-government biases.

The other two terrestrial channels, launched in 1997, are commercial ones, that is to say, they raise revenue from advertisements. They are in fierce competition with each other, poaching media stars from each other and even copying each other's programmes. For long, prime time on both channels was dominated by Latin American soap operas but recently competition has forced them to launch original programmes and the soap operas moved to the afternoon hours.

After the first years of deficit, TV-2 realized a profit in 2001, one year before it was expected. Its main rival, RTL Klub, was profitable one year earlier, in 2000. In the second half of 2001, RTL Klub succeeded in getting into the market leader position.

There are several cable companies but their economic strength varies greatly. In the middle of February 2002, more than half the 170 cable networks of the country belonged to three companies: UPC (thirty), Matáv (twenty one) and Fibernet (fourty eight). In Budapest, which has twenty three districts, UPC gives service in thirteen of them, Matáv in nine. UPC, an affiliate of the Dutch multinational corporation, has built up a large, perhaps too large, network of optic cable and tries to bind customers to itself. Matáv, the Hungarian telephone company with a large ownership share of Deutsche Telekom behind it, also makes great efforts to strengthen its market position in the cable television business. There are other companies as well, threatened by these two. Since 2000, customers have raised a huge number of complaints against the cable companies (90 per cent of the complaints are against UPC and Matáv) because of the high prices and the frequent changes in the assortment of programmes offered.

One can also find fifty regional and local terrestrial television broadcasting companies. Antenna Mikro is the biggest of them because it serves the surroundings of the capital. Its package (twenty two channels plus HBO and a sports channel, for extra fees) is rather small compared with that of UPC, but its prices seem to be much more acceptable to the audience, particularly since UPC raised its prices considerably at the beginning of 2002.

At the beginning of December 2001, one could watch twenty four television programmes in the Hungarian language. Five were free satellite programmes, the rest were broadcast via cable companies. Most of them were the dubbed or subtitled versions of foreign channels: HBO, National Geographic Channel, Animal Planet, Discovery, Eurosport, etc. It means that the cable channels are mostly specialised ones.

One always finds the main German programmes (*Sat-1, Pro-7*) in the packages, usually also MTV Europe, the French TV-5, the Italian RAI Uno and the Austrian ORF-1. The broadcasters also offer programmes for children either in the original (Cartoon Network) or in Hungarian (Minimax, Nickelodeon). A Hungarian-language music channel (Viva+) has been launched.

As far as audience shares are concerned, public television has been losing viewers ever since the private companies began to broadcast in 1997. At the beginning of 2002 m1, the terrestrial public channel, had a share of 11.2 percent, while RTL Klub, the market leader, had reached 33.3 per cent and TV-2 30.5 per cent. Since 2000 the share of other channels has grown from 21.2 per cent to 25 per cent.

### Radio

Five radio channels have national broadcasting possibilities. Three of them belong to public radio (Magyar Rádió); the other two (Danubius and Sláger) are privately owned. Two more companies, Juventus and Radio 1, actually reach more than half the territory of Hungary, but via a network of radio stations; consequently they are in fierce competition with the former, causing much trouble to them in obtaining enough advertising earnings. At the beginning of March 2002 twenty five regional radio channels were in operation, nine of them being the regional stations of public radio. The number of local radio stations reached sixty four, some of them belonging to the network of national or regional companies.

Public radio has three channels, but the audience data are favourable for none of them. Only the news magazine programmes of the first (Kossuth Rádió) have a high audience share, otherwise the public channels are not widely listened to. This is true particularly in the case of the third channel (Bartók Rádió), which broadcasts classical music and literature programmes only: its share is always below 1 per cent. The second channel (Petöfi Rádió) tries to meet the challenge of the commercial music channels – without much success. After years of more or less sane financial conditions, public radio was in deficit in 2001, because both advertising revenue and subscription income were far below the expected level and the sale of a whole frequency as well as staff reduction was not enough to turn the tide.

Most of the commercial radio stations broadcast pop music; there is no jazz radio station. One can tune into news radio (Inforádió), which has an 8 per cent share in the region it reaches. Klubrádió, one of the commercial channels, has modified its profile and launched very serious programmes on politics and social questions; some of the anchor persons came from public radio and television. Pannon Rádió is considered to be extreme-rightist. It has an ownership relationship with a radical right-wing party, and the National Radio and Television Commission claimed the situation to be illegal. The commission has also punished the channel because of its programmes' antiminority biases. A large group of Hungarian musicians tried to boycott the channel by forbidding the use of their songs in its programmes. Rádió C, a special channel for Hungarian Gypsies, has been launched in the region of Budapest; several non-Roma media celebrities help the channel as anchor persons. The genre of talk radio is still unfamiliar in Hungary. However, one can find some shorter programmes on different channels that are reminiscent of talk radio.

### Film and video
In 2001, 173 films were shown in cinemas. The size of the audience and the income of the cinemas both grew considerably. Total cinema admissions reached 15.7 million, a ten per cent rise since 1997. The audience for Hungarian films grew even faster. While the total box office income amounted to Ft 10 billion, which is 29 per cent higher than in the previous year, Hungarian films produced 35 per cent income growth. For years, two-thirds of the films in cinema programmes

have been of American origin, less than 10 per cent of them are French, and there are fewer than ten works from the United Kingdom, Italy and Germany each. Hungary had produced about twenty films per year, but in 2001 the number reached thirty.

There is a special cinema network in Budapest of ten members. They are called art movie houses, because they show artistic films of Hungarian and foreign origin. Although for years they have had a very stable audience of approximately 800,000 moviegoers per year, they cannot survive without massive subsidies.

The financial background of film production is rather unstable, and that was one of the reasons why Hungarian films, which used to be quite famous in the world, almost disappeared from the film festivals during the 1990s. Now that tendency has returned; the state and other sponsors have begun to subsidize film production substantially. In particular the state's involvement has led to much debate whether politically biased films are to be made as a result.

Public television used to be a remarkable producer of films, but since it ran into financial difficulties there are almost no films made by or for television companies. Parliament is working on a new film law that may fix the share of the film subsidies in terms of GDP.

## The Internet and related on-line media

The level of development of the Internet and related media is relatively low. According to the data for the end of 2001, only 17 per cent of the population over fourteen had access to the Internet and 66 per cent of them spent more than five hours per month using that media. The increase was outstanding, however, reaching 70 per cent for the year, by which time the same number of people had access to the Internet from home as from the office. The use of the media was more intensive from home. Internet cafés are very popular: in Budapest, one can find fifty of them with reasonable prices.

In 2001, 77 per cent of primary and secondary schools had access to the World Wide Web, but the distribution was rather uneven; in Budapest the figure was 87 per cent, in other cities 91 per cent, while in the villages it was 65 per cent only. All secondary schools had access, and one-third of schools had a Web site of their own. All the universities had both access and Web sites, and two-thirds of them had built up an intranet as well.

A special sphere is e-government. The government of 1998–2002 invested large sums in the development of e-democracy, particularly in the local and central government portals and services. More and more local government portals opened in the country, with the help of which more and more services became accessible to citizens via the Net but so far the public administration has used the possibility mostly for one-way information and not for communication. Another popular form of Internet use is the so-called Teleház system: local governments establish and finance places where citizens without access can communicate with the administration via the Net.

The data are much more favourable for business. The intensity of use is in direct proportion to the size of the companies. Ninety seven per cent of firms with more than 300 employees have access to the Internet; only 71 per cent of the small ones (with five to nine employees) have the same possibility. In the same time, the growth in that respect was also fairly steady in 2001 and managers were planning to develop the companies. Business used the Web mainly for sales and much less for internal purposes. The central government has been trying to communicate with business via the Internet. For example, all public procurement is soon planned to be carried out with the help of the Internet.

All the main off-line media have launched their on-line portals or Web sites and new on-line media have also appeared. In February 2002 the two most visited Web services were Origo and Index with more than 11 million page impressions each per week, with the next most popular having only 2.5 million. The financial situation of on-line media is rather unstable. Index has been in deficit for long and waiting for investors, just like other Internet companies. Ringier and Vivendi, that is, companies from other spheres of media (press and telephone respectively), seem to be interested in buying, the latter planning to become the Internet market leader.

## POLITICS, POLICY, LAW AND REGULATION

Political forces take freedom of the press as an abstract ideal for granted. One can say that the ideal is realized in the everyday life of the Hungarian media. There are some regulations concerning content, but they are no stricter than in most European countries; they protect minorities and the children, and concern certain religious and sexual questions. One may even say that they are less strict than they should be. For example, public denial of the Holocaust is not yet forbidden despite the frequency of attempts by different governments to pass a law on the issue.

Several laws and decrees concern the sphere of the media. It means that there is no comprehensive regulation for all the aspects of the field. The most important difference is between the press and the electronic media. While the law on the press dates from 1986, that is, from the state socialist period, the law on electronic media is quite recent. Yet the former does not give rise to many problems and debates, particularly because it was modified at the beginning of 1990, while the latter does. That bifurcation is true concerning the regulatory agencies too; the electronic media have a separate commission and a complaints commission above that, while the courts handle the press cases.

### The Press

The press is free in Hungary. Anyone is entitled to launch a paper, no permission is needed, the publisher is only supposed to register the paper or the periodical, and the registration can be rejected only on grounds of criminality.

Press censorship is sometimes a topic of debate and the number of libel suits is growing.

The most questionable regulation is the so-called principle of objective responsibility. According to the principle, applied by the courts, journalists have total responsibility for the truth value of their reports even if they just give an account of someone else's views; if that someone else told an untruth or something that proves to be untrue and journalists put that untruth in the paper or in the programme of an electronic media, they may be condemned by the court, even if they did so in good faith.

Further questionable cases occur in connection with state secrets and privacy. There have been several suits where journalists were sentenced because they had published documents containing state secrets. In other cases the media allegedly infringed on the privacy or the dignity of certain persons, mostly politicians or other public personalities.

There is one problem of free speech that is very delicate and seemingly insoluble for the legislation: so-called hate speech. The issue is one of protection against publications and communications that attack the dignity of a social group. That is especially true of extreme rightist books that cast doubt on the Holocaust and spread antisemitic propaganda. So far legislation has proved unable to reconcile the right to free speech and a free press with the protection of human dignity.

Although the regulations and the problems of censorship concern not only the press but also the media in general, most of the objectionable cases that reach the courts occur in the press, particularly in book publishing, because there are two special bodies concerned with regulation of the electronic media.

After 1998, that is, since the previous majority began to counterbalance the media, there have been two Bills, presented by the members of the majority party in parliament, on the right of response in the media. The first proposed that anyone feeling harmed by an opinion published in a newspaper or broadcast in a radio or television programme should be given the right to respond (with equal prominence). The law would concern not only facts but opinions. The Bill also proposed to establish a fund that would assign part of the profits of best-selling titles to the injured party. The Bill was rejected, but re-emerged in a narrower version in a second Bill concentrating on the right to respond. Parliament passed the law, but the President of the Republic presumed that it might be unconstitutional and asked the Constitutional Court to examine it. The court did raise certain arguments against parts of the law.

Journalists have three main media associations, the rest (for example, the Association of the Hungarian University and College Press, or the Association of Hungarian Catholic Journalists, the trade union of that sphere) work without too much publicity. The first and oldest one (the Association of Hungarian Journalists) used to be the only organization of journalism in the state socialist period. Because of their reformist activity and the sudden privatization of the press on the eve of the first free elections in 1990, the transition did not result in any change of staff in the media. Consequently the old association also survived and is still the most important organization in its field. In 1992 rightist journalists felt obliged to establish a new organization (the Community of Hungarian Journalists) in order to make room for conservative journalism.

Finally, given recent attacks, the journalists of the public media launched their own organization (the Association of Hungarian Journalists of the Electronic Media) in February 2002.

The April 2002 defeat of the previous government has been considered to threaten the survival of the rightist titles. In order to protect them, the late Prime Minister called with success on the voters of the right to subscribe to those weeklies and to *Magyar Nemzet*, the rightist daily.

Since all the important political forces promise a law against hate speech and against Holocaust denial, we can presume that such legislation will begin soon, though the Hungarian Constitutional Court has always preferred freedom of speech against any kind of limitations.

## The electronic media

The Hungarian Broadcasting Act, that is, the law on radio and television, was passed in 1995 and has been in force since 1996. The Act is one of the lengthiest pieces of media legislation in the world. Its size is closely related to all the doubts and fears the legislators felt and with their endeavour to regulate every minuscule part of the sphere and to create legal security. And yet the law did not solve the problems of the media. In fact, it has proved to make it possible for the government to exert as much influence on public radio and television as the previous legal conditions did.

The law created a dual system in the media landscape: the duality of the public and private electronic media. The duality is not very strict because the private media may, and to a certain extent should, broadcast public programmes, while the public media are entitled to broadcast advertisements.

The law also established the National Radio and Television Commission (NRTC), a body to supervise the electronic media. The NRTC has a Complaints Commission and it has to conduct the activities of the Broadcasting Fund, the third important establishment.

The NRTC is responsible for ensuring freedom of speech in the field and for the independence of broadcasters. It also has to carry out anti-trust activities. The commission has a monitoring service that helps the NRTC check: whether the media are following the regulations on programme content; whether the news and news magazines are balanced politically; whether the different companies give enough space to the Hungarian and European-made work in their programmes; whether they exceed the quota of advertisements; whether they follow the rules concerning violent and sexual content; etc. In order to do that, during the 2002 election campaign the commission monitored more than seventy radio and television programmes and published the results daily in the case of the larger broadcasters, weekly or monthly on the activities of the local channels.

The Complaints Commission has to deal with cases where the media companies allegedly violate the rules concerning the content of the programmes. The Broadcasting Fund is to finance works that are not profitable commercially but are important to preserve certain values, to maintain the diversity of the programmes and to serve certain public goals. The sources of the fund are various: licence fees, subscription fees, penalties, and subsidies from the central budget.

The law also changed the legal status of the public media. Accordingly, there are three public broadcasting companies: Hungarian Television, Duna Television and Hungarian Radio. While the NRTC supervises the public media as far as the content of programmes is concerned, boards of trustees supervise the three companies from a financial point of view and they are entitled to select the president of a given company. Each board has a presidium, at least eight members of which are elected by the parliament in such a way that the number of those elected by the parliamentary majority should equal the number of those elected by the opposition. The rest of the members of the boards are elected by social organizations.

And that is the main problem with the public media. The law does not make it clear which parties in parliament are to be regarded as belonging to the government side and which to the opposition; there may be parties that give support to the government without having a representative in the Cabinet. Another trap is that the law presupposes that each side is able to agree about its own nominees, who will then be appointed by the parliament. But after 1998 the opposition proved unable to do that, consequently the presidiums of the boards worked without members sent by the opposition.

The existence of the incomplete boards and, previously, the events that led to their incompleteness caused extremely heated debates between the majority party and the opposition because under such conditions the government had considerable uncontrolled influence over the public electronic media. Even the representatives of the European Union and international journalist organizations raised objections against the situation. Again, both sides agreed that the law had to be amended, but since it needs a two-thirds majority there is no solution to the problem.

The law created the Broadcasting Fund and entitled the public media to have revenues from different sources, but still their financial situation is generally very bad and public broadcasters are very much dependent on state subsidies. One of the reasons is that although every citizen under sixty five with a television set is obliged to pay a licence fee, a considerable part of the population evades the obligation. Moreover, the law compelled the second channel of Hungarian Television to move to satellite and give its frequency to the new private media companies. Together with Duna Television, they broadcast via satellite, although only a very low percentage of the population has the facility to watch their programmes free, and not many people subscribe to the cable services. Consequently their income from advertising is rather low. The political forces have agreed several times that the financial difficulties of the public media should be solved but nothing effective has been done so far, perhaps because subsidies are considered to be a very useful way for governments to keep the public media under control.

In April 2002 a new, leftist government came to power but its minimal majority will probably not be enough to avoid the new battles of the decade-long media war. In any case, the necessity of a two-thirds majority concerning media legislation will probably block or at least slow down even the European adjustment of the Broadcasting Act.

The politicization of the private media is a remarkable tendency in Hungary. Magyar ATV has launched several political programmes anchored by leftist and rightist journalists. The extreme right has tried to establish a network of press, radio, television and Internet-based media by giving space and time to the same journalists on Pannon Rádió and on Szent László Televízió, as in the weekly of the MIÉP, the radical right-wing party in parliament between 1998 and 2002. After its defeat, the right is working to establish the first Hungarian news television channel.

Journalists in the electronic media usually belong to the two main organizations, mainly the older one. In February 2002 a new organization was established for journalists who work in the electronic media. Its profile is not quite clear yet, though the organizers referred to the old journalist association as too leftist, to the other journalist community as too rightist, which suggests that the aim was to create a middle-of-the-road organization. It is remarkable, however, that the founding persons are the presidents and vice-presidents of the public media, that is, figures of the right.

## The Internet and related on-line media

There is no comprehensive law on the Internet, and the political parties agree that the laws already in force should be modified in order to meet the challenge of the new technologies. Three important laws concerning the field were passed by the parliament: on telecommunications, on digital signature, on electronic commerce. The need is urgent to modify the law on copyright, for example.

On 15 February 2001 the leading content providers established their own association. The association was to be the form of self-regulation in the sphere concerning the rules and norms and to give certification to Web sites that meet these norms and requirements.

The Internet is one of the few issues where one can find agreement among the parties, particularly if one takes these plans into account. All political forces would like to develop the sphere considerably, but the actual goals are different: while the right is planning to advance the central services, the left would like to make it possible for citizens to buy computers and have access to the Internet. Independently of the results of the 2002 elections, the parties promise to keep the existing government institutions of e-democracy and e-government, and the new government has even established a separate Ministry of Informatics for supervising the fields of telecommunications, informatics, research and development, etc. All the parties consider it important to develop the Hungarian content of the Internet, to support such initiatives and to urge the dissemination of electronic literacy. All of them would widen government services on the Net.

## STATISTICS

| | |
|---|---|
| Population (1 February 2001) | 10,195,513 |
| Number of households (1 February 2001) | 3,840,000 |
| Movie admissions, 2001 | 15,700,000 |
| Source: HVG. | |
| Books published, 2001 | 8,783 |

**Print media**  Circulation of main newspapers, January–March 2002

| | |
|---|---|
| National | |
| Political | |
| *Népszabadság* | 211,000 |
| *Magyar Nemzet* | 96,000 |
| *Magyar Hírlap* | 50,000 |
| *Népszava* | 36,000 |
| Sports | |
| *Nemzeti Sport* | 107,000 |
| Free | |
| *Metro* | 327,000 |
| Tabloid | |
| *Blikk* | 248,000 |
| *Színes Mai Lap* | 114,000 |
| *Mai Nap* | n.a. |
| *Kurir* | n.a. |

Regional

| | |
|---|---|
| *24 Óra* | 23,000 |
| *Békés Megyei Hírlap* | 30,000 |
| *Délmagyarország* | 34,000 |
| *Délvilág* | 21,000 |
| *Észak-Magyarország* | 51,000 |
| *Fejér Megyei Hírlap* | 52,000 |
| *Hajdú Bihari Napló* | 52,000 |
| *Heves Megyei Hírlap* | 24,000 |
| *Kelet-Magyarország* | 59,000 |
| *Kisalföld* | 81,000 |
| *Napló* | 55,000 |
| *Petöfi Népe* | 44,000 |
| *Somogyi Hírlap* | 38,000 |
| *Tolnai Népújság* | 21,000 |
| *Új Dunántúli Napló* | 50,000 |
| *Új Néplap* | 29,000 |
| *Vas Népe* | 61,000 |
| *Zalai Hírlap* | 61,000 |

Source: MATESZ.

**Broadcast media**

Audience share of main terrestrial, cable and satellite television channels, January–March 2002 (%)

| | |
|---|---|
| Terrestrial | |
| Public | |
| *m1* | 11.2 |
| Private | |
| RTL Klub | 33.3 |
| TV-2 | 30.5 |
| Cable | |
| Public | |
| Duna TV | less than 1 |
| m2 | less than 1 |
| Satellite | None |

Source: AGB Hungary.

Audience share of main radio channels, February 2002 (%)

| | |
|---|---|
| Public | |
| Kossuth Rádió | 20 |
| Petöfi Rádió | 15 |
| Private | |
| Danubius Rádió | 31 |
| Sláger | 23 |
| Juventus | 10 |

Source: Szonda Ipsos.

Percentage of households with all main forms of satellite, cable or terrestrial pay-television, October 2001

| | |
|---|---|
| HBO | 8.8 |
| Sport1 | 5.7 |

Source: AGB Hungary.

Percentage of households with:

| | |
|---|---|
| VCR (2001) | 38 |
| DVD player (2001) | 1 |

Source: Medián.

| | |
|---|---|
| Satellite receiver (October 2001) | 8 |

Source: AGB Hungary.

**Electronic media**

Percentage of households with:

| | |
|---|---|
| Digital reception by any means | n.a. |

Internet access, December 2001

| | |
|---|---|
| Internet penetration in the population above age fourteen | 17 |

Mobile phone

| | |
|---|---|
| Number of active subscribers, May 2002 | 5,695,410 |
| Companies' market shares (%) | |
| Westel Mobil | 50.8 |
| Pannon GSM | 38.5 |
| Vodafone | 10.7 |

Source: Communications Authority.

**Advertising spend, 2001 (%)**

| | |
|---|---|
| Terrestrial television channels | 57.5 |
| Daily newspapers | 14.0 |
| Magazines | 13.5 |
| Cable television channels | 2.0 |
| Other | 13.0 |

Source: Médiagnózis.

**Ownership**

Main media companies and approximate size of their press and television holdings

Daily press
Ringier: *Népszabadság* (49.9 per cent), *Magyar Hírlap, Blikk, Nemzeti Sport.*
Gruner & Jahr (Bertelsmann): *Népszabadság* (17 per cent).
Nemzet (AAB Marketing Services): *Magyar Nemzet.*
Axel Springer Magyarország: *24 Óra, Békés Megyei Hírlap, Heves Megyei Hírlap, Nógrád Megyei Hírlap, Petöfi Népe, Somogyi Hírlap, Tolnai Népújság, Új Dunántúli Napló, Uj Néplap.*
Pannon Lapok Társasága (Westdeutsche Allgemeine Zeitung): *Fejér Megyei Hírlap, Dunaújvárosi Hírlap, Vas Népe, Napló, Zala Hírlap.*
Inform Média (Funk Verlag & Druckerei): *Észak-Magyarország, Kelet-Magyarország, Hajdú-Bihari Napló.*
Lapcom (Associated Press): *Kisalföld, Délmagyarország, Délvilág.*

Television
Magyar RTL (in 1997) (CLT-UFA 49 per cent, Matáv 25 per cent, Pearson group 20 per cent, Raiffeisen group 6 per cent): RTL Klub.
MTM-SBS Televízió (in 2002) (Scandinavian Broadcasting System Co. 81.5 per cent, MTM Kommunikációs 16 per cent, Tele-München 2.5 per cent): TV-2.
Sources: Médiakönyv, 2000–1; Napi Gazdaság, 12 February 2002.

# REFERENCES

Argeó, Éva (ed.) (1998) *Jelentesék könyve*, Budapest: Új Mandátum.

Cseh, Gabriella and Sükösd, Miklós (1999) *Médiajog és médiapolitika Magyarországon* I, *Médiajog* Budapest: Új Manátum Könyvkiadó.

Csermely, Ákos (ed.) (2000/1) *A média jövője*, Budapest: Média Hungária Kiadó.

Enyedi Nagy, Mihály et al. (eds.) (1988) *Médiakönyv* (volume of papers, summaries and data on the Hungarian media scene, annual since 1998), Budapest: Enamiké.

Lánczi, Andras and O'Neil, Patrick (1997) 'Pluralization and the politics of media change in Hungary', in Patrick O'Neil (ed.) *Post-communism and the Media in Eastern Europe*, London: Frank Cass.

Sparks, Colin with Reading, Anna (1998) *Communism, Capitalism and the Mass Media*, London: Sage.

Sükösd, Miklós (1997/8) 'Media and democratic transition in Hungary', *Oxford International Review*, winter, pp. 11–21.

Varga, Domokos György (2001) *Elsőkből lesznek az elsők* I–II, Budapest: LKD.

# 10: Ireland

## WOLFGANG TRUETZSCHLER

## NATIONAL PROFILE

On the periphery of Europe, in area the Republic of Ireland is 70,283 km². With a population of 3,917,336 inhabitants (CSO, 2002), it is the country with the second smallest population in the European Union. The population is not evenly distributed, more than half living in the eastern region. The high concentration in Dublin (29 per cent of the population live in the city and its environment) particularly contributes to this regional imbalance. There are two official languages in the state, namely Irish and English, but English is the mother tongue of the vast majority of the people. Only 2 per cent of the population live in the Gaeltacht, the native Irish-speaking areas situated mainly on the west coast.

Although Ireland has traditionally been seen as a predominantly agricultural country, continuing industrialization has changed this. Continued (in Ireland's history unprecedented) economic growth in the period 1995–2001 reduced the unemployment rate (until the mid-1990s traditionally one of the highest in Europe) to around 4.5 per cent of the labour force in 2001. Ireland's industrial development is that of dependent rather than indigenous industrialization. Central to the state's industrial strategy since 1960 has been the attraction of export-oriented foreign companies to invest in Ireland and of retaining the foreign companies by offering them the lowest corporation tax in the European Union.

The economic policies of the two major parties, Fianna Fáil and Fine Gael, tend to be centrist, with a commitment to economic rectitude on the one hand, but also, given Ireland's large dependent population, committed to maintaining welfare policies. All parties, and the great majority of the population, are also committed to membership of the European Union. The more left-wing party, the Labour Party, usually receives around 10–15 per cent of the vote. The 1997–2002 government, formed by Fianna Fáil and the smaller Progressive Democrats, was re-elected in June 2002.

## STRUCTURE AND OWNERSHIP

### The print media

#### The newspaper press

The press consists of four national dailies and two national evening newspapers, five national Sunday newspapers, around sixty-five regional and twelve local newspapers as well as approximately thirty-two mainly urban-based free (advertising-financed) newspapers (see statistics below). Newspapers other than the dailies tend to be published on a weekly basis. Roughly 600,000 national newspapers and 650,000 regional newspapers are sold each day and week respectively. The figures above do not include newspapers published in Irish.

Irish-language newspapers consist of two weekly newspapers (*Foinse* and *Lá*) and a monthly newspaper on events in the Irish language (*Saol*). These newspapers are circulated in the republic and in Northern Ireland and are subsidized (to the tune of £120,000 in the case of *Lá* and £4,500 per issue of *Foinse*) by Foras Na Gaeilge, the state body responsible for the promotion of the Irish language throughout the whole island of Ireland.

Ireland's booming economy has had a positive effect on its newspaper industry in that there has been a modest increase of around 2.2–2.5 per cent in newspaper sales since 1999. The daily readership of newspapers has also increased in a similar manner.

Most Irish newspapers are politically conservative and have a middle-class orientation. British newspapers (especially the tabloid ones) can be bought all over Ireland. UK newspapers are cheaper in Ireland than Irish ones, as Ireland (unlike Britain) imposes value-added tax on the printing of newspapers. In 2001 approximately 28 per cent of daily and over 34 per cent of Sunday newspapers sold in Ireland were British.

Regarding concentration of the press, the biggest and only Irish 'media concern' is the firm Independent News & Media, a company headed by Ireland's 'press baron' Dr Tony O'Reilly. Independent Newspapers publishes the *Irish Independent*, the daily broadsheet with the highest sales figures in Ireland, two of the five national Sunday newspapers, the national evening newspaper *Evening Herald*, approximately 20 per cent of the regional/local press and the Irish edition of the UK *Daily Star*. Dr Tony O'Reilly also owns newspapers in Australia, New Zealand, South Africa and the United Kingdom (the *Independent*, the *Independent on Sunday* and regional newspapers such as the *Belfast Telegraph*).

Independent Newspapers is the dominant actor in the Irish newspaper industry in that around 80 per cent of Irish newspapers sold in Ireland in 2001 were sold by companies fully or partially owned by Independent Newspapers. This situation has been reviewed by the Irish government and the Irish Competition Authority on a few occasions. The conclusion reached by these reviews has usually been that the newspaper industry shows sufficient editorial diversity not to warrant intervention in the newspaper market.

This diversity is provided by Ireland's main quality daily broadsheet *The Irish Times* and to a lesser extent (lower circulation figures) by the daily *Irish Examiner* and by the quality *Sunday Business Post*. The latter two newspapers are part of the *Examiner Group* owned by the Thomas Crosbie Group, Ireland's second largest media company. There is, arguably, less competition in regional newspapers, as these tend to have monopolies in their respective localities.

Ireland's regional or provincial newspaper market is expected to consolidate substantially in the next few years as smaller operators are targeted by larger ones. In July 2002 there are four companies that own a sizeable section of the regional newspaper market: Independent News & Media (twelve regional titles). Scottish Radio Holdings (six regional titles), Examiner Publications (seven titles) and Leader Group (eight titles). Finally, most of the regional newspapers in County Donegal are now owned by the British Mirror Group.

To date there is some cross-ownership between the print, the audiovisual and the on-line media in Ireland. The main instances of it are the shareholdings in seven local commercial radio stations by some local/regional newspapers (shareholdings are no longer restricted to 25 per cent of the shares as was the case until 2001/2) and the involvement of Independent News & Media in Chorus, the second largest cable operator in Ireland. Scottish Radio Holdings owns the national commercial radio service Today FM. The chairman of Independent News and Media also chairs the Valentia consortium that bought, in 2001, the company Eircom, the privatized and former monopoly telecommunications operator. Eircom operates one of the largest on-line services in Ireland, eircom.net.

The booming economy and the healthy state of the newspaper industry (increasing profitability due to a higher advertising spend in the period 1999–2001) seems to have changed the traditional lack of interest in the Irish newspaper market by foreign (British) investors. This signals a change from the situation in which British newspapers simply increase the print run of their papers for the Irish market to one where British newspaper publishers acquire Irish newspapers – seeing that there are no explicitly stated restrictions on foreign ownership of media services. Some British tabloid newspapers publish an Irish edition.

Judging by the developments in changes of newspaper ownership in the period 2000–2, when most of the changes took place, the sale of smaller but very profitable newspapers is set to continue over the next few years. In the region of forty regional titles are still in local ownership and are likely to be bought by bigger indigenous or foreign (British) newspaper operators.

The only newspaper that is currently in financial difficulties is *The Irish Times*, Ireland's main quality broadsheet. It was particularly badly hit by a slump in advertising revenue subsequent to the events of 11 September 2001, when the Irish economy suddenly reverted temporarily to a static growth rate. This affected all Irish media except the regional newspapers. By May 2002 *The Irish Times* had undergone a number of cost cutting exercises such as streamlining its management, introducing charges for its on-line services, reducing the number of its foreign correspondents, etc.

### The periodical and magazine press

In the magazine sector, Irish titles continue to sell well despite the strong competition from the United Kingdom. Many popular UK titles such as *Bella, Hello!* and *OK!* sell very well in Ireland, while many specialist publications from the United Kingdom have the resources that make it difficult for similar Irish titles to compete in a market of only 2.8 million adults. Because of the size of the market Irish magazines must rely more heavily on advertising than their UK counterparts. In most women's glossies, for example, the editorial/advertising ratio is 60:40. Unlike some of the big circulation UK tabloid newspapers which add Irish content for the Irish market, UK magazines do not follow suit.

Irish periodical and magazine publishers are organized in the Periodical Publishers' Association of Ireland (PPAI). It has forty companies with around 140 of a total of 160 magazine titles in membership. Most companies are quite small, publishing only one or two titles. This would suggest that the market will experience consolidation over the next two years as some magazines may find it difficult to survive without the financial backing of a large publishing house such as Smurfit Communications, which is part of the Jefferson Smurfit Group, one of Ireland's largest companies with an annual turnover of €4,512 million in 2001.

The most successful magazine, with 145,146 copies sold per issue in 2001, is the *RTÉ Guide*, the weekly guide to radio and television published by the public service broadcaster RTÉ. The highest-selling monthly magazine in the country, with an audited circulation of 33,529 per issue in the first six months of 2001, is *VIP*, Ireland's answer to the UK's *Hello!* and *OK!*

Magazines are financed by advertising (only 2 per cent of the annual advertising spend) and over-the-counter sales (73 per cent of total revenue in 2000). Subscription sales are small (5 per cent of revenue in 2000) but on the increase according to the PPAI (Cawley Nua, 2001).

### Book publishing

Despite the fact that the Irish book publishing industry has always been faced with overwhelming competition from UK publishers, there are about sixty serious book publishers, as well as many others who publish titles on a once-off basis. In 2001 educational publishers are estimated to have turned over around €40 million, while general publishers turned over about €25 million. There are no figures available for the total value of the Irish book market, in particular. The retail market value for UK-published books was last estimated in 1994 as being in the region of IR£58 million (€73 million) (Horvath Bastow Charleton, 2000.)

There is a certain amount of state support for book publishing, the main instance being the financial support given to individual authors, to literary organizations and to publishers by the Arts Council of Ireland (Arts Council of Ireland, 2001). In 2000 this financial support amounted to €1.65 million or 3.5 per cent of the total Arts Council budget. Other and smaller forms of state support are primarily aimed at authors and publishers of works in Irish.

## The electronic (audio-visual) media

### Television

Broadcasting has been dominated since the 1920s by Ireland's public service broadcaster Radio Telifís Éireann (RTÉ) and this is still the situation in 2002 to the extent that RTÉ is a major player in Ireland's broadcasting scene. RTÉ operates two national television services: RTÉ-1, a fairly typical public service channel with an emphasis on news and current affairs programming and Network 2, a channel that has tried to give itself a more youthful image. Since October 1996 Ireland has a third public service broadcasting channel, the Irish-language Teléfís na Gaeilge (TG-4). TG-4 operates under the statutory and corporate aegis of RTÉ, but will be set up as a separate broadcasting authority according to the Broadcasting Act 2001. According to TG-4's Web site the channel broadcasts over eleven hours per day, with an average of six hours of Irish-language programmes. The creation of TG-4 was a cultural and language policy decision made by the previous

Irish government in response to the demands of Irish-language speakers to increase the use of Irish, Ireland's official first language.

Apart from the public service broadcaster TG-4, the only indigenous competition to RTÉ television is the private commercial television channel TV-3. Even though the TV-3 consortium was awarded a licence to broadcast television as far back as 1988/9 it commenced broadcasting only in September 1998. One explanation for this long delay lies in the fact that it is hard to imagine the financial viability of four national television channels in a country with a population of just over 3.9 million, most of whom can also receive British television, arguably the world's best. Thus in order to start up television broadcasting TV-3 needed strong financial backers from abroad. TV-3 received such backing in 1997 when CanWest Global, the Canadian television company, took a 45 per cent stake in TV-3 – the maximum allowed under EU legislation. CanWest runs television stations in Australia and New Zealand and is the world's largest non-US purchaser of Hollywood films.

The Canadian company also owns 29.9 per cent of Ulster Television (UTV), the British independent television company of Northern Ireland. UTV is the second most popular television station (in terms of audience figures) in the republic. In September 2000 the British media group Granada Media also took a 45 per cent stake in TV-3. Granada Media is the dominant player in the British independent television sector in that it effectively controls the United Kingdom's ITV network and produces 47 per cent of the network's output, including some of the most popular television programmes in the United Kingdom and Ireland, such as the long-running soap opera *Coronation Street*.

The programming on TV-3 is very much entertainment-led. TV-3 sees itself as an entertainment network although under the Radio and Television Act 1988 it must provide a 'reasonable proportion of news and current affairs programming'. Most of TV-3's programming consists of US, UK or Australian series and films, and advertising, with a minimum of home-produced programmes.

With 51 per cent of Irish households subscribing to cable television at the end of 2000, Ireland had the fourth highest penetration of cable television in Western European countries. About 70 per cent of Irish television homes are in 'multi-channel' areas, i.e., ones which can receive British television signals either off-air or via cable or via MMDS (multipoint microwave distribution system). Cable television homes can receive the four Irish television channels, four British channels (Channel 5 is not available on most Irish cable television systems) and about twelve satellite television stations.

The Irish cable television industry is at the end of a process of consolidation, which has left most cable and MMDS franchises in the hands of two companies, NTL and Chorus. There are also a number of much smaller operators with small single-franchise areas. The US-owned NTL entered the Irish market in 1999 when it bought the company Cablelink, then owned by Eircom and RTÉ. NTL operates, inter alia, cable television in the United Kingdom (including Northern Ireland) and in Paris. NTL Ireland is the largest Irish cable television operator and its franchise area includes the east coast of Ireland with about a third of the Irish population. Chorus Communication is Ireland's second largest cable operator. Fifty per cent of the shares in Chorus are owned by Princes Holdings which in turn is owned by Independent News & Media, publisher and owner of Independent Newspapers. The remaining shares in Chorus are owned by the US company Liberty Media International, which in turn is owned by the US telephone giant AT&T.

Aside from becoming subscribers to cable television, viewers in Ireland can also become subscribers to the digital services of Sky Television at a fairly low cost for the installation of the aerial (satellite dish). Viewers have to subscribe to Sky Digital for a minimum period of one year whereupon they receive free of charge the necessary digital set-top box for their analogue television sets. In May 2002 there were 232,000 subscribers to Sky Digital. In August 2002 Sky Digital is the sole provider of digital satellite television services in Ireland. Subscribers to Sky Digital have a choice of up to more than 100 broadcast television channels as well as a choice of subscription channels and pay-per-view films. (The two cable operators have also started providing digital television in small sections of their respective networks.)

### Radio

RTÉ operates four national radio channels: Radio 1 with traditional public service radio programming, 2 FM, a twenty four-hour music radio station, Raidio na Gaeltachta with public service radio programming in the Irish language, and Lyric FM, a twenty-four hour classical music and arts channel. The Irish public service broadcaster is no longer involved in the provision of local radio subsequent to closing its only local radio station, in Cork, Ireland's second largest city, in 2000 due to its low audience share in comparison with those of the private radio station in Cork now owned by UTV. Since the enactment of the Radio and Television Act 1988 RTÉ is actually excluded from the provision of local radio in Ireland with the sole exception of Cork.

In mid-2002 there are forty eight licensed independent radio stations. These consist of one national independent commercial radio station, twenty four local commercial stations, thirteen community/community of interest stations and three special interest radio stations – the latter three are in Dublin. The remainder consist of hospital and college radio stations. Local radio usually means a county radio station, i.e. the ranges of these stations are limited to their respective county or town boundaries. Community and community of interest stations are run in accordance with the IRTC 1997 Policy on Community Radio Broadcasting and they do not figure prominently in usual audience figures nor are they of any great interest to advertisers. What are significant in terms of audiences and therefore of interest to advertisers are the twenty four local radio stations.

The programming on independent commercial radio stations tends to be quite similar: wall-to-wall music in some form or shape (Top 40 hits or easy listening 'middle of the road' music or country music) interspersed by advertising, jingles, talk or 'prattle' by the disc jockeys and cheaply produced current affairs programmes in order to comply with the legal requirement that 20 per cent of broadcasting time must consist of news and current affairs programmes. However, there are some exceptions to the rule in that some of the more rurally based local radios do provide talk programmes with information about the locality for the local community. On most local radio stations there are very few programmes in the Irish language. Even though the programming on local radio cannot match the diversity and comprehensiveness of the programmes of Ireland's main national public radio channel, RTÉ's Radio

1, the official listenership figures for radio show that Radio 1 has lost its position as the most popular radio station in all parts of the country except Dublin.

A number of other Irish services available to Irish listeners and viewers do not usually figure in advertising statistics or in the usual audience statistics. These other services include cable radio, local television and unlicensed radio stations. There are no cable radio stations as such in Ireland, but the cable operators outlined below do relay Irish and British national radio programmes. Similarly there is no tradition of regional or local television stations of any note. The only local television that does exist consists of local television channels run by the cable operators in different parts of the country.

Unlicensed or pirate radio stations have always existed in Ireland since the start-up of radio broadcasting in Ireland. This was particularly the case in the period 1960–88, prior to the legalization of private local radio. But even in 2002 the listener/radio enthusiast will find, on any day of the year, fifty or sixty pirate radio stations operating in different parts of the republic. Pirate radio stations seem to be run by disenchanted licence applicants for legal radio stations and others who are of the opinion that radio in Ireland offers no real choice other than popular music stations and only one or two 'proper' radio stations, i.e. stations like RTÉ Radio 1, catering for all groups in society. Furthermore the state does not seem to be too bothered to shut down the pirates unless their radio transmissions interfere with those of the emergency services or those of legal broadcasters.

There is no digital audio broadcasting available in Ireland in 2002, neither are there any concrete plans to develop DAB even though the RTÉ Web site states that RTÉ will start broadcasting digital radio. A test transmission of digital radio took place in Dublin in 1999 but no further developments have taken place since then. It seems that RTÉ is more concerned with the development of digital television. There is no mention of digital radio in the Broadcasting Act 2001 described below.

### Film and video

The latest Eurostat cinema statistics show that in 1998 Ireland had sixty six cinema sites with a total of 280 cinema screens (Deiss, 2002). With 3.3 admissions per capita Ireland has one of the highest per capita box office admissions in the European Union (surpassed only by Luxembourg and Spain in 2000). The majority of cinemas are multiplexes owned by the major US film companies, as are the film distribution companies. The latter view the United Kingdom and Ireland as one market, which means it is often very difficult for Irish films to be distributed nationally unless these films are on international cinema release. It follows that the majority of films distributed and exhibited in Ireland are US ones. According to Eurostat, 73 per cent of films shown in Irish cinemas in 1999 were US films, 6 per cent were of national origin and 25 per cent were of EU origin.

Ireland has a number of support mechanisms for the production, distribution and exhibition of indigenous films and television productions (see IBEC, 2001). In 2000 these ranged from tax assistance for investment in film production to the tune of €81.8 million, financial assistance by the Irish Film Board (€4.5 million), by the Arts Council of Ireland (€1.43 million) and commissioning of independent productions by the public service broadcasters RTÉ (€14.6 million) and TG4 (€11.4 million).

However, this level of support does not necessarily guarantee a successful Irish film industry when compared with the US dominance in film production, as was witnessed in the period January to October 2001. During this period of time a record nine films funded by the Irish Film Board resulted in box office returns of €2.8 million. This is generally seen as the most successful year ever for Irish film. This is minuscule in comparison with returns to US distributors. A rough calculation of the box office returns of the US distributors in Ireland for the same period of time shows a turnover of €66.4 million (calculated on the basis of 13.27 million cinema attendances with an average ticket price of €5).

US dominance in film can also be seen in Ireland's video and DVD industry, as a visit to any retail or rental outlet with its displays of US films confirms. The visited outlet is probably one owned by Xtra-vision, Ireland's largest chain of video stores with over 50 per cent of all video shops. Xtra-vision is owned by the US company Blockbuster. The latest published Eurostat figures (Deiss, 2001) show that Ireland has the second highest number of outlets renting videos (29.8 per 100 000 inhabitants) in the European Union. The annual sales of videos in 1997 amounted to €37 million, video rentals in the same year came to €77 million. These figures are likely to have increased substantially in 2002 with the introduction of DVD players since 1997. No details are available on the share of indigenous productions in the video/DVD market.

## The Internet and related on-line media

According to the Irish telecommunications regulator, the Office of the Director of Telecommunications (ODTR) (ODTR, 2002), Internet penetration has grown over the last five years and in June 2002 approximately 34 per cent of Ireland's population had home Internet access via ordinary narrowband phone lines and dial-up modems. Broadband access to the Internet tends to be limited to organizations such as large companies and third-level educational establishments with broadband access via leased lines. ADSL was introduced only in the second half of 2001 on a trial basis and with a subsequent monthly charge of just under €110 it is too expensive for the majority of home users.

The active Internet universe, i.e. the number of people who have Internet access at home and who have used it during the month, stands at 16 per cent of the population. The average home user spent just under four hours on-line in April 2002. Internet penetration in business is substantially higher than residential Internet penetration, with 98 per cent of Irish businesses using the Internet on a regular basis.

Internet access is provided primarily by Ireland's telephone companies Eircom and ESAT (a company owned by British Telecom since 2000/1). UTV also provides dial-up Internet access, the first company to do so on an all-Ireland basis (i.e. Northern Ireland and the republic).

New Web-based media in Ireland encompass streaming audio over the Internet, which is provided by some of the legal radio stations as well as by some private individuals. Web radio offers a way of broadcasting which is untouched by regulation, and a few disgruntled applicants for a local radio licence are now 'broadcasting over the Net'. The period 1994–2001 saw many Irish businesses, and government departments/agencies, develop a Web presence enabling easier access to information by the citizen/customer. Online services by educational institutions tend to consist in the provision of information rather than in the provision of online courses, although this is likely to change over the next few years judging by the developments in the United States. Online access to government and parliamentary information is well established in Ireland, but online access to politicians and government officials is not so highly developed. The year 2001 in general saw an increase in the provision of state information for business and the public.

The only instance of Web television in Ireland, whereby Internet content can be accessed via an analogue television set using a set-top box, is that provided by the portal of the Independent Newspaper Group. According to company information, Unison had just under 23,000 set-top box subscribers at the end of 2001. Portals where users can access a variety of different services also exist. Of particular interest in the context of this chapter are the two portals of the 'traditional' media companies: the *Irish Times* portal and the one of the public service broadcaster RTÉ. Both these portals provide information that goes beyond their remit as a newspaper or a public service broadcaster. However, both portals have been loss-making since their inception.

# POLITICS, POLICY, LAW AND REGULATION

In early 2002 the US magazine *Foreign Policy* ranked Ireland as the most globalized nation in the world in the year 2000, in a study of sixty two advanced economies in the world. This ranking is based on numerous indicators spanning information technology, political engagement in international organizations, international travel and tourism, trade and economic integration (including inward investment, capital flows and personal communication). Some of these indicators are reflected in the development of the national media system as outlined in this chapter: foreign investment in Irish media companies, privatization of state assets and a decrease in state subventions, an advanced telecommunications infrastructure for business and, most importantly, the low (12.5 per cent on profits) corporation tax which attracted a substantial capital inflow by US companies in the information technology and telecommunications sector,

as well as the lack of restrictions on the repatriation of profits.

Concerning Ireland's media, the move towards globalization has been implemented and facilitated by two main regulatory agencies: the Office of the Director of Telecommunications Regulation (ODTR) and the Broadcasting Commission of Ireland (BCI). The ODTR was established in 1997 to oversee the deregulation of the Irish telecommunications market that occurred in 1998. The ODTR not only regulates telecommunications but is also responsible for overseeing the technical side of broadcasting. The BCI was set up in 2001 and is a new super broadcasting authority to regulate Ireland's private broadcasting services and to award the new digital content contracts that will ultimately determine the content of the digital television channels not yet allocated to anybody. Ireland's public service broadcasters are not regulated by the BCI although it is the stated aim of the BCI to include the currently self-regulated RTÉ and TG-4 in its remit.

## The press

The press in Ireland, unlike the broadcast media, is not subject to specific legislation, i.e. to a specific press law. The right to freedom of the press is derived from the express right to freedom of expression as enshrined in the constitution. However, this right is subject to a number of restrictions arising out of considerations of public order and morality, the authority of the state, etc. It is curtailed if it amounts to the publication or utterance of blasphemous, seditious or indecent matter.

Furthermore, there are a large number of statutes with implications for press freedom, such as, for example the Defamation Act, the Official Secrets Act, the common law concept of contempt of court, etc. (Boyle and McGonagle, 1988: 5–8). There is neither a press council nor a specific right to reply incorporated in the various statutes that are of relevance to the press. However, some newspapers have voluntarily appointed 'newspaper ombudspersons' as a means of investigating complaints by the readers and of avoiding litigation which may result in the courts awarding high damages for libel.

Monopoly formation in the press industry is subject to specific cartel legislation. This enables the Minister of Industry and Commerce to refer to the (government-appointed)

Competition Authority any changes in the control of newspapers of more than 30 per cent of the shares in the relevant newspaper. The Minister then has the power to prohibit such a take-over or merger between newspapers.

The current policy issues of concern to the newspaper industry are ones for which the industry has been awaiting a government response since 1996: changes in the libel laws in order to minimize the cost of court awards and the implementation of a self regulatory system for press complaints, the prevention of alleged below-cost selling by UK newspapers, and a lowering of the value-added tax of 12.5 per cent on newspapers. A change in these three issues seems unlikely as of 2002.

## The electronic media

The main applicable legislation for the electronic media is the Broadcasting Act 2001. The Act is a major piece of legislation and sets out the legal framework for broadcasting in Ireland – a framework that includes the operation of digital terrestrial television (DTT). It also makes major changes in Ireland's existing broadcasting legislation (von Trützschler, 2002), namely the Radio and Television Act 1988 (for private broadcasters) and the Broadcasting Authority Acts 1960–93 (for the public service broadcaster).

The Act envisages the setting up of a transmission company which is designated by the Minister with responsibility for broadcasting to transmit analogue and digital broadcast television services, including those of existing television broadcasters, in accordance with arrangements entered into with the multiplex company which is also established under the Act. As of mid-2002 no such companies have been set up and therefore no new digital television channels have started. All that has happened is that the three existing television channels are available in digital format on Sky Digital since April 2002.

Concerning public service broadcasting, the Act defines the public service character of public service broadcasting, establishes a new and separate broadcasting authority Teilifís na Gaeilge with the same public service remit as that of RTÉ but with no clear provision on the funding of this new authority, and increases the amount of money that RTÉ has to spend on programmes commissioned from the independent production sector. Concerning private broadcasting services the Act changes the name of the

IRTC to the Broadcasting Commission of Ireland (BCI) and increases the duties and functions of the BCI to include the drawing up of codes of broadcasting standards for all broadcasters in Ireland and to conduct research to assess the needs of the community for broadcasting services.

Thus the regulatory situation in mid-2002 is such that the BCI has been transformed into the main regulatory authority for the content of broadcasting and has been given some powers concerning the operation of public service broadcasting that were part of the duties of the RTÉ Authority. It is therefore not surprising that the BCI is endeavouring to become the sole regulator of the content of broadcasting in Ireland to include all the functions of the RTÉ authority in its remit. Were the latter to happen it would be a worrying scenario for supporters of public service broadcasting, as the BCI is a 'light touch' regulator in terms of ensuring the compliance of broadcasters with the existing regulations.

In 2002 the future role and financing of public service broadcasting in Ireland is in the hands of the Forum in Broadcasting which was set up by the government in March in response to mounting losses by RTÉ (of €14 million in 2000 and €71 million in 2001) and in order to examine the role of broadcasting in Ireland, especially that of RTÉ. The Forum has received submissions from the majority of actors in Ireland's media, all of which are available on the Web site http://forumonbroadcasting.ie, giving a comprehensive overview of the actors and interests in Irish broadcasting. The Forum will submit its final report to government at the end of August 2002.

## The Internet and related on-line media

A number of recent legal developments are of relevance to on-line services: The first concerns changes in telecommunication laws and regulations. Most of these concern the pricing and licensing of telecommunications services and they are detailed on the website of the ODTR.

Secondly, the Child Trafficking and Pornography Act 1998 is the result of the European Union's deliberations on illegal and harmful material on the Internet. The passing of this legislation was preceded by the publication of a very informative 1998 report by the Working Party on Illegal and Harmful Use of the Internet. The purpose of the Act is to strengthen the legislative protection of the sexual exploitation of children. It gives a detailed definition of child pornography and makes the possession of pornographic images a crime.

A third new legislative measure is the Electronic Commerce Act 2000. This law makes electronic signatures as legally binding as handwritten ones and may increase business over the Internet (e-business).

Finally the Copyright and Related Rights Act 2000 updates existing copyright law, incorporates EU directives and brings the law into the age of the Internet.

## STATISTICS

| | |
|---|---:|
| National population, 2002 | 3,900,000 |
| Number of households | 1,270,000 |
| Movie admissions, 2000 | 14,885,668 |
| Source: Carlton Advertising. | |
| Number of book titles published, 1999 | 995 |
| Source: Horvath Bastow Charleton. | |

**Print media**    Circulation of national and regional newspapers, July–December 2001

| | |
|---|---:|
| Sunday newspapers | |
| *Sunday Independent* | 311,260 |
| *Sunday World* | 305,019 |
| *Sunday Tribune* | 86,030 |
| *Sunday Business Post* | 50,949 |
| *Ireland on Sunday* | 53,265 |
| Dailies | |
| *Irish Independent* | 170,075 |
| *Irish Times* | 120,397 |
| *Star* | 104,944 |
| *Irish Examiner* | 65,274 |
| Evening newspapers | |
| *Evening Herald* | 103,838 |
| *Evening Echo* | 28,874 |
| Regional newspapers (three with highest circulation) | |
| *Kerryman* | 29,000 |
| *Connacht Tribune* | 30,216 |
| *Limerick Leader* | 26,659 |
| Irish-language newspaper (highest circulation) | |
| *Foinse* | 7,859 |

Sources: http://www.medialive.ie, http://www.abc.org.uk.

**Broadcast media**    Main cable television channels

| Service | Audience (%) | Audience share +/- 2000/1 |
|---|---|---|
| Public | | |
| RTÉ-1 | 28.2 | -2.0 |
| N-2 | 8.9 | -2.6 |
| TG-4 | 1.8 | +0.3 |
| Privately owned | | |
| TV-3 | 10.3 | +3.6 |

UK television channels

| | | |
|---|---|---|
| UTV | 15.4 | +1.3 |
| C-4 Channel 4 | 4.5 | +0.7 |
| Sky One (satellite) | 3.4 | -1.3 |
| Sky News (satellite) | 1.5 | 0 |
| BBC-1 | 10 | -0.5 |
| BBC-2 | 4.8 | -0.2 |
| All other stations | 9.2 | +0.7 |

Source: Loughrey (2001).

Audience share of national and local radio (weekdays, national figures %)

| | Listened yesterday | Audience share |
|---|---|---|
| Public | | |
| RTÉ Radio 1 | 30 | 27 |
| RTE-2 FM | 28 | 19 |
| RTÉ Lyric FM | 3 | n.a. |
| Private | 3 | |
| Today FM | 14 | 8 |
| Any local station[a] | 55 | |
| Home local stations | 50 | 38 |
| Other local station | 8 | 5 |

[a]More detailed figures can be found on two Web sites: www.irtc.ie and www.medialive.ie.
Source: JNLR/MRBI (2001).

| Percentage of households with: | |
|---|---|
| Pay-television (ODTR, 2002) | 20 |
| VCR | 78 |
| DVD player | 10 |

| | Percentage of population with: | |
|---|---|---|
| **Electronic media** | Digital television reception | 20 |
| | Internet access (ODTR, 2002) | 34 |
| | (Amarach, 2002) | 38 |
| | Mobile phone (ODTR, 2002) | 77 |

| | | |
|---|---|---|
| **Advertising spend, 2000 (%)** | Press | 42 |
| | Television | 19 |
| | Radio | 10 |
| | Cinema | 1 |
| | Exterior advertising | 7 |
| | Direct marketing | 21 |
| | Source: von Trützschler (2002) | |

| | |
|---|---|
| **Ownership** | Main media companies: Independent News and Media publishes around 80 per cent of all newspapers in Ireland.<br>The main provider of digital television is BSkyB. |

# REFERENCES

Amarach (2002) *Trendwatch Technology*, Quarter 2. Dublin: Amarach Consulting.

Boyle, K. and McGonagle, M. (1988) *Press Freedom and Libel*. Dublin: National Newspapers of Ireland.

JNLR (Joint National Listenership Research) (1996) Dublin: Market Research Bureau of Ireland.

Arts Council (2001) *Annual report 2000*. Dublin: Arts Council.

Cawley Nua (2002) *Ireland World Magazine Trends 2001/2002*. Dublin: PPAI.

CSO (Central Statistics Office) (2002) *Census 2002: Preliminary Report*. Dublin: Stationery Office.

Deiss, R. (2001) *Cinema Statistics*. Eurostat Statistics in Focus: Industry, Trade and Services. Theme 4–3.

Deiss, R. (2002) *Audiovisual Services*. Eurostat Statistics in Focus: Industry, Trade and Services. Theme 4–4.

*Foreign Policy Magazine* (2002) 'Globalization's last hurrah?' January/February.

Horvath Bastow Charleton (2000) *Orosh Book Publishing Survey 2000*. Dublin: Horvath Bastow Charleton.

IBEC (Irish Business and Employers 'Confederation)' (2001) *The Economic Impact of Film Production in Ireland 2001*. Dublin: IBEC.

JNLR (Joint National Listenership Research) (2001) Dublin: Market Research Bureau of Ireland.

Loughrey, P. (2001) *The Competitive TV Market-place in Ireland*. Dublin: RTÉ.

ODTR (2002) *The Irish Communications Market Quarterly Review*, June. Dublin: ODTR.

RTÉ (2002) *Annual accounts* 2001. Dublin: RTÉ.

Von Trützschler, W. (2002) 'Irland', in Hans-Bredow-Institut, *Internationales Medienhandbuch 2002–2003*. Hamburg: Nomos.

Comprehensivee information on Ireland's media can be found on the following Irish Web sites (links active in August 2002):

www.nni.ie/ (National Newspapers of Ireland)
www.ireland.com (*The Irish Times*)
www.unison.ie/ (Independent Newspapers portal)
www.rte.ie (Radio Telefis Eireann)
www.publishingireland.com/ (portal for the book publishing industry in Ireland)
www.icdg.come.to (Irish cable and digital guide)
www.iftn.ie (Irish Film and Television Network)
www.filmboard.ie (Irish Film Board)
www.ppa.ie (Periodical Publishers' Association of Ireland)
www.irlgov.ie (Irish government)
www.cso.ie (Central Statistics Office Ireland)
www.forumonbroadcasting.ie (Forum on the Future of Irish Broadcasting.)
www.artscouncil.ie/ (Arts Council of Ireland)
www.irtc.ie (Broadcasting Commission of Ireland)
www.odtr.ie (Irish telecoms regulator)
www.medialive.ie (site for Irish media data)
www.tg4.ie (Irish-language television channel)
www.infosocomm.ie (Information Society Commission)
radiowaves.fm (comprehensive listing of licensed/unlicensed radio)
www.broadcastireland.com/ (streaming video/audio)
www.irelandlive.com/ (streaming audio)
www.irelandlivetelevision.tv/ (streaming video)
www.asai.ie (Advertising Standards Authority of Ireland)

# 11: Italy

GIANPIETRO MAZZOLENI

## NATIONAL PROFILE

Italy, with over 56 million residents, is one of the most populous countries in Europe. Almost one-third of its population is concentrated in forty nine cities with more than 100,000 residents, four of which (Rome, Milan, Turin and Naples) are metropolitan areas and have more than 2 million residents.

The structure of the population is characterized by a high percentage of middle-aged and elderly and the natural population growth has been slowly but steadily declining since the 1970s, although this trend appears to have been reversed thanks to immigration. Various minorities can be found within the country's borders, to a total of less than half a million people: French in Valle d'Aosta, Germans in Trentino Alto Adige, Slovenians in Friuli Venezia Giulia and Albanians in Puglia. Such minorities are protected by the constitution and enjoy economic, administrative and educational privileges, such as special radio and television broadcasts and newspapers and schools in their own language.

Geographically, Italy is surrounded in the north by the Alps and in the centre and south by the Mediterranean Sea. The mountainous character of large areas (one-third of domestic territory) and the long distances (more than 1,700 km from Trieste to Palermo) have had an impact on the development policies of the mass media in the country.

Politically, until 1992 (the year of the big '*Tangentopoli*' scandal), Italy was characterized by the high instability of its coalition governments (about fifty in forty years), always led by the Christian Democratic Party (DC) – often in alliance with the Socialist Party (PSI). Such a long hegemony had major repercussions on the country's economic (banks, finance and industries) and cultural sectors – and therefore on the media. There also were some ill effects, such as the *lottizzazione*, that is, the partitioning of power among all parties, opposition included, over public resources and over state television (RAI), newspapers, press agencies and, to a certain extent, also over commercial television channels. Following the collapse of the old political establishment caused by judicial investigations into corrupt political parties and leaders, a new phase, called the 'Second Republic', started. A new electoral law in 1993 introduced a mixed system (75 per cent majoritarian, 25 per cent proportional), with the expectation that the reduction in the number of parties would make domestic politics more transparent and government coalitions more stable.

This phase of renewal brought on to the political scene players previously not related to the political system. The most relevant example was the electoral victory in 1994 of Silvio Berlusconi, a Milanese entrepreneur and powerful media baron. His election, cheered by most as the inauguration of a period of more concrete and effective political action, soon revealed that the widespread popular expectations of a 'revolution' in the Italian political arena were illusory. The centre-right Berlusconi government resigned after only seven months because of conflicts among the partners in the governing coalition. A period of political ambiguity followed, until 1996, when a centre-left coalition, led by Romano Prodi, won the general elections. While Berlusconi came under investigation for alleged corrupt practices in his financial affairs (including charges of corrupting judges), the centre-left government coalition did not prove to be a stable alliance: after Prodi's fall, three governments (D'Alema I, D'Alema II and Amato) managed to finish the five-year term of the legislation. In 2001 Berlusconi, his judicial troubles notwithstanding, won the elections by a large margin in both chambers.

Italy's economic system has been characterized for decades by extensive state intervention and interference in all sectors. In the 1990s, however, a series of government policies, most of which were prompted by EU directives, initiated gradual pull-out from all sectors by means of the privatization of public estates and shares. In the field of the media and electronic communications, the state no longer holds a radio and television monopoly; it was rescinded in the 1990 Broadcasting Act (law No. 223). The liberalization of telecommunications services has also been completely enacted. A significant exception is public broadcasting, which is still contracted by the state to the publicly-owned RAI, in spite of referendums and rulings of the Constitutional Court asking for partial privatization. The postal service has been separated from direct ministerial management and transformed into a public SpA.

# STRUCTURE AND OWNERSHIP

## The print media

### The newspaper press

With regard to Italian press history, it is possible to identify the following periods.

*The decade 1945–54.* This was a period of rebirth and normalization for the entire media system. The main dailies (*Il Corriere della Sera, La Stampa, La Nazione, Il Resto del Carlino, Il Messaggero, Il Mattino*) regained and consolidated their traditional leadership.

*The years from 1955 to 1979.* These were the years of a vast internal migration, of the so-called "economic boom" and of the race towards the affluent society. It was a stagnant period for the press with regard to ownership patterns and circulation figures. The two most notable exceptions were the launching of the progressive (and aggressive) news magazine *L'Espresso*, and of the daily *Il Giorno*, both breaking new ground in the news-making domains. The daily circulation remained stable around the 5 million copies that had been a constant pattern for decades.

*From 1970 to 1985.* The Italian media went through an "ordeal by fire", as witnessed by rapid changes in technology, lifestyles and political outlooks. The daily press especially showed signs of awakening and was in fact in the vanguard of the country's political and cultural evolution. The old dailies inaugurated a type of journalism more keen on monitoring social dynamics. Moreover, new and prestigious newspapers were established (*Il Giornale, La Repubblica*). However, this was also the period of financial difficulties for the whole press sector, which opened the way for powerful interest groups to seize control of the major newspapers. The Press Law of 1981 attempted to rescue the ailing press and introduced legal barriers to the concentration of ownership in the hands of industrial trusts. While the financial subsidies worked, helping the publishers to get over the crisis, the anti-trust measures were unable to uphold the cherished pluralism: a group of industrialists led by Fiat established the RCS (Rizzoli-*Corriere della Sera*) trust, a giant with assets in all publishing areas (books, periodicals, dailies).

During the *late 1980s* the press sector did well. The crisis experienced in the previous years had been fully overcome. The marriage between marketing and advertising and the news industry became very strong. The expansion of advertising investments, thanks mostly to the revolution in the television domain, drew a large amount of financial resources to the press as well, easing the process of transition to the new technologies and opening the way to sales promotion operations. By resorting to bingo, gadgets, prizes, folders, etc., in order to increase the entertainment value of the news, the daily press circulation reached a peak of 7 million copies in 1989. The sporting dailies and the small, local newspapers were the ones that registered the highest growth rates.

In 1989–90 another major press concentration took place: Slivio Berlusconi, the commercial television tycoon, and already owner of *Il Giornale*, a leading daily newspaper, bought out Mondadori, Italy's biggest publishing house.

*The 1990s.* The 'political revolution' which started in 1992 and led to the dismissal of the old political class, also had an impact in the press precincts. Italian journalism, traditionally subservient to the political parties, began to free itself from the political logics and to take sides with the prosecutors and with the country's public opinion, infuriated with the old parties and leaders. During the 1994 political campaign and the seven months in which Berlusconi was in power, the press distinguished itself through its criticism of the Premier's policies. However, with the new victory in 2001, a political realignment of the moderate press seems to be taking place. From the industrial and financial perspectives, the 1990–2000 decade appears to be fairly stagnant, registering crises for a number of dailies, a decrease in circulation rates, diminished profits of the biggest papers, and a less lively marketing aggressiveness.

*The current situation.* According to the Authority for Communications, in 2001 there were 138 daily newspapers published by 110 press enterprises. However, the most important dailies are owned and controlled by a few financial trusts (for details on circulation, refer to the statistics section). The publishing firm *l'Espresso* owns *La Repubblica*. The Hdp-RCS group, formerly RCS, owns the biggest-circulation national newspaper, the *Corriere della Sera*, and the most read sport daily, the *Gazzetta dello Sport*. The Fiat group owns *La Stampa*, and Monti-Riffeser (Poligrafici Editoriale) publishes *Il Resto del Carlino – Quotidiano Nazionale, La Nazione* and *Il Giorno*. Finally, the Caltagirone group owns *Il Messaggero* and *Il Mattino*.

In addition to these major groups there are other minor companies, which are very important in that they generate vital interactions among the media, politics and economics. For example, "Democrats of the Left" party (ex-Italian Communist Party) no longer retains the ownership of *L'Unità* (today owned by Dalai Editore), but it is able to influence its editorial line. The Industrialists' Association (Confindustria) publishes *Il Sole 24 Ore*, the most widely diffused financial newspaper.

Italy does not have a tabloid market, although there have been some attempts to create such a market (e.g. *L'occhio* in 1981 and *Telegiornale* in 1995), mainly owing to the fact that there exists a very well developed periodical popular press and also because of the tendency to consider daily newspapers as products for the elites.

Another important characteristic of the newspaper market is the significant presence of a regional and local press: 90 per cent of the 138 daily newspapers are regional and

local. Nevertheless, many local newspapers are also controlled by the main publishing trusts. For example *L'Espresso* group both publishes and has shares in sixteen daily local newspapers, with a combined circulation of over 500,000 copies.

In the past few years, the newspaper market has been characterized by ups and downs. Data by FIEG (Italian Association of Newspaper Publishers) and referring to a sample of sixty two highly representative newspapers in the national publishing scene show that since 2000 there has been growth in the average daily distribution (over 6 million copies). This is partly due to the fact that a substantial number of new sale points have been added to the existing ones, thanks to the experimental scheme provided for in law No. 108/99, in order to liberalize sales through new channels of distribution. However, the traditionally strongest point of sale remains the news-stand, accounting for 86 per cent of copies sold in 2000.

According to World Press Trends (WPT), compared with other European countries, Italy still scores very low in the classification of number of copies sold per 1,000 inhabitants: only 105 copies in 2000.

Between 2001 and 2002 the newspaper sector has been touched by a number of significant phenomena:

1 The rapid and successful diffusion of the free press, with a daily circulation of about 2 million copies.
2 The substantial increase in the price of daily newspapers in connection with the introduction of the euro (from €0.77 to €0.90).
3 The crisis of advertising expenditure, due to the more general uncertainties of the global economic markets. As 57 per cent of the newspapers' total income comes from advertising versus 43 per cent from sales, the decrease of 6.1 per cent in the advertising money has worried the publishers, who lobbied the government to cut down VAT and to take other measures favourable to the press industry.

### The periodical and magazine press
According to the 2002 report of the Authority for Communications, overall

there exist 4,134 magazines, most of which are 'out-market', that is, circulated through non-commercial channels (such as news-letters, advertising sheets, religious and local publications with non-regular periodicity). Only 434 magazines deserve the definition of commercial enterprises. However, no more than 150 have the lion's share of the domestic market.

The weekly press is made up of fifty one magazines (including supplements to daily newspapers), with a total circulation of almost 14.8 million copies. The most impor-tant are *Gente, Oggi, Panorama, Donna Moderna, Grazie, Famiglia Cristiana, TV Sorrisi e Canzoni, L'Espresso, Il Mondo, Avveni-menti, Chi* and *Visto*.

The monthly press scores the highest number of magazines: approximately 100, with a circulation of 12.3 million copies. The most successful ones are *L'Automobile, Airone, Quattroruote Capital, Focus, PC Professionale, Casa Viva, Silhouette Donna* and *Max*.

### Book publishing

According to the 2001 report by the Italian Publishers' Association (AIE) the book market, with its total revenue of approxi-mately €3,460 million, is far from being marginal compared with the other sectors of the publishing industry.

In 2000 52,288 books were published (including reprints), and the total sales were approximately 260 million copies. In the same year there existed 4,226 book publish-ing enterprises.

The sector shows a low level of inter-nationalization (few exchanges and strategies aimed at foreign markets) with the excep-tion of the major publishing groups (Mondadori, Rcs, De Agostini and Gruppo San Paolo) and university press publishers (Il Mulino, Bulzoni, FrancoAngeli, Carocci).

Bookshops are still the preferred sales channel, especially the independent ones, compared with those belonging to chains (Feltrinelli, Mondadori, San Paolo, Fnac, Demetra, Librerie del Centro, Messaggerie Libri). A new opening is the big department store or the supermarket.

Books with electronic support (e.g. a CD-ROM) enclosed are a popular novelty. Between 1997 and 1999 these products scored a growth of 16.3 per cent (66.1 per cent of it only CD-ROM), and in the year 2000 the gross income was about €330 million.

The number of book readers rose signifi-cantly from 1988 to 2000. In 2000 those who claimed to have read "at least one book" in the last twelve months were about 21 million (38.8 per cent of the entire popu-lation). The monthly expenditure per capita (according to ISTAT estimates) was €4.19, distinctly lower than the European average and mainly clustered around novels (59.4 per cent) and cheap and paperback books (57.4 per cent).

Since the 1990s the state of the book market has been marked by five structural factors:

1  A tendency for women to read more than men.
2  An average reading propensity higher among young people.
3  Increasing readership among the elderly, owing to the rising levels of education.
4  A territorial unbalance of readership between north and south: 46 per cent and 30 per cent of the population, respectively.
5  A higher number of readers in metro-politan areas (43.4 per cent) and in towns with more than 50,000 resi-dents, with respect to the rural areas.

## The electronic (audio-visual) media

### Television

Italy's television service came into being in January 1954 when the public company RAI officially inaugurated its first television channel, followed, in November 1961, by a second one and, in 1979, by a third (this lat-ter based on a network of regional centres of production and aimed to contrast the numerous local commercial broadcasting stations emerging in those years).

The first private television stations popped up in the years 1974–8, following the partial (and unintended) deregulation of (cable) television, while the first channels broadcasting at a national level were estab-lished between 1981 and 1982. Never-theless, in 1984, because of financial difficulties, two of those channels (Rete-4, owned by Mondadori and Italia 1, owned by Rusconi, both press publishers) were bought up by Silvio Berlusconi, who had already set up a successful commercial television network, Canale 5.

In general the television broadcasting scene is characterized by the following features:

1 The offering of terrestrial channels is quite rich and diversified: in most parts of the national territory it is possible to receive the thirteen national channels and between ten and fifteen local stations.
2 The duopolist structure of the television marketplace is quite solid: the two biggest groups (RAI and Mediaset) share 90 per cent of the audience and of the television advertising resources (RAI: 32 per cent; Mediaset 58 per cent).
3 Over 50 per cent of the total advertising expenditure destined to the media sector is attracted by television.

The scene is likely to change radically in 2006, when all national television networks will have to convert by law from the analogue system to a digital one, thus leaving the terrestrial analogue frequencies to the local stations. Nevertheless, there are some reservations about the actual feasibility of such a conversion programme before 2006, given the organizational and technological delays that the television system suffers from, not to mention the economic and financial uncertainties of the audio-visual market on the global scale.

*RAI.* The RAI group represents the public pole of broadcasting. The public service is contracted every three years by the state to RAI. It is a publicly owned company, governed by a board appointed by the Speakers of the Chamber of Deputies and of the Senate. It enjoys the financial privilege of getting its income from both the household licence fee (50 per cent) and advertising (30 per cent). Sales of programmes and other commercial activities account for the remaining 20 per cent. Beside broadcasting, through a number of subsidiary companies, RAI undertakes a series of related activities: publishing, records, advertising, programme sales. It employs about 10,500 people, and transmits 27,077 hours of nationwide and 6,822 hours of regional and minority television broadcasts and a total of 53,130 hours of radio programmes (2000).

RAI controls three television channels, five free satellite channels and seven pay-television channels, included in the D + package (Tele +).

Table 11.1 *Structure of RAI programmes, 2000*

| Programme type | % of total |
| --- | --- |
| News | 16.6 |
| Information and culture | 25.8 |
| Sports | 7.2 |
| Film | 10.3 |
| Television fiction | 15.3 |
| Children's | 5.8 |
| Entertainment | 9.1 |
| Other | 9.9 |
| Total | 100.0 |
| (Total hours) | (24,655) |

Source: Annuario RAI 2001.

The three RAI channels (with 46 per cent share of the total audience in June 2002) are: (1) Raiuno, the most popular and 'familiar' network with a typically rich offering of news, entertainment and fiction, (2) Raidue, a channel which attempts to gain the loyalty especially of the young audiences with ad hoc transmissions, (3) Raitre, more keen to identify with the original 'public service' mission of RAI, by offering culture, in-depth information, regional programmes, etc. The contents of the public company's transmissions have the structure shown in Table 11.1

*Mediaset.* The commercial broadcasting group is quoted on Milan's stock exchange but 48.3% of its shares are firmly controlled by Fininvest, Berlusconi's personal financial holding. Through the same holding the Premier-media baron controls 50.3 per cent of shares of the publishing house Mondadori, 99.9 per cent of football team AC Milan, 36.2 per cent of Mediolanum Bank and 100 per cent of Medusa film distribution. The 2000 revenue of Mediaset was €36 billion (all figures from *The Economist*, 28 April 2001).

Today the Mediaset group, with its three channels (Italia 1, Rete 4 and Canale 5, with 41.6 per cent audience share in June 2002) and its satellite channels and other assets in the field is second only to the public company *RAI*.

The 'generalist' channels controlled by the Berlusconi's trust, are: Canale 5, that repeats the main features of its public competitor Raiuno by offering a wide programme range of information, entertainment and fiction. Rete 4 has an audience where the elderly and housewives are overrepresented. Finally, Italia 1 is the 'young' channel, addressed to children, teenagers and youngsters.

Table 11.2  *Structure of Mediaset programmes, 2000*

| Programme type | % of total |
| --- | --- |
| News | 11.6 |
| Information and culture | 6.0 |
| Sports | 2.5 |
| Film | 18.9 |
| Television fiction | 31.7 |
| Children's | 6.2 |
| Entertainment | 18.3 |
| Other | 4.8 |
| Total | 100.0 |
| Total (hours) | 21,808 |

Source: Annuario RAI (2001).

The Mediaset channels aired a total of 21,808 hours of programmes in 2000.

Table 11.2 shows the range of the whole programme provision by the three commercial channels.

Compared with the variety of the programming of the public channels, the offering of the commercial ones appears quite inclined towards entertainment, and commercial television is perceived as such by the viewers. In January 1991, however, the three commercial channels inaugurated a regular daily news service, thus presenting themselves as well as key information outlets, in competition with the previous news monopoly of public television.

*The third pole: La7.* The birth in 2001 of the third television pole in a media market place almost completely dominated by the 'duopoly' of RAI and Mediaset was very troubled and controversial. In the last few years, the film producer Cecchi Gori, owner of the Italian channels of TeleMonteCarlo (TMC and TMC-2), because of serious financial problems, sold TMC-2 to the MTV group and, in January 2001, TMC to Seat– Yellow Pages (controlled by Telecom Italia). Seat renamed the old TMC network La7 and tried to set up a channel that voiced the interests of all those – cultural, political and industrial – who did not, or would not, identify with the two opposed giants. However, whilst La7 was still being launched, the Pirelli industrial group, more interested in telecommunications than in the television sector, bought up Telecom Italia. The original industrial plans (and ambitions) were eventually downsized and fewer financial resources were pumped into the La7 venture by the new bosses of Telecom Italia. Consequently the 'third pole' is struggling for

survival, unable to seize more than 3.9 per cent audience share in June 2002.

Beside the three major poles there exist a number of other commercial networks which are actually syndications or associations of local stations that maintain a fairly large autonomy in programme schedules, advertising collection and financial structure. The total number of small and medium-size independent, private, local television stations is about 1,000.

*Digital television.* Because of the massive television programme supply by the public and commercial broadcasters, Italian viewers for about two decades (the 1980s and 1990s) did not show much interest in other channels of television content. The situation started to change fairly rapidly in the late 1990s and early 2000s.

At present, digital television can be viewed only via satellite. Two companies provide pay-television services via satellite: Stream (controlled 50 per cent by Telecom Italia and 50 per cent by Murdoch's News Corp) with 800,000 subscribers in 2000 (and losses of €390 million); Tele + (98 per cent controlled by the French Canal Plus – Vivendi group and 2 per cent by RAI) with 1,800,000 subscribers (and losses of €215 million).

Both Stream and Tele + have suffered a serious financial setback, much in line with similar crises of pay-television in other countries.

In April 2001 the two companies merged, in an attempt to reduce the enormous losses. Nevertheless, in June 2002, following the notorious events regarding Vivendi, the Australian-American tycoon Rupert Murdoch made a bid to buy 100 per cent of Tele +. After receiving the European Union's green light for the acquisition he established a brand new group named Sky Italia, born out of Tele + and Stream. Telecom Italia still has a 19.9 per cent share in the new group. Italy is one of the few countries in the European Union in which a single company has a monopoly of the entire pay-television market.

A picture of the situation that has developed in recent times, before the crisis, has been given by the Authority for Communications in its 2002 report:

1  Pay-television has seized 13 per cent of the total resources of the television sector.
2  It has also scored a significant increase in the audience, mirrored in

a net loss of terrestrial television viewers of 380,000 in early 2001.
3 Households with satellite receivers range between 15 and 20 per cent.
4 Piracy reached 4 million illegal access cards.
5 There has been a proliferation of satellite channels, about 220 of them using the platform of either Stream or of Tele +.
6 Market research shows that the pay-television audience is 9.5 million to 10.5 million viewers.

### Radio

Italian radio broadcasting service was created in 1924, but it acquired its modern structure only in 1950, when the three national RAI channels were set up.

As happened in the television sector, the 1970s were characterized by unplanned deregulation, which tolerated the emergence of an enormous number of private, mostly local, stations (about 2,500), which attracted an increasingly high number of listeners, especially among the young.

At present the structure of the radio sector is similar to that of television. The public broadcasting company RAI controls three national AM/FM channels (Radio 1, Radio 2 and Radio 3). On the whole, public service radio has a stable and dominant market share of about 50 per cent, whilst the fourteen major commercial networks account for the other half of total listening.

Radio 1, with 13,159,000 listeners per week (June 2002), is the main national radio. It is the most 'generalist' of all channels, offering a wide programme range of news, sport and culture. Radio 2 (average listening 9,425,000) offers mainly entertainment and pop music and is addressed to a young audience. Radio 3 (4,379,000) broadcasts cultural updates, debates and mainly serious music.

Worth mentioning among the private networks are: Radio Montecarlo, launched as a foreign station in 1966, it broadcasts in Italian, and accounts for 6,091,000 listeners a week; Radio One-O-One, established in Milan in 1975 with 4,921,000 listeners; Radio Deejay, established in Milan in 1982 and by far the most listened-to radio network (12,451,000); RDS (Radio Dimensione Suono) (11,618,000), Radio Italia Network (10,383,000) and RTL (10,019,000); Radio 24

(3,092,000), founded by Confindustria (the employers' association), the first network in Italy to offer news twenty four hours a day, dedicating most of its air time to financial and economic issues.

### Film and video

According to the last report by SIAE (the company that administers royalties), 2001 was a fairly positive year for Italian cinema. Over 100 films were produced; there was more investment, especially in European productions, through co-productions, which have partly replaced American imports, the number of which remains high.

In 2001 188 Italian films were released, twelve more than the previous year.

Overall, Italian cinema scored a positive increase both for audience and for profits. In fact, in 2001, 15 million tickets were sold for Italian films or co-productions, as against 13 million sold in 2000.

According to a 1999/2000 report by the research institute Cinetel, concerning the distribution of movie theatres, fifty eight new screens have been inaugurated. Such growth is to be attributed to the increase of multiplex facilities, which in 2001 amounted to forty five structures. Multiplex cinemas, especially those owned by the major international corporations (Warner Village and UCI), attract more than 25 million spectators, that is, 31.5 per cent of the total of cinema viewers.

The Italian cinema industry has always been an object of state attention. In 1958 the government established the Ente Autonomo di Gestione per il Cinema (National Board for Cinema). The main task of the Board was to co-ordinate public investment in the field and to promote the diffusion of national productions both domestically and internationally. In 1993 the Board was converted into Ente Cinema and in 1998 it became Cinecittà Holding. The latter owns Istituto Luce (an organization that deals with the production and distribution of films and documentaries) and is a shareholder in Cinecittà Studios (allegedly the only cinematographic organization in Europe that holds all the technical and professional instruments of film production, editing and special effects features).

According to the data collected by Cinecittà Holding, there are in Italy 255 producers, the most important of which is, per volume of films produced, *Medusa Film* (in 2001–2 market leader with 21 per cent of the total), owned by the Premier, Silvio

Berlusconi. The largest group is the Cecchi Gori group, followed by RAI Cinema. As for distribution, along with the Italian subsidiary companies of the big international distributors (Warner Bros, Buena Vista, UIP), Medusa, Cecchi Gori and Rai & Studio Canal Distribution occupy leading positions.

With regard to home video, according to the 2001 report by Univideo (National Union of Audio-visual Publishing), since 1999 the market has registered an increase. As to video rentals, the report claims that in 2001 1.8 million VHS videos were rented (almost 100,000 less than the preceding year). Moreover, 200,000 DVDs were rented in 2001 (but the data cannot be compared with any previous finding). Among the most popular VHS titles, action films and thrillers represent almost half the market, followed by comedies.

## The Internet and related on-line media

In Italy, as in many other countries, data concerning the exact number of Internet users are less than reliable, owing to the customary tendency to overestimate this phenomenon. Nevertheless, according to a study in 2001 by the research institute Eurisko, it seems appropriate to believe that between 9 million and 11 million people use the Internet every day. The 2002 report of the Authority for Communications hypothesizes about 18 million. Although the Internet is still not a means of communication accessible to everyone, it is on the other hand true that its popularity has steadily grown since it first arrived in the country.

Thanks to Tiscali's "free Internet access" formula in 1999, the number of Internet users tripled and quadrupled in one year. Nevertheless, this growth does not correspond to an effective increase of use of the Net. Eurisko confirms this tendency: 74 per cent of those who own a computer have Internet access, but only 45 per cent use it.

Italy suffers from serious delays in financial investments, in public and private policies, and in technologies, delays that have hampered wider diffusion of the Internet and of the several Web services. Recent governments have introduced financial incentives for those companies investing in this sector and established an Agency for the Informatization of Public Administration (AIPA).

Among the causes of the limited diffusion among the wider population is the age factor (those over fifty five show scant propensity to use the Net) and the 'digital divide' that excludes large sections of lower and less educated classes.

# POLITICS, POLICY, LAW AND REGULATION

## The press

Several laws and codes were enacted in the years following the end of the Second World War relating to information conveyed by the print media.

Of course, the constitution guarantees "freedom of expression" to all citizens (article 21), but the legislation foresees a series of conditions (and restrictions) to be met in order to exercise that freedom. Press Law No. 47 of 1948 is the first legislative Act regulating this complex matter. It has undergone obvious and continuous updating. The law provides basic norms dealing with the journalists' profession: it regulates the right to secrecy, safeguards moral standards, the right to reply, defamation and libel, the penal responsibility of editors and reporters, and the like.

The Press Law of 1981 (with updates in 1984 and 1987) contains more detailed legislation aimed at regulating the information industry. It introduced a series of subsidies that helped Italy's press out of financial and structural crisis. Besides the subsidies the law represented a true turning point both in policy and in the development of the entire sector. The most significant innovations it inaugurated referred to:

1 Transparency in the ownership of publishing companies (ownership must be made public and owners may not be active outside the publishing field).
2 The institution of the Guarantor (a sort of high authority of publishing with several enforcing powers and supervising tasks).
3 The National Press Register (all daily newspapers, periodicals, press agencies and *advertising* selling *companies* to the press must register in order to operate).

4  Transfers of shares (should be communicated to the Guarantor). Concentration among the daily press (the acquisition of newspapers leading to a dominant position in the market is regulated by a series of detailed norms).
5  The establishment of co-operatives of journalists (in case of cessation of publication of a newspaper by the former owner).
6  The cover price of newspapers (formerly fixed by government, liberalized in January 1988).

Between the end of 1999 and the beginning of 2001 significant legislation was passed, capable of modifying in the medium term the existing equilibrium in the press market. Law No. 108/1999, aimed to stimulate the ailing sales of press products, changed the traditionally rigid newspaper distribution system, by allowing supermarkets, tobacconists, petrol stations, cafés and book shops to sell newspapers and periodicals.

An anti-piracy law (No. 248/2000) carrying "new norms for the protection of copyright" introduced innovative regulations regarding reproductions of books, music and video.

## The electronic media

After more than twenty years of dominance of the public service, contracted through a charter to RAI, but actually under the strict control of government, in 1975 parliament passed a reform law (No. 103/1975) that, besides placing RAI under the control of parliament, permitted a very limited private exercise in cable television. That was the proverbial hole in the dam: the first private enterprises appealed to the Constitutional Court for broader acknowledgement of the 'right to publish', also via broadcasting. The court ruled in 1976 that private enterprises could broadcast – but only in limited geographical areas, as the national frequencies were assigned to the public service. With that prononucement started the wild 'deregulation' of the late 1970s and of the 1980s that triggered an explosion of commercial broadcasting. The failure of governments and parties to work out for more than a decade pro-active, comprehensive regulations

allowed those entrepreneurs who engaged in the private radio and television businesses to find their way wide open, with no regulatory limits whatsoever. It was in fact called the 'broadcasting Wild West' where the strongest could wipe out all the (financially and politically) weakest competitors. The Berlusconi empire took enormous advantage of this 'a-regulation'.

As noted, the Italian tycoon succeeded in controlling the three major commercial television channels, in direct competition with the three channels of RAI. The 'duopoly' guaranteed a sort of distorted 'balance' of the broadcasting system but obstructed any plurality.

*The Mammì Law (No. 223/1990).* After long disputes about a general reform of the electronic media system, finally the political forces found a compromise. It was the Broadcasting Act of 1990 (the so called Mammì Law, from the name of the Minister of Communications at the time), which was soon nicknamed the 'photocopy law' and was blamed for legitimizing the existing duopoly of RAI-Fininvest. However, it brought some fixed points into the legislation, especially the prohibition of media cross-ownership:

1  Broadcasting is no longer a state monopoly and private enterprises can apply for a licence to run stations.
2  Private companies may broadcast live, nationwide, by means of technical link-ups.
3  The Guarantor of publishing is given authority also over broadcasting.
4  Programmes may have advertisement breaks, with a number of limitations, according to EU directive No. 89/552.
5  Advertising should not exceed 15 per cent of the daily transmission time and an hourly quota of 18 per cent.
6  Content and programme schedules may not be influenced by sponsors.
7  A National Register of Broadcasting Organizations was established.
8  Cross-ownership of media must meet the following conditions:

(a)  Anyone controlling over 16 per cent of total daily newspaper circulation may not hold any licence to run a national television network.

(b) Anyone controlling 8–16 per cent of the total daily circulation may hold only one licence.

(c) Anyone controlling less than 8 per cent of total daily circulation may hold two licences.

(d) Anyone with no shares in the daily newspaper publishing companies may hold up to three licences.

9 Private licensees broadcasting nationwide are obliged to transmit news bulletins.

10 Forty per cent of annual transmission time has to be devoted to programmes produced in Europe in the first three years following the granting of the licence, 51 per cent in following years; no less than 50 per cent of these have to be of Italian production.

11 The household licence fee is maintained in favour of the public broadcasting company (RAI).

12 A Board of Viewers was appointed as a consultative body to the Guarantor.

The Broadcasting Act of 1990 continued to be a target of criticism, especially from the left, which never accepted that Berlusconi could control so large a part of the broadcast media. After a series of attempts by the opposition to introduce new, more binding norms into legislation, in 1994 the Constitutional Court ruled that one of the anti-trust measures of the Mammì Law (article 15, para. 4) was unconstitutional because it allowed a single enterprise to own three private networks. However, in 1994 Silvio Berlusconi became Prime Minister and his political victory caused an even more exasperated dispute on the need to adopt anti-trust measures. Also the three referendums promoted in spring 1995 by the opposition to bypass the parliamentary stalemate and to bring in some drastic anti-concentration measures missed the target. In fact, the majority of citizens voted against the proposed prohibition on ownership of more than one television channel (referendum No. 1), against the ban on commercial breaks in broadcast movies (referendum No. 2) and in favour of partial privatization of RAI (referendum No. 3).

After the fall of the first Berlusconi Cabinet, the succeeding governments of the centre left passed a series of more restrictive Bills.

The most significant piece of legislation was Law No. 249/1997 (the so called Maccanico Law after the name of the Minister of Communications of the Olive Tree governing coalition).

*The Maccanico Law (No. 249/1997)* attempted to harmonize Italian media policies with the EU guidelines with regard to access, plurality and fair competition. It introduced new anti-concentration thresholds: no one can control more than 30 per cent of total television market resources or more than 20 per cent of total communication resources (i.e. press, radio and television).

It promoted a master plan of frequencies, regulated the liberalization of telecommunications and established the new Authority for Communications.

Before the Maccanico Law, the Guarantor established in 1981 (for publishing) and in 1990 (for broadcasting), and the parliamentary board for RAI, introduced by the 1975 Reform Bill, were the two main control bodies. The Guarantor was a single-person authority, with some control but little power of enforcement. The parliamentary board is still a 'political' authority, made up of dozens of MPs of all parties, which has supervisory powers only over the activity of the public service company, RAI.

The 1997 law abolished the Guarantor and introduced the above-mentioned Authority for Communications, a collegial body with a president (appointed by the government), a council of seven members (elected by parliament) and two committees (one for networks and infrastructures, one for services and products).

This Authority, whose control extends over the press, the broadcast media and the telecommunications sector, among other things:

1 Keeps watch over the enforcement of anti-trust requirements.

2 Polices the relations between the networks' managers and the service providers (in order to avoid discrimination in access).

3 Sets the licence and transmission fees.

4 Prescribes the technical standards for the transmission systems.

Most rules of the Mammì Law and of the Maccanico Law are still enforced today. However, with the return of Berlusconi to power the political climate over the issue of a balanced and truly democratic media system has also returned to being heated and stormy.

The Berlusconi government plans to make several changes in the existing legislation, to partly privatize RAI and to loosen certain limits on media cross-ownership. The opposition charges Berlusconi with attempting to dominate the entire media sector, being himself a media tycoon with personal (and now also political) interests to defend. The recently passed Bill on 'conflicts of interest', according to the opposition, is incapable of guaranteeing any real separation of the interests of the Prime Minister.

In July 2002 a worried President of the Republic solemnly summoned parliament to develop new comprehensive legislation to safeguard plurality against any dominant position in media ownership, to enhance the centrality of the public service, to extend the 'fair treatment' (*par condicio*) regulation to all (i.e. public and commercial) broadcast media.

Following the President's plea, in October 2002 the government made public its reform plan. The draft plan introduces new anti-concentration thresholds (20 per cent of total communication resources) but, unlike the Maccanico Law of 1997, draws no distinction between media and abolishes the existing cross-ownership limits. As far as public broadcasting is concerned, the Bill rules that in 2004 the publicly owned RAI will be partially privatized and its ownership structure will take the form of a 'public company', controlled by the 'golden share' of the Economics Ministry.

## The Internet and related on-line media

During the last few years the technological evolution of the new media has opened the question of whether and to what extent the new means of communication should be the target of regulation, much like the older media. However, the peculiar nature especially of the Internet media makes it hard for the legislatures of individual countries to address effectively the (mostly unprecedented) problems it raises. Italy is no exception.

Some regulations worked out in the years before the explosion of the Internet phenomenon affect security aspects and areas of individual rights, such as privacy (a right protected by law No. 675/1996). Law No. 518/1992, harmonized to directive 91/250/EEC, concerns the legal protection of software and of the informatics systems. In 1999 such a protection measure was extended to data banks (law No.169). Law No. 547/1993 modified and redefined the penal procedures with regard to informatics crimes.

## STATISTICS

| | |
|---|---|
| National population | 56,300,000 |
| Number of households | 21,500,000 |
| Cinema admissions (source: Mediasalles 2001) | 100,000,000 |
| Books published, 2000 (titles) (source: Associazione Italiana Editori) | 52,288 |

**Print media** — Circulation of main daily newspapers, average figures April 2001–March 2002 (source: Prima comunicazione)

| | Print run | Circulation |
|---|---|---|
| *Avvenire* | 140,521 | 93,820 |
| *Il Corriere della Sera* | 886,512 | 708,699 |
| *La Gazzetta dello Sport* | 563,670 | 411,369 |
| *Il Giornale* | 331,821 | 227,314 |
| *Il Giorno* | 123,427 | 81,754 |
| *Il Manifesto* | 95,835 | 37,742 |
| *Il Mattino* | 141,302 | 102,926 |
| *Il Messaggero* | 383,797 | 285,096 |

| La Nazione | 184,884 | 147,880 |
| La Repubblica | 809,259 | 646,005 |
| Il Secolo XIX | 148,214 | 119,538 |
| Il Sole24ore | 513,596 | 416,179 |
| La Stampa | 554,821 | 413,030 |
| L'Unità | 139,077 | 72,540 |

**Broadcast media**

Audience share of main terrestrial television channels, July 2002 (%)

| | |
|---|---|
| RAI (public) | |
| Raiuno | 21.1 |
| Raidue | 13.8 |
| Raitre | 11.1 |
| Mediaset (private) | |
| Canale 5 | 22.4 |
| Rete 4 | 7.8 |
| Italia 1 | 11.5 |
| La 7 (private) | 3.9 |

Source: *Auditel.*

Audience share of main radio channels, daily average, April/June 2002

| | |
|---|---|
| Total radio audience | 35,700,000 |
| RAI (public) | |
| Radiouno | 8,000,000 |
| Radiodue | 5,400,000 |
| Radiotre | 900,000 |
| Private | |
| Radio 101 | 1,000,000 |
| RMC Radio Montecarlo | 2,200,000 |
| Radio Capital | 1,700,000 |
| Radio Deejay | 5,300,000 |
| Radio Italia Network | 2,200,000 |
| Radio Maria | 1,100,000 |
| Radio Radicale | 500,000 |
| Radio 105 | 3,400,000 |
| RDS Radio Dimensione Suono | 4,200,000 |
| Radio Italia | 3,900,000 |
| RTL | 4,400,000 |
| Radio 24 Il Sole24Ore | 1,400,000 |
| Radio Latte e Miele | 2,100,000 |

Source: Prima communicazione.

| | |
|---|---|
| Percentage of households reached by: satellite pay-television | 14.6 |

Source: Federcomin, 2001.

Percentage of households with:

| | |
|---|---|
| Video-cassette recorder | 79.0 |
| DVD | 8.8 |
| DVD-ROM | 8.0 |
| Satellite receiver | 16.5 |

Source: Federcomin rapporto e-family 2002, referring to 2001.

| Electronic media | Percentage of households with: Digital television reception Internet access (source: Federcomin, 2001) | Data not available 25.5 |
|---|---|---|
| | Mobile phone contracts | (79.4 % of population) 45,500,000 |
| | Source: Federcomin rapporto e-family 2002, referring to 2001. | |

| Advertising spend | Division of advertising expenditure, April 2002 (%) Total expenditure: ¤2,652,884 | |
|---|---|---|
| | Television | 58.2 |
| | Daily newspapers | 21.9 |
| | Magazines | 13.4 |
| | Radio | 3.6 |
| | Posters | 1.9 |
| | Cinema | 1.0 |
| | Source: Nielsen//NetRatings. | |

## USEFUL SOURCES

### Books

Castronovo, V. and Tranfaglia, N., eds (1994) *La stampa italiana nell'età della TV 1975–1994.* Rome and Bari: Laterza.

Menduni, E. (2001) *Il mondo della radio.* Bologna: Il Mulino.

Menuni, E. (2001) *La televisione.* Bologna: Il Mulino.

### Reports

Quinto rapporto IEM, *Quinto rapporto sull' Industria della Comunicazione in Italia: l'era Internet* (2001) www.fondazionerosselli.it/IEM/iem_rapporti.htm

Associazione italiana editori (AIE): www.aie.it

Federcomin: www.federcomin.it

Audience research: www.audipress.it, www.audiradio.it, www.auditel.it, www.audinetsinottica.it

### Policy bodies

Ministry of Communications: www.comunicazioni.it

Authority for Communications: www.agcom.it

Authority for Competition (Antitrust): www.agcm.it

### Specialist magazines

*Prima comunicazione* (monthly): www.italian.it/primacomunicazione/

*Media 2000* (monthly): web.tiscali.it/media2000/

Online magazine: www.ediland.it

### Media

RAI: www.rai.it

Mediaset: www.rti.it

La 7: www.la7.it

Stream: www.stream.it

Tele+: www.telepiu.it

L'Espresso: www.espresson line.it

Caltagirone: www.caltagironeeditore.it

RCS-Corriere della Sera: www.rcs.it

Monti-Riffeser: www.monrif.net/eng/home.html

Mondadori Publishing Group: www.mondadori.it

Telecom Italia: www.telecomitalia.it

## ACKNOWLEDGEMENT

The author wishes to thank Valentina Cardo, Andrea Molle and Alessio Pruzzo for their collaboration in composing this chapter.

# 12: Luxembourg

MARIO HIRSCH

## NATIONAL PROFILE

Although tiny (approximately 440,000 inhabitants) the Grand Duchy of Luxembourg is characterized by an extraordinary variety of media, both audio-visual and press. Six dailies and eight weekly magazines are published in the country alongside six radio programmes with a national coverage and four television channels targeted at the national audience.

The diversity of the media landscape has to do with the fact that most of the press is intimately linked with political parties. The press is perceived as an expression of political plurality and in order to guarantee its permanence, it benefits from a very generous system of direct and indirect public subsidies. The remarkable richness as far as the press is concerned is also related to the multicultural dimensions of Luxembourg's society, which has, with a share of 37 per cent of foreign residents among its population (primarily Portuguese nationals, followed by Italians and Spaniards) plus more than 100,000 commuters from the neighbouring regions of France, Belgium and Germany the highest proportion of foreigners in the European Union. Some 67 per cent of the active population is made up of foreigners, either immigrants or commuters. This is reflected in the multilingual approach of the media. Typically, a Luxembourg newspaper carries stories written in any of the three official languages of the country (Lëtzebuergesch, French, German). As of late, some monolingual publications (French, Portuguese) have appeared. Generally speaking the media take into account the fact that for obvious practical reasons the predominant language of communication has become French, whereas in the past German used to prevail in the press and the local dialect dominated the audio-visual media.

In the audio-visual field the multiplication of offerings came only recently. Up to 1991 the country lived under a *de facto* monopoly enjoyed by CLT/RTL, the Luxembourg-based pioneer in commercial radio and television programmes. The liberalization of the sector, introduced by a 1991 law, took into consideration also the need to address the expectations of Luxembourg's multicultural society and to enrich the programming on offer.

Since 2000 two dominant press groups have emerged (Groupe Saint-Paul and Editpress). Together with CLT/RTL, which still leads the field in the audio-visual sector despite the 1991 liberalization, they have taken the lead, thanks to their strong position in the field of print media. Thanks to mergers and acquisitions they call the shots in most of the relevant sectors, including new media developments. The Groupe Saint-Paul and CLT/RTL have been leaders in their respective fields since the 1930s. They control more than two-thirds of the readership respectively of the audience of all the media. As far as audio-visual media are concerned, a qualification is, however, necessary. Foreign programmes enjoy a high degree of popularity in Luxembourg because for quite some time local programmes were rudimentary and limited to only a few hours a day.

## STRUCTURE AND OWNERSHIP

### The Print media

#### The newspaper press
Six dailies are published. The offering was enlarged in autumn 2001 when two new

titles, *La Voix* and *Le Quotidien*, appeared, written entirely in French and aimed at the resident foreign community. All six dailies offer comprehensive coverage of international, national, local and sports events. They are typically written in the three official languages of the country, with the exception of the two newcomers. Regional newspapers, which used to exist up to the Second World War, have disappeared or been integrated into one or other national paper. By far the largest publication is the *Luxemburger Wort* with a daily circulation of 80,000 copies, almost three times as much as all the other five titles together. The *Tageblatt* has a daily circulation of 22,000, followed by the two newcomers *La Voix* and *Le Quotidien* (estimated circulation of 4,000 each), the *Lëtzebuerger Journal* (3,000) and the *Zeitung vum Lëtzebuerger Vollek* (1,000).

The six dailies belong to four publishing houses which each have their own printing press. The Groupe Saint-Paul, which belongs to the Catholic Archbishop of Luxembourg and has close links with the dominant political party, the Christian Social Party (CSV), publishes both the *Luxemburger Wort* and *La Voix*. It holds a 16 per cent share in the Belgian press group Media@bel which controls the second largest Walloon press group. Editpress, with close links to the Socialist Party (LSAP) and the socialist trade union movement, publishes *Tageblatt* and *Le Quotidien* (the later is jointly owned by Editpress and the French regional press group Le Républicain Lorrain, which used to produce a local Luxembourg edition prior to the advent of *Le Quotidien*). Editpress has a cross-ownership agreement with the French newspaper group Le Monde of 3 per cent. The two smaller papers *Journal* and *Zeitung* are owned respectively by the Liberal Party (DP) and the Communist Party (KPL).

Groupe Saint-Paul is the only profitable publishing group, thanks to the impressive circulation of the *Wort*, which harvests about 80 per cent of the advertising revenue devoted to dailies, followed by the *Tageblatt* with a share of only 13 per cent. The group had a turnover of some €80 million in 2000, including its printing activities. Editpress had a turnover of €37 million. Apart from the *Wort*, all the other publications depend for survival to a large extent on the generous state press aid, which amounts in its various components to more than €10 million. One-third of the aid is evenly distributed among the papers that meet the requirements. (The most important is that they have to employ at least five full-time journalists.) Two-thirds are calculated in relation to the number of pages. Circulation does not enter into consideration when the aid is calculated. In some cases public subsidies represent more than 50 per cent of revenue. For the smaller papers they exceed advertising revenue. In the year 2000 advertising for all the media amounted to €80,300,000. Of this €60 million went to the daily press.

### The periodical and magazine press

The two largest press groups each publish their own weekly magazines. They are family oriented and they carry an extensive coverage of television and radio programmes. *Télécran* (Groupe Saint-Paul) sells about 38,000 copies a week, *Revue* (until 2000, when Editpress bought it, it was produced by an independent publisher) some 25,000 copies. Editpress also publishes a general-interest weekly in French, *Le Jeudi*, with a circulation of 6,500. The influential weekly *d'Lëtzebuerger Land* (some 7,000 copies sold) plays an important role as an opinion former, the more so in that it is the only truly independent Luxembourg publication. *Woxx*, another weekly with an emphasis on politics (circulation around 3,000) has close links with the Green Party (déi Lénk) and the associative movement. The weekly *Luxembourg News* (circulation around 4,500), together with a monthly publication, *Luxembourg Business* (circulation approximately 3,000) is produced by a publisher with close links to the business community. Both publications are in English. Each of the two dominant press groups also publishes a weekly in Portuguese. *Contacto* (Groupe Saint-Paul) leads the field with a circulation of 8,000. *Correio* (Editpress) is estimated at 6,000 copies per week. The satirical weekly *Den Neie Feierkrop* is without any doubt the most widely read publication in the country. It sells some 11,000 copies a week and is published by a co-operative. Among the monthly publications *Agéfi Luxembourg* (circulation 7,000), in French, primarily covers the financial world. It belongs to the Agéfi group, specializing in financial and economic news in France and in Belgium. *Paperjam* is a monthly publication dealing primarily with business and economic issues. It is published by a young entrepreneur, Mike Koedinger (MKé) and its circulation is around 7,000. *Forum*, another monthly (circulation 1,500), published by a group of intellectuals, has a good reputation for its in-depth analysis of politics, social issues and cultural matters.

### Book publishing

On average some 400 books are published each year. Book publishing is heavily subsidized by the Ministry of Culture in order to compensate for the smallness of the market. The publishing industry is largely in the hands of the two dominant press groups. Editions Saint-Paul is the publishing arm of Groupe Saint-Paul. In 2002 Editpress, which has its own publishing house (Editions le Phare), bought the most important independent publishing house, Editions Phi. Some independent publishers like Editions Promoculture, Editions Binsfeld and Editions Schortgen exist.

## The electronic (audio-visual) media

### Television

The liberalization of television came only recently when, in autumn 2001, the government granted licences to four programmes. Up to then, television for local audiences was synonymous with RTL, more precisely its local brand, RTL Télé Lëtzebuerg. Up to autumn 2001 RTL offered a minimal local television service (about one hour per day). In view of the competition it stepped up its offering, proposing eight hours per day, with many repeats and MTV-type programming. RTL Télé Lëtzebuerg claims a cumulated average audience share of 33 per cent, which remains impressive considering the large number of channels on offer in this heavily cabled country. Up to fifty programmes are available to cabled audiences. German programmes are traditionally very popular with Luxembourgers. RTL Television comes first, with 14 per cent, followed by ARD (11 per cent), Pro-7 and ZDF (10 per cent), RTL-2 and Sat-1 (7 per cent). The diaspora programmes of RTP, RAI and RTE are also very popular with the immigrant communities. They are all carried on cable networks and they enjoy an audience estimated at 7 per cent each.

Among the four licences granted in autumn 2001 to cable companies, one ceased to exist after only a few months, Kueb TV. The reason is that only sponsorship is authorized, not advertisement financing. The government is committed to changing the rules. Only one of the newcomers is a dedicated commercial

programme, Tango TV. It offers a twenty-four-hour service of the MTV type and it is run by the mobile phone operator Tango, a subsidiary of the Swedish Kinnevik group. Tango is also one of the three operators that have been granted a UMTS licence in Luxembourg and it is eager to offer content aimed at popularizing the new generation of mobile communications. The two other remaining television programmes are fairly modest operations, limiting their presence on screen to one or two hours per week: Nordliicht TV is a regional programme aimed at the north of the country and Uelzechtkanal is a venture into television undertaken by a high school in the south. Television news for local audiences remains the preserve of RTL.

A pay-television channel, Select TV, by an American businessman, Jeff Jackson, was on offer on cable networks for about a year. It ceased its operations at the beginning of 2002 because of a disappointing take-up level (less than 2,500 subscribers). A television licence has also been granted to a public channel, Chamber TV, entirely devoted to live broadcasts of the public sessions of parliament and operated by the Chambre des Députés. This programme started in early 2002.

To complete the picture, mention has to be made of the numerous programmes which make use of the flag of convenience facilities provided by Luxembourg. Altogether seven programmes make use of terrestrial frequencies granted by Luxembourg and seven more are distributed only by satellite on the Astra system. Most of the time programmes of the RTL group aimed at international audiences fall into these categories, but there are also examples of other international groups such as the French Groupe A/B or Canal Europe Audiovisuel which by making use of the very liberal Luxembourg legislation want to circumvent the stricter legislation in the countries they target. Although compatible with the EU directive on Television without Frontiers, the practice provokes intense debate in the target countries. From time to time the government has to bow to pressure from abroad. Thus in July 2002 it withdrew the licence granted to No Zap, a channel with a marked pornographic content.

Television has a modest share of only 10 per cent of total advertisement spending on the media. The explanation for this anomaly has to do with the fact that until recently only one channel with limited scope aimed at domestic audiences was available, RTL Télé Lëtzebuerg.

Moreover RTL had to observe a ceiling, in order to protect the advertising revenue of the press. Cable programmes were prevented from attracting advertising revenue. Both these restrictions are expected to be lifted.

### Radio

Radio liberalization goes back to the 1991 law on electronic media, which abolished the de facto monopoly RTL had enjoyed since 1929. Some pirate radios had started transmitting well before that date, including one established in neighbouring Belgium. Ten years later, RTL Radio Lëtzebuerg still leads the field, with a cumulated audience share of 75 per cent, followed by Eldoradio with 14 per cent. Eldoradio, in which RTL has a stake of 25 per cent, is a collective endeavour launched by Editpress, d'Lëtzebuerger Land and private investors. Its programmes are aimed at young audiences. None of the other radios with nationwide coverage on offer achieves an audience of more than 7 per cent. Denneie Radio, the radio venture of Groupe Saint-Paul, which tries to imitate RTL with extensive news coverage, has an estimated audience of 7 per cent, followed by Radio Latina (also partially controlled by Groupe Saint-Paul), aimed at the foreign communities in Luxembourg, with 6 per cent and Radio Ara, an initiative of the associative sector, with 5 per cent. The law prevents any single investor holding a stake of more than 25 per cent, but the government has pledged to lift the restriction. Radio has a share of 15 per cent of overall advertisement expenditures. In addition there are some sixteen local radio stations which are banned from financing themselves through advertisements.

Finally, Luxembourg has had a public service radio since 1993, Radio socioculturelle, with national coverage and financed entirely by taxpayers' money. Because of its highbrow programming it has a very limited audience estimated at around 2 per cent.

### Film and video

Film production, although heavily subsidized by the Ministry of Culture, is very modest. On average, about one film is being produced per year. The same goes for television programming material. Video has expanded considerably, thanks to the public Centre national de l'audiovisuel, which thrives on its important archives. A very generous tax break scheme has led to Luxembourg involvement in international film production and to the emergence of a small cinema industry. On average some eight productions per year have benefited from the tax break regime since its introduction in 1992.

## The Internet and related on-line media

Internet and on-line services are underdeveloped despite the high rate of Internet connection (about 50 per cent of households are connected). The more successful ones are by-products of the core business of publishers, broadcasters and telecom companies. Among the more innovative content providers is the young entrepreneur Mike Koedinger, whose company MKé offers some of the most popular sites. No reliable figures are available about the level of use, and on-line advertisements are negligible. As is the case with television viewing, a reasonable guess is that Luxembourgers prefer foreign offerings. An attempt to set up a Europe-wide Internet portal in Luxembourg, Europe On-line, has already failed twice and the third attempt, launched in early 2002, is not looking more promising. Teletext has been offered since 1999 by RTL. Some 100,000 people consult it more or less regularly.

## POLITICS, POLICY, LAW AND REGULATION

Luxembourg had and still has great ambitions in the media and communications fields, despite some setbacks. SES Astra, the satellite operator, which became a global company and changed its name to SES Global following its merger with GE Americom in 2001 and its previous stakes in satellite operators in China, Scandinavia and Latin America, has replaced RTL as the locomotive. It is precisely RTL which causes some worries and headaches for the authorities. The almost complete takeover by Bertelsmann in 2001 of the company that made Luxembourg's fortunes in the audio-visual field for over seventy years, renamed RTL Group when the German media conglomerate took control, has raised some doubts about the future of the group in Luxembourg. Bertelsmann held more than 90 per cent of the shares by mid-2002. It is determined to achieve complete control, but is still engaged in a bitter fight with minority shareholders. Corporate headquarters, which for the time being remain in Luxembourg, as well as local operations, may be affected by the change in ownership of Europe's largest audio-visual group. RTL Group, which for the second time in a row has issued earnings warnings, is in the red, primarily because of a dramatic plunge in its advertisement revenue in Germany, and it wants each of its operational units to become a profit centre in its own right. The local Luxembourg programmes of RTL accumulate losses because of the ceiling imposed on both radio and television revenue from advertisement. The government has tried to compensate for this by subsidizing some of the public service role carried out by RTL radio and television. These programmes are governed by a franchise (*contrat de concession*) which has been extended to 2010 and which contains some public service obligations. Concern has been voiced about what will happen to these programmes when the franchise agreement comes to an end. For the time being the government has excluded the possibility of taking over from RTL the local television channel. This reluctance can be explained by the disappointingly poor performance of public radio. Generally speaking, most of the Luxembourg media do not rest on a sound economic basis. In fact, there are too many media on offer for such a limited audience and advertising market, which has not grown in proportion to the multiplication of outlets. This is equally true of the radio scene and the press landscape. None of the many radio stations is profitable and there is increasing pressure to let them benefit from some kind of public subsidy. As regards the press, most daily and weekly titles survive only because they enjoy generous state aid. Nine titles benefit from it and it is likely to be extended to the two new French-language dailies. The soundness of the system is called into question, the more so in that the subsidies achieve one of the original aim less and less, i.e., to encourage quality reporting. The fact that the system takes account of the number of pages printed, independent of their content, has had perverse effects, among them copy-paste as one of the predominant forms of journalism. Typically, Luxembourg's newspapers rely heavily on material from press agencies, which makes for a certain uniformity in their reporting. A reform of the 1976 law that introduced state aid to the press is being called for.

The legislative and regulatory framework remains fairly rudimentary for all the media. An outdated law that goes back to 1869 and which is characterized by a repressive approach governs the press. A reform of that law will soon be passed by parliament. A Press Council, on which both editors and journalists are represented on an equal footing, deals with matters such as press cards and complaints from the general public. It has no power to penalize journalistic behaviour contrary to the code of conduct of the profession. It can only reprimand. The Press Council's performance in this respect can be seen as a timid and kid-glove attempt at self-regulation. Most complaints in press-related matters end up in the ordinary courts, which apply general principles of civil law, like civil responsibility (liability) and damages suits very much against journalists' liking.

A 1991 law governs the electronic media, which is in the process of being reformed. This law introduced a measure of regulation with the creation of two regulatory or supervisory bodies. The Independent Broadcasting Commission grants broadcasting licences and monitors respect for the obligations imposed on broadcasters. A National Programme Council monitors radio and television programmes. But it acts only in an advisory capacity, so it is limited to drawing the attention of the authorities to violations of the content provisions. The reform of the 1991 law will merge these two bodies into one, the Independent Regulatory Authority. It also will replace the licensing procedure by an authorization procedure, which in some cases will consist of a simple notification or declaration. The ownership restrictions pertaining to radio will be abolished, just as will most of the restrictions regarding advertising financing for both radio and television.

## STATISTICS

| | |
|---|---:|
| National population | 440,000 |
| Number of households | 172,000 |
| Movie admissions (tickets sold) | 1,500,000 |
| Books published (titles) | 408 |

| Print media | Circulation of daily newspapers | |
|---|---|---|
| | *Lusemburger wort* | 79,000 |
| | *Tageblatt* | 24,000 |
| | *LaVoix* | 7,000 |
| | *Le Quotidien* | 5,000 |
| | *Lëtzebuerger Journal* | 3,000 |
| | *Zeitung vum* | n.a |
| | *Lëtzebuerger Vollek* | 1,500 |

| Broadcast media | Audience share of television channels (%) | |
|---|---|---|
| | Private | |
| | RTL Tele Lëtzebuerg | 57 |
| | Tango TV | 17 |
| | Audience share of radio channels (%) | |
| | Private | |
| | RTL Radio Lëtzebuerg | 58 |
| | Eldoradio | 17 |
| | Den Neie Radio | 15 |
| | Radio Ara | 7 |
| | Public | |
| | Radio Socioculturelle | 3 |
| | Percentage of households with: | |
| | Cable | 87 |
| | Satellite | 27 |
| | Video-casette recorder, DVD, etc. | 79 |

| Electronic media | Percentage of households with digital reception devices | 14 |
|---|---|---|
| | Internet penetration | |
| | Household equipment | 63 |
| | Regular use | 43 |
| | Mobile phone owners as % of the population | 68 |

| Advertising spend (%) | Press | 70.0 |
|---|---|---|
| | Radio | 15.6 |
| | Television | 9.9 |
| | Outdoor | 3.3 |
| | Cinema | 1.2 |

| Ownership | Main media companies | |
|---|---|---|
| | RTL group (radion and television) | approx. 54 |
| | Groupe Saint-Paul (press) | approx. 70 |
| | Groupe Editpress (press): | approx. 25 |
| | Number of book titles published: | 408 |

# 13: The Netherlands

KEES BRANTS

## NATIONAL PROFILE

The Netherlands are small and densely populated – almost 16 million people inhabit 41 000 km$^2$, or 475 per km$^2$. The highest point is just over 300 m above and the lowest a few metres below sea level. All parts are easy to reach by broadcasting or cabling and, being approximately 240 km long and 190 km wide at its broadest points, the country as a whole is very accessible (or vulnerable) to cross-border broadcasting with (or without) satellites. To the south it shares borders with Belgium, whose northern half is Flemish (Dutch)- speaking, and to the east and south-east with Germany. Though over-the-air broadcasts from both countries can be seen in a fair part of the country, with a cable density of more than 95 per cent more borders are crossed than just these two. There are two official languages, Dutch and Friesian, the latter spoken only in the province of Friesland, which has just over half a million inhabitants. Thirteen per cent of the population are of non-Dutch origin, mostly Turkish, Moroccan and from Surinam, the former Dutch colony.

The Netherlands is one of the richer countries of Europe, linked with Germany both economically and communication-wise (shipping and road transport). With a gross national product of €401 billion (2000), a positive trade balance, a per capita income of €25,000 (2000), a private consumption of €199 billion (2000) and a relatively low rate of unemployment (2002: 167,000, or 2.4 per cent), the Netherlands counts as one of the more successful OECD stories. On the other hand, at the end of 2002 the economy was slowing down to zero growth, the rate of inflation was double the average of 2.5 per cent in the euro zone, and with a hidden unemployment of almost one million people on more or less permanent sick benefit, the pressure on the extensive (and expensive) social security system increases. The political system – a parliamentary democracy with a constitutional monarchy, four large and a number of small(er) parties with never a clear majority for one party – has created a permanent coalition government.

The recent history of press and broadcasting is closely intertwined with that one word for which the Netherlands has been renowned: 'pillarization', the remnants of which are still around. From the beginning of the twentieth century till the mid-1960s (and notably the first twenty years after the Second World War), Dutch society was a prime example of 'segmented pluralism', with the whole social system and particularly political parties, social movements, voluntary associations, educational and communication systems organized vertically along the lines of religious and ideological cleavages. The two religious 'pillars' – Calvinists and Catholics – included all social strata. The socialists incorporated only one class, while from a social-economic point of view the liberal pillar was the mirror image of the socialist one.

The press in those years had strong links with political parties, both formally – the editor of the newspaper often being the party leader as well – and informally – political journalists getting their news from party officials of the same 'pillar'. About two-thirds of the press had interlocking directorships with one of the four pillars, creating a fairly closed political communication system in which the press functioned as the platform of the pillarized elite. Next to these was a politically more neutral press with, however, a rather conservative undertone.

The origin of Dutch broadcasting lies in the 1920s, when there was a coming together of radio amateurs and the telecommunication industry (Philips). But it was not long before representatives of the pillars quickly moved in. In 1930 the government made special rules for radio in which only broadcasting corporations with strong ties to these 'streams in society' were allowed on the air: the VARA for the socialists, the KRO for the Catholics, the NCRV and the VPRO for the Protestants. The AVRO, originally borne out of commercial interests, aspired to be a national broadcasting corporation, but in reality it had strong links with the bourgeois-liberal sphere.

The last thirty to forty years can be described in three periods: internal competition, external competition, uncertainty. Towards the end of the 1960s the polarized structure changed with the loosening of religious and ideological ties: party, press and broadcasting systems were 'depillarized'. While political parties had to go in search of the floating voter, press and broadcasting engaged in a struggle for as large a public as possible in a volatile media environment where radio and television pirates, operating from the North Sea, introduced popular programme formats which rocked the tenuously balanced broadcasting system. With the coming of commercial broadcasting in 1989 a period of external competition started, with new and often foreign entrants in the media market. The original broadcasting organizations were forced to co-operate, albeit hesitantly and uneasily, and 'branded' themselves for the first time as, and taking pride in, a public broadcasting system in opposition to commercial enterprises that used audiences as numbers to attract advertisers and make money.

Since the elections of 2002, like the social and political system as a whole, the media system has entered a situation of uncertainty. After eight years of coalition government with both Labour (PvdA) and Conservatives (VVD) in power, and a political culture based on consensus and collaboration, the dramatic elections of 2002 resulted in a new and much more adversarial socio-political landscape, the effects of which are as yet uncertain. Nine days before the elections a populist politician, Pim Fortuyn, who according to the polls was about to upset the political balance, was murdered, creating national and very visible emotions never before seen in the country. In spite of his death, the party that bears his name (LPF: Lijst Pim Fortuyn), gained 17 per cent of the vote. Together with the Christian

Democrats (CDA) and the VVD, they now form a government propagating anti-immigration policies and a new 'climate' in which ethnic tolerance and a liberal attitude are said to make way for a strict regulatory and policy regime. Moreover, during its short existence the LPF has been very critical of the press and broadcasting; they were blamed for being co-responsible for the murder because of their critical reporting, while the public broadcasting system was also blamed for overspending. As it happens, the present Media Minister (Secretary of State) comes from the LPF, and so does the Minister of Economic Affairs, who deals with telecoms. The Prime Minister, Jan Pieter Balkenende, is from CDA.

# STRUCTURE AND OWNERSHIP

The media in the Netherlands, as in most countries of Europe, are in a state of flux. Economically there is increasing concentration and competition between press and broadcasting and among the public and private broadcasters; ownership of private television and cable has become predominantly foreign; financially there is stagnation of income; audience-wise, newspapers are confronted with de-reading and the electronic media with fragmentation; technologically, digitalization and the Internet pose both challenges and threats. Given the state of the media landscape the Netherlands thus runs the risk of picturing a present that in the very near future may well look more like the past.

## The print media

### The newspaper press
The newspaper situation has been characterized by waves of mergers, especially at the beginning of the 1970s and again in the 1990s, and gradually disappearing titles. The socialist and Catholic pillars were hardest hit. Between 1948 and 2002 the number of dailies with their own editor-in-chief fell from sixty to thirty: seven national and twenty three regional. The socialist *Het Vrije Volk*, shortly after the war the largest newspaper in the country, the Catholic *De Tijd* and the communist *De Waarheid* disappeared one after the other. *Het Parool*, which began as a socialist underground newspaper during the war, dropped its radical tone and is now barely surviving as an Amsterdam paper. *De Volkskrant* changed its Catholic

label to successfully become the paper of the leftish intellectuals. *Trouw*, Dutch Reformed, held its ground but its publisher merged with that of *De Volkskrant* and *Het Parool*. The neutral papers, *De Telegraaf* and *Algemeen Dagblad*, grew in circulation during this period, and the same can be said of *NRC Handelsblad*, which resulted from a merger in 1970 of two liberal-conservative papers. The merger wave in the 1990s particularly hit the regional and local press.

In these fifty years the number of independent newspaper publishers declined from eighty one to eight, but in practice three own some 90 per cent of the market. The seven national newspapers – with the exception of two peripheral and traditional Christian dailies, *Reformatorisch Dagblad* (circulation 60,000) and *Nederlands Dagblad* (33,000) – are in the hands of no more than two publishers: PCM, which with *Algemeen Dagblad* (328,000), *De Volkskrant* (331,000), *NRC Handelsblad* (270,000) and *Trouw* (126,000) owns 54 per cent of that market, and De Telegraaf Holding, covering 40 per cent with the Netherlands' largest newspaper *De Telegraaf* (794,000). Since 1999 there are two new free circulation dailies (handed out mostly at railway stations), which have introduced the tabloid format (though not so much the 'tabloidized' content since they are mostly based on press agency news): the Telegraaf-owned *Spits* (380,000) and Swedish-owned *Metro* (345,000). The latter is in fact the only example of foreign ownership in the newspaper press.

The sharpest decline is to be found in the regional press, where there are still around forty titles, but usually they share editorial material as well as an editor-in-chief. Depending on the way one counts, there are between twenty one and forty regional daily newspapers. Traditionally one of the strongest publishers here, VNU chose to concentrate on the provision of information for the professional market and in 2000 sold most of its regional and local dailies to Wegener. With De Telegraaf Holding, Wegener now dominates the regional market. In 2002 both of them also decided to scale down the number of editorially independent titles, so that by that year the total number of regional/local newspapers had more than halved in half a century. The total circulation of all Dutch newspapers is 4.4 million, or a reach of 65 per 100 households; in 1998 this figure was still 69, so with a growing population we see a steady decline. The largest population growth and at the same time the smallest readership is to be found among the immigrant population.

Though two official languages are spoken and there are more than half a million Turks and Moroccans, all newspapers printed in the Netherlands and focused on those living there are in Dutch. With the exception of *Spits* and *Metro* they are all broadsheets and, from a comparative point of view, of a quality nature; *Telegraaf* and *Algemeen Dagblad*, however, with big headlines and lots of colour pictures, are often considered more mass market newspapers. Interlocking directorships with political parties, unions or Churches have long since disappeared and though they all have political sympathies showing in their comments and columns, clear party political positions and certainly 'coming out' at election time are a thing of the past. The characteristics of readers of Dutch newspapers is that they are slowly getting older, compared with television viewers they are better-off and better educated, they spend fifteen minutes per day reading the paper and generally subscribe to it. Only *Telegraaf* and, to a lesser extent, *Algemeen Dagblad* have a readership that mirrors the population better. *Spits* and *Metro* attract a younger audience (school and higher education students, young commuters) that has triggered some hopeful comments and more wishful thinking from the publishers.

Around 60 per cent of the turnover of newspapers comes from advertising, and it is here that we see a sharp decline. For the first time in years, the net expenditure on all media dropped in 2001, to €5 billion. The newspaper business, with more than 7 per cent hardest hit, realised an advertising income of €1.15 billion, 21 per cent of total advertising expenditure. Slowly falling circulation (1.2 per cent in 2000) and the attacks on the World Trade Center further accelerated the decline. In that same year costs rose between 15 per cent and 20 per cent, leaving the newspaper publishers biting their nails.

### The periodical and magazine press

Relatively, the Dutch read many magazines: 87 per cent say they do so regularly; women more than men and those above fifty years old less than younger people. An estimated 1 billion magazines are sold yearly, ranging in circulation from 3.5 million for the Dutch Automobile Association's *Kampioen* to a few hundred for highly specialized scientific magazines. Very roughly, women prefer women's magazines like *Libelle* (circulation: 650,000) and *Margriet* (430,000) or gossip magazines like *Prive* (475,000), men read more special interest magazines in the motoring or sport sector. Other high-circulation examples are the listings magazines of the broadcasting corporations (the largest being of *Veronica Magazine*: 1.1 million) and sponsored magazines like *AllerHande* (2.1 million) of supermarket Albert Heijn.

After selling off all its dailies and freesheets in 1999, including the printing presses, the Netherlands' largest and oldest magazine publisher, VNU, in 2001 sold all its magazines to the Finish media concern Sanomawsoy Corporation. For €1.25 billion 250 magazines in seven countries (VNU was also market leader in Belgium, Hungary and the Czech Republic), with a total circulation of 375 million, changed hands. Sanoma Magazines is now the biggest publisher in the Netherlands. The sale of the magazine division, and later its educational division (a return of €195 million), enabled VNU to purchase in 2001 for US$2.3 billion the market research firm A. C. Nielsen, which is operational in more than 100 countries. Two years before, VNU had already bought Nielsen Media Research, as a first step on the way to become a global supplier of marketing and media information.

### Book publishing

In spite of a steady decline in the time people spend reading books (to just over ten minutes per day at the end of the twentieth century), the book market shows a reasonably stable picture in which only the debate about retail price maintenance seems a hot and recurrent issue. Sales in 2000 totalled around 32.5 million general (non-educational) books sold and a turnover of €400 million. Total sales that year earned the 500 book publishers in the Netherlands an income of between €1 billion and €1.5 billion. Translated thrillers from successful authors like John Grisham and the Harry Potter books usually end up in the top ten, but especially from the English-language world there is a solid import market of untranslated books fetching €360 million in 2000. The Dutch do read both English-language literature and scientific books. Most publications are (still) being sold via bookshops, with book clubs and mail order business reaching 21 per cent. Sales via the Internet are increasing but so far have not exceeded 2 per cent of total sales. Whereas we see a fairly rich diversity in the ownership structure of publishers of general books, the scientific book market is dominated by the same two publishers as

with scientific journals: Reed Elsevier, mostly for the medical publications, and Wolters Kluwer in the legal sector.

## The electronic (audio-visual) media

### Television

It was not until the end of the 1980s that the advent of private commercial television drastically changed the still predominantly pillarized structure, but advertising had already been an issue before, particularly shortly after the war, when financial and press interests had lobbied for advertising–financed media. One Cabinet had unsuccessfully proposed a dual system based on the British model, in 1965 another Cabinet fell because of the broadcasting issue, and two years later a Catholic–socialist Cabinet produced a Broadcasting Act which bore all the marks of a compromise. In 1969 the Act came into effect, opening up the system and introducing co-operation and mixed financing. Blocks of advertisements (outside the actual programme) were allowed, commercial broadcasting companies were not. A special non-profit foundation (STER) was set up to handle advertising, the proceeds of which went proportionally to the broadcasting organizations and partly to compensate newspapers for the loss of advertising revenue due to the coming of STER. The Act opened up the pillarized system to new licensees as long as they were aimed at 'satisfying cultural, religious or spiritual needs felt among the population' and added to the 'pluriformity' or diversity between the existing organizations. The allocation of broadcasting time was based on the number of members the organization had and/or the number of subscribers to their listings magazine. A Dutch Broadcasting Foundation (NOS) was set up to provide co-ordination and technical services, but also news and sport. The board of NOS had representatives from the different broadcasting organizations and government-appointed members, including the chairman.

The opening up of the system, though also intended to protect the existing order, turned out to favour a concealed form of commercialization and also those newcomers opting more for entertainment than for culture, information and education, four elements which, according to the Act, were supposed to characterize broadcasting in a 'reasonable ratio'. First TROS, originating from a pirate television station, and later the ex-pirate radio Veronica joined the club and grew explosively in audience and number of members/subscribers. A high cable density (around 80 per cent at the time), which allowed foreign programmes sometimes with advertising aimed explicitly at a Dutch audience, and a favourable political climate paved the way for a further opening up of the system. The Media Act of 1988 set a deregulatory trend in motion that no longer could hold back commercial television. In 1989 Luxembourg CLT/RTL, in combination with the Dutch publisher VNU, started a Dutch-language channel. Within a year RTL-4 attracted a quarter of the audience. In 1993 RTL-5 was launched and two years later five other stations took the step. A dual broadcasting system was established in which the traditional public channels saw their audience share drop from complete monopoly in the 1980s to a mere minority now.

The public broadcasters have a market share of 39 per cent, not least because they still have the rights to the Dutch and European Cup football league. In 1989, before RTL-4 entered the market, it was still 85 per cent. Eight member-based broadcasting organizations – the old pillars VARA, KRO, NCRV, VPRO and AVRO, a new evangelical pillar EO, popular TROS and a new and small broadcaster aiming at a young audience, BNN – the non-member NOS (news, sports and national events) and NPS (mainly culture) and some twenty small (religious, humanist, educational) non-member organizations and regular political party and government information programmes share the three national public channels Nederland 1, 2 and 3. All have been given a five-year concession by the government (NOS for ten years), to be renewed in 2005, and they will be audited as to their performance according to their programme obligations. The member-based broadcasters are expected to provide pluriformity and quality in their programming and to cater for the whole of the population as well as for minority groups. At least 35 per cent of their programming must consist of information and education, and at least 25 per cent should be devoted to culture (half of which should be for the arts). Moreover, at least 50 per cent should be in the Dutch language.

Nederland 1, 'home' of AVRO, KRO and NCRV, is branded as a channel emphasizing morals and values, especially in drama and information. Nederland 2, with TROS, EO, BNN and NOS Sports, focuses more on family viewing, youth and sports programmes. It also houses Teleac educational programmes. Nederland 3, home of VARA, VPRO and NPS, is the more highbrow, cultural channel. Since the licence fee was abolished in 2000, 75 per cent of the financing of public broadcasting comes from a levy on income tax. To safeguard public broadcasting's independence from the government of the day the budget is fixed by law at the 1998 level, with yearly indexing. The budget for 2003 (not yet indexed) was €617 million, but the new centre-right government intends to cut the budget by 5 per cent (€26 million). Twenty-five per cent of public financing comes from advertising. Television advertising is still growing (for television on the whole; STER estimated its income for 2002 at €214 million for television and radio) and now receives some 14 per cent of total advertising expenditure. Though the new government is unhappy with the bureaucratic structure of NOS, the large board had already been trimmed in 1998, when it was replaced by a smaller board of managers, comprising three independent members.

Next to the public broadcasters, two groups of foreign-owned stations dominate the commercial system of eight channels: Holland Media Group (HMG), fully owned by Bertelsmann/CLT, which has 28 per cent of the market with RTL-4, RTL-5 and Yorin, and the Swedish-American SBS group which, with SBS-6, Net-5 and V-8, has a 19 per cent share. With 38 per cent of the advertising market HMG had a turnover of €303 million in 2001, whereas SBS had a turnover of €134 million that year. De Telegraaf holds a 30 per cent stake in SBS Holland, the only one in a very competitive market that makes a profit. The Dutch music channel TMF, bought in 2001 by American MTV, has a 0.5 per cent market share. The volatility of the commercial market is shown by the zigzag course of the former pirate radio Veronica. First, in 1995, it left the public 'family', which it had uneasily joined in the mid-1970s, to go commercial. Then in 2000 it parted company with HMG, to be left with a commercially very successful programme guide but no television or radio programmes; Yorin took over its channel. But, after failing to take over the V-8 channel, at the end of 2002 it started broadcasting again, teaming up with Kindernet/Nickelodeon to share a new cable channel. Whereas the public broadcasters' programming is predominantly informational (54 per cent in 2000), and 27 per cent entertainment (of which 41 per cent is Dutch) and 12 per cent education, the commercial channels show the reverse picture: 59 per cent entertainment (42 per cent of it American), 26 per cent information, 2 per cent education.

RTL-4, audience-wise the most successful of the Dutch channels, has a more family and, as they put it themselves, 'feel good' character; it is popular with housewives. RTL-5 aims at adult males with films, news, reality television, sport and eroticism. During the day it is called RTL-Z, offering financial (stock exchange) news. RTL-4 and RTL-5 are officially Luxembourg channels, though they focus fully on the Dutch audience. Yorin aims at the 'modern human being' with films, drama and reality television. It is the home of Big Brother, the internationally successful format produced by Endemol. This entertainment producer caters for a lot of shows and drama on Dutch commercial television. Its attempt to join the Holland Media Group at the end of the 1990s was blocked by the European Union's competition directorate for creating a too concentrated audio-visual market; Endemol is now owned by Spanish Telefónica. SBS-6, like RTL-4, is more family-oriented. It introduced a more locally inspired and also tabloid style of news. Net 5 aims at the better-educated female audience, with quality series and reality television. V-8 aims at teenagers in the early evening and with (action) films at the adult viewer. Veronica, at the moment of writing, has yet to set its format.

Not only commercial television (production) is predominantly a foreign affair. With the sale of Dutch cable company Casema to UPC in 2002, the Liberty daughter of US media mogul Malone now has a market share of 58 per cent. That dominance is strongly objected to by consumer organizations and the anti-trust authority NMa that has still to decide whether to accept it. With Belgium, the Netherlands have the highest cable density in the world: 98 per cent. The cable networks allow between thirty and thirty five television channels for on average €10 per month (to which a few euros will be added in 2003). Next to the three public service and eight commercial channels, most networks have the public service channels (according to a 'must carry' rule) of Belgium, Britain and Germany, plus RAI Uno, CNN, CNBC, BBC World, Eurosport, Euronews, MTV, The Box, TRT, Discovery, National Geographic, Cartoon Network, and one or more regional and local channels, often with programmes in Moroccan or Turkish. In total they cover 12 per cent of the audience market.

There are thirteen regional television stations, mostly of a public nature. Around 100 local television stations show a mixture of commercial and private.

With all these channels available at a relatively cheap price, digital television is slow in coming. The lack of standardization of the set-top box is not very helpful either. Only 107,000 households (16 per cent) have a subscription. An NOS pilot, which ended in December 2002, was subsidized to the tune of €1.1 million and reached some 60,000 households. The digital terrestrial television 'bouquet' Digitenne, a co-operation of public and commercial media partners, started in October 2002 with the HMG channels in a few provinces. The pay-television channel Canal plus, which has offered a digital package since 2000, has never been very successful. In 2001 it had just over 300,000 subscribers, and at present its future is uncertain since its owner, loss-making Vivendi, is planning to sell it.

### Radio

The Netherlands have five national public radio channels: Radio 1 (information), Radio 2 (easy listening), 3-FM (pop/rock music), Radio 4 (classical music and jazz), and Radio 5 (culture, minorities – AM only). They have a market share of 31.5 per cent (2001). Next to these five channels there are thirteen public regional radio channels financed through a provincial levy and advertising (by law providing at least 50 per cent regional information, culture and entertainment, which they have difficulty in reaching) and more than 300 public local radio stations (local news, sport, culture, plus music and religious programming), that are allowed to carry advertising. Together they attract some 16 per cent of the audience.

Not long after the introduction of private television, several private radio stations sprang up as well. There are around a dozen national private radio stations, financed exclusively by advertising. Since radio advertising is not very popular (for the whole of radio just €200 million), the smaller commercial radio stations come and go. Their total market share is around 43 per cent. The most popular ones are Sky Radio (attracting some 15 per cent of the listeners, owned by Rupert Murdoch's News Corporation, non-stop soft pop music), Radio 10 FM (golden oldies) and Radio 538 (Top 40, dance music). Because public regional and local radio has advertising, there are only a few private local stations.

Originally commercial radio could be reached via cable, but a number of terrestrial frequencies have been allocated on a provisional basis. At the end of 2002 there was disagreement within the new government over whether to auction these frequencies, the favoured option, or to sell them on the basis of a so-called 'beauty contest', which the Minister of Economic Affairs favours.

### Film and video

For a long time after the introduction of television, cinema visits declined dramatically, reaching a low in 1992 with 13.7 million tickets sold. Since then there has been a clear recovery: 17 million in 1995, 19 million in 1998, a dip in 1999, and 20.5 million in 2000. In that year the government-sponsored Production Fund, which also receives money from collaboration with the public broadcasters, (co-) financed forty three Dutch movies while the cinemas showed thirty four (including co-productions) new Dutch films. That is 13 per cent of all the new releases shown in Dutch cinemas that year. The number of independent productions have been favoured by tax measures making buying shares in films an almost 100 per cent success story; in 2000 some €200 million was thus attracted from individual investors.

US films were and always are in the majority, and the blockbusters especially are also the most popular. The market share of American films in 1999 was 80 per cent, while only 6 per cent of the audience visited a Dutch movie. It is often said that part of this success is due to the near-monopoly of four American film distributors in the Netherlands: Buena Vista International, Columbia TriStar Films, UIP and Warner Bros. The export of Dutch films is marginal from an economic point of view.

The video recorder, which was introduced in the Netherlands in the 1970s, is today to be found in almost 90 per cent of households, and is used for playing rented or bought videos, for time-shifting television programmes or for own video productions; in 2000 22 per cent of Dutch households had a video camera. Video rental shops became a normal sight in the 1980s, the total is now estimated at 1900. The hire charge (on average €3 per copy) has fallen since 2000, though turnover is still rising: in 2000 to €105 million with around 33 million copies rented out. Video buying – in 2000 11 million copies and a turnover of €115 million – is stalling too. An important reason is the coming of the digital video disc or DVD, which is catching on rapidly. In the middle of 2002 a DVD player was to be found in every third household, an increase of 300 per cent in one year. Half these DVD players are installed in a computer. In 2001 8.3 million DVDs were rented and another 4.9 million sold; in 2002 *Harry Potter* and *Lord of the Rings* were extremely popular. Philips's version of the DVD, cd-i, which came on the market in the mid-1990s, has clearly lost the battle.

## The Internet and related on-line media

The dot.com crisis has not passed the Netherlands by, as was shown in 2002 by the demise of the Internet backbone provider KPNQuest, the forced sale of the Netherlands' largest Web shop, Bertelsmann-owned Bol.com, and a few years previously the downfall of provider Worldonline, shortly after its high-profile stock market flotation. KPN's bankruptcy was a drama, particularly for Internet users, Worldonline more for its shareholders. Though the crisis is affecting businesses large and small, the Internet as a medium of retrieving, sending and receiving all imaginable forms of information and communication has lost very little of its popularity.

At present, approximately half the population have access to the World Wide Web at home. A reliable figure is hard to give, because it rises steadily and because the definition of access (via the home or at work) is not always clearly distinguished in surveys; no one research shows the same percentage. According to a survey by the broadcasters' audience research bureau, about one-fifth of the population go on-line for thirteen minutes every day (KLO/Nielsen, 2001). This figure is doubled among the young. Being on-line affects other media use: the average television viewing time, as well as time reading newspapers and books are said to be affected between 5 per cent (television) and 14 per cent (books). Though there has been an increase among female users, twice as many men are still to be found on the net. The group that has been rising fastest is senior citizens; in June 2000 10 per cent of the over-sixty five-year olds were on-line weekly, four times as many as in the first quarter of 1999. There is still a social, age and gender gap; not so much in penetration any more – PC (almost 70 per cent) and Internet have become part of the household inventory – but in actual use. In spite of the high cable density, access to the Internet is still mostly (two-thirds) sought via a telephone modem.

After some search engines and starter pages, omroep.nl, the home page of the combined public broadcasters, scores high among the more popular Web sites (27,000 hits per day in 2001). With 20,000 hits *De Telegraaf* does best among the newspapers; the Internet-only news portal nu.nl is a strong competitor. All national newspapers and almost all regional dailies are present on-line. They are often reasonably interactive, with not only access to archives but also feedback via e-mail and discussion groups. In order not to 'canabalize' their 'mother', most newspaper sites are mere affiliates with hardly any regular updating or specific informational extras. Television sites make better use of the multimedia features of the Internet and also offer more hyperlinks.

The broadcasters in particular have discovered the commercial and 'bonding' opportunities of the Internet. The success of the Internet applications of the Big Brother reality television show – on-line discussion groups combined with voting via (paid) sms and other mobile telephone features – has made it clear to commercial broadcasters that more money can be made out of the Internet and the telephone than from actual programming. For the public broadcasters, the Concession Act has enabled NOS to develop new Internet-related services. Following McKinsey advice, NOS will probably build up its explicit guide function (EPG) and a strong portal. Internet activities are expected to grow to €45 million in 2004, but the new centre-right government may well cut this part of the budget.

# POLITICS, POLICY, LAW AND REGULATION

Regulating the media is and has always been controversial. As they are in most liberal democracies at the heart of the public sphere – informing on and controlling the powers that be, from Church and aristocracy in the old days to political and economic powers now – concern over their independence and well-being has always been a political issue. On the one hand, freedom from government and economic interference is considered a prerequisite for the free expression of ideas and opinions and for the freedom of the press. Thus government should keep its distance, and there is a tendency to expect market forces and competition to strengthen and guarantee diversity and plurality. On the other hand, there is a sense that communication freedom can be 'enjoyed' only with some form of government regulation: limiting the effects of a malfunctioning media market, enhancing access to and the diversity and quality of the channels and the content of communication. Media policy in the Netherlands, as in many liberal democracies, has always steered between the Scylla of non-interference and the Charybdis of control.

There are good and pressing reasons for a revitalization of this debate. The newspaper press sees a rapidly declining number of titles and increasing concentration of ownership, triggering a debate about the effect on the diversity of opinions voiced. Magazines, commercial television, film distribution and cable are predominantly in the hands of foreign owners, not only raising the question whether money alone is the driving force of the media industry, but particularly what this might mean for the 'Dutchness' of what some consider the bearers of cultural identity. Public broadcasting is holding its ground *vis-à-vis* growing commercial competition, but content and programme policies seem more based on how to hold and attract viewers than on the Enlightenment-inspired cultural-pedagogic mission which, when it still had a monopoly, was more or less its *raison d'être*. One would thus expect anxious activity and a full agenda in the domain of media policy.

## Actors

Though there is growing convergence in the technology and economics of communication, in the domain of policy making and regulation the integration of the traditional press, broadcasting and common carrier policy models is only slowly materializing. The Minister of Economic Affairs deals with liberalization and competition, and since 2002 he also has telecoms in his portfolio. The Secretary of State for the Media is involved in the more cultural and legal aspects of the media and stays away from common carrier policy. As it happens both are from the same party in the new centre-right government, but for the rest there is still a separation of powers.

Three independent bodies overview the actual implementation and upholding of laws and regulations with regard to communication. The Media Authority (Commissariaat voor de Media) on the basis of the Media Act 'polices' the public and commercial broadcasters and the cable owners at a national, regional and local level. The aim of the authority is to enhance an independent and pluriform media sector. In practice it allots air time, checks programmes for hidden advertising and controls the finances of the public broadcasting organizations. It has the power to punish those stations that do not live up to the rules: in 2000 the Authority received €300,000 in fines, particularly for hidden ads and sponsoring, and mostly from the commercial broadcasters.

The Nederlandse Mededingingsautoriteit (NMa), the anti-trust authority, controls all forms of competition, not only in the media market. It has the authority to uphold mergers which are considered detrimental to sufficient competition in that market. The cable company UPC's buying of Casema, which resulted in a market control of more than 50 per cent, is a case which will be scrutinized by the NMa at the end of 2002. The Onafhankelijke Post en Telecommunicatie Autoriteit (Opta) deals with the post and telecoms market. It assesses (sufficient) access to the cable networks which, according to the so-called Open Network Provision, should allow other Internet providers to their networks, it registers providers in the postal and telecoms market, and enhances competition in the liberalized telecommunications market. In 2005 Opta will merge with NMa. The former would also like to merge with parts of the Media Authority, but as yet that seems politically unviable.

Journalist and advertising organizations have their own self-regulatory authorities: the Journalism Council (Raad voor de Journalistiek) which adjudicates (but cannot fine) on complaints filed by the public and by organizations, and the Advertising Council (Reclame Code Commissie) which decides on complaints by the public on specific ads. Libel cases (slander, discrimination) can only be brought before a court of law.

## The press

The history of the battle for press freedom has made sure that the regulation of newspapers, more than of any other medium, is a light and distanced rein. The fears about continuing concentration, and the effect it may have on the diversity and pluriformity of their quantity and quality, have always been at the centre of the debate on how far governments should go. In this debate it never

came to a media-specific anti-trust law, if only because successive governments argued it might violate the constitutionally guaranteed freedom of expression. In 1993 the newspaper publishers agreed to a self-regulatory code of conduct not to extend their ownership beyond a third of the total newspaper market. So far, it has never happened, but there was always doubt that this gentlemen's agreement would not hold at the *moment suprême* when opportunity knocked. The new anti-trust law of 1998, which covers more than the media alone, made the code obsolete. It prohibits price-fixing agreements, the misuse of positions of economic power and business mergers without prior notice. The NMa is to uphold the law. Specific cross-media ownership regulation does not exist, but publishers are refused a broadcast licence if the enterprise already controls 25 per cent of the daily newspaper market, a rule which applies particularly to local newspapers that in almost all cases appear in one-paper cities.

Rather than prohibiting, press policy is based on the principle of enabling measures to support the existence and enhance the diversity of titles. Apart from a special VAT rate for newspapers of 4 per cent, a special Press Fund has existed since 1974, which gives specific financial support to newspapers in trouble. A continuing debate thereby has been whether further concentration under this system will not lead to support for the loss-making parts of an otherwise economically successful media business. A more specific quality support measure, based on the principal of individuality, is the setting up of a fund for special journalistic projects, which gives grants to individual journalists for research journalism that extends the twenty four-hour news cycle.

## The electronic media

Where with the press the government is very hesitant to interfere, it is different with broadcasting. Traditionally because of the scarcity of over-the-air channels, but also because of the assumed intrusiveness of the medium, broadcasting knows a relatively regulated regime as to its organization and to the pluriformity and quality of its content. Some of the measures apply not only to public but also to private commercial broadcasting.

The licence fee was abolished in 2000 and has been replaced by a levy on income tax yielding the same revenue but being less costly. The public service broadcasting organizations now receive a government subsidy, covering 75 per cent of their costs. By fixing the budget by law at the level of 1998, broadcasting's independence is said to be safeguarded, but the 2002 change of government triggered a fierce debate. Coalition partner LPF, the party of the murdered Pim Fortuyn, proposed a cut in the budget while several of its Ministers and members of parliament have questioned the objectivity and quality of public news reporting of their party. No specific measures have as yet been taken, but references to political control in the pillarized period or to the media problems under Italy's President and media mogul Berlusconi are regularly made.

Diversity in the public system is enhanced by its openness. Potentially new public service broadcasting organizations are in principle allowed access, provided they have 60,000 members and that they and their programmes contribute to the representation of different currents in Dutch society. New associations have to demonstrate that their presence would add to the diversity of programming. At the same time, recent governments believe that the survival of public service broadcasting *vis-à-vis* commercial competition is possible only if the existing corporations co-operate more and in a way play down their own original pillarized 'identity'. A concession of five years should help that process, but could also mean the end of the member-based and ideologically and religiously coloured Dutch model.

Other than with the press, broadcasting knows several measures regulating its content. Firstly, the Media Act explicates that public service broadcasting across the three channels should provide a 'full programme', a variety of qualitative programme categories aimed at suiting the needs of society. At least 35 per cent should be devoted to information and education and should be fair and balanced as to its political content; at least 25 per cent should be cultural programmes, with half of them devoted to the arts; half must be in Dutch, half must be European productions, half must be subtitled for the hard of hearing, and a quarter should be commissioned from independent producers. Secondly, there are measures to protect specific groups in society. Feature films and other programme material that is unsuitable for children under the age of twelve or sixteen should not be scheduled before 8.00 p.m. or 10.00 p.m. respectively – a requirement applying to both public service and commercial broadcasters (with the exception of RTL-4 and RTL-5, because as Luxembourg channels they do not fall under Dutch jurisdiction). Since 2001 there has been a classification system for the kind of content of films, television programmes and video games. It is up to the producers to specifically label these with a pictogram and an age suggestion as to their level of violence, sex, bad language and discrimination; parents can then decide whether or not to allow their children to watch or play.

Thirdly, the law prescribes that advertising should be broadcast only in short blocs in 'natural breaks' and not during programmes (and certainly not during the news): a rule which does not apply to commercial broadcasters. What does apply to all is the rule that advertising may not exceed 10 per cent of the total programming, with a maximum of 20 per cent per hour at prime time. Finally, there are support measures, financial incentives, to ensure and enhance a certain level of programme quality. Examples are a statutory fund for productions of outstanding quality (€14 million available annually) and a joint production fund with Flemish television, the Dutch film sector and the performing arts (€9 million annually).

This summary of rules and regulations may convey a different impression, but the dominant policy rule is still one of government keeping its distance and, as far as possible, letting the market do its work.

# STATISTICS (2002 unless otherwise indicated)

| | |
|---|---|
| National population | 15,900,000 |
| Population density | 475 per km$^2$ |
| Number of households | 6,800,000 |
| Movie tickets sold (2000) | 20,500,000 |
| Books (non-educational) sold (2000) | 32,500,000 |

| | | |
|---|---|---|
| **Print media** | Number of national daily newspapers | 7 |
| | Number of (editorially independent) regional/local dailies | 21 |
| | Circulation of daily newspapers | 4,400,000 |
| | Coverage of dailies per 100 households | 65 |
| | | |
| | Circulation of main newspapers, 2002 | |
| | *De Telegraaf* | 780,000 |
| | *Volkskrant* | 326,000 |
| | *Algemeen Daglad* | 315,000 |
| | *NRC Handelsblad* | 271,000 |
| | *Trouw* | 125,000 |
| | *Reformatisch Dagblad* | 60,000 |
| | *Nederlands Dagblad* | 33,000 |

| | | |
|---|---|---|
| **Broadcast media** | Number of national television channels | 3 |
| | Public Private | 8 |
| | Number of national radio channels | 5 |
| | Public Private | more than 10 |
| | Number of regional television channels (public) | 13 |
| | Number of local television channels (mixed) | 100 |
| | Number of regional/local radio channels | 13/300 |
| | Public Private | Few |
| | Average television viewing time per day(minutes) | 166 |
| | Audience share on peak time television (%) | |
| | Public | |
| | Nederland 1 | 13.0 |
| | Nederland 2 | 17.0 |
| | Nederland 3 | 9.0 |
| | Private | |
| | RTL-4 | 16.0 |
| | RTL-5 | 4.5 |
| | Yorin | 7.0 |
| | SBS-6 | 11.0 |
| | V-8 | 3.0 |
| | Net 5 | 5.0 |
| | | |
| | Audience share of radio | 31.0 |
| | Public Private | 53.0 |
| | | |
| | Cable penetration | 98 |
| | percentage of households with: | |
| | VCR | 89 |
| | Satellite receiver | 8 |
| | DVD | 34 |
| | Pay-television subscriptions | 312,000 |

| | | |
|---|---|---|
| **Electronic media** | Internet users (% of total population), 2001 | 7.2 million (45%) |
| | Mobile phone subscribers (% of over-twelve-year-olds) | 6.8 million (50%) |

| | | |
|---|---|---|
| **Advertising spend (%)** | Press | 29.6 |
| | Magazines | 11.6 |
| | Television | 45 |
| | Radio | 7 |
| | Internet | more than 1 |

# REFERENCES

Bakker, P. and Scholten, O. (1999) *Communicatiekaart van Nederland*. Alphen and de Rijn: Samson.

Bardoel, J. and van Reenen, B. (2002) 'Neiderlanden' in Hans Bredow Institute (ed.) *Internationales Handbuch Medien 2002–2003*. Hamburg: Nomos.

*De Mediamarkt in Nederland en Vlaanderen* (2002). The Hague: Biblion.

*Media Handboek 2002* (2002) Amsterdam: Adfo.

Van der Haak, K. and van Snippenburg, L. (2001) 'The Netherlands' in L. d'Haenens and F. Saeys (eds) *Western Broadcasting at the Dawn of the Twenty-first Century*. Berlin and New York: Mouton de Gruyter.

# 14: Norway

## HELGE ØSTBYE

## NATIONAL PROFILE

Norway is a medium-size European country (325,000 km², excluding the Arctic islands of Spitzbergen; larger than Italy, smaller than Spain) with a small population (4.5 million). Seventy-five per cent of the population live in conurbations with more than 2,000 inhabitants. High mountains, deep fjords and valleys have divided the country into a lot of separate communities with a strong local identity. There is one old ethnic minority, the Sámi population, mainly in northern Norway. Sámi has been recognized as an official language in certain areas. Recent immigration has been relatively limited: 250,000 people living in Norway were born in a foreign country. More than half of these were born in Europe.

During the union with Denmark from 1400 to 1814 Oslo became the cultural, political and commercial centre. Nationalist opposition against the union with Sweden (1814-1905) drew much of its strength from the periphery. One lasting outcome of this periphery protest is two official languages: Bokmål (literary Norwegian), based on the dialect of the upper class in Oslo and strongly influenced by Danish, and Nynorsk (new Norwegian), which is based on country dialects from the western parts of Norway (see Haugen, 1966). Bokmål is now used by 80–90 per cent of the population as their written language. Norwegians will usually understand spoken and written Swedish and Danish. English is widely understood. For more than 150 years the literacy level has been very high.

Protest from the periphery is still an important political factor. In two referendums (1972 and 1994) the people have voted against membership of the European Union. Norwegian legislation is, however, to a large extent adjusted to European standards.

Norway is among the richest countries in the world (GNP per capita). Nowadays 6 per cent of employment is in the primary sector and less than 20 per cent in the secondary sector. Norway has a mixed economy where private capitalism is combined with a few nationalized industries, and a lot of public regulations in the economic sphere. Disagreement on the proportion of public versus private spending is one of the major dimensions in politics.

The largest political party, the Labour Party (Arbeiderpartiet), is a social democratic party of the Northern European type. Labour was in government almost continuously from 1936 until 1965, most of the time with a majority in the parliament. Since 1965 Labour has been in and out of power several times. There are three parties to the left of Labour, but only one of them, the Left Socialists (Sosialistisk Venstreparti), is represented in the parliament. There are five non-socialist parties. The Conservative Party (Høyre) is the largest. Important changes in media structure took place after the formation of a Conservative minority government after the election of 1981. The basis of the government was broadened in 1983, when the Christian People's Party (Kristelig Folkeparti) and the Centre Party (Senterpartiet) joined. The Christian People's Party used to represent a fundamentalist, Lutheran type of Christianity, but it has gradually changed into a more European type of Christian Democratic party. The Centre Party is an agrarian party. The Liberal party (Venstre) has a glorious past, but is now struggling to gain representation in the parliament. The Progressive Party (Fremskrittspartiet) represents right-wing politics: anti-taxation, anti-bureaucracy and anti-immigration protest, with substantial support among the population. Following the general election in 2001 there is a minority non-socialist government, dependent on support from the Progressive Party.

# STRUCTURE AND OWNERSHIP

Political and cultural dependence on Denmark until 1814 delayed the development of Norwegian book printing and newspapers. The first newspapers emerged in the 1760s, the first daily paper in 1819. The constitution of 1814 abandoned advance censorship for the print media and granted the population a certain degree of freedom of expression.

## The print media

### The newspaper press
During the period from 1860 to 1920 Norway developed a geographically and politically scattered newspaper system. Most towns and cities used to have three or four papers, each representing one party.

Today the Norwegian press has a strong position, compared with most other European countries. No other country has a higher level of newspaper sales per capita (approximately 600 daily copies per 1,000 inhabitants) (de Bens and Østbye, 1998). In contrast to most of the press in other developed countries, Norwegian newspapers have not suffered a decline in their total circulation. Until 1990 there was a general increase in circulation. Since then, there have been some ups and downs, but no systematic downward trend. But the situation of the newspapers is unstable. The popular newspapers have lost some of their readers, perhaps due to increased competition from other media (television, the Internet, etc.). For the rest of the press, the main threat comes from changes in advertising volumes. Until the arrival of commercial television (gradually from 1988), the advertising market mainly consisted of newspapers and magazines. This situation has changed, especially for national advertising. The newspapers have become more vulnerable to changes in the general economy.

One explanation of the position of the newspapers is that there are strong newspapers at three different geographical levels: national, regional and local (Gustafsson, 1996). The number of newspapers is approximately 220, of which sixty five are dailies (six or seven issues per week). There are two national popular papers, *VG* and *Dagbladet*. The national level also includes a handful of national 'opinion' newspapers and some weeklies, and accounts altogether for a quarter of the national circulation. Four or five regional papers account for another sixth, and the local papers a little more than 50 per cent.

Since World War II there have been several distinct trends in the newspaper structure: (1) monopolization of local newspaper markets; (2) the foundation of new newspapers in places with no previous paper; (3) the establishment of a national popular press from 1965 onwards; (4) depoliticization, in the sense that direct links between parties and newspapers have disappeared since the early 1970s; and (5) concentration of ownership (Ottosen et al., 2002).

In order to halt or slow down the local concentration in ownership, a system of press subsidies was introduced in 1969. Most of the press and other print media are organized in private stock companies. Some newspapers and publishing houses have a very limited number of stockholders. Ownership of the press has traditionally been local, and very few owners used to control more than one paper. This changed during the 1980s, and there is now strong concentration of ownership. There are three major groups in the newspaper business: Schibsted, Orkla and A-pressen.

The largest newspaper owner is the Schibsted group. In 1860 Amandus Schibsted founded *Aftenposten*. During most of the twentieth century *Aftenposten* was the largest-selling newspaper in Norway, with two editions a day (morning and afternoon). In 1966 the *Schibsted* group bought *VG*, then a small evening paper with serious economic difficulties and a circulation of less than 30,000. The new owners developed *VG* into a modern tabloid, and had great success in the market. *VG*'s circulation exceeded *Aftenposten*'s in 1981. The daily circulation in 1994 was almost 390,000, which means that more than one in three Norwegians read this newspaper on an average day. The Schibsted group also owns a minority of the shares in four of the largest regional newspapers (*Fædrelandsvennen*, *Bergens Tidende*, *Stavanger Aftenblad* and *Adresseavisen*) and a regional newspaper chain (*Harstad Tidende*). If we include the regional newspapers, the group accounts for more than half the total Norwegian newspaper circulation and

*Aftenposten* and *VG* alone account for almost 40 per cent of the newsprint.

A more recent development in the industry structure is a chain of dominant local newspapers with a non-socialist history. The formation of the chain started in the first half of the 1980s. The owner is Orkla, a former mining company, now one of Norway's largest financial and manufacturing companies (based on the production of chemicals and consumer goods). Orkla Media owns more than twenty newspapers with 11 per cent of the national circulation.

Both Schibsted and Orkla have expanded in other Nordic countries and in Eastern Europe. Schibsted owns two of Sweden's lagest papers, *Aftonbladet* and *Svenska Dagbladet*. In the autumn of 2000 Orkla bought Denmark's largest newspaper group, Berlingske.

A lot of the newspapers that had been established by the labour movement survived the depoliticization of the press. They were owned mainly by local trade unions, but papers co-operated in taking some editorial material from a separate news agency, in the advertising market and when purchasing new equipment. In 1992 thirty two out of approximately thirty five previous labour newspapers merged into one holding company. During the first few years, the labour movement became the main shareholders, but gradually financial investors and media companies have become major shareholders. Today, A-pressen controls between forty and fifty newspapers with almost 20 per cent of the national circulation.

Very few middle-ranking or large Norwegian newspapers are independent of the three major owners. Until the 1980s the newspaper industry was territory for idealists with a message (political or ideological). During the post-war period a lot of the papers made a loss most years. Some newspapers, however, made a substantial profit, but most of the surplus was reinvested in the paper. Recent changes of ownership have led to an increased focus on profit in some parts of the industry. Newspapers have become businesses.

### The periodical and magazine press

A distinct form of popular magazine emerged in the late nineteenth century, weekly magazines with a general content aimed at the whole family. Danish magazines were introduced on to the Norwegian market in these early days (at the time written Danish and written Norwegian was identical), and two Danish companies, Hjemmet

and Aller, established Norwegian subsidiaries and separate Norwegian editions of the magazines were distributed. In the 1930s and 1940s the general weeklies were very popular, and the publishers also developed more specialized magazines, first for women, then for men. In the first post-war years, news magazines and cartoons were introduced. One of the big successes was Hjemmet's distribution of publications from Walt Disney. From the 1960s there has been a reduction in the number of publishers. The two Danish companies and one Norwegian, Ernst G. Mortensen, survived, while most others disappeared. Ernst G. Mortensen was bought by Orkla in the early 1980s.

In 1978 Aller established a new magazine with a new type of content, focusing almost exclusively on the private lives of famous people, mostly royals and people from the entertainment industry. This magazine immediately became a great success, and is now the best-selling publication on the Norwegian market, with a weekly sale of more than 400,000 copies.

In this entertainment-oriented market, there have been established many new magazines. The traditional general weekly magazines used to sell between 300,000 and 400,000 copies around 1980, but sales have dropped considerably (only Hjemmet is now above 200,000). New, more specialized magazines have taken over. But the publishing houses have been able to maintain their dominance. In 1992 Hjemmet and Ernst G. Mortensen merged, and the new company is called *Hjemmet-Mortensen*. This meant that two companies – the Aller group (Danish) and Hjemmet-Mortensen (50 per cent Egmont, 50 per cent Orkla) – completely dominate this sector. A major actor in this new, specialized magazine market is the Swedish multimedia company Bonnier.

### Book publishing

The political ties between Denmark and Norway had been cut in 1814, but a common language tied Norway closely to Denmark in all matters that were linked with literary culture. This cultural dependence lasted until 1925 when the Norwegian division of the Danish publishing house Gyldendal (including the rights to key authors like Ibsen and Hamsun) was bought by Norwegians and established as a Norwegian book publisher.

Along with two well established publishing houses (Aschehoug and Cappelen) Gyldendal became the leading book publisher. In 1961

Aschehoug and Gyldendal started the first major book club in Norway. The Swedish publisher and multimedia giant Bonnier bought Cappelen in 1987. The fourth largest book publishing house is Egmont (which is also the owner of Hjemmet, the magazine publisher). One Swedish and one Danish multimedia conglomerate own two of Norway's four largest publishing houses.

There is strong concentration of ownership in book publishing. The larger publishing houses have expanded, partly by buying up smaller publishers. Gyldendal and Aschehoug compete in some areas, but they also run a lot of joint operations (book clubs, one publishing house, book distribution, etc.). Together, they control approximately 50 per cent of turnover in the book trade. In several contexts they are regarded as one group. The four largest publishing houses (or three, if Gyldendal and Aschehoug are seen as one group) completely dominate the book trade. In the late 1990s both Gyldendal and Aschehoug gained control over a lot of book-shops, and the traditional separation of ownership between book publishing and bookselling is vanishing.

The book trade is regarded as important for Norwegian culture. In two ways the state has decided to support the industry. Since 1965 books have been exempted from value-added tax (VAT). In the same year the 'Purchasing Programme for Contemporary Fiction' was established. This means that a certain number of copies of all new Norwegian fiction books (1,000 copies of books for adults and 1,550 copies of books for children and adolescents) are bought with government money and the books are distributed to libraries all over the country. In principle, all books above a certain literary quality qualify for this purchase.

## The electronic (audio-visual) media

Norwegian newspapers reported clear reception of Dame Nellie Melba's famous radio concert from Chelmsford in 1920. But it was another five years before the first permanent *Norwegian* radio station got started. Following a round of discussions, the government chose a system where private companies were given licences for regional monopolies. There were strict and detailed guidelines for the programmes. In 1933 this system was replaced by a state-owned national public service company: Norsk rikskringkasting, the NRK. The Broadcasting Act of 1933 gave NRK a monopoly of broadcasting from

Norwegian territory. The main aim of the broadcasting company for the next thirty years was to extend the network to cover the whole country. World War II represented a setback. Some transmitters were destroyed, and from 1941 only members of the Nazi party were allowed to keep their radio receivers. From 1945 the dissemination of radio was very fast, and the 1950s were the golden age of radio.

NRK's monopoly from 1933 included the 'transmission of pictures', but Norway was among the last countries in Europe to introduce television. The official opening took place in 1960. Since 1981 the government has licensed local radio and television stations outside the NRK. From 1992 commercial channels have competed with the NRK for the national audience.

### Television

The broadcasting monopoly of NRK lasted for almost fifty years. 1981 was the year when a process of change started an extensive transformation of the broadcasting system. At the start of this process there existed only one radio channel (a second was under construction and officially opened in 1984) and only one television channel. The changes were linked with a change in the political climate, a Conservative minority government starting the changes in 1981. From the start neither community radio nor local television was allowed to carry commercials, but no one could come up with alternative forms of financing, and the government came under pressure to allow advertising.

Licences for local television distributed via cable were granted to six communities in 1981. In contrast to community radio, local television has never become a success. Terrestrial distribution was allowed in 1985 and advertising from 1992, but neither has been sufficient to provide a solid economic basis for this kind of service. In the late 1990s the whole system of licences for local television was changed. Norway was divided into twenty seven areas, each with one operator. The local companies were allowed to co-operate with a national satellite channel, TVNorge (see below). The satellite channel is transmitted via terrestrial transmitters, and the local programmes are transmitted in local windows in the national programme.

In 1981–2 some local community transmitters were licensed to relay programmes from satellites. From 1988 the regulations in this field have been relaxed and cable networks now typically provide a list of around

100 channels which subscribers can choose from. Almost 40 per cent of the population are linked to cable networks. Two important players have divided the cable network market evenly: Telenor Avidi, which is a subsidiary of the old telecommunications monopoly (Telenor), and the international operator UPC.

The introduction of international television channels like Sky Channel created a lot of debate but these channels never got high audience ratings, except amongst schoolchildren. In 1988 the Swedish company Kinnevik launched a commercial pan-Scandinavian channel distributed via satellite. The channel was called *TV-3*. The Ministry of Culture tried to prevent *TV-3* from being distributed via cable networks, but failed. Later *TV-3* was divided into separate channels for Denmark, Sweden and Norway. In the same year two commercial Norwegian channels were established. They too distributed their programmes via satellite. After a short competitive period, the two channels merged. TVNorge has survived since 1988 as the only satellite channel with a Norwegian origin. Scandinavian Broadcasting System, which is American-owned, has a 51 per cent stake in TVNorge. It is this satellite channel which co-operates with local television stations. From the late 1990s, TVNorge has an agreement with twenty one out of the twenty six operators of local television.

NRK's monopoly of national television with terrestrial distribution ended with the establishment of *TV-2* in 1992. Each of three companies with a strong position in other media – Schibsted (newspapers, etc.), A-pressen (newspapers) and the Danish Egmont (magazines, etc.) – owns 33 per cent of the shares in TV-2. TV-2 owns 49 per cent of TVNorge.

NRK has experienced a reduction in its market share since the mid-1990s. TV-2 quickly reached a market share of approximately 30 per cent, but has not been able to increase its share by more than one or two percentage points since 1995. TVNorge and TV-3 have gradually increased their market share, and they are both close to 10 per cent, with TVNorge one or two points ahead of TV-3. Since 1995 NRK has dropped from 45 per cent to 40 per cent, despite the launching of NRK-2 in 1996. NRK-1 is still larger than TV-2.

Both NRK and TV-2 have for several years planned a digital future. In this area the two companies co-operate, and they have established a joint company. A third party in the preparations for digitalization has been Telenor, the old telecommunications monopoly. Telenor has bought from NRK the physical infrastructure for terrestrial transmission, links, etc. In addition, Telenor has been an important operator in the satellite market since the early 1980s. In recent years Telenor has been accused of preparing to establish itself as a broadcaster, with programmes in competition with NRK and TV-2.

### Radio

As noted above, in 1981 there was only one radio channel in Norway, another opening in 1984. After 1981, in several stages, the number of community radio licences increased. From 1988 community radio was made permanent and commercials were allowed. This has led to the professionalization and commercialization of local radio, and to a reduction in the number of operators. Radio 1 is a chain of local radio stations in larger cities. The magazine publisher Aller and the American Clear Channel Communications jointly own the Radio 1 chain. These two owners also co-operate in preparations for a national network of digital radio.

In 1993 there was a total change in the national radio services. The NRK was allowed to open a third channel, and NRK's radio channels became more specialized: *P-1* is the general channel with a broad range of programmes, including regional programmes from seventeen districts. *P-2* specializes in culture and in-depth news. P-3 ('Petre') has young people as its targeted audience. In addition to the three channels from the NRK, a fourth channel, P-4, also started in the autumn of 1993. P-4 is a privately owned commercial radio channel, which attracts most of its audience in the age group between twenty and forty. Most of the content is music.

On average, Norwegians listen to radio approximately two hours twenty minutes per day. NRK's market share is close to 60 per cent (with P-1 alone accounting for 40–5 per cent of the total), P-4 25–30 per cent and community radio 10–15 per cent (data from different sources, collected from the MedieNorge database).

### Film and video

The first movies reached Norway less than a year after the Lumière brothers' first showing of film in Paris in 1895. Only a few years later, the first moving pictures were produced in Norway. From 1913 new legislation introduced advance censorship for movies. A second feature of the Cinema Act was that it authorized the municipal councils to license cinemas in their area. This led to a system where the municipalities very often took over as owners of the cinemas. The system of public ownership of cinemas still exists, and is unique to Norway. The municipal cinemas produce 85–90 per cent of the total ticket revenue, and until the year 2000 this percentage has been increasing as some small, private cinemas have been closed down. A trend towards privatization has started. Some of the major municipal cinema companies (for example in Oslo and Bergen) have been transformed into joint-stock companies with private owners. In addition, some Scandinavian cine-chains have established cinemas in Norway.

The Ministry of Culture subsidizes film production. During the 1990s the number of movies produced in Norway fluctuated between ten and twenty. The dominant production company was the state-subsidized *Norsk film*. In recent years, private investment has become more important in film production. In 2002 *Norsk film* was closed down and all production companies can now compete for production support from the state.

The municipal cinemas established an import and distribution agency for movies. This agency has for a long time been the largest in Norway (at least with regard to the number of imported movies), but its importance has been slowly declining. Some importing agencies are subsidiaries of the large American production companies, others are owned by Scandinavian multimedia companies (like Schibsted, Egmont and Bonnier). In general, the Norwegian film and cinema industry has become more oriented towards competition and profit.

The same commercial actors dominate the video sector: Scandinavian firms (Egmont, Sandrew Metronome, Svensk Filmindustri) import and distribute videos for hire and sale in competition with a few international actors (like Buena Vista and CIC).

## The Internet and related on-line media

The development of the Internet in Norway is similar to the same process in other industrialized countries. The diffusion process started in academic institutions, but in 1996 the net was opened for commercial use. There has been a steady increase in the number of PC owners and Internet users. Especially for the Internet, the autumn of 1999 meant a breakthrough. On an average day in the first months of 2002 more than one-third of the population (thirteen years of age or over) used the Internet, and almost two-thirds had been online during the last month (data from Norsk Gallup, via MedieNorge). Of the different services on the Internet, e-mail, file transfer, chat groups and games are examples of interpersonal communication. The World Wide Web is a provider of mass communication.

Very few major actors are able to make a profit from their Internet activities. Advertising is still divided mostly between the print media and the traditional electronic media. Shopping on the Internet has so far not become a success, despite the level of Internet use in the population.

Norsk Gallup (Gallup WebMeasure) measures the use of a majority of the major commercial Norwegian Web sites. The newspaper *VG* tops the ranking of the sites used, measured by the number of individual visitors in one month (March 2002), with 1.7 million users. All major newspapers and radio and television channels provide Internet news services. *VG* and the other news providers are examples of information providers on the Net. Two other types of sites are also high up on the list: search engines and information gateways.

Ownership of the most frequently used Norwegian Web sites indicates that well established media owners dominate the new media Internet. Two actors are particularly important: Schibsted (the newspaper and TV-2 owner) and Telenor, the old telephone monopoly. One of the major information sites, Nettavisen, started as an independent newspaper on the Net (no paper edition). Nettavisen has been bought by Lycos, which is owned by the Spanish Telefónica. Some other telephone companies also provide popular Internet sites.

Schibsted and Telenor show one important feature of the process of convergence. All media – new and old – produce their messages in digital form. Only the final stages in the production of newspapers, books and magazines – and, for the time being, transmission of radio and television via terrestrial networks – draw on traditional production and distribution methods. But the information in digital form can be distributed through several different channels.

One consequence of the convergence is that the production of media content can be easily separated by putting together a 'package', which can then be sold to the audience. And the 'package' can reach the audience via different channels. The radio programme can reach the audience from terrestrial transmitters, via the Internet or via cable television. Telenor has a very strong position in this last stage of this process. Telenor controls several channels: transmitters; the telephone network, which is upgraded to ISDN and ADSL standards in order to provide high-speed Internet connections; and it owns one of the two nationwide cable operators.

# POLITICS, POLICY, LAW AND REGULATION

Two – partly conflicting – basic principles have been imperative for Norwegian media politics: on the one hand a desire to use the mass media to strengthen democracy, improve the dissemination of culture and important information, and function as a tool for extended freedom of expression. On the other hand, the mass media are regularly seen as a threat to the stability of society by bringing unwanted messages. A system of press subsidies is an indication of the first principle. Advance censorship of movies is an example of the second. The public service monopoly from 1933 to 1981 can be put into both categories.

The trend towards more liberal free-market economic politics from the late 1970s reached Norway in the early 1980s. This led to pressure to deal with the media in the same way as any industrial sector. But even in the last two decades of the twentieth century, public service broadcasting and press subsidies remained two important pillars of Norwegian media politics. In both these areas, a political right–left cleavage is clearly visible. For long the Labour Party, the Left Socialists and the Centre Party supported the broadcasting monopoly, and these parties have also defended press subsidies. Both these policies have been under attack from the Progressive Party and the Conservatives.

Two new and general issues emerged during the 1990s: an increase in questions related to freedom of expression and concern about concentration of ownership. These will be discussed at the end of this section.

Media politics in Norway is not a well integrated area, guided by overall principles. Most regulations have been ad hoc, dealing with topical issues. For a long time different Ministries dealt with media questions. From 1982 a new Ministry of Culture gradually became responsible for most questions relating to the media. But the convergence process has again divided the responsibility between the Ministry of Culture and the Ministry of Transport and Communications.

## The press

Most media are regulated through specific legislation, like the Broadcasting Act or the Cinema and Video Act. There is no press law or similar provision aiming specifically at regulating the print media. One of the few parts of the legislation that is specific to the press is a demand that a paper should have an editor who is responsible for the content. More general regulation protects state secrets, prohibits libel and the publication of some forms of racial discrimination, pornography, etc. This legislation usually limits the individual's freedom of expression when it threatens the integrity of other people or the basic interests of the nation. One important piece of legislation has been in favour of the media: the Freedom of Information Act (*Offentlighetsloven*) was adopted in 1970. It says that all documents in the administration are public unless otherwise decided with reference to the law. And the exemptions from the general principle are relatively few and specific. The state has left it to the press's own self-regulation to work out and enforce a professional code of practice for the newspapers and the journalists. Organizations representing most other news media have also signed this code of practice.

In the post-war period a lot of newspapers were forced to close (see the paragraph about monopolization above). This threatened both political balance and local competition. In 1968 representatives of the industry turned to the government for subsidies. Labour and the Centre Parties backed the proposition, while the Conservative Party opposed it. Newspapers were already exempt from VAT, and since 1969 a system of press subsidies has been in operation. The most important form of subsidy is called 'production support'. Production support is directed towards papers with the weakest structural position in the market (the smallest papers and papers with a minority position in the local market – No. 2 papers), but with set rules so that there should be no fear of state interference with editorial policies.

In total, the subsidies account for less than 3 per cent of the industry's total income, and they have not been sufficient to prevent the monopolization of local markets, only to slow down the process. Since 1981 the Conservative Party has proposed a reduction in the subsidies or to abolish the whole system, but other parties have been in favour of the press subsidies. The future of the press subsidies is a topical issue in media politics in 2002.

## The electronic media

Radio and television are primarily regulated according to the Broadcasting Act of 1992. It gives NRK a permanent licence to broadcast and specifies that everyone else who plans to broadcast from Norwegian territory must have a licence. The regulations also include transmission via cable as long as the signals are aimed at a general public.

Norway is divided into 150 areas for local radio and twenty six regions for local television. For local radio, several licensees can operate in the same area, sharing one frequency or operating on different frequencies (two or three in a handful of areas, six in Oslo). The Mass Media Authority issues licences on behalf of the Ministry of Culture. In addition to the NRK, only one company has been allotted a licence for national television. TV-2 got a ten-year licence which in 2001 was extended until the end of 2009. A similar licence was issued for a private, commercial, nationwide radio channel, P-4, in 1992 (P-4 commenced its transmissions in 1993). A topical issue in 2002 is whether to continue with one commercial radio channel or issue a second, nationwide licence.

Until 1988 a coalition of the political left, including the Centre Party, blocked all attempts to open radio and television up to advertising. Then advertising was allowed on local radio, and from 1992 in all forms of broadcasting outside the NRK. The terms are, however, quite restrictive. There is a ban on advertising for several products, including political and religious organizations. There is also a general ban on advertising aimed at children and young people. Commercials shall, in general, not interrupt programmes, and there are limits to the amount of advertising per hour (20 per cent) and per twenty four-hour period (15 per cent). One problem with this legislation is that it applies only to channels transmitted from Norway, and not to channels like TV-3, which are beamed at Norway but have their uplink abroad. This way, there is uneven competition between the almost unregulated TV-3 and the strictly regulated conditions of TV-2 and TVNorge.

NRK has to some extent been squeezed by developments in the broadcasting sector. *NRK's raison d'être* as a state-owned broadcasting company financed by a licence fee lies in fulfilling public service obligations in a way that satisfies a political majority in the parliament. But the licence fee is under threat. If the audience drops too low, it will be difficult to defend the licence fee. But if NRK, on the other hand, competes and provides the same mix of programmes as its commercially financed competitors, it is difficult to argue in favour of NRK's special position. NRK's attempt to handle this dilemma has been to change the scheduling and to establish a second television channel (NRK-2). The schedule has become more repetitive from day to day and from week to week. Programmes expected to have low audience rating are not being transmitted during prime time (Syvertsen, 1997). Much attention is paid to the schedule for Fridays and Saturdays, when NRK has a particularly strong position. NRK-2 is used for some programmes that are important in a public service perspective, but with low audience ratings.

A new director general of the NRK was appointed in 2001. He had previously been a member of parliament from the Conservative Party. All his predecessors since the position was created in 1948 had had links with the Labour Party.

## The Internet and related on-line media

There have been very few attempts to regulate the Internet-based media. General rules regarding pornography, etc., apply to information on the Web, but regulation is difficult to enforce upon media with such an international orientation as the Web. There has been a lot of debate about what editorial responsibility the owners of Internet sites have or should have.

Several governments, of different parties, have been criticized for not being able to present plans for the future development of the Internet and Net-based services. The state controls two important actors in the process of adapting to the new technology: Telenor and the NRK. But the state has left it to these two institutions to develop their own strategies, and has, neither with regard to policy nor with regard to finance, been able to support or direct these two institutions.

## New issues: concentration of ownership and freedom of expression

Previous sections of this chapter have shown the high level of concentration of ownership in the press and other print media. In radio and television the state-controlled NRK is a dominant actor, and concentration in the private sector is high. But more important, is the high level of cross-ownership. Schibsted, Egmont, the Norwegian state and a handful of others are important actors in several media (see statistics).

Concentration of ownership in the media has been regarded as a potential threat to freedom of expression and democracy (St meld. No. 32 1992–93). In 1997 the parliament passed the Media Ownership Act, which regulates the acquisition of newspaper and broadcasting enterprises. From 1999 the Norwegian Media Ownership Authority was established as an independent public body supervising media ownership for the protection of freedom of expression and media pluralism. The Act has probably prevented the Schibsted group from trying to take over some of the regional newspapers, but otherwise the Act and the Authority have not proved efficient in preventing the continued concentration of ownership in the media. The main problems with the legislation are that it covers only a few media

(newspapers, radio and television) and that it does not take into consideration multimedia concentration.

Regarding freedom of expression, the Norwegian constitution was adopted in 1814. Article 100, which covers freedom of expression, has not been changed. There are two major problems with this article. First of all, the most specific parts cover only the print media (not surprisingly, considering that it was formulated in 1814, but the interpretation of 'freedom to print' has been by the letter), and the general parts can be undermined by ordinary legislation.

In several cases newspapers have been heavily fined for libel, etc., by the courts because some minor aspect of an article has been incorrect. Some of these cases have been brought to the European Court of Human Rights for breaching the European Convention on the Protection of Human Rights and Fundamental Freedoms. The European Court has overturned several decisions of the Norwegian courts.

This is one of the reasons why the government in 1996 appointed a Commission on Freedom of Expression. Three years of work resulted in a document with a broad discussion of the principles of freedom of expression, and proposed amendments to Article 100 (NOU, 1999: 27). If this change in the constitution is passed, the legislation will be more in line with international obligations. The proposed new Article 100 will be more general and not linked with specific media. Access to public documents will be granted under the constitution, and the authorities of the state will have an obligation 'to create conditions enabling an open and informed public debate'.

# STATISTICS

| | |
|---|---|
| Population, 1998 | 4,445,000 |
| Number of households, 1998 | 2,050,000 |
| Movie admissions, 2000 | 11,586,000 |
| Books published (source: National Library) | |
| First editions | 3,948 |
| Translations | 1,588 |
| Total | 4,784 |
| Main daily newspapers, 2000 | |

**Print media**

| Newspaper | Location | Type | Circulation | Major owner[a] |
|---|---|---|---|---|
| VG (Verdens Gang) | Oslo | Popular, national | 375,983 | Schibsted |
| Aftenposten | Oslo | Regional/national | 276,429 | Schibsted |
| Aftenposten Aften | Oslo | Local/regional | 175,783 | Schibsted |
| Dagbladet | Oslo | Popular, national | 192,555 | (Orkla) |
| Dagens Næringsliv | Oslo | Financial, national | 71,364 | |
| Bergens Tidende | Bergen | Regional | 91,956 | (Schibsted, Orkla) |
| Adresseavisen | Trondheim | Regional | 88,885 | (Schibsted, Orkla) |
| Stavanger Aftenblad | Stavanger | Regional | 73,221 | (Schibsted) |
| Fædrelandsvennen | Kristiansand | Regional | 46,185 | Orkla |
| Drammens Tidende | Drammen | Local/regional | 46,70 | Orkla |

[a]Indicates major owner with less than 50% of the shares.

**Broadcast media**

Main television channels, 2000

| Channel | Type of content | Distribution[a] | Financing[b] | Penetration (%) | Market share (%) | Owner |
|---|---|---|---|---|---|---|
| NRK-1 | General (PSB) | T | Lic. | 98 | 38 | NRK (Public) |
| NRK-2 | Supplement | T | Lic. | 78 | 3 | NRK (Public) (PSB) |
| TV-2 | General | T | Com. | 95 | 32 | Schibsted, Orkla, A- pressen |
| TVNorge | General | T | Com. | 83 | 10 | SBS, TV-2 |
| TV3 | Entertainment | T/C/S | Com. | 58 | 8 | Kinnevik |
| 26 local | Local news etc. | C/S | Com. | n.a. | n.a. | Orkla, A-pressen, etc. (TV Norge) |
| SVT1 + 2 | General (Swedish) | C/S | Lic. | 43 | n.a. | SVT (Swedish, public) |
| TV-4 | General (Swedish) | C/S | Com. | 35 | n.a. | Kinnevik |
| Eurosport | Sports | C/S | Com./Sub. | 44 | n.a. | |
| CNN | News | C/S | Com./Sub. | 41 | n.a. | |
| Discovery | Documentary | C/S | Com./Sub. | 38 | n.a. | |
| MTV | Music | C/S | Com./Sub. | 37 | n.a. | |

a T Terrestrial; C Cable; S Satellite. b Lic. Licence fee; Com. Commercials; Sub. Subscription fee n.a. Figures not available.
Source: Carlsson and Harrie (2001).

Terrestrial radio channels, 2000

| Channel | Financing | Market share(%) | Owner |
|---|---|---|---|
| NRK P-1 | Licence fee[a] | 47 | NRK (Public) |
| NRK P-2 | Licence fee[a] | 4 | NRK (Public) |
| NRK PeTre | Licence fee[a] | 8 | NRK (Public) |
| P-4 | Commercials | 28 | *Kinnevik* + others |
| 274 local | Commercials + | 12 | *Aller, Orkla,* |
| radio stations | private subsidies | | *Schibsted* + others |

Channels with satellite, cable or Internet distribution are also available, but do not play an important role.
a There is no licence fee for radio. *NRK*'s radio channels are financed by the television licence fee.

Percentage of households (2000) reached by:
| | |
|---|---|
| Satellite | 21 |
| Cable | 39 |
| Terrestrial pay-television | 0 |

Percentage of households (2000) with:
| | |
|---|---|
| VCR | 79 |
| Satellite receiver | 21 |
| DVD player | n.a. |

**Electronic media**

Percentage of households with: Digital television reception. No exact data available, but probably most cable television subscribers and families with their own satellite antenna are equipped for digital reception (2002)

| | |
|---|---|
| Access to personal computer (2000) | 71 |
| Mobile phones, 2001 (Source: Norwegian PTT Authority) | 83 |

**Advertising spend, 2001 (%)**

| | |
|---|---|
| Newspapers | 40.4 |
| Magazines | 13.5 |
| Television | 38.8 |
| Radio | 4.2 |
| Cinemas | 1.1 |
| Billboards | 2.0 |

Source: MedieNorge, from Nielsen.

**Ownership**

Main media companies:

| Owner | Country | Newspapers | Magazines | Book | Radio | TV | Film/video | Internet |
|---|---|---|---|---|---|---|---|---|
| Schibsted | Norway | ++ | + | + | | ++ | ++ | ++ |
| Norwegian state: | Norway | | | | + | ++ | | ++ |
| Telenor | | | | | ++ | ++ | + | + |
| NRK | Norway | ++ | | | ++ | | + | |
| A-pressen | Norway | ++ | ++ | | | | + | + |
| Orkla | Sweden | + | ++ | | + | + | | |
| Bonnier | Denmark | | ++ | | | ++ | ++ | |
| Egmont | Denmark | | ++ | | ++ | | | |
| Aller | Norway | | | ++ | | | | |
| Aschehoug | Norway | | | ++ | | | | |
| Gyldendal | Sweden | | | | ++ | + | | |
| Kinnevik (MTG) | | | | | | | | |

+ Important actor. + + Very important actor (among the largest).
Source: based partly on Roppen (2000) and Østbye (2000).

# REFERENCES

Bens, Els de and Østbye, Helge (1998) 'Changes in the European newspaper market' in Denis McQuail and Karen Siune (eds) *Media Policy: Convergence, Concentration and Commerce*. London: Sage.

Carlsson, Ulla, and Harrie, Eva, eds (2001) *Media Trends 2001 in Denmark, Finland, Iceland, Norway and Sweden*. Göteborg: Nordicom.

Gustafsson, Karl Erik (1996) *Dagspressen i Norden: struktur och ekonomi*. Lund: Studentlitteratur.

Haugen, Einar (1966) *Language Conflict and Language Planning*. Cambridge MA: Harvard University Press.

NOU (1999) *Ytringsfrihed bdr finde Sted* (report of the Government Commission on Freedom of Expression). Oslo: NOU.

Ottosen, Rune, Rössland, Lars Arve and Östbye, Helge (2002) *Norsk pressehistorie*. Oslo: Samlaget.

Roppen, Johann (2000) 'Medieeigarskap' in Nina Bjdmstad and Dag Grdnnestad (eds) *MedieNorge 1999*. Bergen: Fagbokforlaget.

St meld. nr 32 (1992–93) *Media i tida* (White Paper on the media).

Syvertsen, Trine (1997) *Den store TV-krigen: Norsk allmennfjernsyn 1988–1996*. Bergen: Fagbokforlaget.

Østbye, Helge (2000) *Om eierforhold i norske media*. Bergen: Department of Media Studies, University of Bergen.

# 15: Poland

KAROL JAKUBOWICZ

## NATIONAL PROFILE

Poland is a country of nearly 39 million people (some 12.5 million households) undergoing rapid systemic transformation after the collapse of communism. As a largely ethnically homogeneous nation, Poland has been spared the ethnic conflicts and war that have affected post-communist transformation in so many other countries. Regarded as one of the more successful cases of transformation, and as an EU candidate country in a stage of far-reaching alignment with the Community *acquis*, it shares all the features of post-communism (Schöpflin, 1995) with a relatively advanced case of mimetic development. It has revived and reinstated, or copied and transplanted, the political, legal and organizational frameworks of democracy and the market economy. It now has to wait for them to take root, and for the social, cultural and axiological frameworks that give meaning to those institutions and ensure their proper functioning to emerge in full – a process certain to take a long time. Nevertheless, it is one of a relatively small number of post-communist countries where economic reform has led to the development of a functioning market economy (World Bank, 2002).

Since 1989 the Polish media have undergone a stormy process of change. The old centralized media system has been dismantled, the print media have been privatized and a broadcasting system has been introduced, composed, legally speaking, of public, commercial and civic sectors. Change was mostly politically driven to begin with, and since then has increasingly been market-driven. That was assisted by large-scale foreign investment, especially in the print media,

cable television and terrestrial television (for overviews of this process see, e.g., Filas, 1995; Jarowiecki, 1996; Chorazki, 1999).

The state has almost completely withdrawn from the media. It retains ownership of Ruch, a press distribution agency, and a controlling interest in the Polish Press Agency, pending their complete privatization. Meanwhile government control over them has not provoked significant complaints about their use for political ends.

## STRUCTURE AND OWNERSHIP

### The print media

#### The newspaper press
Changes in the number of newspapers and periodicals published since 1989 tell an interesting story. The number of newspapers grew from fifty three in 1989 to eighty in 1992, only to fall to forty nine in 1999. Meanwhile the number of weeklies grew from 239 in 1989 to 418 in 1999; that of fortnightlies from 130 to 276, that of monthlies from 678 to 1,849, and that of bi-monthlies and quarterlies from 748 to 1,450 in the same period (Central Statistical Office, 2001). The number of sub-local newspapers has grown from about 100 in 1988 to as many as 1,800 in 2000. These include newspapers directed at inhabitants of one city quarter, one town, one county, one parish or one local association (OBP, n.d.).

What was originally a politically inspired publishing boom (every new party and organization wanted its own newspaper) was soon brought down to size by the market, which killed off virtually all party newspapers, responded to demand for previously underdeveloped types of newspapers (regional, local and specialized ones) and showed clearly how few national general-interest dailies can survive fierce competition. The number of such dailies fell from twelve to six, of which only three really count: the liberal *Gazeta Wyborcza*, the right-of-centre *Rzeczpospolita* and the tabloid *Super Express*. There are also the Catholic daily *Nasz Dziennik*, the conservative *Życie* and the social-democrat *Trybuna*. Other national dailies are tailored to specialized markets, dealing with the economy and business (*Puls Biznesu* or *Prawo i Gospodarka*), legal issues (*Gazeta Prawna*) or sport (*Przeglad sportowy* or *Tempo*).

Between 1991 and 2000 sales of dailies fell by one-third, compared with 1988, while the newspapers themselves grew from an average of six to eight pages in 1989 to between sixty and eighty. Local editions and supplements of both national and regional dailies have been developing, and *Gazeta Wyborcza* with its eighteen local supplements (practically full-fledged newspapers in their own right) is the dominant force in the market.

In 2001 there were are about twenty publishers of daily newspapers in Poland. The top publishing company had a 24.5 per cent market share, the three top companies (Agora, Polskapresse, controlled by Neue Passauer Presse of Germany, and Orkla Media, a Norwegian company) accounted for 63 per cent, and the top five for 82 per cent.

Little systematic research on media concentration is published in Poland. According to Andersen, there were twenty five cases of mergers and acquisitions in Polish broadcasting in 2000 (compared with 383 in Europe as a whole). The seventeen cases whose value was revealed added up to €363.1 million, compared with €85.2 billion for the 154 European mergers and acquisitions of known value.

Among ninety leading publishing houses analysed in late 1998, forty one were controlled wholly or partly by foreign owners (of these, fifteen had exclusively foreign owners). Foreign investors involved in those ninety publishing houses come from Germany (eight companies), Switzerland (four), Holland (three companies), the United States (two), Italy (two), Norway (one) and France (three companies with shares in one publishing house).

In 1998, among the forty two publishers of regional and local newspapers, twenty

(i.e. 47.6 per cent of the total) were owned wholly or partly by foreign interests. Among the fifty four regional and local newspapers, twenty were brought out by foreign-owned publishers: Polskapresse, of Germany (eleven titles, many with local and sub-local editions) and Orkla Media Polen (Norway) with nine titles (and a majority shareholder in *Rzeczpospolita*). Both have continued buying up local and sub-local newspapers.

Probably the largest media conglomerate, operating across both print and electronic media, is Agora (13 per cent of its stock is held by Cox Enterprises, an American company), the publisher of *Gazeta Wyborcza*, the leading Polish daily, with its twelve thematic supplements and nineteen local sections. Agora publishes thirteen magazines, owns three printing plants, owns or has interests in twenty four local radio stations around the country and in an outdoor advertising company, and operates an on-line version of *Gazeta Wyborcza*, as well as an Internet portal.

Among other Polish publishers of importance, mention must be made of Infor (which brings out over forty magazines with legal and business information for entrepreneurs); Prószyński i Spółka (publisher of a variety of periodicals), Wydawnictwo Sigma-Not (some forty titles on construction, electronics, power engineering, metallurgy, etc.), Murator (a number of magazines dealing with housing and the construction industry).

Similar media concentration processes are unfolding also at the regional level. For example, Głos Wielkopolski Oficyna Wydawnicza, the publisher of *Głos Wielkopolski*, the leading daily in Poznań, western Poland, has shares in three radio stations and in a cable television system, owns a national monthly magazine, has an Internet company, and in addition owns a private university.

### Advertising

In 2000 advertising spending amounted to US$ 1.5 billion to US$ 1.9 billion. The advertising market is atypical in that television, and not the press, is the main advertising medium. The 1990s have seen an explosion of advertising, fuelled by the country's fast economic growth. According to Zenith Media, advertising spending grew by 60 per cent in 1996, compared with the year before, 52 per cent in 1997, 51 per cent in 1998, 26 per cent in 1999 and 11.3 per cent in 2000. In recent years, recession has had a dampening effect on advertising, leading to sizeable lay-offs in many media organizations, but there is no doubt as to the market's ability to sustain a wide range of media. With per capita spending on advertising of US$ 45 per annum (in 2000), the advertising market still has a long way to go, given that the figure then stood at US$ 279 in the United Kingdom, and at $ 492 in the United State. Nevertheless, given the fact that multinational companies are at the top of the table of advertising spending in Poland and that international advertising agencies (Leo Burnett, McCann-Erickson, Ogilvy & Mather, Hager, Saatchi & Saatchi, J. Walter Thompson/Parintex, Publicis, Lowe Lintas GGK, etc.) are all operating in Poland, it is well integrated with the global market.

Tumultuous change in the press market was accompanied by equally significant changes in readership patterns. First, there was a time of re-evaluation of old titles as a great many new ones appeared on the market. *Gazeta Wyborcza* (*Election Newspaper*), launched by Solidarity in advance of the first quasi-free election in June 1989, became a symbol of the new era and took the market by storm. Many of the old dailies went out of business.

The second half of 1994 marked the beginning of a three-year period when powerful German publishers launched a great number of popular periodicals. The public enjoyed this new offer, as 'readership' changed into 'viewership' of richly illustrated glossy periodicals. In 1998–2000 publishers identified and targeted new market segments and niches. Only two dailies survived in each of the regional press markets, whereas a few years earlier three to five of them were published. Thus what had been uncritical enjoyment of new titles now turned into highly competitive selection, especially in terms of the decrease in the volume of sales. Occasional, irregular readership, especially of dailies, was the prevailing pattern. In the first half of 2001 the sales of all national, regional and local dailies saw a sharp drop. The same is true of the magazine market, though some popular women's weeklies, lifestyle magazines and opinion weeklies held their own. Also magazines devoted to spectacular television events or shows (e.g. *Big Brother*) were very successful.

### The periodical and magazine press

Three opinion weeklies, *Polityka* and *Wprost* and *Newsweek* (whose Polish edition was successfully launched in August 2001), take pride of place in this market as the most influential publications of their kind (in August 2002 *Wprost* claimed sales of 2.6 million, equalling 8.7 per cent of the market for weeklies, with *Polityka* reportedly accounting for 6.4 per cent and *Newsweek* for 6.1 per cent). The former two, both long established, have had to be dramatically redesigned (in *Polityka's* case from a broadsheet into a full-colour, richly illustrated magazine) to keep pace with the changing demands of their readers.

Western, especially German, publishers have launched a great number and variety of periodicals in two waves: first, beginning in 1994, weeklies for women, entertainment/gossip magazines and new television guides dominated the press market. Then, in 1998–2000, publishers identified and targeted new market segments and niches. Many advice magazines (*Olivia*) or people magazines (*Viva!*), or exclusive, lifestyle magazines addressed to women (*Cosmopolitan*) and men (*CKM*) were successfully launched at that time. Also lifestyle magazines addressed to men began to appear. At the same time there was a turn towards popular science periodicals (e.g. *Cogito, Focus* or *National Geographic*). Computer, games and Internet magazines, as well as automobile magazines (e.g. *Auto Świat*) also found many readers.

The fourteen biggest magazine publishers (Prószynski i Spólka and Agora are the major Polish companies among them) publish over 100 titles which are most read, and with a total aggregate circulation of 30 million copies. Many of these magazines are Polish versions of Western European or American magazines (e.g. *Reader's Digest* or *Tina*).

Among the most popular magazines are those, published by German publishers, addressed to girls and women. The variety of magazine types is even greater among fortnightlies and monthlies. Besides magazines for women and girls (such as 'lifestyle'), there are hobby magazines (computer, DIY, interior design, motor, garden, cooking, etc.), children's and youth magazines (computer games, cartoons, etc.), magazines for men (erotica), and Catholic magazines either opinion or social-religious, e.g. *Niedziela* and *Gość Niedzielny*.

A number of national and ethnic minorities (including German, Jewish, Lithuanian, Ukrainian, Belarussian, Tartar and other groups) have their own periodicals.

### Book publishing

In 2001 over 19,000 book titles were published in 74.4 million copies. Of those, 508 titles were published for the first time (61.1 million copies).

## The electronic (audio-visual) media

### Television

Practically all households have a television set. Some 50 per cent of households can receive satellite television (18 per cent via a satellite dish and the rest via cable television). A total of around 400 different satellite channels are available via cable. This includes all the international channels available in Europe. Some fifty of these channels are in the Polish language or have Polish voice-over translation (this includes Eurosport, Planete, Animal Planet, Discovery, Travel, National Geographic, Fox Kids, Hallmark, TCM; soon to come is MTV Polska, a Polish-language version of MTV).

Thirty one per cent of households have a VCR, while some twenty one per cent have a video player. 4 per cent of households now have a DVD player. Some 4 per cent of households have digital television sets. Using these and set-top boxes, 4 per cent of households receive the Cyfra + digital satellite platform, and 2 per cent the Polsat 2 Cyfrowy platform.

The two satellite pay-television channels (Canal plus and HBO) available in Poland are received in 3 per cent of households.

Polish Television (TVP), a public service organization, broadcasts three generalist national channels: TVP-1, TVP-2 and TVP-3 (with regional opt-outs for the twelve regional stations forming part of TVP); a satellite channel (TV Polonia) addressed to Poles resident abroad, but also available to the Polish audience, e.g. by means of cable television.

Terrestrial free-to-air commercial television is controlled by two main players: POLSAT (wholly owned by Zygmunt Solorz, a Polish businessman) and TVN (part of ITI Holdings, 33 per cent owned by SBS Broadcasting).

POLSAT broadcasts a national channel under the same name and indirectly controls TV-4, a sub-national channel. It also supplies programming to the eight local television stations operating in Poland and sells their advertising time. POLSAT operates a digital satellite platform (POLSAT 2 Cyfrowy) with a number of thematic channels, which has some 300,000 subscribers. POLSAT's other holdings and interests include a cable system, two television stations in Latvia and Lithuania, a pension fund, a bank and e-commerce ventures.

TVN broadcasts a sub-national television channel under the same name, TVN-7 (previously RTL-7, owned by the RTL group) – a satellite-to-cable movie channel – and TVN-24, a satellite-to-cable news channel. TVN is the centrepiece of ITI Holdings, a budding Luxembourg-based media empire also involving two production companies (Endemol Neovision and ITI Film Studio), a string of multiplex cinemas, two Internet portals and a software company, in addition to non-media interests.

Another established television player in Poland is Canal plus Polska, an encrypted pay-television film and sports channel. It is also the majority owner of Nowa Cyfra Plus, a digital satellite platform. It provides a wide variety of satellite channels and some interactive services and has 700,000 subscribers.

The market shares of public television and the national and subnational commercial channels are shown below.

Mention must also be made of TV Plus, a Catholic television channel with limited geographical reach. Its programming is provided by Telewizja Familijna (Family Television), a production company created with investments from a number of state companies. It is perennially short of cash and has had to cut costs by eliminating much of its line-up of in-house news and current affairs programming.

The year 2002 saw considerable activity on the television scene, with a number of new satellite services for the Polish audience coming on stream. In addition, a number of international channels (Discovery, Eurosport, MTV, etc.) added a Polish-language version for the Polish market.

Some 4.5 million households are on cable.

Both public radio and television are financed by licence fees and advertising. Polish Television accounted in 2001 for some 46 per cent of the total television advertising spend; Polish Radio and the regional public service radio companies for a combined total of 12.1 per cent of the radio spend. The strong position of TVP (in terms of both audience and advertising market share) is one of the media policy issues under constant debate.

Polish Television derives over 60 per cent of its funding from advertising revenue, with unavoidable consequences for its programme offer, seen by many as too commercialized and entertainment-oriented.

Table 15.1  *The two most prominent programme types of the major television broadcasters (%)*

| TVP-1 | TVP-2 | TVN | POLSAT | TV-4 | TV Plus |
|---|---|---|---|---|---|
| Films and series 36 | Films and series 38 | Films and series 42 | Films and series 49 | Films and series 47 | Films and series 54 |
| Current affairs 16 | News 10 | Entertainment 28 | Light music 17 | Entertainment 21 | Current affairs 9 |

Source: annual report of the National Broadcasting Council for 2001.

Polish Radio is more public service-oriented, but as a result is much less successful in preserving its position in the market and its share of the audience.

Table 15.1 shows the two programme genres were most prominent in the air time of particular public and commercial television stations. This is taken as evidence of excessive commercialization of public television's programming. To get a fuller picture, let us note that among other major genres, news takes up 8 per cent and 10 per cent of air time respectively on TVP-1 and TVP-2, current affairs 16 per cent and 7 per cent, documentary films 8 per cent and 8 per cent, entertainment 5 per cent and 9 per cent, education and practical advice 6 per cent and 2 per cent, sport 5 per cent and 4 per cent, religion 2 per cent and under 1 per cent, advertising and teleshopping 7 per cent and 5 per cent.

### Radio

Polish Radio, the national public service radio broadcaster, broadcasts four national channels and an External Service, composed of national services in different languages. There are in addition seventeen regional public service radio companies.

Poland's active and highly competitive commercial broadcasting sector includes two nationwide stations: Radio Zet in Warsaw, owned by the Eurozet company (49 per cent-owned by French companies), and RMF FM in Kraków, fully Polish-owned.

Facing strong competition from other commercial radio stations, Radio Zet and RMF FM are reorienting their profiles from generalist to music and entertainment, reducing news, current affairs and other programme types.

Radio Maryja, a Catholic network run by the Redemptorist Fathers, is an important social and political force. It devotes up to 50 per cent of air time to strictly religious programming, some 15 per cent to news and current affairs.

Another category is formed by 'supraregional stations', available mainly in big towns: Radio WAWA, 33 per cent owned by Eurocast of Germany, a generalist channel; Radiostacja (49 per cent-owned by Eurozet, owner of Radio Zet), a niche station for young people; Tok FM, a news-and-talk station owned by a number of Polish and foreign companies.

There are also two networks of music-oriented stations: ESKA (twenty local stations broadcasting different programme services, mostly in big towns, formed under the auspices of the multimedia holding company ZPR), and Agora (seventeen local stations mostly broadcasting music, owned or co-owned by Agora.

Twenty four radio stations established by the dioceses and archdioceses of the Roman Catholic Church form a network using the services of Plus, a production company partly owned by the Church, which provides news, current affairs and other programming, accounting for between 40 per cent and 80 per cent of air time in the programming of particular stations.

Apart from that, there are also some twenty other local Catholic stations, three radio stations of other denominations, and seven stations operated by universities.

The audience share of the main national and supra-regional stations in the first half of 2002 is shown in the 'statistics' section.

### Film and video

After 1989, film production was assisted by the State Committee of Polish Cinematography which, acting through specialized agencies, provided co-financing for the pre-production, production, distribution and promotion of selected films. Polish Television and Canal plus Polska also invested heavily in film production. Other television broadcasters were under an obligation to do the same. The film studios (grouping directors, script writers, and other film makers) have to support themselves from whatever funding they can obtain for their films, and the profits they bring. There are in addition independent film producers.

In recent years, state funding for film production has dried up, the committee has been dissolved, and recession has eaten into the profits of television stations (which have therefore reduced their investment in film making). Polish cinema has accordingly been experiencing serious difficulties. Film studios sought financing from banks, but except for a few blockbusters have not been able to return a profit on the investment, so banks have been wary of further involvement. Poland produces around twenty feature films a year. Foreign, especially American, films account for over 90 per cent of films shown in cinemas. In 2001 cinema admissions equalled 27.6 million. Multiplex cinemas are becoming popular.

## The Internet and related on-line media

Twenty three per cent of households have a personal computer. Twenty one per cent of Poles have access to the Internet. Among them, 39 per cent access the Internet at home, 31 per cent at school or a university, 23 per cent at work, 7 per cent in an Internet café, 5 per cent at their friends' homes (Expert-Monitor, www:http://www.expert. wroc.pl/monit-rap.php3). Some 6.5 million Poles (17 per cent) are regarded as regular Internet users.

Among some 500 ISPs and data transmission companies, pride of place is taken by TP, former monopoly telecoms operator, now 47.5 per cent owned by a consortium involving France Télécom.

The two most popular Polish horizontal portals were launched in the mid-1990s: Wirtualna Polska in 1995 and Onet in 1996.

According to April 2002 figures, three leading Polish portals (Onet, Wirtualna Polska and Interia.pl) attract more than 75 per cent of all visits.

# POLITICS, POLICY, LAW AND REGULATION

Poland's 1997 constitution guarantees freedom of speech in language similar to that of Article 10 of the European Convention on Human Rights, as well as freedom of the press and the other media and the right of access to public information. Poland is recognized as a country of free speech and free media.

If one looks a little closer, it is clear that four forces are shaping the media system and its regulatory framework: politics (as befits a partitocratic country where civil society is weak and public life has been 'colonized' by political parties: Grabowska, 2001; Hausner and Marody, 2000), the market, technology and international integration.

The main thrust of media policy has been political and, to some extent, cultural. Technological and economic factors have not been given a great deal of attention. Even though Poland is adopting EU policies (e.g. 'e-Europe') oriented towards developing the knowledge-based society, policy – overshadowed by party-political interests and lingering public definitions of the media as primarily political institutions – is only beginning to become aware of the practical implications of convergence and the interdependence of the Internet and the media, and the need to encompass them both within the ambit of policy making.

Politics mainly impacts on the operation of public media. Commercial media are on the whole free to adjust to the vicissitudes of the market, though some aspects of policy making affecting them may also be politically driven. However, at least at the national level, they are already powerful enough to influence policy and, in most cases, resist encroachments on their freedom. This is not to deny the fact that many media have close ties with politicians of one persuasion or another.

Media politicization is not only a top-down but also a bottom-up process. Many publishers and journalists consider it their civic duty to be involved in the process of reshaping the country and determining its future, also by supporting political ideas and organizations of their choice.

Market competition is now the decisive factor in determining prospects for the survival and development of particular commercial media outlets. Media concentration processes are in full swing, promoted in part by the growing involvement of foreign capital in the Polish media – giving practical effect to their globalization. The market has taken over also in this sense that media users with their remotes opt for *Big Brother*, or *Who wants to be a millionaire?* instead of other, more ambitious content. Of some 200 private radio stations, only a handful offer special programme formats. All the others have had to reorient their programming to the rather undifferentiated tastes of the mass audience. As noted above, only two quality national daily newspapers and three opinion weeklies are successful. The audience is able to impose its tastes and interests on the media, and this has created special difficulties for the public media, which cannot afford to ignore the popular taste yet are always being accused of neglecting their cultural mission.

Technology is promoting a process of convergence, though not a great deal of money is yet to be made by offering convergent services.

Finally, the EU accession process and membership of other international organizations have had a strong impact on the regulatory framework.

The Polish version of 'media wars' pits 'political society' against civil society and media interests. 'Political society' has few administrative means of controlling the media (even public service media are virtually impervious to direct administrative influence by the government of the day), and the political culture (though as yet crude) is mature enough not to permit outrageous use of the law or other means to cow the media. So, even though civil society is still weak and resigned to politicization of the media, the 'war' takes relatively civilized forms. There should, however, be no illusion as to the intention of political elites to control the public media and influence private ones, especially at the local level.

There is growing, though as yet far from sufficient, awareness of the economic importance of the media, especially convergent media, so this factor is not strong enough to influence media policy.

There are no limits on foreign investment in the print media or ownership of cable television systems, but the Broadcasting Act imposes a cap of 33 per cent (to be eliminated when Poland joins the European Union) on foreign participation in broadcast media outlets. Foreign investors try to keep out of political battles for control of the media when they can, and generally play safe. For example, local newspapers owned by foreign publishers are said to be much more cautious in criticizing local power elites than are independent Polish-owned newspapers (Sawkowski, 2002).

## The main regulatory agencies

There is only one media regulatory agency, the National Broadcasting Council (NBC). The Telecommunications and Post Regulatory Office is responsible for frequency management and in this capacity is involved in licensing procedures.

## The press

The 1984 Press Law was amended in 1989 and 1990, lifting all constraints on the press and introducing a simple registration system for new titles. Also in 1990 censorship was formally banned. The 2001 Access to Public Information Act is another element of the regulatory framework, though it has been criticized for accepting that other laws (e.g. on the protection of state secrets) may take precedence over the principle of access to information.

The main advantage of the press law in force is that it does not constrain the media, i.e. mainly the media owners, in any way. At the same time, it is silent on such issues as concentration of ownership, lack of transparency of ownership, journalists' working conditions and abuses of journalistic freedom.

There have been several attempts to draft a new press law. One which would have introduced a regulatory body for the print media and introduced many other constraints on press freedom, was rejected by parliament on its first reading in 1999.

A major row broke out when the social democratic government (dominated by a communist-successor party), in proposing amendments to the Broadcasting Act in 2001, sought to curb excessive cross-media ownership by means of a draft provision banning the ownership of a national radio or television channel by a 'national newspaper'. That was widely seen as a politically inspired move, intended to prevent *Gazeta Wyborcza*, the largest daily newspaper of liberal orientation and Solidarity background, from branching out into national terrestrial television. Some months later, following a massive media campaign against the proposal, an embattled government climbed down and changed the proposed provision so that it would ban ownership of a national television channel by the publisher of any newspaper or newspapers with a 30 per cent market share (*Gazeta Wyborcza* has a share of 17 per cent).

Selective use of public funds to subsidize, or place public advertising in, 'friendly' media is another issue of concern.

The Polish print media system has been described as a 'pluralistic system of party-oriented newspapers', with particular daily newspapers committed to promoting a set of political interests or views (Burnetko, 1995). Most major national general-interest dailies have a clear political identity and support one or other political grouping.

The Press Law envisages the existence of a Press Council, but since it is to be appointed by the Prime Minister, no head of government has used this power since 1989 in the knowledge that such a council would have no credibility.

The print and broadcast media formed a 'Conference of Polish Media' in 1995, as a self-regulatory body. Because of political divisions and conflicts of interest, it has not been able to play a role of importance. The conference has appointed a Media Ethics Council to pronounce itself on what it sees as breaches of journalistic ethics. The council has no teeth and little authority.

The main journalistic organizations are: the Polish Journalists' Association (SDP), the Journalists' Association of the Republic of Poland (these two associations have their own codes of conduct and seek to enforce them), the Catholic Association of Journalists, the Syndicate of Polish Journalists, the Union of Journalists, the Union of Television and Radio Journalists, the European Club of Journalists, the Local Press Association, the Polish Local Press Association and the Polish chapter of the Association of European Journalists.

The major media owners' organizations are: the Polish Chamber of Press Publishers and the Association of the Local Press Publishers.

Polish Chamber of Press Publishers (established in March 1996) represents its members vis-à-vis the authorities and provides legal assistance to them. The Press Circulation Audit Union aims to provide reliable and verifiable information about the print runs and sales of newspapers and periodicals, serving both publishers and advertisers. A Centre for Monitoring Press Freedom, maintained by the Polish Journalists' Association, seeks to expose all curbs on media freedom and access to information, also providing legal advice to journalists.

## The electronic media

Broadcasting is regulated by the 1992 Broadcasting Act which introduced the dual system of public and commercial broadcasting (in 2001 another category was added, that of 'civic broadcasters' for non-commercial private stations serving worthy, mainly religious, causes) and created the regulatory authority, the National Broadcasting Council (NBC).

The NBC is composed of nine members: four are appointed by the lower chamber of parliament, two by the upper chamber and three by the President of the country. The council's chairperson is elected by the members themselves. Members have staggered terms (every two years one-third of them are replaced), so no parliamentary majority can decisively influence the composition of the whole council. The members cannot be dismissed.

The NBC has extensive powers: to issue secondary regulation envisaged in the Broadcasting Act, license commercial broadcasters and allocate frequencies in co-operation with telecommunications authorities, supervise public and commercial broadcasters, etc. The National Broadcasting Council issues secondary regulations when authorized to do so by the Broadcasting Act, where many detailed issues are decided within the general framework created by the statute. Together with the licences to broadcast issued to commercial broadcasters, they affect the content of programming.

The main principles of regulation have been demonopolization and transformation of the state-controlled broadcasting organization into a strong public service broadcasting system, capable of surviving in a competitive market. Another goal has been protection of the national audio-visual market.

With time, regulation has had to respond to new challenges. At the time of writing, parliament is working on amendments to the Broadcasting Act, devoted in part to regulating digital terrestrial broadcasting, as well as to completing the job of harmonizing it with the European Union's 'Television without Frontiers' directive, and aligning it with the Union's 'Telecoms Package 2003'.

The Broadcasting Act describes the programme obligations of public service broadcasters in general terms, but it is proposed that a 'programme licence' (to be granted by NBC) be introduced for them as an accountability mechanism, providing both a detailed list of obligations and a set of criteria for assessing performance. Amendments to the Broadcasting Act are also to improve licence fee collection (Polish Television receives less than 60 per cent of the expected licence fee revenue).

At the same time, commercial broadcasters are, as in many other countries, exerting pressure on successive governments to 'create a more level playing field' – e.g. by reducing the proportion of air time it can devote to advertising (at present there are no differences in this respect between public and commercial broadcasters, except for the fact that public broadcasters may insert advertising only between and not during programme items). The original plan to create strong and independent public service broadcasting may be in danger of redefinition as governments seek an accommodation with private media.

The legal status of public service broadcasters is that of 'one-person joint stock companies of the State Treasury'. The state owns all the shares in these companies and is represented at their general meetings of shareholders by the Minister of the State Treasury. Despite their formal status as state companies, public service broadcasters are not really controlled by either parliament or government. The general meeting of shareholders (i.e. the Minister of the State Treasury) is legally prohibited from affecting the content of programming. Also, it appoints only one out of nine members of the supervisory boards of public radio and television; the remaining eight are appointed by the broadcasting regulatory body.

This system of PSB governance (with six-year staggered terms for NBC members, three-year terms for the supervisory councils of public broadcasters and four-year terms for their boards of management), in which supervisory board members cannot be dismissed, was designed to ensure political balance in the membership of the NBC and the governing bodies of public broadcasters and to prevent undue political influence on them. However, owing to the 'colonization' of public life by political parties, and to the vagaries of electoral results, the appointment of all members is intensely political and their composition is lopsided in favour of left-of-centre parties. Thus public service broadcasters are not seen as impartial; rather as a mouthpiece for one side of the political divide.

Commercial broadcasters are free to choose their allies and usually try to maintain good relations with whoever is in power.

The following self-regulatory organizations should be mentioned: the Convenion of Local Commercial Radio Stations, the Association of Independent Film and Television Producers and the National Industrial Chamber of Cable Communications. All lobby on behalf of their members' interests.

It can be expected that as Poland enters the European Union, the main thrust of its broadcasting and general communications policy will begin to reflect the Union's predominantly economic and technological approach to broadcasting, probably (for quite some time yet) with an admixture of political 'media wars'.

## The Internet and related on-line media

The Internet as such is unregulated. There is, however, a growing body of legislation concerning e-commerce and other business aspects of the Internet, e.g. concerning electronic signatures.

## STATISTICS

| | |
|---|---|
| Population | 39,000,000 |
| Number of households | 12,500,000 |
| Cinema admissions annually | 27,600,000 |
| Book published (titles) | 19,000 |

**Print media** — Average sales of national and regional dailies in the first half of 2002

| National | |
|---|---|
| Gazeta Wyborcza | 443,596 |
| Rzeczpospolita | 189,563 |
| Super Express | 315,161 |
| Trybuna | 39,385 |
| Życie | 33,016 |

| Regional | |
|---|---|
| Gazeta Pomorska | 102,530 |
| Dziennik Zachodni | 92,119 |
| Dziennik Battycki | 81,919 |
| Dziennik Polski | 68,210 |
| Express Ilustrowany | 66,183 |
| Dziennik tódzki | 57,588 |

| | |
|---|---|
| *Trybuna Śląska* | 56,073 |
| *Głos Wielkopolski* | 55,831 |
| *Gazeta Lubuska* | 53,179 |
| *Gazeta Poznańska* | 47,637 |

Source: *Press* 6 (77), 2002.

**Broadcast media**

Market share of main national and subnational television stations (%)

| | |
|---|---|
| Public television | |
| TVP-1 | 26.1 |
| TVP-2 | 20.6 |
| TVP-3 | 3.9 |
| | |
| Commercial television | |
| Polsat | 18.9 |
| TVN | 14.1 |
| TV-4 | 3.8 |
| Canal Plus | 3.0 |
| TVN-7[a] | 1.5 |

[a]TVN-7 has been on the air in its present form since March 2002.
Source: TNS OBOP.

Audience share of main national and supra-regional radio stations (%)

| | |
|---|---|
| Polish Radio channels | |
| Programme | |
| I PR (generalist) | 16.2 |
| Programme III PR (for young people) | 5.0 |
| Programme II PR (high-brow) | 0.5 |
| Radio Bis (educational) | 0.1 |
| Commercial channels | |
| RMF FM | 22.8 |
| Radio Zet | 18.1 |
| Radio Maryja | 3.5 |
| Radio WAWa | 1.5 |
| Radiostacja | 0.5 |
| Radio Tok FM | 0.3 |

Source: Radio Track 2002 survey conducted by SMG/KRC Poland Media.

| | |
|---|---|
| Percentage reached by cable (4.5 million) | 36 |
| Percentage of households with:Video-cassette recorder | 52 |
| Satellite receiver | 6 |
| DVD player | 4 |
| Digital television reception | n.a. |
| Internet use | 21 |
| Mobile phone | 36 |

**Advertising spend, June 2002 (%)**

| | |
|---|---|
| Television | 65.10 |
| Newspapers | 19.75 |
| Periodicals | 13.00 |
| Radio | 6.56 |
| Outdoor | 5.17 |
| Cinemas | 0.34 |

Source: Expert-Monitor, http://www.expert.wroc.pl/monit-rap.php3.

# ACKNOWLEDGEMENTS

The author wishes to acknowledge the assistance of Mr Wojciech Siesicki in preparing this chapter. He has also relied on the report *Media in Poland: an Overview* prepared by the Press Research Centre of the Jagiellonian University in Kraków (OBP, n.d.) for some of the information included here.

# REFERENCES

Burnetko, K. (1995) 'Media a wybory: egzamin, jednak, zaliczony. Z Walerym Pisarkiem rozmawia K. Burnetko'. *Tygodnik Powszechny*, 50, 10 December, p. 36.

Central Statistical Office (2001) *Statistical Yearbook of the Republic of Poland 1989–2000*. Warsaw.

Chorazki. W. (1999) 'Polskie media lokalne i sublokalne 1989–1999', *Zeszyty Prasoznawcze*, 42 (1–2): 59–82.

Grabowska, Mirostawa (2001) 'Partie polityczne jako dzialajacy aktorzy. Partyjne organizacje – programy – elity' in Mirostawa Grabowska and Tadeusz Szawiel (eds) *Budowanie demokracji*. Warsaw: Wydawnictwo Naukowe PWN.

Filas, Ryszard (1995) 'Panorama czytelnictwa prasy 1989–1994'. in A. Stomkowska (ed.) *Pieciolecie transformacji mediów 1989–1994*. Warsaw: Uniwersytet Warszawski, Dom Wydawniczy Elipsa.

Filas, Ryszard (1999) 'Dziesieć lat przemian mediów masowych w Polsce 1989–1999', *Zeszyty Prasoznawcze*, 42 (1–2): 30–58.

Filas, Ryszard (2001) 'Aktywność czytelnicza Polaków przelomu wieku', *Zeszyty Prasoznawcze*, pp. 3–4.

Hausner, Jerzy and Marody, Mirostawa (2000) 'Miekki kraj', *Polityka* 50, 5 December, pp. 24–5.

Jarowiecki, J. (1996) 'Przeksztatcenia prasy polskiej w latach 1989–1995' in A. Slomkowska et al. (eds.) *Transformacja mediów 1989–1995*. Warsaw: Uniwersytet Warszawski, Dom Wydawniczy Elipsa.

Linz, J.J. and Stepan A. (1996) *Problems of Democratic Transition and Consolidation: Southern Europe, South America, and post-Communist Europe*. Baltimore OH and London: Johns Hopkins University Press.

OBP (n.d.) *Media in Poland: an Overview*. Craków: Ośrodek Badań Prasoznawczych. http://www.obp.pl/Transformation1.htm.

Sawkowski, Pawet (2002) 'Czwarta wtadza powiatowa', *Newsweek Polska*, 30 June, pp. 94–5.

Schöpflin, G. (1995) 'Post-communism: a profile', *Javnost/The Public* 2 (1): 63:74.

World Bank (2002) *Transition: the First Ten Years. Analysis and Lessons for Eastern Europe and the Former Soviet Union*. Washington DC: World Bank.

# 16: Portugal

MANUEL PINTO AND HELENA SOUSA

## NATIONAL PROFILE

Portugal is one of the oldest countries in the world. It has been an independent country since the first half of the twelfth century. Located in the Iberian peninsula (south-west of Europe), Portugal covers 92,028 km². Most of its population (10.4 million) live on the Atlantic coast, mainly between the two most important urban centres: Lisbon (the capital) and Oporto, in the north. According to the 2001 census, 3 million people are younger than twenty four and 1.7 million are older than sixty five. In 2001 the unemployment rate was 4.1per cent, and the gross domestic product amounted to €122,900,6 million.

Portuguese is the official language of the country and the entire population speaks Portuguese. In the north-east there is a small community (around 7,000 people) speaking Portuguese and Mirandês, a romanic language recently recognized by the state. In Portugal there are, however, non-Portuguese-speakers, namely foreigners and immigrants, but the media and the state have not paid particular attention to their linguistic specificities as the country is perceived as homogeneous in terms of language.

In addition to the European continental territory, the country has two autonomous regions: the Azores and the Madeira islands which have their own political institutions (regional parliaments and regional governments). In administrative terms, Portugal is divided into *municípios* (which can be compared to councils) and *freguesias* (very small councils). These two forms of local government are almost totally dependent on central government as they get most of their income from it. *Freguesias* are all too small to have any significant power and even *municípios* – with the exception of those corresponding to big cities such as Lisbon and Oporto – have to struggle to put their views across. Although the 1976 constitution envisaged the creation of administrative regions, further legislation to implement the constitutional provisions has never been introduced, which partly explains the non-existence of regional television in Portugal. Portugal has close political and cultural links with its former colonies and territories such as East Timor, Macau, Brazil, Angola, Mozambique, Guinea-Bissau, Cape Verde and Sãs Tomé and Príncipe.

The development of the media has obviously had a close relationship with the country's political history. When Oliveira Salazar came to power in the late 1920s he was faced with an outspoken and relatively diversified press. During the first Republic (1910–26) the press managed to gain freedom from the constraints imposed by the monarchy (Tengarrinha, 1989; Sousa, 1996). As the authoritarian regime became consolidated, in the mid-1930s, press censorship was installed. Showing no interest in owning newspapers, the Salazar regime concentrated on controlling their content. The control of media content, which expanded to the electronic media, had a significant impact on the political, social and cultural development of the country.

The long-standing authoritarian regime was overthrown in 1974 and Portugal became a semi-presidential parliamentary democracy. After a highly unstable decade, the Portuguese democracy started consolidating. In 1986 the country joined the European Economic Community and a centre-right government, led by Cavaco Silva, remained in power from 1985 until 1995. The socialists assumed power after the legislative elections of October 1995 and stayed in government until 2002, when a centre-right coalition (Social Democrats and Popular Party) was elected. Since the mid-1980s structural reforms have been introduced in almost all policy areas, including the media. Despite these reforms, the state apparatus is still perceived as inefficient and non-accountable to citizens.

## STRUCTURE AND OWNERSHIP

Despite the liberalization and privatization of the Portuguese media market in the late 1980s and in the 1990s, the national media market is small, compared with most EU countries. The most important domestic group is Portugal Telecom, with no less than 70 per cent of the media and communications market in 1999. In 2000 Portugal Telecom acquired 58 per cent of the second most important multimedia group, Lusomundo. Portugal Telecom was already the biggest telecommunications operator, having the most important Internet service provider and the main cable television network. Still, with Lusomundo, Portugal Telecom controls two of the most significant daily newspapers (*Diário de Notícias* and *Jornal de Notícias*), and relevant interests in the cinema and press distribution. In 2000 the Portuguese media market was worth €349 million, representing 7.8 per cent of the gross national product (Obercom, 2002).

### The print media

#### The newspaper press

The 1933 constitution, although guaranteeing – in principle – freedom of the press, opened up the possibility of institutionalizing censorship when it stated that 'special laws will regulate the exercise of press freedom … in order to avoid distortion of public opinion in its social function'. This 'special law' was soon passed, establishing that publications 'about political and social issues will be under pre-censorship' (Carvalho, 1973: 55–6). The tight control over content had a negative impact in the quality and quantity of newspapers. 'The main function of the press under the dictatorship was not to inspire, enlighten or convince but to

communicate official attitudes' (Seaton and Pimlott, 1983: 94–5). Restrained in content, with poor distribution facilities and readership, there was a steady decline in the regional press: 'from 210 papers in 1926, to 170 in 1933, 80 in 1944, and to a mere 17 by 1963' (Seaton and Pimlott, 1983: 94); a national press was virtually non-existent. Most city newspapers were family businesses whilst in towns and villages papers were mainly controlled by the Catholic Church. The press was generally underfunded, with very low or non-existent profits.

After the 1974 revolution, major changes were introduced in the press. The 1975 Press Law guaranteed that the freedom of the press will be exercised without subordination to any form of censorship (Article 4). Similarly, the 1976 constitution suggested that the pluralist view of the media was clearly successful. It stated that the freedom of the press was guaranteed and that no group was allowed to exercise censorship or obstruct journalist creativity (Article 39). Nevertheless, these legal instruments do not mean that the press became free after the revolution. Indeed, during the so-called 1974–5 revolutionary period the press, which was still in private hands, was 'transferred' to public ownership. Three days after the leftist *coup* of 15 March 1975 important sectors of the economy such as banking and insurance were nationalized. Because many leading newspapers were owned by strong economic groups and banks, they became state property. The nationalization of the press was never explained as a political option. 'It was presented as an indirect consequence of the nationalisation of the banking sector' (Mesquita et al., 1994: 368). But behind this option was clearly the will to control what was left of government's direct influence. Significantly, the nationalization process was not reversed with the removal of the communist Prime Minister, Vasco Gonçalves, in November 1975.

Indeed, after this revolutionary period the nationalized press played a central role, as newspapers did not lose their readership and did not face any serious competition from the private sector until 1990 when *Público* daily newspaper was set up, becoming in a short period of time a standard for quality. The privatization of leading national newspapers took place in the late 1980s and early 1990s due to Cavaco Silva's media reforms.

Currently, the press sector can be characterized in the following manner:

1 There are six generalist daily newspapers, six weekly generalist newspapers and news magazines and hundreds of local and regional newspapers. More than 600 benefit from state distribution subsidies.

2 The so-called quality press comprises two daily newspapers (*Público* and *Diário de Notícias*), a weekly newspaper (*Expresso*) and a news magazine (*Visão*). The *Diário de Notícias* long-standing position as the most prestigious national newspaper was challenged by *Públics*. Unlike the *Diário de Notícias,* which is more than a century old, *Expresso* was established right before the 1974 revolution, and it has consolidated its position over the decades since. *Visão* was set up in 1993, and despite initial difficulties, it has recently expanded its market thanks to an aggressive marketing strategy and a strong commitment to the subscription market.

3 In the popular newspaper market, the two most important daily titles are *Jornal de Notícias* and *Correio da Manhã*. *Jornal de Notícias* is more than a century old, based in Oporto. *Correio da Manhã* is based in Lisbon and was set up in 1979.

4 Over the last few years, a new phenomenon has appeared in the press: the establishment of several free weekly newspapers. Most of these titles, launched in heavily populated areas, are local editions of *Jornal da Região*, owned by the multimedia group Impresa and by the Belgian group Roularta. These local editions print 50,000–70,000 copies. Contrary to what has happened in other European countries, the introduction and development of free papers in Portugal was not a controversial issue.

5 In the specialist press, there has been a proliferation of titles, particularly in four areas: women's magazines, sport (there are three daily newspapers), television guides and society, and the business press.

6 Most periodicals belong to multimedia groups, Impresa, Lusomundo, Media Capital, Cofina, Impala, among others. Few titles have been set up over recent years outside the scope of the multimedia groups. These groups have been more at ease with the expansion of titles because they have been able to develop group synergies.

7 The local and regional press is still very weak. There are no more than twenty daily regional newspapers selling more than a few thousand copies. Apart from these titles, there are hundreds of very small local newspapers. In 1999, 660 benefited from state distribution subsidies.

Despite the diversity of titles, formats and content, the generalist press occupies a very humble position in terms of circulation. It occupies the second last position in the European Union in terms of circulation figures per 1,000 inhabitants: sixty four copies (WAN, 1999). According to Eurobarometer, only one person in every four older than fifteen reads newspapers on a daily basis; 30 per cent never do. The relatively small size of the market makes periodicals an expensive commodity but the high level of illiteracy must also be considered when attempting to explain these figures.

### Book publishing

There are a great many book publishers. In 1999, 1,290 companies and/or individuals were involved in the publication of at least one book. However, the main publishing association, representing 70 per cent of the book market, has only 186 associates. In 1999, 7,235 new titles were published, 14 per cent more than in the previous year. Translations represent 45 per cent of books published.

## The electronic (audio-visual) media

### Radio

The evolution of the electronic media in the first stages of Salazarism was slow and limited in scope. Amateur radio broadcasts started thriving in the capital in the mid-1920s. After these early beginnings, local and neighbourhood stations emerged in Lisbon and, soon afterwards, in Oporto, as well as some minor regional stations which were permitted to continue their operations during the Salazar regime. The first relevant political intervention by the Salazar regime in the electronic media was the creation of the government station Emissora Nacional (EN) (now called Radiodifusão Portuguesa, RDP). Emission Nacional resulted from the incorporation of almost all existing private stations and began transmitting regular broadcasts from Lisbon on short and medium wave on 1 August 1935. Nevertheless, owing to the country's overall underdevelopment, 'it was not until 1955 that some 80 per cent of the population were technically capable of listening to radio broadcasts, and not until the second half of the 1960s that the country came anywhere near full nationwide coverage' (Optenhögel, 1986: 240).

Recognizing the importance of radio, the Catholic Church – with a traditional involvement in the regional press – also set up its own station, Rádio Renascença (RR), which started broadcasting in 1937. The early days of radio stations were difficult because, up to the 1950s, advertising was not allowed, which caused enormous financial hardship to most private radios (EN was financed by the licence fee). Rádio Renascença and Emissora Nacional were clearly the most significant radio stations[1] whose importance grew not only under Salazism and Marcelism but after the 1974 revolution as well. The so-called radio oligopoly was challenged only in the 1980s with the explosion of illegal radio stations and with the subsequent allocation of frequencies to local and regional stations.

Radio went through a profound transformation after the revolution. As mentioned, the radio oligopoly (RR and RDP) was not dismantled. In spite of deep crisis during the revolutionary period, this model survived until the boom in illegal radio stations and with the subsequent allocation of frequencies to local and regional stations in the late 1980s.

At present there are three national radio stations: Rádio Renascença, Radiodifusão Portuguesa and Rádio Comercial. Rádio Renascença, owned by the Catholic Church, is still the audience leader. Renascença operates three national channels: Rádio Renascença (generalist), RFM (generalist) and *Mega FM* (targeting young people). Rádio Renascença also has a network of regional transmitters which broadcast autonomous programming at certain periods of the day. Overall, Rádio Renascença channels have 40 per cent of the total radio audience (Obercom, 2002).

Like Rádio Renascença, RDP was set up in the 1930s. It is a public service broadcasting station and it is financed by licence fee. RDP operates five channels: Antena 1 (generalist), Antena 2 (culture and classic music), Antena 3 (targeting young people), RDP Internacional (a satellite radio channel for Portuguese communities abroad) and RDP África (a satellite radio channel for African countries whose official language is Portuguese). The third national station is Rádio Comercial, which was privatized in 1993 and now belongs to the Media Capital group. It operates two channels: Rádio Comercial (targeting young people) and Rádio Nacional (Portuguese music only).

At regional level there are two stations: Rádio Nostalgia (mainly music from the 1950s to the 1970s) and TSF. TSF started broadcasting in 1988 and was later bought by the Lusomundo group. This station has had an enormous impact on radio journalism, as it has introduced a new, highly dynamic model based on live political discussions, features, documentaries and frequent news bulletins.

If there are few national and regional radio stations, the same is not true at local level. There are more than 300 radio stations, mostly concentrated along the coastline (like the population). The lack of advertising revenue and the difficulty of finding other sources of financing led the socialist government to develop a framework of subsidies for local radio.

### Television

If Salazar did not object to the development of radio broadcasting, the same did not apply to television. Unlike Salazar, his *dauphin,* Marcello Caetano, was interested in cinema and television and got actively involved in the setting up of Rádiotelevisão Portuguesa (RTP). Marcello believed that 'the survival of the regime depended on its ability to modernize itself and television was perceived as a necessary condition for it' (Gonçalves, 1992). So, overcoming internal resistance, in 1953 a more liberal faction of the regime created a study group to look into the introduction of television. The Grupo de Estudos de Televisão, operating within the confines of public radio station (EN), completed its report, *A televisão em Portugal,* the following year. Whilst this group developed its studies, in January 1955 Marcello – by then Secretary of State of the Presidency – appointed a commission which

183

largely agreed with the EN study group's recommendation that television should be under one company of mixed ownership (see e.g. *TV Guia*, 17 April 1982; RTP, 1992).

On 15 December 1955 the government constituted Rádiotelevisão Portuguesa (RTP), granting the company the exclusive concession for television broadcasting. The government issued this exclusive licence for twenty years, with provision for extending it by consecutive periods of ten years, and an option for the government to purchase the corporation after its first ten years in operation. The RTP's statute was drawn up personally by Marcello Caetano.

RTP's shares were divided into three blocs, held by the government, Portuguese commercial radio stations, banks and other private companies. It was to be financed mainly by licence fee and advertising revenue. Its technical operations were to be regulated by the PTT while its in-house management was to rest with a board of directors partially appointed by the government. RTP initiated experimental broadcasts on 4 September 1956 but regular programming would begin on 7 March 1957. During the first fifteen years, RTP managed only one national channel. This situation changed in 1968 when a second national channel, RTP-2, was introduced. Regular television broadcasts were initiated in the autonomous region of Madeira in August 1972 and in the autonomous region of the Azores in August 1975.

The 1976 constitution stated that no television channel could be privately owned. Therefore, in the following decade no serious attempts were made to alter the broadcasting status quo. Politicians concentrated on the reorganization of the radio sector, whose expansion had been chaotic. When 300 local and regional radio frequencies were finally allocated in the late 1980s, political interest moved to private television. Following a highly intricate political process, on 6 February 1992 the Cabinet made public the allocation of two commercial channels: SIC, led by the former Prime Minister, Francisco Pinto Balsemão, got the third national channels, and TVI, having close links with the Catholic Church, was allocated the fourth channel. From 1993 onwards, the television broadcasting scenario included two national public service channels and two private national channels.

The opening up of television to commercial interests was the most important media policy undertaken since the 1974–5 revolutionary period. The radio sector had already been liberalized but the impact of this policy measure was far greater. The public service operator, RTP, lost its monopoly and in a very short period of time lost its audience leadership. SIC's success coincided with RTP's financial and managerial deterioration. Deprived of the licence fee, with low audiences, and uncertain about its future, RTP entered into an acute crisis. At the time of writing the newly elected centre-right government is considering the closure of RTP and the setting up of a new public service company with a single generalist national channel.

The two private national channels – notwithstanding financial difficulties – managed to establish themselves. In 1995 SIC overtook RTP in terms of audiences owing to an exclusivity contract with the Brazilian Globo. From then on, Globo would sell *telenovelas* only to SIC and with this trump card SIC maintained almost 50 per cent of the total television audience from 1996 to 2000. From the beginning TVI had relatively small audiences but in 2000/1 important changes did occur: with aggressive scheduling of *Big Brother*, TVI moved to first place in audience share. In 2002 SIC fought back, and currently the two private channels are in equilibrium.

Cable television has developed strongly. According to the National Authority for Communications (Anacom) by the beginning of 2002, 62 per cent of Portuguese homes had access to cable, though only 23 per cent had subscribed to cable services. In 1995 a mere 9 per cent of households had access to cable television and 1 per cent subscribed to it. The fast implementation of cable television is certainly related to the increase in the number of thematic channels and pay-per-view services.

The launching of terrestrial digital television is under way. A fifteen-year licence has already been allocated to a consortium that includes RTP and SIC among other entities. This consortium is expected to start operating by 2003.

# POLITICS, POLICY, LAW AND REGULATION

The most comprehensive changes in communications policy and regulation, since the 1974–5 revolutionary period, were undertaken by the social democrats during the period of absolute majority rule from 1987 to 1995 (Sousa, 1999b, 2000). The economy was booming and media liberalization was perceived as inevitable. The pro-business approach of Cavaco Silva's government favoured the privatization of the state media. As we have shown, newspapers which had been nationalized during the revolutionary period returned to private hands. The radio sector was liberalized and one state radio station was privatized. The television public service operator, RTP, lost its monopoly as two national television companies were allowed to operate commercial channels. The socialist government thus inherited a highly reformed but poorly regulated media system, and no structural communications policies were either announced or introduced. Up to 2002, when a centre-right government returned to power, the socialists merely attempted to strengthen regulatory bodies and introduced minor changes in several legal instruments.

## Actors and interests

The structural changes which took place during the Cavaco Silva majority governments and the regulatory/legal adjustments implemented by the socialists were certainly related to the main actors and interests involved in this policy area. When analysing Portuguese media actors, Sousa (1996) identified the state/government as the most relevant, not only regulating but also owning and controlling the political content of public media. During Cavaco Silva's mandates the media were under the tutelage of the Secretaria de Estado da Presidência do Conselho de Ministros. Although Marques Mendes chaired this *secretaria*, the Prime Minister personally handled the most important portfolios, such as the opening up of television to private operators. Marques Mendes dealt with 'politically safe' issues such as violence on television and RTP's broadcasts to the Portuguese emigrant communities and to the Portuguese-speaking African nations. Though the socialists contributed to the development of a more open policy network, the state has not lost its centrality in the policy-making arena. Private actors in the electronic media largely depended on the state to keep their licences and to expand their interests.

Political parties in general and the opposition in particular (inside and outside the parliament context) as well as the President of the Republic tended to pay particular attention to the government's intervention in the media. This does not necessarily mean that these actors determined major decisions, but they created an awareness and visibility of media issues, which had no parallel in other policy sectors. The opposition and the President of the Republic, Mário Soares, frequently put forward their views on media policy and media (essentially public) performance. During Guterres's governments the President, Jorge Sampaio, and the (fragmented) opposition made a more discreet intervention in the sector.

Within the institutional framework, the Alta Autoridade para a Comunicação Social (AACS) was another relevant actor – at least in legal terms. AACS was first envisaged in the 1989 version of the constitution and its objectives were (and still are), inter alia, to guarantee the freedom of the press, to have a say in the attribution of television channels to private initiative[2] and in the selection of public media editors. Despite its constitutional status, the High Authority was perceived as being dominated by the government of the day and as a weak regulatory body. Of its twelve members, one was a magistrate, five were members of parliament, the government itself designated three members and the other elements were so-called representatives of public opinion. The composition of AACS alone would prevent it from operating as an independent entity. During the first Guterres mandate, changes were introduced in the composition of the AACS in order to guarantee that it would operate more independently. The High Authority Law (No. 43/98 of 6 August) reinforced its power and reduced the number of government-appointed members.

Apart from the state actors, Sousa (1996) highlighted the role of two non-state actors: the Catholic Church and the Balsemão media group. The opening up of the television broadcasting sub-sector to private operators was the most relevant media decision during Cavaco Silva's mandates, and these two actors successfully lobbied to determine the outcome that best suited their interests. The Catholic Church and the Balsemão group were granted the two available national television licences in what turned out to be an extremely controversial process.

The Catholic Church is a powerful actor in a number of policy areas and it has a long history of involvement in the media (owning hundreds of local/regional papers and dozens of radio stations, including the highly successful national network Rádio Renascença). The acquisition of a television channel had been a long-standing wish. Recognizing that other media groups were gaining social influence and considering a national television channel of strategic importance to the expansion of Christian values, the Church developed its arguments and has positioned itself as a 'natural' holder of a television licence. However, being more concerned with its influence on society than with the economic aspects of such a venture, the Church soon realized that it had not the financial means to keep the channel (TVI). TVI is now in the hands of the Media Capital group.

The Controjornal group, whose figurehead was (and still is) the former Prime Minister, Pinto Balsemão, had started with the successful weekly *Expresso* and had been consolidating its position in the media market. In addition to *Expresso*, it owned at the time a daily newspaper (*Capital*), several specialist magazines and also had a solid position in the printing industry. The creation of a national television channel (SIC) was the most important development in Balsemão's media strategy.

Though Lusomundo media group did not perceive itself as a potential candidate in the bid for television channels, it certainly was another powerful actor in the media arena under the social democrat governments. Lusomundo started with film distribution and later expanded into exhibitions and real estate. It had a dominant position in the cinema distribution and exhibition sub-sectors. During the allocation of regional radio stations, in the late 1980s, Lusomundo successfully bidded for the northern Portugal frequency (now absorbed by TSF Rádio Jornal, where Lusomundo got a solid position from March 1993 onwards). The privatization of the two most important daily newspapers, *Jornal de Notícias* and *Diário de Notícias*, took place in circumstances favourable to Lusomundo, which seized the opportunity to buy them both.

During Guterres's mandates (1995–2002) the above-mentioned actors remained active (though significant internal changes did occur), and the government did not lose its central position. The Prime Minister's Cabinet and the *Secretário de Estado* for the media, Arons de Carvalho, continued to be nuclear figures in both decision making and non decision-making. Contrary to what took place during the Cavaco Silva period, highly sensitive topics such as public service television broadcasting were not dealt with.

Willing to demarcate themselves from Cavaco Silva's centralist rule, Guterres's governments set up or promoted the development of entities whose main task was to assist policy making and/or to study the media sector so politicians could decide with a better understanding of the alternatives. Amongst other examples, we would mention the Comissão de Reflexão para o Estudo da Televisão (Commission on the Future of Television), the Comissão inter-ministerial para propor acções nos sectores do cinema, audio-visual e telecomunicações (Interministerial Commission to propose Measures in the Cinema, Audio-visual and Telecommunications Sectors), the Instituto da Comunicação Social (Media Institute), the Conselho de Opinião da RTP (Advisory Council of the Public Service Broadcaster, RTP), the Instituto do Cinema, Audio-visual e Multimedia (Audio-visual and Multimedia Institute), and the Observatório da Comunicação (Communications Observatory).

The Instituto da Comunicação de Portugal (ICP), the telecommunications regulator, started operating in 1989 but owing to technological convergence has assumed a new role during Guterres's mandates. The Instituto da Comunicação Social and the Instituto da Comunicação de Portugal (ICP), renamed Anacom (Communications Authority), were put to work together in order to develop common strategies for the converging telecommunications and audio-visual sectors.

The emerging regulatory/advisory entities contributed to the public's perception that policy making was more open to consultation and debate. However, it should not be assumed that these new media policy actors had a real impact on the development and implementation of policies. Indeed, it might eventually be argued that the increasing number of policy actors and their competing views might have contributed to non-decision making due to what can be called a zero-sum game.

The previously mentioned multi media groups have not disappeared but there were changes in their power structure. It could be argued that under the socialists' rule the

Catholic Church lost some ground. Its most important acquisition, TVI, went into debt owing to the lack of advertising revenue and in 1997 SOCI media group and the Scandinavian Broadcasting System bought it. In November 1998 the Media Capital group bought the company, and is now its current owner. Apart from losing TVI, its most important asset, the Catholic Church also saw state subsidies to its numerous (but economically fragile) local newspapers reduced, owing to a policy measure taken during the second Guterres government.

Although all television companies went through serious financial difficulties, the Balsemão group managed to expand its business. The Impresa holding managed to cement its position in the television market with a generalist terrestrial channel (SIC) and three thematic cable channels (SIC Notícias, SIC Gold and SIC Radical). In the press, it has acquired the news magazine *Visão* and it has reinforced its magazine offer in segments such as business, society and tourism.

Apart from the traditional media groups, newcomers have joined the policy network. The biggest telecommunications operator, Portugal Telecom, has entered the television distribution business, with TV Cabo, but it also became a multimedia group in 2000, when it bought the Lusomundo group. The group does not have a terrestrial generalist channel but it is very strong in cinema distribution, the press, and owns the highly influential radio network, TSF. In addition, two other multimedia groups (Media Capital and Cofina) gained relevance in the media sphere. Media Capital made important investments in the radio sector and controlled the national television channel TVI. Recently this group has expanded into on-line services, cable television and television production. Cofina is an extremely recent group with a strong position in the newspapers and magazines markets.

Having put forward the main actors and interests in this arena, we will now briefly mention the principal legislative tools and recent regulatory developments in the press, electronic media and Internet-based media.

## The press

As stated in the 1995 government programme, independence in the media public sector and journalists' rights were high on the agenda. Therefore, both the Press Law

and the Journalists' Statute were altered. The new Press Law (No. 2/99 of 13 January) intended to expand pluralism and independence among media companies and to reinforce journalists' rights. The freedom of the press, free access to the market and the impossibility of any form of censorship are basic principles of this legal tool.

## The electronic media

In the broadcasting arena, a new television Act was also passed (law 31-A/98 of 14 July). The new television Act introduced changes in access to television activity. For the first time, the possibility of creating local, regional and thematic channels was enshrined in law. Until law 31-A/98 was approved, the television broadcasting system already included a number of channels: two public national channels (RTP-1 and RTP-2), two private national channels (SIC and TVI), two public regional channels (RTP-Açores and RTP-Madeira), and two public international channels (RTP África and RTP Internacional). Cable television and satellite television reception were also well established realities but companies were not allowed to produce their own programmes. Only third-party transmissions were legally possible.

The new television law opened up possibilities in terms of cable channels and terrestrial television channels soon entered this market. SIC, for example, has associated itself with the Brazilian network TV Globo and the biggest national cable operator, TV Cabo, in order to develop the Premium TV project. Premium TV has been offering two codified movie channels (Telecine 1 and Telecine 2) since June 1998. RTP in February 1998 signed a contract with TV Cabo, and with a company with multiple interests in sports, Olivedesportos. This consortium has operated, since September 1998, a codified sports channel, Sport TV.

The proliferation of television channels does not necessarily mean that the financial situation of broadcasting companies has improved during the Guterres government. In fact, television stations had important financial losses over recent years. The advertising market is small and, apart from SIC, terrestrial broadcasting companies have had highly unstable management mainly due to the lack of advertising revenue and debt accumulation. When the broadcasting market was opened up to private initiative, in 1992, the

Cavaco Silva government abolished the television licence fee and sold RTP's transmission network to Portugal Telecom. These political decisions, which were not reversed by latter governments, put RTP in a difficult economic situation and transformed a so-called public service broadcaster into an ordinary commercial television company, i.e. RTP had to fight for audiences to achieve a meaningful slice of the adverting cake.

In the radio broadcasting sphere, the socialist government has also revised an important legal tool: the Radio Law. Law No. 2/97 of 18 January sets out the basis of the overall Portuguese radio system and makes it compulsory for local radio stations to produce their own content (most were simply broadcasting national radio stations' feed). The Guterres governments have also for the first time expanded the press incentives to local radio, subsidizing technological modernization, providing institutional advertising, and reducing telecommunications costs (due to an agreement with Portugal Telecom).

## The Internet and related on-line media

In the information society arena, some relevant measures have effectively been taken. In 1997 the government published the Information Society Green Paper, an attempt to develop and implement policies within the 'information society' framework. In the aftermath of this Green Paper, a number of political measures were implemented. The National Science, Technology and Society Network was set up. This scientific network plans to bring together national researchers and to stimulate and consolidate R&D. In a move very similar to the one being developed in Britain, the Ministério da Ciência e da Tecnologia (Science Ministry) made an effort to introduce the Internet into every school in the country (from the fifth to the twelth grade), universities, libraries and research centres. 'Computers for all' was another project. The 'Computers for all' project has the objective of increasing the number and use of Internet-connected computers at home. Other small-scale initiatives, such as the creation of tele-work centres, were also on the agenda.

Specific legislation for on-line services and content has not yet been developed but this is not to say that no legal means exist to punish crimes committed on electronic services. Indeed, the constitution, the penal law and the civil law envisage a number of issues which are relevant to on-line material and on-line services and these might be used to prosecute 'on-line' crimes such as injury, defamation, among others.

As we have already mentioned, changes in the media regulatory body, the High Authority for the Media, were introduced as well. Indeed, this entity was perceived as highly politicized and its influence was very limited. The socialist government altered its composition and widened its powers. According to law No. 43/98 of 6 August, the High Authority for the Media has a very important set of responsibilities: it should guarantee freedom of expression and access to information, it should ensure objectivity and impartiality in media content, it should guarantee that the media act independently of the political power, it should ensure that radio and television channels comply with the law, it should protect the public interest, etc.

Despite its wide range of responsibilities and despite its formal independence from the government of the day, the High Authority for the Media has not yet found the human and financial resources to become a respected independent regulator. The media regulator is perceived as a weak body, unable to make the operators comply with the law. In order to circumvent this difficulty, the High Authority has itself promoted self-regulatory protocols to try to get the media to comply with the legislation. For example, on 18 September 2001 all television operators signed an agreement to respect human dignity in television programming. In the first clause of the agreement, the operators state that they will obey the Television Law (No. 31-A/98 of 14 July), namely its twenty-first article regarding the limits on programming freedom. Other clauses confirm the intention of television operators to comply with the legislation in terms of bad language, violence and sex. This agreement, which does not go any further than the existing television law, clearly demonstrates that television operators have not complied with the legislation and that the regulatory body does not have the means to fulfil its job.

## NOTES

[1]In addition to RR and EN, there were a few local radio stations and Rádio Club Português, a radio station owned by the Botelho Moniz family, a traditional ally of Salazar and Marcello.

[2]The AACS was not able to put forward its view on the allocation of television channels to private operators. But, as its opinion was required by the constitution, the High Authority decided for 'technical equality' and no candidacy was excluded.

## STATISTICS

| | |
|---|---:|
| National population | 10,400,000 |
| Population density | 112.5 per km$^2$ |
| Percentage with higher education degree | 10.6 |

Source: 2001 census, INE.

| **Print media** | | |
|---|---|---:|
| | Number of daily national newspapers | 6 |
| | Number of daily regional newspapers | 20 |
| | Circulation per 1,000 inhabitants | 64 |
| | Percentage over fifteen years old who read newspapers | 25 |
| | | |
| | Circulation of periodicals, January–September 2000 | |
| | *Maria* (popular women's magazine) | 322,000 |
| | *Nova Gente* (society magazine) | 185,000 |
| | *Selecções Reader's Digest* | 178,000 |
| | *Expresso* (weekly quality paper) | 138,000 |
| | *Jornal de Notícias* (popular daily) | 108,000 |

Source: AIND.

| **Broadcast media** | | |
|---|---|---:|
| | Radio and television | |
| | | |
| | Number of national radio channels | 8 |
| | Number of regional radio channels | 2 |
| | Number of local radio channels | approx. 300 |
| | | |
| | Number of national television channels | 4 |
| | | |
| | Percentage of households with: | |
| | Access to cable television, 1995 | 9 |
| | Access to cable television, 2002 | 62 |
| | Subscription to cable television, 1995 | 1 |
| | Subscription to cable television, 2002 | 23 |

Source: Anacom, 2002.

| **Electronic media** | | |
|---|---|---:|
| | Percentage of households with: | |
| | Personal computer, 1997 | 25.8 |
| | Personal computer, 2002 (first quarter) | 40.2 |
| | Access to the Internet from home, 1997 | 2.2 |
| | Access to the Internet from home, 2002 (first quarter) | 23.3 |

Source: Marktest 2002.

# REFERENCES

Anacom (2002) *Redes de distribuição por cabo* (first quarter 2002), www.anacom.pt.

APEL (n.d.) *Estatisticas da edição de livros relativas ao ano de 1999*, http://www.apel.pt/livro/estatisticas/estatisticas.html

Assembleia da República (1987) *Programa do XI Governo Constitucional*, Apresentação e Debate, AR-Divisão de Edições, Lisbon.

Assembleia da República (1992) *Programa do XII Governo Constitucional*, Apresentação e Debate, AR-Divisão de Edições, Lisbon.

Assembleia da República (1995) *Programa do XIII Governo Constitucional*, Apresentação e Debate, AR-Divisão de Edições, Lisbon.

Cádima, F. R., ed. (2000) *Anuário da comunicação*. Lisbon: Obercom.

Carvalho, Arons (1973) *A censura e as leis de imprensa*, Lisbon, Seara Nova.

Eurobarometer (2002) *Europeans' Participation in Cultural Activities*. Brussels: Eurostat.

Gonçalves, Maria Augusta (1992) '35 anos de televisão em Portugal: um Percurso de dependência' in catalogue *Televisão na Europa dos Doze*. Madrid: Madrid, Capital of Culture.

Mesquita, Mario, et al. (1994) 'Os meios de comunicação social' in António Reis (ed.) *Portugal: vinte anos de democracia*. Lisbon: Circulo de Leitores.

Obercom (2002) 'O Sector da comunicação em Portugal', *Newsletter*, January.

Optenhögel, U. (1986) 'Portugal' in H.J. Kleinsteuber et al. (eds) *Electronic Media and Politics in Western Europe*. Frankfurt: Campus Verlag.

Pinto, Manuel, et al. (2000) *A Comunicação e os media em Portugal*, Comunicação e Sociedade series. Braga: Instituto de Ciências Sociais da Universidade do Minho.

Pissarreira, Agostinho, ed. (1999) *Os media em Portugal*. Lisbon: ICS.

RTP, Departamento de Relações Externas (1992) *RTP: 35 anos de experiencia*. Lisbon: TV Guia.

Seaton, Jean and Pimlott, Ben (1983) 'The Portuguese media in transition' in Kenneth Maxwell (ed.) *The Press and the Rebirth of Iberian Democracy*, Westport CT: Greenwood Press.

Sousa, Helena (1996) 'Communications Policy in Portugal and its Links with the European Union', Ph.D. dissertation. London: School of Social Sciences, City University.

Sousa, Helena (1999a) 'Portugal' in *Legal Guide to Audio-visual Media in Europe*. Strasbourg: European Audio-visual Observatory, Council of Europe.

Sousa, Helena (1999b) 'The Liberalisation of the Media and Communications in Portugal', paper delivered at the conference 'Portugal and the Millennium', London, 21 May.

Sousa, Helena (2000) 'Políticas da comunicação: reformas e continuidades' in Manuel Pinto et al. (eds) *A comunicação e os media em Portugal*, Comunicação e Sociedade series. Braga: Instituto de Ciências Sociais da Universidade do Minho.

Tengarrinha, José Manuel (1989) *História da Imprensa Periódica em Portugal*, 2nd edn. Lisbon: Caminho.

# 17: Russia

## ELENA VARTANOVA

## NATIONAL PROFILE

The territory of the Russian Federation is the largest of any nation in the world (17 million km²). It is unevenly populated by nearly 146,100,000 people. The majority of the population are concentrated in several areas around industrial centres in the European part of Russia, but regions of Siberia and Far East are populated sparsely. Russia has borders with fourteen countries in Europe and Asia. Among neighbouring countries there are former Soviet republics, China (in the south-east and south, length of the border 3,645 km). Russia's border with Finland (north-west, 1,313 km) is also the border with the European Union.

Russia has several time zones with the maximum time difference between them of eight hours. The geographical profile of the country is a crucial factor for the media infrastructure, heavily affecting both the distribution of print media and transmission of broadcast signal. Consequently, national television and radio channels are transmitted mostly via satellites, but there also exists a developed system of terrestrial transmission located mostly in the European part of Russia. Satellite earth stations provide access to the Intelsat, Intersputnik, Eutelsat, Inmarsat, and Orbita systems.

Russia is a federal republic, comprising eighty nine federal administrative units (sub'ekt federatzii) subordinate to the central government. They include twenty one republics, six regions (krai), forty nine provinces (oblast), ten autonomous districts (avtonomnyi okrug), one autonomous area (avtonomnyi raion) and two cities. Since May 2000 Russia also has been divided into seven federal regions (okrug) headed by plenipotentiaries appointed by the President to control the execution of federal laws on the territory of the Russian Federation.

The Russian language is the official state language but many ethnic groups populating the country speak nearly seventy other languages. Russians make the largest group (81.5 per cent), other big ethnic groups are Tatars (3.8 per cent), Ukrainians (3 per cent), Chuvashs (1.2 per cent), Bashkirs (0.9 per cent), Byelorussians (0.8 per cent), Moldavans (0.7 per cent) and others (8.1 per cent). The major religion is Russian Orthodox, but Muslim, Buddhist and Jewish are also dominant for some ethnic groups.

Russia's economic situation remains poor despite its rich natural resources (oil, natural gas, coal, etc.). There are serious obstacles of climate, terrain and distance which hinder exploitation of natural resources. Traditional economic disintegration of regions arising from the country's big territory and the strong autonomy of local authorities also prevents economic progress, and many Russian political leaders before and after the Socialist Revolution (1917) made strong efforts to consolidate various regional markets into one economy.

Russia is a parliamentary democracy. The bicameral Federal Assembly consists of the Federation Council with members appointed for each of eighty nine federal administrative units and the State Duma, consisting of 450 members elected every four years by proportional representation from party lists (50 per cent) and from single-member constituencies (50 per cent). Political parties are numerous (more than 150 registered with the Ministry of Justice) but only some of them obtain strong positions among the Russian electorate, in particular the left-wing Communist Party and agrarians, centrist 'United Russia', right-wing Union of Right-wing Forces (SPS), 'Yabloko' and the nationalist Liberal Democratic Party.

Historically, Russia played an important role in European and even world politics. In 1917 power was seized by the communists, and the Soviet Union was established in 1922. It played an important role in defeating the Hitler coalition in World War II and after that it became the new centre of power in the post-war world. After Stalin's death there was an attempt at ideological 'thaw' which resulted in rapid, but uneven, modernization of industry and science, especially in the military sectors. The planned Soviet economy stagnated in the following decades until M. Gorbachev introduced *glasnost* and *perestroika* in an attempt to reform the Soviet system, but he failed and in December 1991 the Soviet Union was split into fifteen independent states. Since then, Russia has been struggling to build a democratic political system and a market economy to replace the political and economic control of the socialist period.

The first print newspaper *Vedomosty* was set up in 1703 by a reformist tsar, Peter the Great. The development of the press was strictly controlled by the political elite. Catherine the Great issued a magazine in which she promoted high moral values among educated Russians. After the French Revolution, however, she suppressed most publications, and her son, Pavel I, introduced advance censorship. In the nineteenth century Russian journalism developed unevenly. The existence of censorship hindered the progress of the press. Until the reform of 1865, literary magazines predominated, and private newspapers circulated only in St Petersburg and Moscow. The foundations of the regional structure of the newspaper market were laid down in the 1850s and 1860s but the system mostly included official regional newspapers subordinate to governors' offices. Only in 1880 did the number of newspapers come to outnumber magazines. Early in the twentieth century, after the first Russian revolution, numerous political parties and their newspapers began to operate legally. Press freedom was legally introduced in April 1917, in the course of the bourgeois revolution. In the Soviet period the media were used instrumentally to promote the dominant communist ideology, therefore their political role was extremely important though different from the role of media in the market democracies.

# STRUCTURE AND OWNERSHIP

The dominant structure of the Soviet media was a pyramid hierarchy which subordinated all levels of print and broadcast media to the central media. This pyramid was controlled and owned by the Communist Party and the state, thus safeguarding the political and economic functioning of Soviet society. The media played an important role in promoting communist ideas among the population. High political involvement of the Soviet media was achieved under Lenin's guidelines, defining a newspaper as 'a collective propagandist, collective agitator and collective organizer'. It was built into the foundations of the media system. To ensure political accuracy media content was supervised by representatives of Glavlit, the special agency of the Soviet censorship. This also led to the emergence of an informal system of self-censorship and professional norms which still affects the activity of Russian media professionals. After the demise of the Soviet Union, Russian media experienced a radical change in structures, ownership, modes of operation and professional values.

## The print media

### The newspaper press

As a result of post-Soviet transformations, newspapers have lost their central position in the media system, but they still play an important role in regional and local markets. About 80 per cent of Russians read at least one newspaper every day. The number of titles increased significantly from 4,863 in 1991 to 5,758 in 2000. However, total newspaper circulation radically dropped from 160.2 million in 1990 to 108.8 *million* in 2000 (a decrease of 32 per cent). The clearest shift within the newspaper system concerned the correlation between national, regional and local dailies. In 1990 the share of nationally distributed newspapers in the national circulation was equal to 67 per cent, but it fell to 36 per cent in 2000 despite the fact that the total number of national newspapers increased 7.7 times during this period. The average circulation of a national newspaper diminished as well, from 2.58 million in 1990 to 118,000 in 2000 (*Pecht' RF in 2000*).

Russia's vast territory and multi-layered administrative system are the main reasons for the existence of various newspaper types. Two basic characteristics, namely area of distribution and periodicity, play an important role in defining the type of a newspaper. Newspapers published in Moscow are considered national because of their national distribution and national news coverage. Accordingly, regional dailies cover events within large administrative and economic areas (*oblast* or *krai*) which coincide with their distribution zones. Newspapers of lower levels (city or district) have a narrow community focus. National data indicate that the Russian newspaper system is comprised of national (5.8 per cent of all newspapers), republic (4.8 per cent), regional (15.2 per cent), city (29.3 per cent), rural district (24.9 per cent), lower-level (lower than city or district, e.g. factory, enterprise, etc., 16.3 per cent) and other (mostly free non-daily sheets, 3.7 per cent) newspapers. At the national level, newspapers are distributed by subscription; the role of retail distribution is essential only in big cities.

Regional newspapers have managed to get rid of pressures from Moscow newspapers and do not take them seriously as rivals for local audiences. Understanding these realities, the most profitable and innovative Moscow dailies developed new modes of expansion to local markets. *Moskovsky Komsomolets* (1,400,000), *Komsomolskaya Pravda* (daily circulation in CIS 756,000), *Izvestiya* (234,500) have started to produce regional inserts and established joint distribution systems with regional leaders. While many Moscow dailies promote themselves as national, their distribution is restricted to the capital area and to some industrial centres of central Russia. The largest share of readers of nationally distributed Moscow dailies (40.2 per cent) outside the capital is represented by state and municipal officials, political activists, high and middle-level managers, intellectuals and students (Resnyanskaya and Fomicheva, 1999: 97).

Newspaper markets in many regional centres are characterized by competition between regional newspapers themselves and between regional and national dailies. At the regional level, competition occurs between former Soviet dailies, still owned and controlled by local authorities, and private newspapers set up in post-Soviet years. However, in many families the reading of a regional/local daily is often supplemented by the reading of a national weekly. This is true both of mass circulation newspapers targeted for wider audiences like *Argumenty i Facty* (3 million),

the weekend editions of *Komsomolskaya pravda* (circulation in CIS 2.8 million) and *Trud* (1.58 million) and of quality analytical news magazines such as *Itogy* (85,000), *Expert* (75,000), and *Kommersant Vlast'* (73,500) for educated and well-paid readers. There are also numerous indications of existing gaps between mass circulation and quality newspapers in the regional and national markets. Many former national dailies still have a reputation as serious analytical media, but their influence is in reality marginal. With circulation no higher than 100,000 copies, quality dailies like *Kommersant Daily* (86,000) or *Nezavisimaja Gazeta* (50,000) cannot compete with local tabloids or nationally distributed mass circulation dailies outside Moscow.

Russian newspapers and print media have two basic sources of revenue: advertising and circulation sales. However, the shares of the two vary considerably, since retail prices for newspaper copies are too low to cover production costs. After the financial crisis of August 1998 the Russian advertising market was almost ruined. In 1999 the total decrease in media advertising revenues was 57 per cent compared with the year 1998. The press suffered from advertising cuts less than did other media (40 per cent). However, in 2000 advertising revenue started to rise and in 2001 expenditure on advertising reached US$ 1.73 million. The volume of newspaper advertising was equal to US$ 310 million (29 per cent growth compared with the previous year). Nevertheless, the advertising market share of Russian newspapers – 18 per cent – is lower than the share of television (28 per cent).

Taking into account the limited size of the commercial advertising market, the uneven and complicated state of the national economy as well as the low purchasing capacity of Russians it is important to point to other sources of income less traditional in conditions of a market economy. They are:

1  A considerable amount of hidden advertising which poses serious moral problems for media professionals and negatively affects the reliability of the Russian press and media in general.
2  Political advertising, especially important to the regional and local press during local election campaigns.

3  In-house subsidies from profitable non-media affiliates such as resource or financial sectors, industrial or service enterprises.
4  State and municipal subsidies.
5  Hidden or informal financial support to regional and local newspapers by the executive power.

In the 1990s the free press including both advertising sheets and free dailies demonstrated progress in competition for advertising money and audience attention with traditional newspapers. Mass circulation advertising papers offer job vacancies, second-hand cars, apartments, and therefore they have come to reach about 40 per cent of adults. The Moscow underground daily *Metro* (500,000) has captured the second biggest share – 4.5 per cent – of the Moscow daily market.

Compared with other countries, the degree of concentration in the newspaper market may seem rather low. However, there are not enough reliable statistics to illustrate the trend. Until now no substantial studies to measure the level of concentration have been conducted at the national level. However, there is evidence of increasing concentration in the newspaper industry. In the 1990s four Moscow-based newspaper companies seized the leading positions in the national market by creating diversified companies with ownership in different media. Prof-Media, a media branch under the financial umbrella of the largest oil company, LukOil, acquired more than forty newspapers and magazines in Moscow and other cities, television channels in Rostov, Norilsk, several radio stations, numerous Internet sites, a business news agency. The total circulation of print media outlets published by the company has already passed 50 million. The company's share of the print media retail market – nearly 20 per cent – is also among the top indicators. The Speed-Info Company, specializing in publishing sensational tabloid weeklies and magazines, is regarded as the second largest print media company in terms of the gross circulation of its outlets (over 8 million). The Argumenty i Fakty newspaper holding company (forty two periodicals with total circulation 6.4 million) and the Redaktsiya gazety MK share holding company (69 periodicals with a total circulation 2.35 million) are the next largest print media companies (Vartanova, 2001: 134). A unique media proprietor nowadays is the Russian state. State agencies completely or partly control 300 national, regional and local television companies and 2,140 print media (15 per cent of all print media titles). The central government holds a 100 per cent stake in *Rossiiskaya gazeta*, the ITAR-TASS news agency, the VGTRK broadcasting company and a number of related businesses.

### The periodical and magazine press

The rise of weeklies has become a response to various problems of the post-Soviet period, but mostly to the problem of costly and late distribution which negatively affected the position of dailies. Russian weekly newspapers are reminiscent of Britain's mass circulation tabloids not only in format and large circulation but also in content and style of writing. *Argumenti i Facty* (*AiF*, circulation about 3 million) is not only the most popular but also one of the most economically viable media outlets. It has created a variety of thematic offsprings on health, gardening, leisure and family issues. Newspapers of the 'AiF family' built up their success by including regional inserts to better satisfy readers' interest in national and regional information, but also to stimulate regional distribution and advertising revenue. Other popular weeklies like *Mir novostei* (850,000) or *Megapolis-Ekspress* (500,000) try to pursue the same strategy but with much more scandalous stories and less success in national distribution.

The market for popular magazines is developing by filling up various thematic niches. Illustrated television guides, a relatively new type of weekly magazine, triumphed as the most popular publications. The rivalry between *7 dnei* (1 million plus), *Antenna* (487,000), *TV park* (298,000) and *Tsvetnoi televizor* (162,000) is fierce, but still newcomers appear, making the situation truly competitive. The unmistakably most successful target audience in Russia are women, and *Liza* (90,000), a weekly with a mixture of practical advice for working females, cookbook summaries and fashion patterns, is the most popular among magazines. Glossy magazines represent a comparatively small but vigorous sector of the magazine industry. The importance of the Western experience was crucial to their success. The German company Burda (23 per cent of the magazine retail), the Dutch-owned company Independent

Media (nearly 5 per cent of retail) have adapted to the Russian market a set of well known international periodicals like *Burda moden, Playboy, Good Housekeeping, Harper's Bazaar* and *Cosmopolitan*. In 2000 the growth of advertising revenue in the Russian magazine industry was 43 per cent, the second indicator within the media industry after television.

### Book publishing

Russian book publishing lived through a crisis period in the 1990s. The state has almost withdrawn from the industry, and many state-owned publishing houses have almost lost their position in the market. At the moment they produce no more than 18 per cent of all titles and about 15 per cent of the total book production. Thus the competitive structure of the Russian book publishing industry leaves space for numerous small and medium-size companies specializing in textbooks, encyclopedias, technical and business books. On the other hand, as a result of growing concentration private publishers like the Vagrius, Drofa and Olma-Press gained leading positions in the market by promoting post-Soviet best-sellers about the Russian 'mafia' and criminality. V. Dotsenko's detective stories about 'Furious' paved the way for mass circulation low-quality novels by adapting commercialized Western formats and promotion patterns to Russian realities. A female policy analyst, a hero of A. Malinina's criminal novels, became popular because of her non-heroic but independent individuality, thus securing the highest book sales in post-Soviet Russia at the level of 26 million copies.

The top positions in national retail lists are traditionally occupied by Russian and foreign classic novels, but there is a growing tendency towards 'entertainization' resulting in the increasing production of mostly domestic 'light' science fiction, fantasy, women's novels and detective stories. The variety of titles, flexibility in response to demand, diversity of formats ranging from illustrated hard-cover art albums to pocket-size paperbacks have become the main features of Russian book publishing (Alekseyeva, 2000: 121).

## The electronic (audio-visual) media

### Television

In recent years Russian television has taken the central place in the media system. It is the most powerful medium, with 94 per cent of Russians watching television every day. The average time spent watching television is nearly three and a half hours a day. Ninety-nine per cent of Russian households have at least one television set and half of all households have two or more; about two-thirds have colour sets, but 45 per cent still possess black-and-white sets. The number of television sets per thousand people is 421, and compared with other post-socialist countries of Eastern and Central Europe this is close to the average.

All basic systems of television transmission, including air, satellite, cable and Internet, exist in Russia but they are very unevenly spread across the territory. Major national television channels are transmitted from the Ostankino tower in Moscow through terrestrial networks to cities in the European part and are also sent out via satellite to regions in Siberia and the Far East. Regional and local stations mostly broadcast their programmes on the air.

According to the data provided by the Ministry of Press and Broadcasting, the total number of broadcast licences issued in 2002 was 1,276 for television broadcasting and 1,002 for radio broadcasting. However, the figures are approximate, as they do not indicate the number of operating stations. The core of the national television market is comprised of nine channels available to more than 50 per cent of the population. They include:

1 Three all-national federal channels, though of different ownership: Obshestvennoye Rossiiskoye Televidenie (ORT, Public Russian Television) with a mixed structure of state and private shareholders, the state Rossiiskoye Televidenie (RTR, Russian Television), and the private NTV.

2 Four federal television networks: TVS, broadcasting on the frequency previously given to TV-6 and being its successor, Ren-TV, CTC and TNT.

3 Two regional channels with national distribution: the state-owned and financed Kultura (Culture) and the Moscow municipal TVC (TV Centre).

Historically, the dual state–Communist Party dominance remained the most significant feature distinguishing the Soviet television model from the two major models, e.g. the US privately owned commercial and Western European public service models. The concept of public service broadcasting as a possible form of television industry was never considered publicly until the year 2000, since state control of television was and still is used to safeguard existing political elites.

The state remains the main actor in the television business. By controlling the holding company VGTRK it has control over two nationally distributed television channels – RTR and Kultura, the radio channel Radio Rossiyi – and partly over the radio news channel Mayak, in which it owns more than 50 per cent of the shares. VGTRK also includes a network of sixty eight state-controlled regional television stations and 100 centres for the transmission of television and radio signals. In 2001 the structure of the company was transformed and the transmission centres were separated into an independent company. In 2000, VGTRK employed more than 4,000 people. In 2001–2 the company started experiments with digital television but the lack of financial resourses makes this activity really marginal.

Despite control over programming policies and the appointment of top management, the state cannot completely finance the activities of RTR and ORT (it provides subsidies to both channels and 30 per cent of the operating costs of RTR), and they have to attract advertising. Their strong position in the advertising market is obvious and the unfair competition is heavily criticized by privately owned channels, but for now state-controlled television dominates the national airwaves. More than 50 per cent of viewing time is provided by ORT and RTR; 70 per cent of television advertising revenue is received by them as well. In the budget structure of modern Russian television, advertising and sponsorship provide the largest revenue source.

National channels operate as television networks, although three all-national brands, ORT, RTR and NTV, operate as networks only in technical terms. The national status of the three is secured by their technical availability. Practically all Russians receive two national channels: ORT is available to 98 per cent of the whole population, and RTR is received by 95 per cent of

Russians. NTV is available to nearly 75 per cent of the population. Three other channels transmitted from Moscow have also secured firm positions at the federal level: TVS is received by almost 60 per cent of all Russians, TVC by 39 per cent and Kultura by 36 per cent. However, technical availability and the popularity of channels essentially differ: 41 per cent of Russians prefer ORT to other channels. It is followed by NTV (25 per cent), RTR (13 per cent) and commercial networks (altogether, 11 per cent). It is notable that 6 per cent of the audience has no consistently voiced preference.

The Moscow-based private television companies Ren-TV, STS and TNT have also attained national penetration but at lower rates. They operate as commercial networks, forming alliances with regional and local stations targeted at joint programming and advertising policies. This results in the complete predominance of Moscow channels in national and in many cases also in regional broadcasting. In terms of programming, the competition for viewers among major channels is especially intense among evening news and current affairs programmes and political reviews on Sunday evenings. The growing popularity of entertainment genres, cultural and non-political programmes compared with political ones in the early days of *glasnost* has brought to light both the rebirth of old Soviet attitudes towards television as a home art and aesthetic medium and the revelation of the global trend towards television infotainment.

Not surprisingly, the development of regional television has grown into a kind of indicator of the economic situation in the regions. The most advanced and wealthy parts of the country are characterized by the highest numbers of private television channels. Out of all eighty nine regions, territories and republics of the Russian Federation, only twelve economically underdeveloped regions do not have any non-state television channels. In the most developed fifteen regions, including Moscow and St Petersburg, the number of television programmes ranges between a maximum of fifty eight in the capital and fifty seven in the Krasnodar region to approximately fifteen in the Tver, Vladimir and Novosibirsk regions and Bashkortostan. The overall number of channels available in these regions ranges from twenty to seventy two (Freedom of Speech Audit, 2000).

The new realities of the commercial television market have proved the interdependence of programming policy and the tastes of viewers. The preferences of Russians are similar, in general, to those of the television audience in many European countries. For an average Russian, television is one of the major ways of spending leisure time. In the course of time this tendency is gaining in influence, reflecting a different perception of television by politicians, those in power, and the audience. Sociological surveys show that Russians tend to watch more feature films, entertainment, family, cultural, educational, children's and sports programmes. The shift away from politics towards 'entertainization' is obvious (Rantanen, 2002).

A particularly entertaining role of Russian television is illustrated by the fact that an average citizen traditionally watches a lot of feature films on television. In recent years domestic movies have outnumbered American ones. Popular Soviet films, mostly comedies and melodramas, make up a kind of 'Golden Top Thirty', each broadcast by national channels fifteen to twenty times in the last five years. The top managers of the leading television channels even claim that they try to co-ordinate schedules for broadcasting these 'best-showers'. Consequently, the key resource that helps national channels to keep friendly relations with the audience is made up of popular Soviet movies and new Russian low-budget serials which are increasingly challenging content imported from the United States and Latin America.

In relation to the principles of public service broadcasting, the Russian situation remains truly controversial. Commercial interests challenged the national television, consequently advertising and entertaining genres (talk and quiz shows, soap operas, serials, reality shows) dominate all programme schedules, commercial and state channels alike. The only channel which carries non-commercial programmes (high culture, elitist films, quality documentaries, classical music) is the state-run Kultura. By including Euronews news shows in its programming schedule (2000) Kultura came close to the idea of public service in television.

Terrestrial television will undoubtedly enjoy a central position in the media system for the foreseeable future, but the role of cable and satellite alternatives is also expected to increase. The cable sector began to develop in 1989–1990 on the basis of the particular technical infrastructure of the late Soviet period, when collective cable systems were installed in apartment blocks. Cable systems operated on a semi-legal base and offered a variety of previously unknown genres, chiefly pirated American movies, entertainment, music and pornographic programmes. Even in a rudimentary form new cable systems caused serious problems for the major television channels mostly in terms of audience attitudes. Cable networks were the first to pave the way for more individualized patterns of viewing and to promote video as an alternative to national television.

Cable television was seriously affected by the crisis of August 1998, but in subsequent years the interest of private operators grew significantly. In sum, the state and municipal authorities have issued 258 licenses for cable television networks, eighteen for satellite transmission and twenty for combined air and cable operations, but statistics show that there are 3,000 relatively large cable companies operating and delivering programmes to nearly 12 million households. The choice of programmes remains fairly limited, but the lack of specific regulation and uncertain financial basis (viewers not ready to subscribe and advertisers sceptical of cable networks' competitiveness) have an impact on the state of the industry.

The development of satellite television in Russia is very slow compared with most European states. The two leading companies, NTV Plus and Kosmos-TV, could attract an audience only in Moscow and several big cities. Their programming offers do not vary much and include Russian-language programmes and the most popular international channels like CNN, BBC World, Euronews, Discovery, Cartoon Channel, etc.

### Radio

Today, radio enjoys more popularity than ever before. In 1999, 82 per cent of Russians listened to radio because, in their view, it meets the requirements of the audience better than television. 76.9 per cent of Russians are satisfied by radio programmes while only 65 per cent hold a similar opinion about television.

Commercial-format radio based on pop music and advertisements began to make its appearance in the major cities in 1990. Evropa plyus created the first radio network with a clear commercial focus on serving the music tastes of its well defined target audience based on definite parameters such as age, income and education level. Ekho Moskvy integrated the programming and polemic experience of Soviet political radio, Western news criteria and music formats.

The present structure of the radio industry involves a mixture of state and private channels. The state channel Radio Rossiyi, received by 66 per cent of the population, and Mayak (55 per cent) retain their position as the major national channels with the largest reach. Their almost universal technical accessibility is the main reason for their popularity. In many cities access is provided through the still existent connections of home radio receivers with radio cable networks created in the Soviet era. Another reason to legitimize the predominance of state-controlled radio channels is their informal fulfilment of public service obligations. Radio Rossiyi has drama and classical music as visible components of its programming policy and Mayak is well known for its information and news programmes, which undoubtedly remain the most diverse in the national radio landscape.

In the radio sector a significant role is played by commercial networks. The success of the Russkoye radio network formed of 257 local stations is ensured mostly by music programming based upon Russian pop and light music. The network has risen to third national radio channel (45 per cent reach) and Evropa plyus has become the fourth (43 per cent). In big cities commercial music radio stations have succeeded because of increased professionalism in developing formats and establishing relations with both advertisers and listeners. Other stations gained popularity among specific audiences, positioning themselves as sources of specialist programmes like women's interest (Nadezhda), drivers' radio (Avtoradio) or religious channels (Radonezh). The general increase in the number of commercial radio stations has been accompanied by growth in the advertising money channelled to radio. Today almost 21 per cent of local advertising goes to local radio stations.

### Film

The film industry survived the problems of post-Soviet transition. Cinemagoing was one of the most popular leisure activities in the Soviet Union. The average citizen went to the cinema twenty times a year. By the end of the 1980s the popularity of cinemas began to decline but the real crisis occurred in the early 1990s when state financing of the industry came almost to an end. Domestic production dropped from 178 films in 1992 to forty six in 1995. In these years many cinemas were transformed into night clubs, discos, or closed down. By the end of the 1990s in some big cities, including Moscow, there emerged signs of revival. After the renovation of some cinemas, moviegoing is becoming a fashionable way of spending free time. The most modern cinemas are operated by two Russian rental networks – Imperia Kino and Karo-Premier. Foreign films are imported mostly from Hollywood companies, but the French Unifrance is also an active foreign player in the Russian movie market, which is supposed to become the largest in Europe.

In 1991 the Russian state was almost a monopolist in the film market, but in 1996 domestic films almost disappeared from cinemas (8 per cent market share), and the share increased only slightly in 2000 (20 per cent). The enormous popularity of Western, especially American, movie formats did not last long and in the late 1990s Russians began to express nostalgia for domestic films. Currently, thanks to increasing state support, the production of Russian films is growing in terms of both quality and audience demand. The most appreciated by the public and critics at home have been *Brother II* by A. Balabanov, *Burnt by the Sun* (the Oscar winner in 1996) and *The Barber of Siberia* by N. Mikhalkov, *The Delicate Age* by S. Soloviev and *Moloch* by A. Sokurov.

## The Internet and related on-line media

The Russian-language sector of the Internet, Runet, has become the clearest indicator of the latest media changes. Technically it existed in the Soviet Union as an academic computer network with a very limited access. Use of the Internet increased greatly between 1993 and 1997, when the number of users doubled each year. Now the maximum number of users stands close to 12.8 million (8.8 per cent of population). The progress of the Internet initially took place in big cities, especially in Moscow, but in recent years the inequality of geographical regions has been steadily decreasing. Now residents of Moscow and St Petersburg represent less than 20 per cent of Russian users. The share of female users stands close to almost 40 per cent. However, users are mostly educated, better-paid urban male residents (aged twenty to thirty-five), including state officials, politicians, businessmen, journalists, students and schoolchildren.

The Russian media have made up the core of the Runet. Several popular newspapers like the *Nezavisimaya Gazeta* began to explore the Internet as early as 1994. The first on-line media projects were started by postmodernist literary writers who launched the *Russkii Zhurnal*. At the time of writing there are about fifty television companies, sixty radio sites, thirty three Internet news agencies and almost 1,200 newspapers, of which 70 per cent represent the Internet versions of paper publications (defined as 'clones' and 'hybrids') and the rest are Internet-only papers ('originals'). The most popular on-line sources are RBK.ru, Gazeta.ru, List.ru, Lenta.ru and Polit.ru. They have no analogues in the traditional media and, owing to constant updating of information, objectivity and non-political involvement successfully compete with analogue media. Today the Runet contains almost infinite content resources in the Russian language and the languages of other ethnic groups.

The active role of the Internet news media in the parliamentary (1999) and presidential (2000) elections was especially important for the media. Several sites run by the state-supported Fond Effectivnoi politiki played a propagandistic role in the creation of public images of leading politicians. Through the Internet political image makers appealed directly to those forming public opinion, mostly journalists and intellectuals. The Internet served as a mediator between the political powers and this important but limited part of Russian society. Citing from on-line sites made available by the traditional media during the election campaigns guaranteed the enormous popularity of the Net. On the other hand, the political use of the Internet led to very critical attitudes on the part of users. Today, many Russians consider information from the Internet rather unreliable. Of all Russian users, 36 per cent do trust Internet information, while 35 per cent do not trust anything on the Net.

# POLITICS, POLICY, LAW AND REGULATION

The central actors in media policy are the state Duma, government bodies, associations of the media industry and unions of journalists. The main regulatory agency in the field is the Ministry of Press, Broadcasting and Mass Communications. Its main tasks are to issue licences for broadcasting and for some printing activities, to register media outlets and to distribute a number of subsidies. The number of industry and professional associations is growing; among them the most influential are the Guild of Publishers, Russian Book Printing Union, National Association of Broadcasters, Association of Advertisers, Russian Association of Advertising Agencies, Union of Journalists and Media Soyuz.

After the disintegration of the Soviet Union in 1991, media policy experienced a radical change, and new strategic goals and ways to accomplish them had to be identified. However, Russian legislators had to begin by setting up the basic legal conditions for the media to operate in the new political and economic conditions. About thirty federal statutes for the mass media field were adopted by the Duma in 1991–2000, thus creating a sound and operational but slightly controversial basis for the mass media.

The new Russian media legislation has inherited the basic values of the Soviet Law on Press and other Media (1990), the most significant achievement of the *glasnost* media policy initiated by M. Gorbachev. It guaranteed freedom of speech, freedom of expression and abolished censorship completely. The law also introduced private ownership in the media and declared editors' and journalists' independence from media owners.

The law lasted until the fall of the Soviet Union and was replaced by the Law of the Russian Federation on the Mass Media which came into force on 27 December 1991 (Nordenstreng et al., 2001: 218–50). During the 1990s the media had a definite slant towards a personal approach by politicians and state executives which had its historical roots in the instrumental use of the media by Russian decision makers. The key feature of the media situation in the 1990s was the great personal influence of B. Yeltsin, the first President of the Russian Federation. In many cases he supported a media policy tolerant of the creation of media offshoots by political and financial 'oligarchs'. This was exactly the case of media concentration in 1994–8 when large media empires owned by B. Berezovsky (through the Logovaz or Ob'edinenniy Bank companies), V. Gousinsky (Media-Most) and V. Potanin (Oneksim) emerged under the umbrella of privatized industrial or new financial companies. The 'oligarchs' struggle for political influence, new property and financial advantage was supported by the activity of their media outlets. Yeltsin's re-election in 1996 became a kind of a reward from the 'oligarchs', whose media effectively manipulated public opinion during the election campaign in conditions of Yeltsin's dramatically low approval rating.

Aside from personal interventions, the development of media policy in post-Soviet Russia also became a multi-faceted societal process which gradually combined the results of the constructive and destructive activity of legislators, politicians, state officials and media professionals, and an emerging, but still weak, civil society. In relation to the immediate tasks of the political elite, the construction of media regulation might be divided into four distinct stages (Richter, 2001: 116–26).

The first stage (1990–3) was characterized by Yeltsin's fight to free the media from the control of the Soviet Communist Party and central authorities. This was especially true of the last Soviet years when Yeltsin strongly opposed Gorbachev. Two laws mentioned above, the revolutionary Soviet Law on the Press and other Mass Media and the Russian Law on the Mass Media, became of predominant importance for all media. Since then, however, no detailed specific regulation of individual media has been elaborated. In particular, Russia still lacks laws to regulate issues regarding access to information and broadcasting.

After the foundations of media activity were laid down, documents to regulate some particular issues were adopted. They were the 1993 Copyright Statute and Decree on Minimum Standard of Requirements for Television and Radio Broadcasting (March 1993). In the new constitution of 1993 (Article 29) among other basic rights and freedoms guarantees of free speech and a free press were provided as well. Yeltsin's personal approach to instrumentally use the 'free media' was revealed in his decision to set up the Judicial Chamber on Informational Disputes (December 1993, abolished in June 2000).

The second stage of media policy (1994–5) is mainly associated with the privatization of the economy that also involved denationalization of the first channel of the national television. It showed the growing tolerance by the state of concentration of the media in the hands of 'oligarchs'. The media politics of the third stage (1995–6) was entirely determined by the necessity to ensure the re-election of Yeltsin. State legislative activity, in particular, included the adoption of the presidential decree on the full-time licence for the national Channel 4 to NTV in violation of existing procedures. However, at this period two statutes on economic support for the press came into force. Although subsidies were not enough to cope with the crisis, the attention paid to the economic problems of the print media was noteworthy. The fourth stage of media policy (1996–9) was characterized by safeguarding the status quo in media policy. The principal role of the executive in media regulation and the dominance of state-run media became the main features of the situation. President Yeltsin viewed himself as the guarantor of constitutional rights, including certainly freedom of speech. Besides, the personal involvement of state officials remained essential. This was especially true of the non-transparent system of issuing broadcasting licences at the federal and regional levels and of the distribution of state and municipal subsidies among loyal newspapers.

Lobbying by business was the factor behind the adoption of, or hindrances to, a number of Bills (the Law on Advertising, Law on the Dissemination of Products of a Sexual Character). Lobbying of government bodies was also a factor behind some statutes (the Law on Information, Informatization and the Protection of Information, on Communications). At the regional and local levels this was proved by the existence of specific local regulation used by federal and local authorities together with corporate business to exert fierce informal pressure on local media, especially during election campaigns.

There is clear evidence that the fifth stage began after the parliamentary (1999) and presidential (2000) elections by strengthening the role of government bodies and Presidential Administration (PA) in media policy. On the one hand, numerous official statements were made about the eventual withdrawal of the state from the media industry and closing the Ministry for Press, Broadcasting and Mass Communications. This should secure fair competition and provide equal conditions for all companies in the media market. On the other hand, the government and PA are intensifying their efforts to determine policy for the media more efficiently. They have already inspired a number of draft laws (on the Internet, on restrictions on foreign ownership of the media, a new version of the media law) aimed to increase the role of state decision making under the flagship of protecting the 'national interests'.

The dichotomy between *étatism* and the market-driven economy is undoubtedly a distinct feature of Russian media policy. Examples are numerous. Journalists' and civil society organizations emphasize the importance of public service broadcasting, but they have to reckon with the commercial interests of corporations and advertisers who aggressively protect their presence in national television. Lack of state financial support became the reason for successful lobbying for the new integrated taxation for the print media conducted by media industry associations (since 2002). While financially viable enterprises have obviously benefited, small and medium-size media companies are facing new financial risks. In relation to this, the attempt to create a powerful media lobby of media associations is considered to be an important stage in Russian media policy.

In two media sectors, film and the Internet, state interference is accepted more positively. In the film industry the government has introduced (2001) tax exemptions for investment in film production with the aim of increasing the number of domestic films and to foster the construction of a new film studio in Sochi with the most advanced equipment to eventually produce twenty to thirty films a year to replace all the southern studios lost after the collapse of the Soviet Union. In the area of ICT and the Internet political documents are numerous, including the *Concept of State Information Policy* (1998), a document which was the first to introduce the building of the information society as a major goal of national development, the *Concept of Building the Information Society in Russia* (1999) and the *Doctrine of Information Security of the Russian Federation* (2000). Two profound federal programmes to develop ICT and the Internet were approved by the government in 2001. They are 'Electronic Russia in the Years 2002–2010' and 'The Development of the Unified Information and Educational Space in 2001–2005'. The documents reflect a new understanding of the key role of info-communications and the Internet in developing civil society, promoting a power–citizen dialogue and increasing the effectiveness of education.

Self-regulation exists in the form of the code of practice adopted by the Union of Journalists and the codes of professional associations (National Association of Broadcasters, Russian Association of Advertising Agencies) or the informal professional requirements of media companies (NTV, Interfax news agency). Although basic principles formally correspond to general principles, the relevance of self-regulation in Russian conditions is very low. The economic difficulties of the media industry are the main reasons for the general decline in standards and the acceptance of concealed advertising as an addition to the low salaries of journalists.

Media policy trends are contradictory. On the one hand, they are directed towards strengthening market-based principles in the economics of the media, with the eventual removal of the state from the media business. However, it is hard to believe that fair competition and transparency would be realized under conditions of growing commercialization and concentration of the media business. Increased attempts to form a powerful media lobby are another reason to be sceptical.

On the other hand, the state has to become a more active actor in future media policy. Under present conditions some state interventions such as support for satellite and digital television, safeguarding media diversity, encouraging domestic film production, providing universal public access to the Internet are demanded by society. However, any interference in the activity of media companies, manipulation of news flows or media content is viewed as an infringement of basic human rights.

# STATISTICS

| | |
|---|---:|
| National population | 146,100,000 |
| Number of households | 45,300,000 |
| Cinema admissions | n.a |
| Books published (titles) | 67,000 |

| **Print media** | Circulation of main national daily newspapers | |
|---|---|---:|
| | *Komsomolets* | 1,400,000 |
| | *Komsomolskaya Pravda* | 756,000 |
| | *Izvestiya* | 234,000 |
| | *Kommersant Daily* | 86,000 |
| | *Nezavisimaya Gazeta* | 50,000 |
| | *Metro* | 500,000 |

| **Broadcast media** | Audience share of main national television channels (%) | |
|---|---|---:|
| | ORT (state) | 41 |
| | RTR (state) | 13 |
| | NTV (private) | 25 |
| | Audience share of main national radio channels (%) | |
| | Radio Rossiyi (state) | 40 |
| | Mayak (state) | 28 |
| | Russkoye Radio (private) | 26 |
| | Europa Plus (private) | 21 |
| | Percentage of households reached by satellite television, cable or pay-television | 20 |
| | Percentage of households with: | |
| | Video-cassette recorder | 25 |
| | Satellite receiver | n.a. |
| | DVD | n.a. |

| **Electronic media** | Digital television reception | n.a. |
|---|---|---:|
| | Internet use | 9 |
| | Mobile phone ownership | n.a. |

| **Advertising spend, 2001** | Television | 28 |
|---|---|---:|
| | Press | 18 |
| | Radio | n.a. |
| | Other | n.a. |

# REFERENCES

Alekseyeva, M. (2000) 'Knigoizdaniye Rossii na rubezhe vekov' (Russian book publishing in the threshold of centuries) in Y. Zassoursky and E. Vartanova (eds) *Ot knigi do interneta* (From print books to the Internet). Moscow: Moscow University Press.

Dialog (2002) 'Industriya rossiiskich sredstv massovoi informatsii' (The Russian mass media industry), draft report, Russian–American Media Enterpreneurship Dialogue. http://www.smi.rusmedia.ru/industrial.

Freedom of Speech Audit (2000).

Nordenstreng, K., Vartanova, E. and Zassoursky, Y., eds (2001) *Russian Media Challenge*. Helsinki: Kikimora.

*Pecht' Rossiyiskoi Federtsii v 2000 godu* (The press of the Russian Federation in 2000) (2001) Moscow: Rossiyiskaya knizhnaya palata.

Rantanen, T. (2002) *The Global and the National: Media and Communication in post-Communist Russia*. Lanham MD: Rowman & Littlefield.

Resnyanskaya, L. and Fomicheva, I. (1999) *Gazeta dlya vsei Rossii* (Newspaper for the Whole Russia). Moscow: IKAR.

Richter, A. (2001) 'Media regulation: foundation laid for free speech' in K. Nordenstreng, E. Vartanova and Y. Zassoursky (eds) *Russian Media Challenge*. Helsinki: Kikimora.

*Sredstva massovoi informatsii Rossii* (1997) *Analiz, tendentsii, prognozy.*

UNESCO (2000) *Statistical yearbook, 2000*. Paris: Unesco.

Vartanova, E. (2001) 'Post-Soviet media model in Russia: diversity of structures, variety of pressures' in Yassen N. Zassoursky and Elena Vartanova (eds) *Media for the Open Society. West–East and North–South Interface*. Moscow: Faculty of Journalism/Ikar.

Yevstafiev, V. (2002) 'Reklamnyi rynok v 2001 godu' (The advertising market in 2001), *Vestnik Moskovskogo Universiteta,* series Zhournalistika, 3: 74–6.

# 18: Slovakia

ANDREJ ŠKOLKAY

## NATIONAL PROFILE

Slovakia became a fully independent state on 1 January 1993, but its economic and cultural development was different from other regions of the states it was part of during the twentieth century. Consequently, the print media and – to a lesser degree – broadcast media have reflected this difference. It was also partly due to a different language and partly due to different issues. Radio broadcasting has played a very important role in politics and in cultural life in Slovakia, argues historian Ivan Kamenec (2001). Táborský (1961: 551) believes that radio listening was always more widespread in Czechoslovakia than in other countries of Eastern Europe, and there has been a steady and substantial rise in the ownership of radio receivers in the post-war years. Johnson (1995: 223) argued that during the reform movement in Czechoslovakia in 1968 people voted for democracy by listening to the radio newscast in the evening, a newscast they viewed as independent.

Television's impact was smaller, since only about half of households had it, and they were unevenly distributed across the country. There seems to be agreement that during the communist era radio broadcasting was a major source of independent news from abroad. Thus Brown and Wightman (1979: 185) argue that when censorship within Czechoslovakia itself withered away in 1968, only 17 per cent of Czechoslovak respondents listened to foreign broadcasts. This contrasts with 47 per cent in June 1967 and 56 per cent in March 1969. Similarly, Köpplová et al. (1993: 203) argue that in sharp contrast to the established custom towards the press was the widespread habit

of listening to foreign broadcasts, especially Czech- and Slovak-language programmes transmitted by the Voice of America, Radio Free Europe (RFE) and the BBC. Importantly, the number of listeners to Western radio broadcast stations significantly increased in the 1980s, i.e. during the growing internal, although mostly less visible, crisis of communism in Czechoslovakia (see *Názory* 2 (2) 1991: 32). By contrast, in June 1989 the unofficial opposition press (*samizdat*) was read regularly only by 1 per cent of the population, while 8 per cent read this press very occasionally (Krejčí, 1991). This tradition had some important impact on the role of radio broadcasting in the first crucial years of the transformation of society. Although Slovakia has become effectively a typical television media culture country by the 1990s, it has sustained higher programme quality and higher political independence of public radio to this today.

For historical reasons there is a large 9.7 per cent ethnic Hungarian population in Slovakia. These Hungarian-speaking citizens primarily rely on Hungarian and secondarily on Slovak-Hungarian media or Slovak language media.

Because of the hilly terrain terrestrial broadcasting costs about the same as in the geographically twice as large Czech Republic. This fact certainly contributes to the financial weakness of both public service broadcasters, but especially television, which by law has to cover the whole territory.

There is widespread corruption in the Slovak media. It is not clear whether some editors are first of all businessmen or indeed guarding some ethical rules. It is not unusual to find *adversials*, i.e. articles presented as journalism but in fact mixing, at best, journalism with advertisements. This is related to lack of professional management and the sometimes questionable independence of the media. It is particularly problematic outside the capital, Bratislava, where it is difficult to find a job. There are two dominant television companies, one private (TV Markíza) and one public (STV, with two channels, *STV-1* and *STV-2*). There is one dominant radio station which belongs to the public Slovak Radio, SRo (with five major channels, plus foreign broadcast and on-line broadcast), followed at some distance by three nationally important private radio stations. In some regions regional radio stations are more important than these national private radio stations. There are three important daily newspapers out of a total of less than twenty daily newspapers, including regional daily papers. There is a relatively important daily and weekly regional press. The first private radio – Fun Radio – started broadcasting on 10 June 1990, without proper legal regulation at the time. There were twenty five private radio stations broadcasting including foreign affiliations during 2001, but one radio station ceased broadcasting in early 2001. There is one state-sponsored wire agency, TA SR, and one private agency, SITA (established on 15 January 1997).

The specific feature of Slovak media is low transparency of ownership, especially of the press. An oddity is that although after long deliberations there is a voluntary system of verifying the circulation of print media, neither clients nor customers are really interested in the data. There are three reasons for this phenomenon. First, not all print media are included in the process. Secondly, some believe that some competitors still do not behave fairly, but sell part of the print run to some quasi-buyers. Thirdly, when there is a period of collection of statistical data, some publishers increase their print runs.

The government has no clear media policy. This applies both to the daily press (for example, there are no subsidies) and to the public electronic media, especially television.

The daily press, and some smaller radio stations, often serve as free-of-charge training centres for larger media. Once young journalists get enough experience, those who are best and brightest move into the electronic media, especially television. In addition, a significant number of journalists moved to jobs in press departments after the 1998 parliamentary elections and to PR agencies throughout the last decade. This trend from the late 1990s was facilitated by a trend from the early 1990s, when for political reasons many of the older generation of media professionals were forced to leave their jobs, especially in television. For these reasons, but also because of the boom in the media market, there are a large number of young journalists in the media. Ironically, many of these journalists have no university education, including a few of the best ones.

There is no potential new market of readers for the daily press. Not even young people read newspapers as relatively often as they did in the past. The weeklies benefit from daily newspapers' reporting and the tendency among readers to get some summary information once a week. Often, weekly newspapers take tips from daily papers or only put together daily reporting of dailies in the past few days and add some photographs.

In an effort to decrease costs, some newspapers have already established their own printing plants. Although foreign owners seem to be more balanced in the level of politicization of their media, these owners are not immune to attempts to co-operate with politicians nor, at a minimum, do they forget to take into account the possible impact of criticism of the political parties in power on their business activities.

## STRUCTURE AND OWNERSHIP

### The print media

While there were 326 registered titles of print media in 1989, the registered number of periodicals was 1,465, with an overall circulation of 487 million copies in 2000. However, some media exist only for a short time. The most used second language in newspaper publishing was Hungarian. There was one daily newspaper (*Új Szó*), five weeklies, and ten other newspapers published in the Hungarian language. In addition, there were six weeklies published bilingually in Slovak and Hungarian, and ten additional newspapers published less often but in both the Slovak and Hungarian languages (*Vybrané ukazovatele*, 2000: 21).

### *The newspaper press*

Following the UNESCO definition, there were 451 newspapers with a circulation of 281.5 million copies in 2000. The number of newspapers decreased by eighteen, and their circulation decreased by 35,500 copies in comparison with the previous year (*Vybrané ukazovatele*, 2000: 7). Of the 451 newspapers, sixteen were published five to seven times a week, 100 were published once or twice a week, and the rest were published less frequently. These newspapers had a total circulation of over 205 million copies. In practice (not following the UNESCO categorization), there were less than twenty dailies in 2002. Of these, half were national dailies (including one advertising daily), six were regional and three were local dailies (including evening papers). The chain of regional daily newspapers shares substantial parts of its content with national daily *Sme*.

The specific feature of the daily press is that domestic owners often do not own the media exclusively for making a profit from publishing, but tend to use the press as a tool for their occasional unfair lobbying. This is a result of the high politicization of Slovak society during the previous era (up to 1998). The trend seems to have changed to a 'normal', or at least more standard situation, with the clear exception of TV Markíza and affiliated media, like the daily *Národná obroda*.

Most print media lack a transparent ownership structure. Another specific feature of the daily press is that in its professional development it follows examples found in the Czech Republic and Austria. This phenomenon could be observed in layout as well as in content (style of writing), especially in the late 1990s. In two cases, Slovak owners hired Czech editors in order to improve the quality of their media (the daily *Pravda* and news television channel TA3).

The German publishing house Gruner & Jahr owns the most popular daily newspaper, *Nový Čas*. The daily *Pravda* is owned by the Slovak concern Harvardská investičná spoločnosť' (Harvard Investment Fund). The daily *Sme* is majority owned by the German Verlagsgruppe Passau. This group owns the largest regional daily press network in Slovakia. The Verlagsgruppe Passau publishes in company with Petit Press three dailies (*Sme, Új Szó* and *Rol'nícke noviny*) and three weeklies (*Domino fórum, Vasárnap, The Slovak Spectator*) and a number of regional papers. Half of Petit Press shares are owned by the Slovak VMV company. The daily *Hospodárske noviny* is published by the US-German Dow Jones/Handelsblatt group.

The year 2001 was significant, with changes in layout and/or full-colour printing of some pages of major daily newspapers (*Nový èas, Pravda, Sme*) and some less popular newspapers (*Práca, Hospodárske noviny*). The print media, especially the daily press, owing to its smaller circulation and smaller market, is very little resistant to pressure from advertising agencies for special rates.

Many print media suffered heavy losses when the major distributor of the press collapsed in late 1998 and early 1999. This distributor collapsed when the main printing plant connected with the distributor diverted the money collected for pro-governmental media to dubious operations. But perhaps more important is that the current distributors (especially the major one, PONS, owned by the Slovak Post) are not motivated to sell – they do not suffer losses if they do not sell, because they take their profit from distribution, not from selling. For example, PONS suggested in early 2002 an increase in prices for distribution of 15–20 per cent. Under normal circumstances, the major daily newspapers at least do make a profit.

The older generation of readers usually do not trust the media. Older readers are used to reading 'between the lines'. Almost 45 per cent of the population does not read the daily press regularly. The most popular daily newspaper, *Nový čas* (*New Times*), is a tabloid. It was read by around one-fifth of the population and about one-third of all readers of the daily press in the years 1996–2001. However, there was a significant decline in the circulation of this newspaper in 2001 due to citizens' satiation with scandals and negative news as well as the increasing cost of the press and the financial weakness of the population. Citizens do still widely read this newspaper – there were 23.5 per cent reporting 'read yesterday' in March 2002. Many copies circulated among friends. This market leader was followed by the daily *Pravda* (8.6 per cent), *Sme* (8 per cent), *Šport* (7.5 per cent) and the Hungarian-language *Uj Szó* (4.3 per cent). The daily *Pravda* is a former Communist Party paper, now without a clear ideology but representing the business and political interests of the owners. The daily *Sme* is more oriented towards the right of the political spectrum. Then there are dailies with a national but low circulation like *Národná obroda* (4.2 per cent), *Hospodárke noviny* (3.2 per cent), *Práca* (2.9 per cent), *Nový den* (2.7 per cent) and some regional dailies with about the same readership in their regions. These included some less popular national dailies such as

*Korzár/Východoslovenské noviny* (Šrámek, 2000: 36). Regional dailies were read by 9.7 per cent of all citizens in early 2002 (*Sme*, 28 February 2002, p. 2). The daily *Nový deň* supports the strongest political party in Slovakia – the Movement for a Democratic Slovakia.

There is a general declining trend of circulation and readership of the daily press in Slovakia. There is no tabloid daily press (like *Das Bild* in Germany or *Blesk* in the Czech Republic).

### The periodical and magazine press

The number of magazines was over a thousand with a total circulation of 205.7 million copies in 2000. This means that there was an increase by 193 titles and 13.9 million copies in contrast to the previous year. The highest circulation was among the advertising magazines (47 million copies), the lowest circulation was among the magazines of political parties (41,000 copies) (*Vybrané ukazovatele*, 2000: 7). There were 134 weeklies published in 2000. Of these, forty four were national, seventy nine regional and eleven local weeklies.

The most read weeklies were *Plus 7 dní* (19 per cent readership in late 2001 and over 200,000 circulation), *Markíza* (19 per cent), *Život* (14 per cent readership and 127,000), *Eurotelevízia* (11 per cent and 150,000) and *Slovenka* (10 per cent). *Plus 7 dní* is a weekly of the *Time* variety, but with less international politics and more scandal. *Život* is a family weekly but covering almost everything. *Slovenka* is a weekly for women. These weeklies were followed by the weeklies *TV komplet* and *Moment* (7 per cent and 5 per cent respectively, 115,000 and 50,000 circulation). The weekly *Markíza* was established by TV Markíza. *Markíza* focuses on domestic and international celebrities. *Eurotelevízia* is mainly a television programme weekly. *Moment* is a more serious family weekly, with a declining circulation in 2001. *Vasárnap* is a Hungarian-language weekly.

Among the most popular monthlies are the family-oriented *Rodina* (70,000), those for women (*Dorka, Eva*, 50,000; *Emma*, 90,000; *Zenský magazín*, 85,000), leisure interest (*Minikrízovky, Lišiak*, 50,000; *Tabu*), hobby and health (*Zdravie, Záhradkár*, 85,000) and *Reader's Digest Výber* (50,000).

The German publishing house Gruner & Jahr launched the weekly *Čas* (similar to the German weekly *Focus*, with a circulation of about 50,000) in May 2001. In late 2001 and early 2002 Gruner & Jahr planned a merger with the Ringier publishing house operating in Slovakia. Gruner & Jahr would get a 51 per cent share of Ringier's media in Slovakia. This merger would create the biggest media publishing house in Slovakia. The Swiss Ringier published five out of fifteen of the most popular magazines in Slovakia (most of them were published before 1989): *Život, Eurotelevízia, Telemagazín, Rodina* and *Eva*. Tele-programme magazines *Eurotelevízia* and *Telemagazín* together shared 41 per cent of the market in its segment.

The most important Slovak publishers are Spoločnos' 7 Plus (it publishes weekly *Plus 7 dní* and four monthlies) and Perex (which publishes the daily *Pravda* and the weekly *Moment*). *TV Komplet, Profit* and *Lišiak* were bought in early 2002 by the A-ha public company.

## The electronic (audio-visual) media

### Television

There were 98.9 per cent of households with television sets in 2001. There were five national terrestrial or cable channels broadcasting from the territory of Slovakia in 2002: STV-1, STV-2, Markíza, JOJ and the news cable channel TA-3. Territorial coverage of the main terrestrial television stations at the end of 2001 was as follows: STV-1 covered between 97.3 per cent and 99 per cent, STV-2 covered between 89.4 per cent and 95.1 per cent, Markíza covered between 63.5 per cent and 79 per cent of the national territory (and 94 per cent of citizens) and cable and terrestrial television Global (since March 2002 JOJ) with an estimated territorial coverage of 30 per cent but an estimated 65–70 per cent coverage in March 2002 (market share 1.41 per cent in October 2001).

TA-3 broadcast via the cable network (and planned to broadcast also via digital satellite) with about 35 per cent coverage, 12–14 per cent daily audience but only 0.86 per cent market share in September–October 2001 (STV, 2001: 2; *Stratégie*, October 2001: 74). TA-3 replaced *TV Luna*, which broadcast for less than two years by way of the cable networks. JOJ TV increased its coverage in early 2002 to become about equal with TV Markíza. It is expected that JOJ TV will in two years' create serious competition for TV Markíza.

TV Nova was received by 40 per cent of households but in March 2002 it was withdrawn from cable networks, officially because of copyright issues, but in practice because the new JOJ TV replaced it effectively. Currently JOJ TV broadcasts old programmes from TV Nova archives. The Czech TV Nova played an important role in the Slovak television market until early 2002. Its market share in October 2001 was 9.6 per cent. TV Nova can still be received in parts of western Slovakia terrestrially.

The Czech public ČT-1 was accessible by 46 per cent of the population and its second channel ČT-2 by 32 per cent of households (with about 4 per cent market share together), while 28 per cent of households in Slovakia had access to other Czech television stations. Other Czech television stations were present in the Slovak cable network, including the Prima television channel (3.27 per cent market share) and TV-3 (0.78 per cent market share) (Šrámek, 2000: 31). There was discussion as to whether this is in line with international copyright.

There are also Hungarian television stations which can be received terrestrially in southern parts of Slovakia. These channels are watched by ethnic Hungarians in Slovakia as mentioned above. A specific feature of the Slovak electronic media market is the news television channel TA-3, which has been broadcasting since September 2001.

The STV-1 market share in October 2001 was 21.3 per cent, while STV-2 had a market share of only 3.7 per cent at the same time (STV, 2001: 28). Among the most popular programmes at the end of 2001 was news, followed by two sports programmes. There is no great need to discuss the situation in the public Slovak Television. It is enough to quote its director-general, Milan Materák. In his words, there are no rules in STV, there is a crisis of creativity, a bad enterprise culture and a lot of incompetent people (*Sme*, 17 January 2002: 5).

Public television is financed by fees, state subsidies, advertisements and by its own limited business activities (like selling videocassettes of its programmes). Owing to rising costs and fixed fees (these are not increased regularly), as well as non-transparent management, there is a permanent financial crisis in the public television service.

TV Markíza is majority-owned by Slovak owners and the minority owner (49 per cent) of the service organization for TV Markíza is CME. CME also obtained a 34 per cent share in the licence organization of TV Markíza, including control rights, in early 2002.

New JOJ TV is owned by Czech entrepreneurs from Česká produkční invest, which is owned by MEF Holding. The news television channel TA-3 has been majority-owned by a British company, Millenium Electronics, since early 2002.

Slovakia is probably the only country in Europe without live broadcasting of football matches in the national football league. The public television argues that the fees are too high, while its private competitor TV Markíza believes that the quality of the game is too low. Ironically, football was the most popular sport in 1999 among the male population and the second most popular sport in general (*Stratégie*, June 2001: 17).

There are very few programmes (for example, in contrast to Poland and Russia, with much bigger markets) with subtitles in Slovakia, and there is virtually no television movie with voice-over. But the trend is towards an increasing number of television movies with subtitles. There were 10,777 hours broadcast by both public television channels and 470,477 hours by all other television stations (mainly by regional and local television) in 2001. STV broadcast 71 per cent in-house programmes, including 48 per cent of repeats. This partly explains the low popularity of STV-1, only 32 per cent of viewers in mid-2001. But this was also the first year when there was no decline in the audience of *STV*.

About 93 per cent of citizens watch broadcast television. TV Markíza dominates the market, followed by STV-1. The daily audience of TV Markíza was 35 per cent in October 1996, passed 50 per cent between April and December 1997, reached almost 67 per cent in November 1999 and was 62.2 per cent in March 2000. STV-1 followed a reverse pattern: from 52 per cent in March 1996 to as low as 35.4 per cent in December 1997 and back to 40.3 per cent in March 2000. The third television channel, TV Nova, attracted daily between 11.5 per cent and 18.4 per cent of viewers in the period from March 1996 to March 2000, with 18.4 per cent of the daily audience in March 2000. STV-2 followed the general pattern of STV-1, with a decrease in daily audience from 25 per cent in March 1996 to 11.3 per cent in March 2000. STV-2 data were thus close to the daily audience data of CT-1 in Slovakia, with 7.2 per cent of the daily audience in March 2000 (Šrámek, 2000: 32).

The market share at the turn of 2001/2 for major television stations is in the statistics section; for STV-2 it was 3.6–4.7 per cent, for TV Global 1.3–1.7 sper cent, for TA-3 (0.9 per cent and for others 16.9–18.1 per cent. The new JOJ TV (which replaced TV Global) audience was 8 per cent in March 2002. The data cited here are from two different research organizations, and are based on various methodologies. There was some discussion in early 2002 of introducing people-metres for monitoring the popularity of television stations. Smaller stations in particular argued that the current system of measuring popularity favours bigger stations.

### Radio

There are four types of radio stations: national (public radio – Rádio Slovensko, Rádio Devín, Rádio Rock FM), multiregional (seven), regional (nine plus two public) and local stations (seven). There were twenty-four private radio stations broadcasting in late 2001, including AWR Europe broadcast from abroad, RFE/RL and the BBC World Service. The public radio covered the whole territory on medium wave, and 82 per cent of territory by FM.

The public Slovak *Radio* runs six channels. There are three national channels and three more specific ones: regional Rádio Regina, for minorities Rádio Patria and the international broadcaster *Radio* Slovakia International. In addition, there is broadcasting via the Internet, called *Radio* Net. Rádio Slovensko has universal programming, broadcast on medium wave and FM. Rádio Devín specializes in high-quality educational and classical music radio, broadcast on FM. Rádio Rock FM is a commercially oriented public radio channel focused on the young generation.

The most popular radio stations in early 2001 were: Rádio Slovensko (27.2 per cent 'listened yesterday'), Rádio Rock FM (11.7 per cent), Rádio Okey (9.4 per cent), Fun Rádio (9.4 per cent), Rádio Twist (6.0 per cent), Rádio Regina (5 per cent), Rádio Východ (4.4 per cent), Kiks (3.9 per cent) and N Rádio (3.2 per cent) (AISA Slovensko).

In 2000 the commercially most successful radio stations were multi-regional and national stations: Rádio Twist, Fun Rádio, Rádio Slovensko and Rádio Rock FM (www.radia.sk).

The majority of small private broadcasters face financial problems. The clear exception so far is Rádio Express, which started to broadcast on 1 January 2001. Its shareholders are the European Bank for Reconstruction

and Development, the European Union via one of its foundations and three Slovak businessmen. It is a radio for drivers.

All important private radio stations are wholly or majority-owned by Slovak owners, with the exception of foreign stations also broadcasting from Slovakia, like the BBC and RFE. SRo broadcast 44,345 hours (including 25,061 hours of music) while other radio stations broadcast 196,530 hours in 2001. News and current affairs created about one-fifth of all programmes. There was rapid expansion in private radio broadcasting between 1999 and 2000.

About 80 per cent of citizens listen to radio broadcasting. The most recent audience figures of the most popular radio stations ('listened yesterday') can be seen in the statistics section. These major radio stations are followed by the private Fun Rádio with 12.8 per cent, Rádio Twist with 11 per cent and the public Rádio Regina with 10.5 per cent. Among the most popular radio stations one can find Rádio Východ (6.2 per cent), Rádio Hviezda FM (5.4 per cent), Rádio Expres (5.5 per cent) and Rádio Patria (4.6 per cent). The 'most often listened to' stations are Rádio Slovensko (36.1 per cent), Rádio Rock FM (9.8 per cent), Rádio Okey (7.5 per cent), Fun Rádio (7.4 per cent) and Rádio Twist (5.6 per cent). Among foreign radio stations the most important ones are the Hungarian stations Danubius Radio (3.8 per cent), Slágerradio (3.4 per cent) and Kossuth Radio (2.5 per cent) (www.slovakradio.sk).

### Film and video

Two evening full-length feature movies were produced in 2001, and three in 2000 as well as in 1999. Altogether eighty three various short and evening movies were produced in 2000, including three in co-production with foreign companies. It was expected that the number of new evening movies would be as many as five in 2002. There were 135 movie premiers in movie theatres in 2000. Of these, 60.7 per cent came from the United States and 10.4 per cent from the Czech Republic, followed by France and the United Kingdom. Only four movies were dubbed into the Slovak language and sixty three movies had Slovak subtitles. The number of movie theatres decreased by fifty six in 2000 to 279 and the number of visitors by 384,000 to 2,646,000. The movie theatres organized 57,214 showings. There were 250 video rental places in Slovakia in 2000 (*Vybrané ukazovatele*, 2000: 7,19).

## The Internet and related on-line media

There were sixty four Internet service providers in 1999 compared with forty nine in 1998. The most popular Internet providers in late 2001 were Slovak Telecom (majority owner Deutsche Telekom) with a 30.7 per cent market share, followed by Nextra (Norwegian) and Kiwwi, owned by Globaltel. Kiwwi provides free Internet access. Additional companies are Euroweb, owned by the Dutch KPN, and Slovanet, owned by US Advent International. Two agencies claimed that overall Internet penetration is Slovakia in mid-2001 was around 18–19 per cent and perhaps as many as 25 per cent of citizens regularly used the Internet in 2001 (see also the statistics section). Probably 23–30 per cent of citizens used the Internet at least once in their life (Bella and Durkovic, 2001: 674). Access to the Internet in Slovakia is amongst the most expensive of all OECD countries in purchasing power parity. This development led to protests by users (sending e-mails) and by the government in early 2002. As a consequence, the Prime Minister met representatives of Slovak Telecom. The result was an initiative called eSlovensko. This project should make the Internet accessible to more people at lower rates.

The first on-line daily 'newspaper' started on 9 September 1999. It was a free electronic newspaper and survived for only about one year. In 2001 another Internet daily started but this time it is not daily for universal readership but for business and economy news (www.fini.sk).

# POLITICS, POLICY, LAW AND REGULATION

The government has no clear media policy. The main actors in policy matters are: the Council for Broadcasting and Retransmission, the Association of Independent Radio and Television Stations, the Slovak Syndicate of Journalists (2,645 members in 2000) and the Slovak Association of Journalists (500 members). Both private and public electronic media are regulated by the Council on Broadcasting and Retransmission. This council awards and takes away licences, checks the diversity and independence of broadcasts as well as ethical and legal standards. In addition, both public service media have their own supervising councils, also elected by the parliament.

## The press

In March 1990 parliament passed a Press law (No. 445). Some journalists do not know that such a law even exists, others complain that it does not sufficiently protect journalists. The President – and especially in the past sometimes other politicians – sued some very critical journalists under the libel/defamation laws. The 1990 law regulates distribution and tries to curb the sale of pornographic material. There are no other special principles of regulation except those mentioned above.

The state does not support press diversity by way of any specific policy. This is related to VAT, distribution network functioning or up-to date press legislation as well as press plurality (which exists due to a still not consolidated market).

Similar to what happens in the domain of the electronic media, politicians try to establish close links with the news professionals. There has been a Press Council since March 2002. A code of ethics has existed since 1990 but is morally binding only upon members of the Syndicate of Slovak Journalists. Some of the best journalists are not members of this professional body, which for some time also acted as a trade union organization. Some important media, including *STV* and the daily *Pravda,* in 2000–1 adopted their own code of ethics/professional conduct. This is certainly a sign of professionalization of the media.

It is expected that the new government will pass a comprehensive new media law in 2002–6.

## The electronic media

Since summer 1992 there has been a state-established supervisory body for the electronic media, now called the Council on Broadcasting and Retransmission. In principle, Slovak media legislation was harmonized with the EU electronic media legislation in 2000. There are about five major media laws (each has on average been changed about five times in the last ten years) and up to fifteen laws relating directly or indirectly to broadcasting, plus amendments.

There is no need for a licence for the retransmission of programmes unchanged, a provider needs only to register. Radio licences are valid for eight years, while television licences are valid for twelve years. It is possible to extend a licence for one additional term without repeating the procedures.

Advertising is allowed for 3 per cent of daily broadcasting in public media (and up to 10 per cent including tele-shopping). Private radio stations can broadcast 20 per cent of advertisements and private television stations 15 per cent of their air time (plus an additional 5 per cent for tele-shopping). It is possible to advertise alcohol only after 10.00 p.m. (with the exception of beer, which has no restriction). It is not permissible to advertise tobacco products, but till 2006 it is possible to broadcast sports programmes with sponsoring by tobacco trade marks.

Further conditions are set by the Council on Broadcasting and Retransmission. For example, broadcasters are obliged to respect the usual conditions such as avoiding vulgarity and discrimination. Changes in broadcasting structure must be reported to the council within fifteen days. There is a right of reply for citizens and state authorities, among others, if information published is incorrect. The time limit is two months. On radio, Slovak music should form at least 10 per cent of all music broadcast. An interesting requirement is that top managers and programme directors must have no criminal record. In the case of television broadcasting, 90 per cent of employees must be Slovak citizens. Any planned changes in ownership structure must be reported to the council in advance. The Slovak language is compulsory in broadcasting, while the Czech language is allowed in programmes that overall do not exceed 20 per cent of the station's total broadcasting time.

The major problem is that the law does not give the council enough enforcement powers. Subsequent measures have introduced further limits on the supervisory tasks of the council. Until early 1999 the government was not really interested in media reform or at least it was not a priority. However, some MPs often initiated changes in media laws. Sometimes the changes were motivated or at least influenced by the business interests of big media owners. New Bills relating to changes in the laws on broadcasting, public television and radio, as well as on advertising, and the so-called new comprehensive big media law (in two versions) were submitted to the parliament in the years 2000–1. Only two of these laws, regarding advertising and broadcasting, were passed. In early 2001 the government submitted some Bills relating to the public media but there was insufficient consensus on the form that regulation and reform should take. To summarize, there is still no coherent media policy in Slovakia.

## The Internet and related on-line media

There is no special legislation. There are no special principles of regulation other than those relating to other media. Politicians have started using the Internet for on-line discussions with citizens in recent years. Parts of these discussions sometimes appear in the print media. There is a plan on the part of Slovak Telecom and the government to increase the diffusion of the Internet but no details are available.

# STATISTICS

| | | |
|---|---|---:|
| Population | | 5,379,455 |
| Number of households | | 1,832,484 |
| Overall movie admissions, 2001 | | 2,850,000 |
| Books published (titles) | | 7,200 |

| **Print media** | Circulation of main daily newspapers, 2003 | |
|---|---|---:|
| | National | |
| | Nový Čas | 148,000 |
| | Šport | 70,000 |
| | Pravda | 78,000 |
| | Sme | 70,000 |
| | Regional: six daily newspapers together print only 33,000 copies. | |

| | | |
|---|---|---:|
| **Broadcast media** | Audience share of main television channels, 2003 (%) | |
| | Public | |
| | STV-1 | approx. 17–20 |
| | STV-2 | 4–5 |
| | Private | |
| | TV Markíza | approx. 38–44 |
| | JOJ TV | 10–11 |
| | TV Nova (withdrawn from cable networks in 2002) | approx. 5–6 |
| | | |
| | Audience share of main radio channels (%) | |
| | Public | |
| | Slovak Radio (Rádio Slovensko) | approx. 48 |
| | Rádio Rock FM | approx. 21 |
| | Three other major public channels | |
| | Private | |
| | Rádio Okey | approx. 13 |
| | Fun Rádio | |
| | Rádio Twist | |
| | Rádio Východ (regional) | |
| | | |
| | Percentage of households reached by all main forms of satellite, cable or terrestrial pay-television | |
| | Percentage of households with cable television, early 2002 | 43.5 |
| | Percentage of households with satellite dish | 30.5 |
| | Percentage of households with: | |
| | Video cassette recorder 2000/1 | 52 |

| | | |
|---|---|---:|
| **Electronic media** | Digital television reception | n.a. |
| | Personal computer, late 2001 | 22 |
| | Internet access at home, late 2001 | 11 |
| | Mobile phone, early 2002 | 45 |

| | | |
|---|---|---:|
| **Advertising spend, 2001** | Television | 46.6 |
| | Press | 34.8 |
| | Radio | 10.4 |
| | Other | 8.2 |

## Sources

Interviews with Milan Stanislav, deputy editor-in-chief, *Pravda*, 15 January 2002; Vladimír Miškovský, editor-in-chief, *Práca*, 29 January 2002; Anna Sámelová, editor, news department, Radio Twist, 31 January 2002; Tatiana Veselá, editor-in-chief, weekly *Moment*, 15 February 2002; Tom Nicholson, editor-in-chief, *The Slovak Spectator*, 15 March 2002.

# REFERENCES

Bella, Tomas and Ďurkovič, Marian (2001) 'Internet', in Miroslav Kollar and Grigorij Meseznikov (eds) *Slovensko 2001. Suhrnna sprava o stave spolocnosti*. Bratislava: IVO.

Brown, Archie and Wightman, Gordon (1979) 'Czechoslovakia: revival and retreat' in Archie Brown and Jack Gray (eds) *Political Culture and Political Change in Communist States,* (2nd edn). London and Basingstoke: Macmillan.

Hapak, Pavel (2002) 'Prognozy naplnene – je tu rast!' *Strategie* 2: 21–3.

Havros, Richard (2002) 'Tlak na telekomunikacie pre cenu Internetu rastie', *Sme*, Supplement Pocítac, 17 January p. 1.

Havros, Richard (2002) 'Omyly Slovenskych telekomunikacif', *Sme*, 31 January, p. 19.

Johnson, Owen V. (1995) 'Mass Media and the Velvet Revolution', in Jeremy D. Popkin (ed.) *Media and Revolution: Comparative Perspectives*. Lexington KY: University of Kentucky Press.

Kamenec, Ivan (2001) 'Fenomen rozhlasu v modernych (slovenskych) dejinach' in *Prispevky k dejinam rozhlasu 6*. Bratislava: Slovensky rozhlas.

Köpplová, Barbora, Jirák, Jan and Kaplan, Frank, L., (1993) 'Major trends in the Czech mass media after November 1989' in Al Hester and Kristina White, (eds) *Creating a Free Press in Eastern Europe*. Athens GA: James M. Cox Jr Center for International Mass Communication Training and Research.

Krejčí, Oskar (1991) 'Preco to prasklo?' *Pravda na nedel'u,* 25 January, p. 5.

Lamplova, Zuzana M. (2002) 'Pomoc, pravo a vol'ný pohyb', *Sme*, 17 January, p. 9.

Smatlak, Martin (2001) 'Medialna problematika na Slovensku sa spaja s kompromismi', *Otazky zurnalistiky* 44 (3–4): 146–54.

Šrámek, Ludovit (2000) 'Publikum medii na Slovensku v roku 2000' in Denisa Vlkova, Lucia Petranska and Anna Chynoradska (eds) *Adresar medii Slovenskej republiky*. Bratislava: MIC.

STV (2001) *Tyzdenny ohlas divakov v 42 tyzdni*. Bratislava: STV, odbor medialneho vyskumu a informacif.

Táborský, Edward (1961) *Communism in Czechoslovakia 1948–1960*. Princeton NJ: Princeton University Press.

*Vybrané ukazovatele za kulturu v SR* (2000) Bratislava: Statistical Office of the Slovak Republic.

*Yearbook of Transport, Posts and Telecommunications* (2000) Bratislava: Statistical Office of the Slovak Republic.

Sprava o stave vysielania v Slovenskej republike a o cinnosti Rady pre vysielanie a retransmisiu za rok 2001. Bratislava: Ndrodna rada Slovenskej republiky II. volebne obdobie, tlac *c*. 1347, March 2002.

www.slovakradio.sk/radioinet/index5/index5_pri eskurn.html.

www.eb.sk/spravy/mon.ltc?ID=58.

europa.eu.int/comm/public_opinion/.

# 19: Slovenia

VIDA ZEI

## NATIONAL PROFILE

The Republic of Slovenia is one of the youngest and smallest European countries. Before its independence in 1991, Slovenia was one of the republics of the Socialist Federal Republic of Yugoslavia. Today, Slovenia is a multi-party parliamentary democracy, the 176th member of the United Nations, and a full member of various European institutions. Official governmental representations of Slovenia's position in the world stress two ideas: Slovenia's European historical tradition, geographical position, and close economic ties with the West, and its political and ideological distance from its former position as a Balkan state.

Slovenia is small in terms of its territory (20,273 km$^2$) and its population (1,966,000, according to the 1991 census). Demographically, Slovenia represents an ageing country with a slow-growing, ethnically fairly homogeneous population. The main reasons are the two world wars, in which Slovenes suffered great losses, and emigration. The latter was strongest in the decades before the First World War, when people left mostly for economic reasons to overseas destinations, and between both world wars, when they moved mainly to Western Europe. The process of ageing would be even faster had Slovenia's population not been rejuvenated by immigration between 1971 and 1981, when mostly young and economically active individuals from other Yugoslav republics settled in Slovenia's urban and industrial areas.

Slovenia's active working population today includes 49.5 per cent of the total population, including nearly half of all women. Twelve per cent of all Slovenes between the ages of twenty five and sixty four have a higher education; in 1998 Slovenia had a ratio of thirty students per thousand inhabitants.

According to the 1991 census, 88 per cent of the people consider themselves Slovenes. Italians, Hungarians, and recently also Romanies (according to a new law) are considered indigenous ethnic minorities with rights protected by the constitution. The members of 'other' nations are Croats (2.7 per cent), Serbs (2.4 per cent), and Muslims (1.4 per cent). A majority of Slovene citizens are Roman Catholics, other religious preferences include Orthodox (2 per cent), Islam (1.5 per cent), and Protestant (1 per cent). For 88 per cent of the citizens the mother tongue is Slovene, while the languages of indigenous ethnic minorities – Italians (0.2 per cent), Hungarians (0.5 per cent) and Romanies (0.1 per cent) – were spoken by fewer people than the languages of immigrants.

The use of the Slovene language has been historically the most important part of the national and cultural identity. In 2000 the government established an Office of the Slovene Language, following an earlier, informal 'Language Court' and the example of Scandinavian countries – anticipating language problems with the expected entry of Slovenia into the European Union. The Office has linking, harmonizing, advisory and promotional roles in the planning and implementation of active linguistic policies. Slovenia's legislation takes into account also the specific needs of Italian and Hungarian ethnic communities in ethnically mixed regions. In Slovene Istria, for instance, Koper/Capodistria radio and television stations play a special role in the development of the Italian ethnic community, while members of the Hungarian ethnic minority may view and listen to Hungarian programming from a Lendava station. Efforts directed at providing the Romany ethnic community with media services are only in their initial stage.

About 300,000 Slovenes live outside Slovenia's borders as ethnic minorities in Italy, Austria, and Hungary, or as emigrants overseas and in other EU countries. They represent an important part of Slovene media production, with their press and radio and television programming in Slovene. Their communication activities depend largely on legislatures in the host countries and ever diminishing financial support from Slovenia.

The beginnings of the Slovene media are linked with the specificity of Slovene political history and the cultural history of media developments in Europe. Publishing began with the first two Slovene books, the *Catechismus* and *Abecedarium*, published by Primož Trubar in 1550, followed by fifty six books published by Slovene Protestants between 1550 and 1599. The first modern Slovene publisher was L. Schwentner, who produced about 200 books of Slovene literature, poetry, and educational content between 1898 and 1938.

The first Slovene periodical was the *Slovene Calender*, published for a general readership in 1557. Anti-reformation activities slowed down the development of a Slovene press until 1797, when the first Slovene newspaper, *Lublanske novice*, became a centre of the Enlightenment movement.

Radio Ljubljana was the second radio station that started to operate in the Kingdom of Yugoslavia in 1928, and kept its name until 1991, when it became part of Radiotelevizija Slovenia.

Regular television programming in Slovenia started in 1958 as part of the Yugoslav Radiodifusion, but shared time with studios in Zagreb and Belgrade, the latter providing the centralized evening news programme. In 1966 colour television programming operated experimentally to become a regular feature in 1974 (PAL system). In 1968 Television Ljubljana introduced a central Slovene-language evening news programme.

Prior to the 1990s, the media were socially owned and largely subordinated to party and state authorities. Their primary role was the spread of general information and knowledge and contributions to political and cultural education. After the political change in 1990, the period of transition was marked by a number of paradoxes in the media sphere, similar to those in other countries of Central and Eastern Europe. Because of their importance before and during the political changes of the late 1980s, the media became a significant political issue regarding questions of privatization and freedom. Today the restructuring of the media, and of national public broadcasting in particular, shows that the new political elites, the ruling coalitions as well as the opposition parties are trying to use the media as a source of power and generator of funds. Thus the change from socially owned to privately held media involved a fusing of political and economic controls, in which advertising revenue plays an important role; in 2001 it represented total revenue of €120 million.

## STRUCTURE AND OWNERSHIP

### The print media

#### *The newspaper press*
During the 1990s the print media was strongly affected by political changes. In 1994 a new Mass Media Act institutionalized the privatization and liberalization of the print media market and, as a consequence, revealed the monopolization and commercialization of the media. The new government expected that former socially owned print media enterprises would be invaded by European and US corporations. Instead, a small number of local owners with stakes in numerous affiliated companies took control of the majority of the media market (Hrvatin and Milosavljević, 2001: 7). Privatization led to increasing dependence on advertising revenue. The largest advertisers in the print media are foreign companies, such as Procter & Gamble, Henkel, and Renault, and, among the Slovene advertisers, mobile phone operators Mobitel and Si.mobil.

Today there are about 1,500 print media published in Slovenia, with about 6 million circulation. They include 205 newspapers, among them five major dailies with a combined circulation of about 356,000 copies, more than fifty weeklies and regional papers with a circulation of about 1.6 million copies, thirty four fortnightly newspapers, and about 300 monthlies.

All major daily newspapers (except *Slovenske novice* and *Finance*) originated in the previous political system; they were privatized through internal buy-outs and internal distributions of shares. After 1990 three new dailies, *Slovenec*, *Republika*, and *Jutranjik*, filled the press vacuum on the political right, but they failed after a short time owing to lack of start-up capital to keep them afloat through the first few years when even the most successful media operate at a loss. Today the four largest media companies (Delo, Dnevnik, Večer, and Slovenske novice) control more than 90 per cent of the daily newspaper market. In contrast to the experience in other East and Central European countries, the proportion of foreign capital in the daily press is insignificant.

The largest national daily is *Delo*, a serious general circulation newspaper in Ljubljana, that was established in 1959. Its slogan, since 1990, is 'The right to know'. The average circulation is 93,369, 60 per cent of which is sold through subscriptions by regular readers from industrial urban areas (Ljubljana, Kranj, and Postojna) between the ages of twenty and seventy five; over 60 per cent completed higher education and belong to the highest income categories. *Delo*'s share of advertising revenue amounts to 48.8 per cent of all dailies. In terms of ownership, the share of internal owners – in the 1990s originally 60 per cent – fell by half, while the shares of external owners increased, especially through the concentration of capital by one owner, Krekova družba. The latter represents mainly 'conservative' (Christian Democrat) capital which controls 37 per cent of Delo stock. Interest among foreign investors (Maxwell, Great Britain; OVB, Germany; WAZ, Germany) was rebuffed by *Delo* management, which expressed interest in co-operation on the principle of equality (Hrvatin and Milosavljević, 2001: 24).

A similar daily, *Večer*, has been published in Maribor since 1945. It has an average circulation of 67,500 copies. About 70 per cent of *Večer* is sold through subscriptions in the Štajerska, Prekmurje, and Koroška regions, but the newspaper is gaining popularity in the rest of the country because of its pronounced critical and objective editorial policy. Its share of advertising revenue among dailies is 23.2 per cent. In contrast to *Delo*, *Večer* focuses on establishing business links with local media in the region, including local radio stations and advertising agencies, owned to a large extent by employees and various state investment funds. The other dailies, *Slovenske novice* and *Dnevnik*, are published in Ljubljana; the first, established in 1991, with the highest circulation in Slovenia (85,312 copies) because of its tabloid content, has a readership that is fairly evenly spread across generations, gender, region, and income groups. Its share of advertising revenue is 23.2 per cent. *Dnevnik*, established in 1951, is a lighter, general information daily with a circulation of about 80,000 copies and a readership in and around Ljubljana. Its advertising share is 29.3 per cent. *Finance*, since 1992 the first Slovene business newspaper, turned from a weekly to a daily in 2001. Because of its aggressive editorial policy it is considered a newspaper on the rise, receiving 4.6 per cent of advertising revenue. *Finance* is an exception among Slovene newspapers in terms of its foreign ownership: Dagens Industri (Bonnier) owns 75 per cent.

### The periodical and magazine press

Among the bigger regional newspapers is *Primorske novice*, Koper, published three times a week, with a circulation of 27,000 copies and 60 per cent subscriptions. Its advertising revenue is about 10 per cent of all periodicals. The two biggest political weeklies, with different political background and readership, are *Mladina* and *Mag*.

Slovene magazines cover various interests, ranging from current affairs, the economy and finance to home, family and children, men's and women's issues, culinary topics, religion, and sport, among others. Seventeen magazines are connected with Delo, the two biggest have 15 per cent of the market and all of them control more than 50 per cent of the magazine market. Ten new computer magazines have appeared on the market since the 1990s, but those addressing personal relationships, fashion and women's topics are most numerous. The oldest one, *Naša žena*, has changed radically since 1941 and its early days of militant agitation (its average circulation is 67,000 copies and its readership share is 8.3 per cent). Readers are highly educated high-income women of all generations, even though its new editorial policy is now much closer to *Jana*, the most popular women's magazine since 1972. *Jana*'s readership share is 14 per cent, and its advertising revenue reaches nearly 10 per cent of all periodicals. Readers of *Jana* are women of all generations mainly with medium education in the upper middle income bracket of society. The newer women's weekly magazine, *Lady*, appeared on the market in 1990; its logo, 'The tabloid with the highest circulation in Slovenia', reflects the appeal to lower middle-class women. It prints, on average, 75,000 copies.

### Book publishing

Book publishing contributes enormously to the sense of Slovene national identity. In the twentieth century book publishing developed as in the rest of Europe. After the Second World War the publication of original Slovene literature in socialist Yugoslavia was highly subsidized but under the control of Agitprop. In the 1950s self-management allowed more freedom. The Publishing Law of 1978 attached special social importance to publishing and included the right to subsidization; nevertheless, financial support diminished in the 1980s. At the end of the decade there were some twenty publishing houses actively involved in publishing over 2,000 titles a year, participating in international co-productions, appearing at international book fairs, and raising the quality of printing and book illustration. Slovene publishers also developed the production of music records and cassettes.

After 1990 a host of new small private publishers arrived at the scene, but their number quickly diminished. In 1995 there were still about fifty book publishers. The Publishing Law of 1978 is a dead letter and book publishing is regulated like any other economic activity. However, some original works in Slovene still receive subsidies that in 2001 amounted to about €1.5 million and helped 215 books appear on the market.

Of 3,917 books published in 2000, a little over 900 titles were translations. Slovenia represents a small publishing market; print runs are rarely large (3,000 copies represent a bestseller!), and books are made even more expensive by the newly introduced 8.5 per cent (value added) tax. Nevertheless, in 2000 one-third of all published titles were original Slovene works. Less than two decades ago, Slovenia was the European record holder for the number of new titles published per capita; today people obtain books mainly from libraries: around 15 million books are lent annually.

The major Slovene owner in the publishing industry is Državna založba Slovenije (DZS), previously a publishing house that turned into a commercial company which sells and buys more than it actually publishes. Državna založba Slovenije also owns 26.4 per cent of Dnevnik and is slowly moving into broadcasting properties. Most of the larger, now privatized publishing houses (the biggest, Mladinska knjiga, publishes about 400 books a year) are owned by internal shareholders, by DZS, and by various investment funds.

Book publishing also takes place among Slovenes abroad, as in Italy (Trieste and Gorizia), Austria (Koroška), Germany (Munich), Argentina (Buenos Aires), and the United States (Cleveland). For many decades their publishing activities have been overlooked; today they are a recognized part of Slovenia's cultural history and are present on the book market.

## The electronic (audio-visual) media

### Television

There are more than forty television organizations in Slovenia, according to the Broadcasting Council of the Republic of Slovenia. The national public service broadcasting company, Radiotelevizija Slovenija, consists of Radio Slovenia, Television Slovenia, RTV Koper-Capodistria, RTV Maribor, Transmitters, and of three organizational units of radio, television and music production. Its operation is monitored by the Council of Radio and Television Slovenia. Another body, the Broadcasting Council of the Republic of Slovenia, is an independent regulatory agency of the broadcasting industry. It was established in 1994 to monitor all the broadcasting channels.

Radiotelevizija Slovenija operates three national television programmes (SLO-1, SLO-2, TV Koper-Capodistria) alongside three national commercial programmes, which reach more than 80 per cent of the population (Kanal A, Pop TV, TV-3). The development of a cable network, run by over 100 cable operators, has set off an increase in local commercial television programmes. In addition, there are nine local public (non-profit) television programmes reaching smaller audiences. A public television programme for the Italian ethnic minority, Television Koper-Capodistria, operates as part of Radiotelevizija Slovenija but is independent in terms of the management of programme policies and in directly influencing the appointment of programme directors. Television Koper-Capodistria began operating in 1971 with target audiences in

Slovenia and Croatia; it broadcasts more than eleven hours per day.

Television viewers in Slovenia have access to about 360 hours of programmes each day. Since 1997 the first and second public service national television programmes may be seen over the Hot Bird 3 satellite and, since 1995, over the Internet. The reception of foreign television programmes offers a variety of choices. Viewers may choose from about ten English-language programmes (e.g. BBC World, BBC Prime, CNN, Sky, or the Discovery Channel), a host of German-language programmes (such as 3-SAT or ORF), the European ARTE, the Italian RAI, the Spanish TVE, the French TV-5, and various programmes produced by television studios in the former Yugoslav federation, featuring Croat, Serbian, Montenegrin, Albanian, Bosnian and Macedonian languages.

Until the mid-1990s Radiotelevizija Slovenia had practically no competition, but dramatically lost a large share of viewers (except in entertainment and sports programmes) as a result of the introduction of commercial television, cable, and the Internet. As a result, Radiotelevizija Slovenia changed, and became more commercial; it expanded entertainment, reduced information, commentary, documentary, and in-house drama programmes, introduced more US films, and even started to insert commercials into the longer popular programmes. It also introduced television shopping, developed its presence on the Internet, and started to broadcast by satellite. In 1998 it produced about 13,000 hours of programming; more than half the imported programmes were of European origin.

Radiotelevizija Slovenia is largely financed from subscription fees and, to a smaller degree, from advertising. In the 1990s its advertising revenue increased, but is limited by law. In addition to a programming crisis of public television during the 1990s there were constant serious financial problems and monitoring by a politically divided Broadcasting Council. Consequently, it was once again transformed into a vehicle for promoting political interests. Currently, the situation has improved financially because of access to electricity customers: inhabitants of Slovenia who pay for electricity also pay for a television licence!

Commercial television programmes, like Kanal A, that started to operate in 1991 specifically, had similar problems at the time: the initial starting capital was only modest

and resulted in insufficient funding for good programmes or for in-house quality productions, even though the Mass Media Act of 1994 prescribed a very low programming quota for them, i.e. one-tenth of broadcast time. Pop TV, which was initially only a 'trade mark' of a programme producer (ProPlus, a company owned by a US corporation, CME) introduced a network system in 1995 and became the first large foreign investment in Slovene media (US capital was represented to the public as a loan), thus becoming the first serious competitor of public television. Pop TV featured popular films and television hits from the United States, Great Britain and other European countries, without any information programmes, except for the evening news. The Americanization of Pop TV (which has since merged with Kanal A) is confirmed by surveys which show that cheap US imports often constitute up to 79 per cent of the broadcast content, narrowing it culturally while reducing costs by reducing if not eliminating in-house productions (Hrvatin and Milosavljević, 2001: 60). Advertising revenues of ProPlus (marketer of Pop TV and Kanal A) in 2001 are close to 60 per cent of television advertising expenditure. Nevertheless, none of the national commercial television organizations operates profitably, according to official reports of the Broadcasting Council (Gerl, 2001: 36).

TV-3, the third Slovene commercial station with a national audience, started on Christmas Eve 1995 and continues with programming for children, youth, the family, and the Catholic community. It is owned by the Catholic radio, Ognjišče, the diocese of Maribor, the diocese of Koper, Mohorjeva Družba (a predominantly religious book publisher), and the Economic Forum of the Christian Democratic Party.

### Radio

The radio scene consists of eighty nine radio programmes with a total transmission of 71,500 minutes of programming per day. Thirty eight programmes are commercial, twenty six local, regional and non-profit, while fifteen programmes target Slovenes abroad; there are also two student stations, and eight public service programmes operated by Radiotelevizija Slovenia, including two for ethnic minorities. Radio Koper/ Capodistria transmits programmes in Italian – beginning with a few hours in 1945 and ending with a fourteen-hour daily service today. The Hungarian ethnic community receives its radio and television programmes from studios in Lendava.

In 2000 public Radio Slovenia produced 23,321 hours of programmes. Advertising reached up to 2.5 per cent of programming time. The three main channels (Program A, Val 202, Program ARS) offer four main programme types: information (about 23 per cent), music (26 per cent classical, 32 per cent popular, 0.4 per cent folk–national), the arts (4 per cent drama, literary programmes), and entertainment (about 9 per cent sport, contact, talk shows, and humour). Some of the most popular programmes on public radio are very old, including the radio drama programme or *Slovenes around the world* and *Good night, children*, which have been broadcast at the same time and on the same day for decades, some since 1936!

Local radio programmes broadcast in 1999 totalled 412,618 hours, divided among music (over 50 per cent), information (about 14 per cent), and entertainment (6 per cent), while less than 1 per cent were artistic and educational programmes. Advertising amounted to about 29,000 hours. While interest in new radio stations is increasing, according to the Broadcasting Council, the local radio market in urban areas is saturated, which gives rise to sales and mergers. However, the Telecommunications and Broadcasting Agency of the Republic of Slovenia still offers new frequencies to potential broadcasters.

### Film and video

The film industry in the former Yugoslavia was nationalized and film production highly subsidized by the state. Slovenia had its own film production company, Triglav film, later Viba film, a monopoly. With financial support from the Republic Film Fund and 'help' with script selection, Viba film produced ninty two feature films (sixty one original Slovene, thirty one co-productions).

The Film Fund Act of 1994 re-created the Film Fund of the Republic of Slovenia, abolished the monopoly of film production and set out to create the right conditions for feature film, video and short film production, stimulate script writing, promote Slovene films abroad, organize Slovene film festivals, and support student film production at the Academy of Film in Ljubljana. The fund has limited financial resources and subsidizes feature films on the basis of public tenders. The fund is supervised by a supervisory board whose members are appointed by the government. Co-productions help finance new Slovene films, and national television plays one of the key roles despite its own financial problems.

Since the 1970s, when 10 million tickets were sold in Slovene cinemas, audiences have been decreasing. Also, Slovene film distributors, by choosing to rely on Hollywood blockbusters, are victims of commercial television stations, which increasingly broadcast more films. A low point in attendance was in 1992 with only 1.5 million tickets sold, increasing to nearly 3 million before dropping in 1999 to less than 2 million. According to a 2001 Mediana survey, less than 6 per cent of the population may be considered regular moviegoers. Research is needed to detect changes with the opening of multiplex cinemas in Ljubljana and Maribor, although there are indications that movie theatres in urban centres have had much better attendance all along. In Ljubljana the Cultural Centre Cankarjev dom and Slovene Cinemateque are the focal point of Art Fest, the Short Film and Documentary Video Festival, and other promotions of quality films of mostly European origin.

Some changes may also be due to the success of Slovene cinematography. About 140 feature films and a few hundred documentaries and short films have been produced so far. Between 1995 and 2000 the Film Fund of the Republic of Slovenia subsidized the production of thirty feature films and fifty six short film projects. Films by a new generation of film directors (Igor Šterk, Janez Burger, Vito Taufer, Jan Cvitkoviè) have been received very favourably at home, where they have rejuvenated the movie audience, and abroad, where reactions from international film festival juries have been very encouraging. For example, at the fifty-eighth Venice Film Festival in 2001, the Slovene film *Kruh in mleko* (*Bread and Milk*), written and directed by Jan Cvitkoviè, received the Lion of the Future award.

## The Internet and related on-line media

The use of computer technologies and the Internet is on the rise in Slovenia. Internet users are between fifteen and twenty four years old (35 per cent), have higher and/or university education (about 24 per cent), and belong to the highest income groups (37 per cent). Forty six per cent of Internet users are women. The number of personal computers in 2000 per 100 inhabitants was 27.3 (in 1998: 21.2, in 1999: 25.3) and there were 1,089 hosts per 100,000 inhabitants (1,029 in 1998, 1,159 in 1999).

Acquisition of general information through the Internet is pervasive (close to 70 per cent), followed by entertainment and e-mail (both close to 60 per cent). About 15 per cent of Internet users engage in e-banking (7 per cent in 1999), and about 10 per cent use e-shopping (0 per cent in 1999). About 25 per cent have access to the Internet at home and about 20 per cent at work. Elementary and secondary schools are not yet well equipped with computers; there are only about five computers per 100 pupils. Nevertheless, practically all of them have access to the Internet and about 80 per cent through ISDN. Half of elementary schools and nearly all secondary schools have their own home pages.

The regular use of computers is also on the rise commercially. In 2000 small companies with five to fifty employees were the fastest to embrace the new technology; more then half of them use computers regularly (there are 5.6 computers per ten employees). While 88 per cent have access to the Internet, close to 50 per cent have their own Web site, and 78 per cent have an ISDN line. Medium-size companies (51–250 employees) and large enterprises (over 250 employees) show smaller numbers. About one-third are regular computer users (less than three computers per ten employees), but they have close to 100 per cent access to the Internet. More than 60 per cent of the larger companies have their own Web sites.

Regarding media use, it is important to realize that more than a quarter of Internet customers use it for reading the news. All dailies, and many other periodicals, have on-line versions with advertising. Most of them limit access to their archives, however. *Delo* has a special, shortened version, *Delofax*, which can be accessed only with Acrobat Reader. It serves about 400 to 600 daily readers, has no advertising, an extensive archive, can be downloaded and used for clipping; about 300 copies are sent by e-mail daily to readers around the world.

# POLITICS, POLICY, LAW AND REGULATION

During the time of Yugoslavia, Slovenia was one of the first republics to adopt a Public Information Law in 1973. Amended in 1985 – even though the media were, at least indirectly, owned and controlled by the state and did not operate as autonomous economic entities – the law explicitly mentioned 'freedom of information' and 'the right to be informed'. The foundation of Slovenia's current legislation remains an ongoing political and economic reform; it is a process since 1990 that aims to develop compatibility with standards prevailing in the European Union.

The first step in this process was the Mass Media Law of 1994, and the specific Act on Radio-Television Slovenia, setting forth specific rules regulating media ownership, prohibiting mergers and cross-ownership, as well as multiple ownership of the media (print, news service, or broadcasting). The Mass Media Act of 1994 was expected to affirm democracy and a plurality of media, and secure legal and financial conditions for media freedom. But the law provided an opportunity for a dangerous concentration of capital, cross-ownership, and the kind of media privatization that allowed the media to avoid public accountability. The law proved to be deficient and did not allow for enough supervision of the non-transparent concentration of media ownership and of numerous violations of the law – for which there were no sanctions. For instance, the largest commercial television producer, ProPlus (owned by CME) was able to by-pass the law by establishing a production company which was registered not as a broadcaster but as a producer, and contracted three local television stations to broadcast its programme (*Pop TV*) exclusively.

A new Mass Media Law (running to 168 articles), passed in 2001, has been strongly criticized. Regarding ownership, the law limits concentration by prescribing that a publisher of a general information-providing daily newspaper (including any natural or legal person, or a group of associated persons who have more than a 20 per cent share in the capital or property of that publisher, or more than 20 per cent of management or voting rights) may not be an owner or co-founder or broadcaster of a radio or television programme, and may not engage in radio and television activities. The same restriction applies to a radio or television broadcaster, who may not become a publisher of a general information-providing daily newspaper. Any acquisition of an ownership share of more than 20 per cent, or management or voting rights, is subject to prior approval by the Ministry of Culture – which approves or rejects according to its assessment of the media (advertising) market. This task is practically impossible to achieve unless transparency of media ownership is achieved first. With the political changes of the 1990s regulatory mechanisms were abandoned, but the independence of media owners from the state and politics was not secured, because political parties have considerable shares in investment funds that own the media, especially the press.

The second part of the new Media Law specifically deals with radio and television programmes and defines local, regional, student, non-profit programmes, and programmes of special importance for Slovene culture and that could be financially supported by the state budget. The programming of non-profit radio and television should consist of at least 30 per cent of their own daily news, culture, arts and educational programming. The Media Law also prescribes new ratios of in-house, local, Slovene and European production and states that all television programmes (public and commercial) must broadcast each day at least 20 per cent of their own production – at least one hour during prime time (between 18.00 and 22.00 hours) – and at least 30 per cent of their own production is prescribed for radio programmes. In addition, radio programmes must ensure that at least 10 per cent of daily music programmes is of Slovene origin; for television, the law prescribes at least 2 per cent of Slovene audio-visual material per year and suggests that television companies should strive to increase Slovene audio-visual material to 5 per cent a year (which is considered a considerable share).

The new Media Law also regulates commercial television advertising. Programmes shorter than thirty minutes should not be interrupted by commercials, longer ones only once every forty five minutes. Public television must not interrupt longer programmes at all, and advertising should not exceed 15 per cent of daily broadcasting time; during prime time advertising should not exceed nine minutes per hour. Slovene public television retains practically the same rights for advertising as commercial programmes, except for prime-time limits, because licence fees alone cannot finance new Slovene audio-visual productions.

The Public Service Broadcasting Act of 1994 has been amended several times regarding fees, naming editors-in-chief, and similar, and a new Telecommunications Law was passed in 2001 that established a Telecommunications and Broadcasting Agency of the Republic of Slovenia which continues the activities of the former Telecommunications Administration. Among its most important duties is the allocation of radio frequencies.

To ensure the development of information technologies and the promotion of an information society, the government created a Ministry of the Information Society in 2001. Its priorities are, among others, to enable inhabitants of Slovenia to have equal (or free) access to information technologies and services, to promote a knowledge-based economy and e-business in the private and public sectors and in public administration. Its regulatory tasks include monitoring and proposing legislation, implementing regulation of the infrastructure for e-business, harmonizing Slovenia's legislation pertaining to this sector, and preventing Internet misuse, although Internet-related media are not mentioned. Slovenia also adopted the Convention on Cyber-crime, among other international conventions that regulate this area, but not much work has been done regarding use of the Internet. The latter is regulated indirectly by several related laws, among them the Electronic Business and Signature Law and the Consumer Protection Law. There are no laws regulating pornography or spamming, however, and Internet-related media are only partly covered by the new Media Law of 2001. This creates confusion, since, for instance, *Delofax*, the Internet daily version of *Delo*, could be registered as a new medium, and not as an on-line paper.

The media in Slovenia are to a large extent directly (in the case of public radio and television) or indirectly (licensing, political advertising, and other 'soft influences' and pressures on programme directors) under state control, since political parties continue to be strongly involved in the choice of editor and the programme policies of both press and broadcasting, while the integration of the media and political elites is evident in the continuing mobility between journalism and politics.

# STATISTICS

National population, 1991    1,965,986
Number of households, 1991    640,195

Overall movie admissions, 1999:

| | |
|---|---:|
| Cinemas | 85 |
| Seats | 24,529 |
| Performances | 33,138 |
| Tickets sold | 1,965,000 |

Number of book titles published

| Year | Total | Original works | Translations |
|------|-------|----------------|--------------|
| 1985 | 2,328 | 2,119 | 209 |
| 1990 | 1,853 | 1,272 | 581 |
| 1995 | 3,194 | 2,219 | 975 |
| 1997 | 3,647 | 2,484 | 1,163 |
| 1999 | 3,976 | 2,926 | 1,050 |
| 2000 | 3,917 | 2,985 | 932 |

Sources: *Statistical Yearbook 2001, Mediana 2001, Marketing Magazin MM.*

| | | |
|---|---|---:|
| **Print media** | Circulation of main newspapers, 2000 (%) | |
| | Dailies | |
| | *Slovenske novice* | 18.2 |
| | *Delo* | 13.2 |
| | *Večer* | 12.0 |
| | *Dnevnik* | 8.8 |
| | *Finance* | 2.0 |
| | Weeklies | |
| | *Nedeljski dnevnik* | 28.3 |
| | *Slovenski delničar* | 28.1 |
| | *Vikend magazin* | 25.9 |

| | | |
|---|---|---:|
| **Broadcast media** | Main television channels | |
| | Audience share of public service national television (%) | |
| | SLO-1 | 42.6 |
| | SLO-2 | 12.4 |
| | TV Koper-Capodistria | 2.3 |
| | Audience share of commercial national television (%) | |
| | Kanal A | 23.8 |
| | Pop TV | 57.2 |
| | TV-3 | n.a. |

Audience share of main radio channels, public and private (%)

Public service

| | |
|---|---|
| Program A | 13.9 |
| Val 202 | 15.5 |
| Program Ars | 3.1 |
| Radio Koper-Modri Val | 3.5 |
| Radio Maribor – MM1 | 5.2 |
| Slovenski turističniRadio | 3.7 |

Commercial

| | |
|---|---|
| Radio Maribor | 5.2 |
| Radio City | 4.2 |
| Radio Hit | 4.5 |
| Murski Val | 2.9 |

Percentage of households with:

| | |
|---|---|
| Television | 97 |
| Video-cassette recorder, satellite receiver, DVD player | 57 |

**Electronic media**

Percentage of households with:

| | |
|---|---|
| Digital television reception, by whatever means | n.a. |
| Personal computer | 46 |
| Internet access | 21 |
| Number of personal computers per 100 inhabitants | 27.3 |
| Mobile phone | 75 |

**Advertising spend (%)**

| | |
|---|---|
| Dailies | 29.3 |
| Other print media | 17.0 |
| Television | 35.1 |
| Radio | 8.7 |
| Posters | 9.9 |

# REFERENCES

European Commission (1998) *The Development of the Audiovisual Landscape in Central Europe since 1989*. Luton: University of Luton Press/John Libbey Media.

Hrvatin, Sandra B. and Milosavljevič, Marko (2001) Media Policy in Slovenia in the 1990s: Regulation, Privatisation, Concentration and Commercialisation of the Media. Ljubljana: Peace Institute/Mediawatch.

Jancic, J. (2002) 'Recesijo obcutijo tudi slovenski mediji' (Recession hits Slovenian media too), *Marketing Magazine* 22 (1): 14–17.

Mediana (2001) *Raziskava medijev v Sloveniji*. Ljubljana: Inštitut za raziskovanje medijev.

Gerl, Matjaž (2001) *Radijski in TV programi v Sloveniji*. Ljubljana: Svet za Republike Slovenije.

*Statistical Yearbook of the Republic of Slovenia* (2001) Ljubljana: Statistični urad Republike Slovenije.

*Uradni list* (2001) 'Zakon o medijih' (Media law), No. 35, (May): 4017–42.

www.gov.si.

www.ris.org.

# 20: Spain

ROSARIO DE MATEO

## NATIONAL PROFILE

Spain covers an area of 507,782 km² and has a population of 41,116,000 inhabitants. The population density is seventy nine inhabitants per square kilometer. However, its distribution is very uneven: in the coastal regions the density is 100 inhabitants per square kilometer, whereas in the interior of the peninsula it is only twenty five. The metropolitan areas Madrid and Barcelona are the main nuclei of population with about 4.5 million and 3 million inhabitants respectively. Economic activity is focused on Madrid, Catalonia, the Basque Country and Valencia. However, the region with the highest income per person is the Balearic Isles. This is due to tourism.

Following the dictator Franco's death in 1975, the transitional period to democracy started, and old and new values coexisted for a time. This gave way to the formation of the present mass media structures. With the constitution of 1978 Spain became a parliamentary monarchy. A regime was established which recognizes the existence of diferent regions and cultural particularities. Seventeen autonomous regions (*Comunidades Autónomas*, CCAA) were set up, each having its own parliamentary and governmental system. The state administration is distributed between the central and the regional governments. The regional governments handle issues concerning culture, health, urbanism, security, etc., with some variations. Defence and foreign policy are the prerogative of the central government.

The constitution acknowledges the linguistic plurality of Spain. Spanish (or Castilian) is the official language of the whole country. Catalan, Basque and Galician are official languages in their respective regions. In 1986 Spain entered the European Union (EU) and has been obliged to restructure its legislation in economic affairs, adapting it to the Union. The new situation in Europe has made it easier for foreign capital to enter most branches of production, including communications.

## STRUCTURE AND OWNERSHIP

### The print media

#### The newspaper press

There are about 140 daily newspapers. Only three of them are national newspapers of general information (*El Pais*, *ABC* and *El Mundo*), two are national daily sports newspapers (*Marca*, *As*) and three are national daily business newspapers (*Expansión*, *Cinco Dias* and *La Gaceta de los Negocios*). Most of the 140 daily newspapers are published in Spanish. Only six of them are in Catalan and one in Basque, and a few more are bilingual, Catalan/Spanish, Galician/Spanish and Basque/Spanish. Newspapers printed in Catalan receive economic help from the government of Catalonia, in order to mitigate their economic difficulties. The circulation rate of these newspapers is about eighteen copies per thousand inhabitants.

The three daily newspapers with the highest circulation are the national newspapers but in most Autonomous Communities they are exceeded in sales by the main regional newspapers. Among these newspapers we find the next two daily newspapers with the highest circulation, *El Periódico* and *La Vanguardia* in Catalonia. We find too *El Correo* and *El Diario Vasco* (Basque Country) and *La Voz de Galicia* (Galicia), among others. In 1999 and 2000 the total circulation of the five most important newspapers went down, increasing a little in 2001. In 2002 two titles (*El Pais* and *El Mundo*) also increased their circulation a little. *El Pais* is the daily newspaper with the highest circulation (436,302 copies) and with the biggest readership (1.6 million). That represents only 4.2 per cent of the total Spanish population. *ABC* and *El Mundo* have a circulation of almost 292,000 and 302,000 copies respectively, and *El Periódico* and *La Vanguardia* more than 184,000 and 191,000 copies respectively. In comparison with other countries, these daily newspapers have a very low rate of penetration. However, they are daily newspapers of reference and they shape public opinion.

In 2000 the total circulation of sporting daily newspapers decreased in relation to 1999 and stood at 787,204 copies, with a small increase since. *Marca* had the highest national circulation and its audience was 6.5 per cent of the total population. *As*, the second most important daily sports newspaper, is published in Madrid, as is *Marca* and had an audience of 1.8 per cent of the total population. *Mundo Deportivo* and *Sport* are published in Barcelona and have an audience of 1.3 per cent and 1.1 per cent of the total population, respectively. In 2000 the total circulation of daily business newspapers was a little more than 100,000 copies and increased a little from 1999. *Expansion, Cinco Dias, La Gaceta de los Negocios* had the following circulations: 62,925, 28,287 and 13,753 copies, respectively. These are rather low figures.

The median rate of circulation of Spanish daily papers is 30,000 copies per day and only thirty newspapers have a higher rate. The circulation rate of daily newspapers is among the lowest in Europe but it has been growing slowly in recent years. In 1987 the rate was seventy nine copies per thousand inhabitants, while in 2000 it had grown to 107 copies per thousand inhabitants. In the last few years these rates have stabilized. The rate is lower, however, if we consider only general information daily newspapers and disregard sports and economic dailies. In this case the circulation rate went from sixty nine copies per thousand inhabitants, in 1987, to ninety copies in 2000. In the northern regions the rate is higher – in Catalonia about 115 copies per thousand. In 2000 total circulation and total audience were higher in the northern region. Per Autonomous Region, the rates of

penetration over the whole population are as follows: Navarra (60.2 per cent), Cantabria (58.6 per cent), País Vasco (58.4 per cent), Asturias (51.5 per cent), Baleares (49.2 per cent), La Rioja (40.5 per cent), Aragón (40.4 per cent), Castilla–León y Cataluña (39.5 per cent each), Canarias (39.2 per cent), Galicia (37.6 per cent), Canarias (32.4 per cent), Madrid (32.3 per cent), Murcia (30.0 per cent), Extremadura (28.5 per cent), Andalucía (27.4 per cent) and Castilla–La Mancha (19.6 per cent).

The concentration of circulation of daily newspapers fits (for 90 per cent at least) into the following twelve groups:

1. Prisa, with three national daily newspapers, one of general information, *El Pais*, one of sporting information, *As*, and one of business information, *Cinco Dias*, and four provincial daily newspapers.
2. Recoletos, with two national daily newspapers, one of sport information and with the higher circulation of the newspapers, *Marca*, and one other of business information, *Expansión*.
3. Correo, with eleven regional and provincial daily newspapers.
4. Zeta, with ten regional and provincial daily newspapers. Between them, one of sport information, *Sport*, and one of general information, *El Periódico de Catalunya* are very important, having dual language editions, one in Spanish and one in Catalan.
6. Prensa Española, with one daily newspaper of general information, *ABC*, and eight regional and provincial daily newspapers.
7. Godó, with a regional daily newspaper, *La Vanguardia*, and other sport information daily newspaper, *Mundo Deportivo*.
8. Unedisa, with nine regional and provincial newspapers, one of them, *El Mundo*.
9. Prensa Ibérica, with thirteen regional and provincial daily newspapers.
10. Voz, with two regional newspapers.
11. Joly, with four.
12. Serra, with three, and La Region, with two.

Since 1 January 2002 there have been only eleven because the Correo and Prensa Española groups have combined.

To be more precise in describing this model of small firms and 140 low-circulation daily newspapers, it should be added that in several cases the daily newspapers are versions of one master edition because many daily newspapers are owned by the press or multimedia groups. The ten daily newspapers with the highest circulation have nearly 45 per cent of total circulation.

There is a trend towards concentration of ownership and production. A mere twenty among 140 daily newspapers control nearly 70 per cent of the total circulation of the newspapers and almost two-thirds of these newspapers are owned by daily press groups or multimedia groups. Foreign capital has found it much more difficult to enter the Spanish daily press. There are only two foreign groups represented in the daily newspaper press: the British group Pearson, with the majority of the capital of the Spanish group Recoletos, and the Italian group Rizzoli, with a majority of the capital of the Spanish group Unedisa. These groups have formalized their presence in newspapers by acquiring part of the capital of newspaper publishing companies. None has created its own newspaper. The expansion of the Spanish press groups into foreign markets is not very significant. Only the Prisa group owns part of the capital of foreign publishing companies, for instance, Publico (Portugal) and La Prensa (México). Prisa also has an agreement to exchange information products with *Le Monde* (France), *La Reppublica* (Italia) and *The Independent* (United Kingdom).

The financing of daily newspapers comes from subscriptions, from direct selling copies and from advertising. Subscription revenue is not very important except in a very few cases of daily newspapers of general information like *La Vanguardia*, with about 27 per cent of its total revenue from this source, *La Voz de Galicia*, with 18.4 per cent, and nearly twenty five other low-circulation dailies, with about 25 per cent of their total revenue derived from subscriptions. As a source of revenue it has been in continuous decline for the last two decades. As for the remaining daily newspapers, including the national newspapers (*ABC*, 8.2 per cent of its revenue from subscriptions, *El Mundo*, with 5.6 per cent, and *El Pais*, with 1.9 per cent) the sources of revenue are almost exclusively direct sales of copies and advertising.

In recent years, the revenue from direct sales has been going down. In 1999 it represented 49 per cent of total revenue while in 2000 it was only 43 per cent. In the same years, advertising contributed 51 per cent and 57 per cent, respectively, to the total income of the daily newspapers. From January to September 2001 total advertising investment in the media went down about 7 per cent by comparison with 2000. In the same period the revenue from advertising in daily newspapers went down by about 10 per cent. The economic outlook for daily nwspapers is not very promising

A little less than two-thirds of the total population do not habitually read daily newspapers. In 2000 the rate of reading was 36.3 per cent of the total population, a little above 1999. The majority of readers are: men; living in cities of more of 10,000 inhabitants; of upper, upper middle and middle social class; on average forty years old; and in employment. In recent years the total circulation of the Sunday supplements of the national daily newspapers has decreased. However, that of the supplements of some regional daily newspapers has increased, for instance, *El Semanal*, *El Semanal TV* and, since 1998, *Mujer de Hoy*. These three supplements are published by Taller Editores, the majority of whose capital is owned by the Correo group. In 2000 the audience for these supplements was 11.6 per cent, 7.6 per cent and 6.2 per cent of the total population, respectively.

In general, in 2000, the circulation of daily newspapers had stabilized and the circulation of some of them had decreased. In the near future it seems that newspaper circulation is going to decrease further. This is due to the existence of the free daily press published, for the moment, in Madrid and in Barcelona by Indice Multiprensa and Metro Internacional. This means new competition for advertising revenue. For instance, Metro Internacional has plans to distribute in Madrid and Barcelona 450,000 copies of its free daily newspapers and covers more than the traditional daily newspapers. In 2001 investment in advertising and the readership of the media went down, owing to the global economic crisis. So there are two reasons to say that the daily newspapers have a poor future outlook.

### The periodical and magazine press

In the broad field of the non-daily press, Spain has an enormous quantity of periodicals. Some 7,000 are produced by about 1,000 publishing companies of the non-daily press, most of them having a small circulation. Only about 100 titles count as important, with only a few exceeding 500,000 copies. Unlike the newspapers, most magazines have a national reach. This fact makes it easier for them to survive. In Catalonia there is a local Catalan-language press. In 2000 the total audience of the periodical and magazine press was 53.6 per cent of the total population, much the same as in 1999. The audience is clearly lower than it was between 1988 and 1997. The weeklies have a larger readership than the other periodicals but the monthly market has been increasing. The audiences for general information weeklies are a little more than 6 per cent of the total population. The most important of them is *Interviú* with a circulation, in 2000, of 158,690 copies and its audience was 2.7 per cent. The circulation of the rest is less than 50,000 copies and the audience less than 0.5 per cent.

The yellow weekly press (*Prensa del Corazón*) has the highest circulation and audience (70 per cent) of non-daily press. In 2000 the most important journals by their circulation and audience were the following: *Pronto* (circulaton 981,223 copies and 10.3 per cent of audience); *Hola* (circulation 573,914 copies and 6.6 per cent of audience); *Lecturas* (circulation 301,212 copies and 4.4 per cent of audience); *Semana* (circulation 243,310 copies and 4.3 per cent of audience). The rest are under the 4 per cent audience level.

Television weeklies have about 10 per cent of the total audience. The most important are: *Teleprograma* (circulation 185,992 copies and 2 per cent of audience); *Telenovela* and *Supertele* (circulation 1 million copies and 15 per cent of audience, each).

The most important monthly journals and their audiences are the following: *Canal Plus* (8.9 per cent), *Canal Satélite Digital* (5.3 per cent), *Muy Interesante* (5.1 per cent), *Quo* (3.3 per cent) and *El Mueble* (3 per cent). At the level between 2 per cent and 2.8 per cent of audience there are six journals; between 1 per cent and 1.9 per cent of audience there are thirteen; the rest are under 1 per cent of the audience.

The non-daily press has two sources of revenue: the direct sale of copies and advertising. In 2000 the revenue from advertising was €619 million, increasing 9 per cent by comparison with 1999.

The majority of publishing companies of the non-daily press have an important amount of foreign investment. Among them are the following companies: Hachette–Filipachi, Edipress, Heres, Gruner & Jahr, Axel Springer. The Spanish company publishing the yellow weekly journal *Hola* has invested in Great Britain and in France.

The readers of the non-daily press (the majority of them reading *Prensa del corazón*) are predominantly: women; living in cities of over 10,000 inhabitants; middle-class; and averaging thirty eight years old. The audience in different Autonomous Communities is as follows: Galicia (42.4 per cent); Castilla–La Mancha (44.9 per cent); Andalucía (48.7 per cent); Extremadura (50.2 per cent); Cataluña (60.7 per cent); Asturias (61.1 per cent); Baleares (65.7 per cent) and Cantabria (67.2 per cent).

### Book publishing

There are nearly 2,000 private book publishing houses. About 25 per cent belong to the main groups. The process of concentration and transnationalization began in the 1970s. The most important Spanish group, Planeta, is going to be a multimedia group. It has business in Latin America and several agreements with other companies, the most important with Agostini. There are some Spanish companies belonging to media groups such as Prisa, Correo or Prensa Española. There are many foreign groups in this industry and the most important are Bertelsmann, Havas (Vivendi), Hachette (Lagardère), Pearson and Mondadori. All these groups have bought Spanish companies.

Book production in terms of ISBNs has increased since 1997, numbering 67,106 titles in 2001. In 2000, 93 per cent of the books published were in Spanish languages (more then 80 per cent in Spanish, 12 per cent in Catalan, 2 per cent in Galician, 2 per cent in Basque and the rest in other languages), 3.9 per cent in foreign languages and 3.1 per cent were multilingual. The median print run is about 4,000 copies. Book sales in the Spanish market in 1999 were worth about €2,500 million. Exports were worth about €400 million. In 2001, as always, readership is low, at only 58 per cent of population and with only 36 per cent reading books often.

## The electronic (audio-visual) media

### Television

There are two national public television channels, Televisión Española, in the RTVE corporation. There are ten regional public television channels belonging to regional radio and television corporations: TV-3 and Canal 33, in Catalonia; ETB-2 and RTB-1, in the Basque Country; TVG, in Galicia; Telemadrid, in Madrid; Canal Sur and Canal 2 AND, in Andalucía; Canal 9 and Noticies 9/PUNT 2, in Pais Valenciano; and TVA, in Aragón.

The private television companies have, among others, as their main shareholders Spanish and foreign communication groups. The shareholders of private television companies are as follows.

1 Antena 3 TV: Telefónica (48 per cent); Santander Central Hispano Bank (29 per cent); RTL (16 per cent). At the same tima RTL is participated in by Pearson (22 per cent), Bertelsmann (37 per cent), GBL (30 per cent), and others (7 per cent).
2 Telecinco: Berlusconi (40 per cent), Kirch (25 per cent) and the Correo and Planeta groups, 10 per cent each.
3 Canal Plus Sogecable (pay-television): Canal Plus Francia and Prisa, 20 per cent each; Group March (13 per cent); Bilbao Vizcaya Argentaria bank (5 per cent); Caja Madrid and Eventos, 4 per cent each; and 5 per cent on the stock exchange.
4 Canal Satélite Digital, a digital satellite platform: SogecableGroup Prisa (82 per cent); Warner Brothers (10 per cent); Antena 3 TV and Proarda, 5 per cent each.
5 Via Digital, the other digital satellite platform: Telefónica (16 per cent), SMM (16 per cent), Televisa (10 per cent), Direct TV (7 per cent) and the rest of the capital is owned by Mediapark, Recoletos and the autonomous public television channels TVG, Canal 9 and Telemadrid.
6 Quiero TV, digital terrestrial television: Retevisión (48 per cent); Mediapark and Sofiscable, 15 per cent each; regional Cajas de Ahorros (10 per cent); Carlton Com (8 per cent); and Ivercatalunya cable (4 per cent). There are two companies that will operate with new terrestrial digital open channels and their capital involves the following companies:
7 Net TV: Prensa Española (25 per cent); Pantalla Digital (25 per cent);

Viaplus/Altadis (18 per cent); Euoproducciones (9 per cent); TF-1, SIC and Sauzal Intereconomía, 7 per cent each; others 3 per cent.
8 Veo TV: Unidesa (26 per cent); Recoletos (25 per cent); Iberdrola (20 per cent); J. Abelló (15 per cent); others 14 per cent:
In March 2002 both platforms signed an agreement, which the government will approve before 20 December, to become a single digital satellite platform.

In each Autonomous Community the law permits two cable operators: one for Telefónica and another for Retevisión or Cable Europe. Cable is not much developed in Spain. In 1999 there were 741 local terrestrial television stations with distribution on cable television. There are numerous different types of ownership, management and technological balance. Their future is not clear, especially with the coming of digital television.

Public and private television companies base their income on advertising. There are no television licence fees. However, public broadcasting corporations can receive funds from the state and Autonomous Communities if they do not receive enough income from advertising to finance themselves. From 1982 to 1992 TVE did not receive any state funding because of its high advertising revenue. Since 1993 RTVE has received public funds. In 1999 the total income from advertising was €2,072 million and in 2000 it was €2,275 million. The majority of this income (85 per cent) went to TVE, Telecinco and Antena 3 TV. Two per cent was for Canal Plus because it is pay-television, with 887,000 suscribers in 2000. The rest went to autonomous television stations (40 per cent of it to TV-3 and Canal 33) and other television stations, including local television.

In 2001 the total television audience was near 90 per cent of the total population. The median consumption in 2000 was 222 minutes per day.

Television programming is highly dependent on advertising, forcing public and private enterprises to choose programmes likely to attract a large audience: light entertainment (talk shows, variety, etc.), films, series and sport, mainly football. Rarely do cultural programmes get shown, and never in prime time, except on the two public television channels, La 2, national, and Canal 33, regional. Among the other television channels there is no great difference between the public and the private programming policies. The only exception is pay-television, which does not rely on advertising and broadcasts basically films, sport and other thematic content. The reduction in the number of films shown in prime time on open television channels has been compensated for by Spanish-produced series. Of the films shown on television, public and private, about 60 per cent were from the United States and only about 22 per cent were Spanish. The entry of Warner Brothers in the social capital of Canal Satélite Digital of Sogecable, owned by Prisa group, has reinforced the position of this group in the control of audio-visual content. This group also has agreements with Walt Disney/Buenavista, Paramount, Columbia Tristar and Polygram, among others.

Telefónica has also enlarged its production of content, buying 25 per cent of Mediapark and Endemol. Via Digital and Antena 3-TV have agreements with Filmax, Twentieth Century Fox and Movierecord Cine.

### Radio

There is a public national network of Radio Nacional de España in the RTVE corporation. Some regional radio stations are owned by regional radio and television corporations. In 1998 there were 621 public local radio stations owned by town councils (*radios municipales*). The majority of private radio channels are owned by Spanish media groups, because there is almost no internationalization. SER and Antena 3 Radio belong to the Prisa group. Onda Cero belongs to the Telefónica group and transmits national digital radio too. COPE is 74 per cent owned by the Catholic Church, but the Prensa Española and Correo groups have 5 per cent of the social capital each. In the development of digital radio there are or will be the following media groups: Telefónica, Prisa, Unidesa, Recoletos, Planeta, Correo, Retevision, among others.

National public radio has no advertising income, only regional and local radio (*radios municipales*). Private radio bases its income on advertising. In 1999 the total income of advertising was €466 million, and in 2000, it was €502 million. It was divided as follows:

Union Radio (SER plus Antena 3 Radio) of the Prisa group 40 per cent, COPE 25 per cent, Onda Cero of the Telefónica group 17 per cent. Thirteen per cent went to other private radio and the rest to autonomous radio.

In 2000 the national average of listeners was about 53 per cent and the average of consumption time was ninety five minutes a day. Radio listeners are: predominantly men; more in cities of over 10,000 inhabitants; of all social classes; with an average age of forty two; and in employment.

A near majority of programmes are produced by the radio channels themselves. But some production companies exist with close ties to radio channels. For instance, the media group Zeta and the radio channel Ona Catalana have created the Radio Sports Catalunya company to produce sports information for this radio channel and other audio-visual media of the group.

In 1999 the Autonomous Communities awarded licences for FM radio. This is a very concentrated sector, so it is difficult for independent radio to work. The total audience for radio is decreasing, perhaps because of music listening on the Internet.

### Film and video

In 2000 there were about 1,305 exhibition cinemas and 3,505 screens. 292 Spanish films and 1,464 foreign films were exhibited (see statistics section).

## The Internet and related on-line media

There are still very few media companies distributing only by the Internet, because the majority of them have as an information source the same content as the traditional media. Almost all newspapers, radio and television stations are also on the Internet. This is not the case with magazines.

Almost all the media groups have created new companies to develop their Internet business. An example is Prisacom, of the Prisa group, but there are not enough statistics available to allow an analysis of the on-line media separate from the traditional media. The mass media have reached their own definition of the Internet role on the basis of their own traditional trademark. They want to secure a share of possible future business. More and more, television, radio and newspapers distributed by the Internet offer complementary services like chats, forums, etc.

Some local and regional newspapers have been created for distribution solely by the Internet, such as *Estrella Digital, El confidencial.com, Madridiario* (all in Madrid) and *Vilaweb* in Barcelona, which, in 2000, had 425,000 visits. There are also some radio stations distributing only on the Internet, like World Wide Radio and El Mundo Radio. Some media groups set up services to distribute by the Internet, for instance Unedisa and Recoletos, which created expansión y empleo.com, or group Telefónica, which uses Terra to give services through its own media.

In February–March 2001 users of the Internet numbered 6.9 million. From these, 1.97 million were consumers of electronic newspapers, 803,000 of magazines, and 613,000 of radio. The number of visits, according to the media, were the following: 11 million for general information newspapers; 3.3 million for sports newspapers; 187,000 for business newspapers; 13.4 million for monthly magazines; 10 million for weekly magazines; 18 million for radio; and 31.3 million for television. In March 2001 the media having most visits were: *El Mundo* (5 million); *El Pais Digital* (4.5 million); *Marca* (1.5 million); the weekly magazine *Hola.com* (4.5 million) and *Plus.es* (0.9 mllion).

In 2000 the profile of the Internet audience was: more men (63 per cent); living in cities; middle-class (37.1 per cent); upper middle-class (27.6 per cent) or upper-class (24.1 per cent); lower middle-class (9.8 per cent) and working-class 1.5 per cent. The average age was 30.4 years and they are in employment. In 2000 the total advertising revenue for the Internet was €53 million, two and a half times above that for 1999.

The media on-line are at the beginning of their development. In the long term it can be expected that the media will provide more services by the Internet, with lower technical but higher marketing costs, and by creating pay services.

## POLITICS, POLICY, LAW AND REGULATION

In defining policy we refer to different actors and their interests. These include: the national government; the regional governments; the large communication groups; financial groups; basic service groups (e.g. electricity); foreign media groups; regional or local companies; and audio-visual programme producers.

Regulation and public policy have driven the creation and the development of the private commercial communication groups, both for the industrial benefits of competition groups and for political reasons. For instance, the socialist party (PSOE) during its period in power (1982–96) favoured the growth of the Prisa group in several ways. Among other things, by awarding licences for FM radio; or allowing the merger (concentration) between the two important radio companies (SER and Antena 3 Radio); or by awarding a licence for private television (Canal Plus). In 1996 the conservative party (Partido Popular) came to power. Indirectly, it promoted the establishment of a new communications group led by Telefónica. At the same time this company was in the process of being privatized.

Owing to the varied regulation of the television industry, it is difficult to get a picture of the whole. We can say that two general trends already apparent in 1997 are still under way. One is privatization and liberalization. There are other interrelated media trends: cabling, digitalization (and hence, from both, channel proliferation, concentration of ownership and of media activities and convergence of telecommunications, cable and broadcasting). The liberalization of broadcasting and the concession by the state of licences for digital radio and television have closely followed the liberalization of telecommunications. In 2000 the state allocated the licences for third-generation mobile telephony and for cordless telephones, and completed the liberalization of the television distribution channels.

The convergence of telecommunications, broadcasting and the rest of the mass media has been expected to occur along with entrepreneurial convergence. The latter increased when new concessions were awarded for running a business in the mass media or in telecommunications services. Some of the shareholders of the groups that obtained licences for telecommunications are also in the audio-visual and other mass-media businesses. On the one hand, the mass media groups like Prisa, Unedisa and Recoletos entered the telecommunications market through the cordless telephone business. On the other hand, the companies coming from the telecommunications market, like Telefónica and Retevisión, entered the cable television market, the new digital television market and the mobile telephone market. With France Télécom, these two companies will carry the signal of terrestrial digital television.

The conventional private television companies that are members of the Union of Open Commercial Televisions (UTECA), have demonstrated their interest in being in the business of carrying the terrestrial digital television signal, whether by agreement with the existing network operators, or by creating their own network. The electrical companies, like Endesa, Unión Fenosa and Iberdrola, have investments in cable television and in the new telephone licences. Also, banks, savings banks and other investment companies have invested in audiovisual and telecommunications companies.

It is also necessary to consider the convergence between the content of the media and the telecommunications business. This opens the way for the content industry to move into other services distributed through radio, television and the Internet. The first consequence of this behaviour is the change in size of the competitor companies. On increasing the capacity of transmission, telephone traffic (like the distribution of electrical energy) becomes a raw material and its price decreases. Then the infrastructure companies, like Telefónica, Iberdrola or Endesa, seek to enter new business services that allow them to increase their profit margin. That is why they have invested in the production and distribution of broadcasting content and services.

Arising from the need to enlarge its scale of operations in a globalized and very competitive market, the group Santillana merged with the Santillana group; Telefónica created a new company at the end of the 1990s, Telefónica Media, in order to control its business in the Spanish and Latin American mass media (in 2001 it reorganized the company and promoted Admira to be the top company of the holding). From 1 January 2002 the Correo group and Prensa Española became one company. Prisa and Telefónica are now listed on the stock exchange.

For the future, nobody knows what the response of consumers will be in the face of an increasing supply of existing or new content and services arising from these types of convergence.

There are some regulatory agencies. The Commission on the Telecommunications Market (CMT) does not work directly on the mass media but it advises on interconnection rates, on cable, and on the use of the airwaves. In general CMT has to oversee all aspects of (broadcast) transmissions. There is no national authority of the audio-visual. Only in Catalonia is there an Audio-visual Council of Catalonia (CAC).

Royal Decree 991, of 1998, established the Council on Sports Broadcasting and it determines every year those sports events of national interest which have to be broadcast on open television. There are national and regional parliamentary commissions for the control of public television and radio. In Catalonia there is a self-regulation agency – the Information Council – that is dependent on the journalists' association (Colegio de Periodistas de Cataluña). In addition to the initiative of journalists, some communications companies have editiorial statutes, which apply generally to questions of journalistic ethics.

## Press policy

With reference to the legal framework, the press in Spain is not controlled by any specific legislation since the promulgation of the 1978 constitution. Formerly, the law of 1966 was an impediment to the normal development of press activities. The activity of the press is now free, subject only to legislation protecting honour and individual privacy, the new penal code, approved by parliament in November 1995 and the constitution. Therefore, there are no limitations on the ownership or the financing of publications. The participation of the press companies in radio, television and Internet is allowed.

In 1986 the entry of foreign capital into the Spanish press was liberalized, so as to adapt Spanish legislation to the regulations of the European Union. Since then many press groups have started activities in Spain, most of them in the field of the non-daily press, like Bertelsmann, Hachette, Bauer, Springer, VNU. Other groups were established in Spain earlier, by taking advantage of some loopholes in the law, like Gruner & Jahr.

From 1988 onwards there has been no help from the state, directly or indirectly, to the press (only a reduction in postal and telecommunications rates). The governments of some Autonomous Communities with their own language (Catalonia, the Basque Country) give economic help to the press (magazines and newspapers) to make up for the difficulties of sustaining a press with a language other than Spanish.

In order to overcome the economic consequences of low circulation and increasing costs, especially of paper, and low advertising investment in 2001, newspapers created a number of parallel strategies in the 1980s and 1990s, still continuing. Some of the national newspapers publish special editions in some Autonomous Communities (for instance, *El Pais*), in order to increase their sales regionally. Another strategy is to establish new press groups, publishing regional newspapers in some Autonomous Communities, sharing news with other Communities (Grupo Z, which publishes *El Periódico de Cataluña, La Voz de Asturias, El Periódico de Extremadura* and *El Periódico de Aragón*; Prensa Ibérica, with newspapers bought from the state in 1984; Comecosa, set up by the Correo group and regional newspapers). Finally, by concentrating ownership, as the Correo group and the Prensa Española group did in 2002.

For the first time, in 2001, a collective industrial agreement was signed between unions of journalists and publishers of newspapers (Aede).

As in recent years, the main non-daily press publishing companies continue with the same strategy. They launch or close some magazines to cover market niches, but, in fact, they launch magazines for a short time in segments occupied by other magazines or by the same non-daily press publishing company. Thus they try to eliminate competition.

## The electronic media: television and radio policy

After Franco's death in 1975, in the radio sector public and private ownership and management coexisted, and freedom of information was introduced in 1977. However, all legal structures and the organization of radio were maintained until 1987. In October 1956 the first official television broadcasting began. In 1965 the second official television channel was launched. In the 1980s and in the 1990s there was an important change in the legal regulation of television, radio and the other electronic media. Its effects continue today.

Television reached adulthood in 1980, when the Radio and Television Statute was promulgated. This statute superseded the previous television regulation, which was chaotic and partial. In television, the 1980 statute established the Radio Televisión Española (RTVE) monopoly. Under the control of parliament, RTVE developed the state jurisdiction in television, and also managed the public radio channels (Radio Nacional de España, RNE). In 1983 the passing of the 'third channel law' allowed the Autonomous Communities to create a television channel for their geographical area in addition to the two RTVE channels and under the same charter as RTVE. The regional parliaments were in control and could use the Third Channel broadcasting network of RTVE. Retevision had the monopoly to broadcast until 1999; it was a public institution now privatized.

A law passed in 1988 allowed private companies to run three national channels. Foreign participation was limited to 25 per cent. The same limit applied to Spanish newspaper publishing companies. In 1999 this law was changed to permit, among other things, an enlargement of the limits of participation in social capital on the part of the television companies (49 per cent), for foreign as well as for Spanish companies. The companies are also permitted to go to the stock exchange.

At the end of 1992 a law was passed in order to regulate television by satellite. In spite of initial opposition by the private companies, in July 1994 the 'Television without Frontiers' law was passed, bringing Spanish legislation into line with EU Directive 89/552. After more than two years of debate a law regulating satellite and cable telecommunications was passed in December 1995 and the technical directions for the execution of this law were approved in February 1996. The law defines cable communications as a public service and satellite communications as not a public service. The law on terrestrial local television was approved in 1995 and permits two television channels in every place. Licences are awarded for existing local television but they do not enlarge the phenomenon. Law No. 66 of 1997 approved terrestrial digital radio and television. The royal decree of 1998 approved the national technical plan for terrestrial digital television.

Royal Decree 1462 of 1999 established the right of the consumer to have information about the content of programmes. Law No. 22 of 1999 was passed bringing Spanish legislation into line with the European directive on 'Television without Frontiers'.

In 1987 the Telecommunications Regulation Law (LOT) was passed. Radio broadcasting is considered a public service, with state control of operating licences. In 1989 a technical plan for FM radio was approved. The latest technical plan for FM radio was approved in 1998. The Autonomous Communities can issue licences to operate on the FM band. After twelve years without any regulation, in April 1991 a law was passed allowing municipalities to broadcast local radio financed by their own budgets and local advertising. Royal Decree 1287 of 1999 (the technical national plan for digital terrestrial radio) was passed for national radio. Regional and local digital terrestrial radio are not yet regulated. On 4 October 2002 the government modified the law on private television companies of 1998. It will be included in the General Budget Law (*Ley de Acompañamiento de los Presupuestas Generales*) of 2003. It will ease the limits on participation by television companies in the social capital (100 per cent) of foreign as well as of Spanish companies.

At the end of 2000 the government completed the award of national digital radio licences. They went to two communication groups: Correo and Godó. At the beginning of the next year, the government awarded ten more licences. The process of awarding the licences for regional digital radio is open because the government has awarded only the licences for the Autonomous Community of Madrid.

However, the development of digital radio could be slow and some studies say that it will take at least five years for digital radio to change the radio map, because of the following circumstances: the high price of the radio receivers; the lack of experience of dealers; and the competitive development of the mass media, especially by Internet.

In 2000 the government extended its allocation to the three private national terrestrial television networks. The government gave them two years for the transition to terrestrial digital television and awarded two open national television channels operating with digital technology. The government took this decision because of the pressure from the communication groups. They want to complete their audio-visual mass media structure as quickly as possible.

Because of that urgency, digital television licences have been allocated without defining the role of national and regional public television or the means of financing them.

It could have adverse effects in the audio-visual industry in the future if there arose an economic crisis and less advertising investment.

The whole legislation liberalized and established the requisites for the awards and has had an effect on the structure of the mass media. The trend of the legislation has been to eliminate the limits on private activity (for instance, satellite is not a public service; companies are able to have 49 per cent of the social capital in the television business; to award licences for digital radio and television, the legislation regards it as positive if companies have financial capacity, experience of the industry and large size). Increasingly, there are fewer limits on media concentration.

From the incorporation of the EU directive into Spanish legislation comes the requirement for television companies to invest 5 per cent of their revenue in independent production. But there is no definition of what are the independent audio-visual production companies. As a result, television companies both buy audio-visual products from these companies or buy their social capital, which makes them less independent. Content regulation applies to advertising content and its duration and also regulates content for reasons of the protection of childhood, minorities, etc.

In 2001 the Promotion of Cinema and Audio-visual Law was passed. This concerns national subsidies for production, distribution, promotion and the preservation of the audio-visual heritage through the Cinema and Audio-visual Institute. The Autonomous Communities also have programmes to help the audio-visual industry.

In coming years, the Spanish audio-visual scenario will change. There will be more operators competing for a slow-growing and more fragmented audience. Some specialists say that the business of the open television networks will decrease. As with the audio-visual map, the programme production industry will face up not only to growth but also to the problem of entering the market without losing its personality and without becoming just one appendix of the audio-visual operators.

Reduced advertising investment in 2001 and the creation of channel networks between local television and communications groups, without a legal framework, could influence the future audio-visual scenario.

## Policy for the Internet and related on-line media

The role of the state is mainly confined to regulatory and tariff questions. The government has begun programmes to encourage an expansion of Internet use. The law of 1999 is concerned with the certification of electronic signatures. Royal Decree 7 of 2000 concerning urgent measures in the telecommunications field established a programme of telephone tariffs designed to introduce a flat rate for Internet connections. Since November 2000 it has been possible to choose metropolitan call telephone operators (until that date only Telefónica controlled these calls). The rate system for consumer telephones and access to the Internet was brought in. In March 2000 a regulation was passed to allocate domain names under codigo.es. That opens the door to the private companies. There is a project of law concerning the information society and electronic commerce, affecting content.

## STATISTICS

| | |
|---|---|
| National population | 41,116,800 |
| Number of households | 12,100,000 |
| Movie admissions (ticket sales), 2001 | 135,400,000 |
| Books published, 2001 | 67,000 |

**Print media**

Circulation of main national dailies, 2001

| | |
|---|---|
| El Pais | 436,302 |
| El Mundo | 302,122 |
| ABC | 291,950 |
| Marca (sport) | 403,049 |
| As (sport) | 158,780 |
| Expansion (finance) | 62,925 |
| Cinco Dias (finance) | 28,287 |

Regional dailies

| | |
|---|---|
| La Vanguardia | 191,673 |
| El Periodico de Cataluna | 184,251 |
| El Correo Espanol/El Pueblo Vasco | 132,113 |
| La Voz de Galicia | 107,850 |

Source: OJD.

**Broadcast media**

Audience share of television channels, 2001 (%)

| | |
|---|---|
| TVE-1 (national and public) | 29.7 |
| La 2 (national and public) | 5.3 |
| Public regional television | 17.4 |
| Telecino | 21.2 |
| Antena 3 | 19.5 |
| Canal Plus | 2.8 |

Soure: EGM-AIMC.

Audience share of radio channels, 2001 (%)

(Conventional)

235

| | |
|---|---:|
| Ser | 34.3 |
| Onda Cero | 19.9 |
| RNE-1 (public) | 14.4 |
| COPE | 12.8 |
| Catalunya Radio (public, regional) | 4.4 |
| Canal Sur (public, regional) | 2.2 |

Music – 'formula radio'

| | |
|---|---:|
| Cadena 40 | 25.1 |
| Cadena Dial | 17.7 |
| Other musical | 22 |

Source: EGM-AIMC.

Number of households with:

| | |
|---|---:|
| Cable or pay-television (2000) | 3,570,000 |

Percentage with:

| | |
|---|---:|
| Video-cassette recorder (2001) | 71.0 |
| Satellite television (2001) | 11.4 |

| | | |
|---|---|---:|
| **Electronic media** | Number of households with digital television | 2,300,000 |
| | Number of Internet users (2001) | 7,390,000 |
| | Personal computer ownership, 2001 (%) | 33.3 |
| | Mobile phone ownership, 2001 (%) | 71 |

| | | |
|---|---|---:|
| **Advertising spend (%)** | Newspapers | 35.0 |
| | Magazines | 10.0 |
| | Television | 42.6 |
| | Radio | 7.4 |
| | Other | 5.0 |

# 21: Sweden

## OLOF HULTÉN

## NATIONAL PROFILE

Sweden is the third largest country in Western Europe, after France and Spain, covering a land area of 449,964 km², with a population of about 9 million people. There are only three very big cities, the capital Stockholm being the biggest, with 1.3 million inhabitants, including suburbs. The majority of the population live in smaller towns and cities.

During the last thirty years Sweden has experienced fairly substantial immigration, first from neighbouring Finland, then from south-eastern Europe, the Middle East and former Yugoslavia. Today 11 per cent of the population are first-generation immigrants, and in the capital region 17.3 per cent.

Sweden is mostly known for its extensive welfare system, financed by high taxes. Big changes in Swedish economic life and industry have, since the 1990s, put the welfare system under pressure. There is still broad support among the population for such things as the public health system, day care centres for children and unemployment insurance. In other areas, a mixture of public and private solutions has been introduced, most notably perhaps with school vouchers, outsourcing of community services and the state retirement plan (which since the year 2000 funnels the regulated percentage of wage earners' income to the fund(s) chosen by each individual). A number of state-owned services have been opened to private competition, such as railway transport, telecommunications and the postal service.

After a long period of strong Social Democratic governments, general elections since 1976 brought in a mixture of non-socialist coalition governments and minority Social Democratic ones. Sweden was severely affected by the banking crisis of the early 1990s. During the mid-1990s big cuts had to be made in state, regional and local public budgets to achieve a better balance in public finances. This affected welfare services, as well as increasing the rate of unemployment. After a period of low inflation, foreign trade surpluses (aided by a decrease in the exchange value of the krona) and shrinking unemployment, households enjoyed an increase in private spending power in the early years of the new millennium.

Swedish industry is particularly concentrated in a relatively few large and mostly internationally oriented corporations, many of which have also passed into the hands of foreign owners. There has been a growth of high-tech and research-based enterprises, in biotechnology and IT. Especially in the mobile phone infrastructure and software industry, Sweden has attracted venture capital. On the whole, Sweden is one of the most export-dependent economies in the world.

## STRUCTURE AND OWNERSHIP

A special dimension of Swedish cultural affairs during a good part of the twentieth century is worth mentioning here: there was a predominantly negative attitude towards the effects of commercialism and its influence in the cultural sphere, including broadcasting. Newspaper owners were not shy of supporting this idea and attitude, as did public broadcasters themselves. Public service broadcasting is still (2002) not allowed to sell advertising but must rely almost exclusively on the mandatory licence fee every household with a television set has to pay.

Since Sweden entered into the European Union (1 January 1995), domestic media markets have been directly affected by EU regulations. Market logic prevails. Demands on public budgets clash with political ambitions to preserve viable national cultural industries. Concentration of ownership and market dominance of a limited number of commercial actors are perceived as a threat to healthy competition and to the opening up of markets for new media entrepreneurs.

There are some significant structural trends which affect the Swedish media landscape, but there is also a considerable degree of stability, both in supply and in demand. Newspapers still enjoy a strong and prestigious position in the market and in the daily media consumption pattern. Private broadcast media are growing in economic importance, but the public broadcasting media are still attracting good shares of the audiences' viewing and listening time. Internet use has expanded rapidly in recent years, mainly thanks to high household penetration. The Internet has quickly achieved a level of daily use on a par with many established media. Broadband infrastructures (high-speed multimedia two-way connections) by cable and fibreoptic networks are beginning their household diffusion, but expansion will be moderate until subscribers are offered a wide range of services.

## The print media

### The newspaper press

The first modern newspaper in Sweden, *Aftonbladet*, was launched in 1830 by a wealthy nobleman, Lars Johan Hierta, who wanted to promote free trade and voting rights. The first mass-market newspaper, *Dagens Nyheter*, was started in 1864. This newspaper is today the leading morning newspaper in the country, while *Aftonbladet* has become the dominant afternoon tabloid paper, as well as having the single biggest circulation.

The number of newspaper titles reached its peak in 1920, then numbering some 240 independent titles. While the number of different newspapers has since decreased (in 2000 there were 160, many of which belonged to the same owners) particularly between 1945–60, the total number of copies printed continued to grow. Dominant

newspapers grew at the expense of secondary titles. In 1971 a state press support system was introduced after many years of political debate, which helped a number of newspapers to survive. Consumption of newspaper copies peaked in 1980, with 580 copies per 1,000 inhabitants. Twenty years later, however, it had dropped by about 20 per cent (to 475). Sweden, none the less, is still among the top newspaper-reading countries in the world.

Swedish newspapers used to be affiliated to a political party, but today that relationship is much looser, most newspapers preferring to call themselves 'independent'. The Social Democratic press has been reduced in recent years, and newspapers with an independent liberal orientation dominate. The daily press still has a prominent and significant political and cultural position. Thanks to a strong local presence and loyal readers the press manages to keep a large share of total media advertising revenue.

Some newspaper owners have nevertheless been active in building local private radio stations, introduced in 1993. Publishers were not allowed to own radio stations, but many managed to invest anyway. The Bonnier group, the leading newspaper owner in Sweden, quickly established control of one national network, Mix Megapol.

There is no regulation against cross-ownership between newspapers and other media, locally or nationally, in Sweden. In the capital, Stockholm, the Bonnier group for example owns three daily newspapers (of six), two radio stations (of ten) as well as being the dominant owner of the national TV-4 network and its local channel in Stockholm.

The newspaper press consists of four traditional categories: metropolitan morning papers, afternoon tabloids, provincial morning dailies and smaller complementary papers, appearing once or a few times per week. The biggest individual newspapers belong to the first of these categories, the metropolitan morning press (see statistics at end of chapter), the national circulation of which has, however, been reduced in order to reduce costs. The most prestigious newspaper is *Dagens Nyheter* in Stockholm. *Svenska Dagbladet*, also a morning Stockholm paper, has struggled to survive and has so far succeeded, after repeated capital infusions from different owners as well as annual state press subsidies.

The government expressed its disapproval when *Dagens Nyheter* proposed to take over its rival and the Bonnier group withdrew. Instead, Norway's biggest newspaper publisher Schibsted bought *Svenska Dagbladet*. Schibsted has suffered big losses as well. At the beginning of 2002 the new owners were, however, cautiously optimistic about the future of the paper, as circulation had started to rise again in its core market, Stockholm.

Free morning papers have become an important phenomenon in metropolitan newspaper markets. Launched in 1995 in Stockholm, *Metro* quickly grew to become the second biggest newspaper there, as well as reaching profitability. *Metro* has local editions in Götsborg and Malmö as well, which in total yield a daily circulation of *Metro* in Sweden of 380,000 copies. The owner is the MTG Group of Sweden. It is today an international media company, growing out of one single satellite television channel, TV-3, launched by MTG's parent, Kinnevik. *Metro* is today published in a growing number of cities in Europe and the Americas (twenty two editions in fourteen countries in April 2002). *Metro* created a model for other free newspapers owned by competing publishers.

In the second category, afternoon tabloids have been hit by a decrease in readership and sales. Young people do not read them as frequently as before. There are four titles in this category, three of which have been bought by Bonnier. Bonnier established *Expressen* in 1944, which grew to be the biggest daily in Sweden and the Nordic region, with a peak circulation of 580,000 copies in 1986. Today, *Aftonbladet* is the biggest in this category. It pioneered Internet publishing and www.aftonbladet.se is today the most frequently used Web site in Sweden. The previous owner, the Swedish National Organization of Labour Unions (LO) sold *Aftonbladet* to Schibsted in 1996. The new conservative owner pledged to retain the ideological orientation of the editorial section.

The third category, provincial daily newspapers, is the most stable of the four press groups, least affected by structural changes so far. Most of these newspapers enjoy monopoly status. Only in three locations in Sweden, outside Stockholm, is there direct competition between rivals of similar size. The most common type of competition is between a dominant primary paper and a weak secondary one.

Advertising revenues are less volatile for local newspapers compared with newspapers in the capital region. Provincial newspapers also have a higher proportion of regular readers and less competition from other media. Many local papers might have low levels of circulation, but they are often very profitable operations. Some publishers are in the process of building regional chains, by acquiring titles in neighbouring towns. Some co-operate by jointly owning printing plants and by creating other forms of joint ventures such as in advertising, sales and marketing. Syndication of features and news has narrowed the quality gap between provincial papers and metropolitan papers with bigger resources. Investments in local radio and the Internet are made in order to protect advertising revenue and make use of cross-promotion.

The fourth category of newspapers, with low frequency of publication (once or twice a week), make up about a third of the total number of newspaper titles, thus adding to the pluralism of the press, perhaps mostly in theory. Circulation is low and few of them would survive without annual press subsidies from the state.

In total, as an industry, newspapers had one of their economically best years ever in 2000. The total volume of advertising had been bigger ten years earlier, but publishers had become more cost-efficient and profit-oriented during the 1990s. While critics of the press lament the loss of publishers' idealism and their profit orientation, other observers defend the new market ethos of publishers as their best bet for survival in a future with more competition from old and new media.

Sweden will, no doubt, have problems in maintaining the present number of independent newspapers. Swedes are avid newspaper readers, however. Consumption studies reveal newspaper readership in the population at a stable thirty minutes per day. Fewer readers, however, might subscribe or buy single copies, and a continued slow decline in total circulation is to be expected. Free newspapers, like *Metro*, have increased reading and recruited new readers among urban commuters rather than diverted them from competitors. So far, the consequences of Internet use have not hit readership levels or frequency.

Most readers take out a subscription and expect to find their newspaper in the mailbox early in the morning. Publishers have organized their own distribution carrier services, covering a big part of the country, supplemented by the postal service in some non-urban areas. Hence, distribution is a major cost item. A specific part of state press support is earmarked for newspapers delivering copies from other publishers.

There is a trend toward more concentration in the press industry. The biggest publishing group is Bonnier, owned by the family of the same name (see statistics at end of chapter). Bonnier have gradually expanded their newspaper interests outside the capital and outside Sweden. Successive Labour governments have struggled with the powerful position of Bonnier in the media industries, but in late 2001 (once again) gave up the idea of legislation on media concentration. Media legislation is a complicated political matter, and a constitutional matter as well, requiring very broad parliamentary agreement. Norwegian Schibsted is now the second biggest newspaper owner in Sweden in terms of circulation. It is one of the few foreign owners of newspapers. The six biggest press publishers accounted for 60 per cent of total turnover.

### The periodical and magazine press

Weeklies and monthlies are an important form of mass media in Sweden. There are a large number of them, more than 3,000 titles are registered, reading is increasing for the sector as a whole, and advertising revenues expand. There are several sub-sectors of periodicals, such as traditional women's weeklies, monthly magazines for numerous leisure time activities, professional and trade journals and non-commercial periodicals for national membership organizations.

Traditionally, family and women's weeklies had large numbers of copies in circulation. However, first television, later daily newspapers, have taken a big toll. Swedish women work outside the home as frequently as men, more and more in professional fields. Total circulation in this category has gone down, and all titles have been sold to publishers in other Scandinavian countries.

Another genre of publications which has been affected negatively by other media are comic books. They are predominantly read by youngsters, who today have access to numerous television channels, computer games and the Internet. Total circulation halved during the 1990s.

Some hundreds of non-commercial titles on science, technology, the economy and culture are published thanks to special state support, aimed at promoting freedom of expression and pluralism. Among commercially published titles of consumer interest, the largest circulation figures are found in motoring, sailing, sport, gardening and other hobbies. Professional and organizational journals remain prolific and they are less concentrated in the hands of a few dominant publishing houses.

The level of internationalization is growing in the market for commercial magazines. Swedish publishers launch their titles in other countries, and Nordic and other foreign companies introduce their products on to the Swedish market. Successful titles can travel as 'concepts' and benefit from well known international trade marks. On the Swedish market, *Elle* from France has been introduced by Hachette, *Cosmopolitan* was launched by the Dutch publisher TTG under licence from the American Hearst Corporation, and *National Geographic* appears in a Swedish edition. As trade marks, journals and magazines support and cross-promote television channels, video productions and Web sites with the same names, and vice versa.

The Bonnier group is an important publisher in the market for specialist magazines, especially lifestyle and interior decoration. The Danish Allers and Egmont, French Hachette and IDG of the United States are among the most important foreign publishers in the Swedish periodical market. The biggest circulation among all subscribed weeklies is the family-oriented magazine *ICA-Kuriren* with 340,000 copies. The highest circulation among women's weeklies is 250,000 for *Allers*. The biggest computer magazine is *Computer World* with 105,000 copies. *Illustrerad Vetenskap* (*Popular Science*) has a circulation of 145,000 copies.

So far, the Internet does not seem to have diminished the role and function of printed magazines. On the contrary, many Web operations also publish printed magazines, because people like to read printed magazines with excellent picture and text production values. Print copies are user-friendly and the physical product can be socially exhibited in ways that do not apply to Web sites.

### Book publishing

The volume of printed book titles published in Sweden had in 2000 fallen back to the level of the mid-1980s. Most of the decrease is accounted for by non-fiction books, which seemingly more and more frequently find their home exclusively on the Internet.

However, the number of fiction titles has fallen during the 1990s, while books for children show a stable level. In total, 10,976 book titles were published in 2000, of which 10 per cent were fiction and 10 per cent books for children.

Structurally, book publishing is undergoing profound changes. There is concentration of ownership by the four biggest companies on the one hand and a number of small publishers on the other, with almost none of the traditional medium-size companies left in the middle. Book clubs are important channels of distribution for the bigger publishers, while traditional booksellers are the most important channel for small publishers. Public libraries are important for both categories. Outlets such as department stores are a significant sales channel (a quarter of total book sales in 2000) for mass-appeal titles, ever since the system of fixed and regulated prices was abandoned in 1970. The Internet accounted for about 10 per cent of book sales in 2000.

The state supports the publishing of books as well as authors and readers. Publishers can apply for direct production support for individual titles, at present about 750 titles per year. Buyers of books enjoy a reduced level of sales tax on books, the same level as newspapers and cultural products. Authors get remunerated when their books are borrowed at public libraries. Local governments are obliged to provide free public libraries. Public libraries are important: they make, on average, ten loans per Swede a year.

Reading books remains a stable activity. Women read more than men, younger people more than older people and those with higher education more than others. There are no signs of competition from the Internet to the reading of printed books. Major publishers have launched electronic books, so far, however, without much success. Few e-books are sold. However, sales of printed paperbacks have doubled since the mid-1990s. User-friendliness and low price are the most likely reasons. The book publishers' association and the writers' guild have not yet been able to agree on electronic copyright.

## The electronic (audio-visual) media

### Television

The television market consists of three separate sectors: national public broadcasting, domestic commercial channels and foreign satellite channels. Public service television was established in 1957 with one channel; in 1969 a second channel was added. Private competition was introduced in 1988, when the first commercial Swedish-language channel, TV-3, launched in London. It was carried by satellite and cable. A domestic private channel, TV-4, was allowed to start terrestrial broadcasts in 1992. TV-4 has enjoyed a legally protected monopoly on the sale of advertising on terrestrial television, in exchange for serving the whole country with news, information and entertainment.

Today, there are three general entertainment commercial channels (two by satellite and one terrestrial) accounting for 45 per cent of all viewing in Sweden, there are two national public service television channels with an audience share of 42 per cent, and all other channels (most of them satellite-delivered subscription channels) divide the remaining 13 per cent share of viewing between them. There are two rival pay-television platforms (bouquet of services), Swedish-owned Viasat and Norwegian-owned Canal Digital, offering a few premium channels in addition to a number of thematic channels, most of them international services adapted to Swedish audiences, with translations (subtitles). Some of these thematic channels offer windows with domestic programmes.

Competition between public service broadcasting and private channels is a mixture of different trends, and to a large degree similar to what happens in other European countries. There is division of labour between them: private channels offer much more American fiction and movies, more Swedish soap operas and docu-drama, and tabloid format information. Public service channels keep their traditional broad output, with a high proportion of news and information and more expensive Swedish drama and fiction. Public channels broadcast about 75 per cent domestic content, TV-4 about 50 per cent domestic, while the two biggest satellite channels, TV-3 and Kanal 5, show 80 per cent foreign content, mostly from the United States. While there is competition for viewers there is no competition for advertising, since *SVT* is financed by licence fees and very limited sponsorship revenue (in sport).

Viewing trends show a steady growth for private channels since the early 1990s, with a greater loss among young adults for the public channels. Still, fifteen years after the introduction of satellite and cable services, three out of ten viewers are content with having access to only the three national terrestrial analogue channels. Introduction of more channels in digital terrestrial broadcasts in 1999 has not changed this pattern.

In 2000 advertising sales grew bigger than the total revenue of public television for the first time. As private channels have enjoyed higher income, they have invested more in domestic content and their competitive strength has grown. Pay-television operators have so far not been in a position to invest in domestic programmes, until now mostly in sport (domestic football and ice hockey).

Cable television accounts for about half of all households, about a quarter receive directly from satellite and the remainder receive only terrestrial signals. There is a slow increase in multi-channel reception, that is, in access to satellite and cable. Swedish households are on average not fond of paying high monthly fees for their television channels.

Since 1999 a bigger but still limited terrestrial output is offered by digital transmissions in Sweden. Four digital frequencies carry about twenty channels, in a mixture of subscription and free-to-air channels. Sweden was the second country in Europe, after the United Kingdom, to introduce digital terrestrial broadcasts. In early 2002 only a few per cent of households had chosen this service. Digital satellite transmissions were in more demand, 10 per cent. Digital cable accounted for as many as the terrestrial service. In total, digital decoders were available to about 15 per cent of the audience. Broadband is a fourth infrastructure to bring television to the home in the future. So far, it is limited to bringing high-speed Internet access to households demanding better and faster surfing. In 2002 some broadband operators were introducing television channels and limited on-demand services.

On the whole, the introduction of digital television has not been a success. So far, digital services are synonymous with subscription to pay-television. Operators of such services have converted their customers to digital reception by supplying them with subsidized decoders. The further diffusion of digital receivers in households is held back by decoders which are too expensive and by a market too fragmented by different standards and operating systems. What is needed is a combined effort by the government, broadcasters, commercial operators and manufacturers to create an open and seamless environment. As it stands in 2002, digital television offers viewers services of too little extra value, at higher cost than analogue television.

The conclusion in 2002 is that viewers must be offered more free channels and less expensive decoders in order to convert to digital. Broadcasters are eager for a short conversion period, in order to be able to turn off all analogue transmissions. This will save money as well as offer new opportunities to develop new kinds of interactive services. Public service broadcaster SVT therefore, at the end of 2001, called for a new strategy: giving one free digital converter (a simple digital box capable only of receiving broadcast signals) to all households who pay the television licence fee. SVT proposed that households should be given a choice of transmission platform, and thus given a voucher to cover the cost of a standard converter for digital reception for cable, satellite and terrestrial. Successful conversion could make it possible to shut off analogue transmissions around 2005, rather than some ten to fifteen years later.

### Radio

Until 1985 there was only public service radio, with three national channels and twenty five regional stations sharing a fourth nationwide network. A first break with the public service monopoly came when very local, non-profit public access radio was introduced in 1979 and made permanent in 1985 to accommodate a growing demand from religious, political and various other social groups for air-time. Frequencies were allocated in accordance with requests for transmission time, and different organizations had to share broadcast hours. Some of these so-called neighbourhood stations formed the nucleus of private commercial radio, introduced ten years later. Since 1993 public access radio has been allowed to sell advertising.

The number of broadcasting licences reached a peak during the late 1980s. By 2000 it has fallen by half (to 1,200), sharing 175 transmitters around the country. The composition of organizations has changed slightly over time. At the beginning, political groups accounted for almost a third of all licences; these have now diminished to 10 per cent. Ethnic groups have increased instead and accounted for 20 per cent in 2000. The largest number of licensees are related to Churches and spiritual movements (25 per cent).

In 1993 private commercial radio was introduced. About eighty FM frequencies were auctioned off by the government to the highest bidders, and will be renewed after ten years. According to the law, each licensed station is an autonomous local business, serving its listeners with a certain amount of locally originated broadcasts, and to encourage plurality, newspaper proprietors may not own local radio stations. Quickly, however, the new stations were consolidated into five networks, leaving very few independent stations. Newspapers are prominent owners in many cases. NRJ, the big French radio company, operates the biggest network, with twenty one stations; the Bonnier group owns a network of fourteen stations. Little local news or information is provided (with a few exceptions), as the law accepts the playing of recorded music at night as station-originated broadcasting.

Parliament changed the law in 2001 to bring it more in line with reality, and also in order to strengthen the rules about local origination. Some ten new FM licences are to be allocated, selected on content promises in exchange for lower annual fees to the government. All commercial licences will expire in 2008.

Public service radio is operated by Sveriges Radio (SR), broadcasting on four national FM networks and a number of local and regional stations, and Utbildningsradion (UR), a designated educational broadcaster, transmitting on FM-4. The national FM networks serve different audiences, FM-1 being the only exclusive news and information station. FM-4 has the biggest audience share of all radio stations in Sweden, with a mixture of music and regional news and information. Youth-oriented FM-3 lost three-quarters of its audience share to private stations. Public service radio has a stable and dominant market share of about 65 per cent. Private stations account for a third of total listening and neighbourhood stations 2 per cent.

Digital radio (DAB) was started in Sweden in 1995 by SR, but it has failed to grow an audience because DAB receivers are too expensive. SR invested significant resources to develop digital services, reaching 90 per cent of the population. A new Finnish-speaking DAB service was introduced in 1998, and several music services are being planned. In 2002 the government decided to reduce funding for DAB transmissions, to the biggest cities only. The government and private stations were until then unable to agree on the regulation of commercial DAB operations, deemed necessary to make digital radio succeed in the market. New attempts are being made to resolve the impasse. Private broadcasters have asked for new forms of digital advertising to be permitted before they will commit resources to DAB.

### Film and video
Film production and cinemas were greatly affected by television in the 1950s. The number of cinemas decreased and the number of cinemagoers in 2001 was 20 per cent of what it was fifty years earlier. The number of new foreign and new domestic films shown in Swedish cinemas has, however, remained stable since the 1990s. Cinemas are still very important for the circulation of movies on television and video. The biggest change during the 1990s in Swedish cinemas has been the shrinking number of foreign films exhibited. The reason is an expanding home video market and more television channels.

Production of domestic films is supported by a fee on every cinema ticket sold, every rental cassette released as well as a mandatory budget allocation from the terrestrial national television companies SVT and TV-4. Of the 223 movies which premiered in cinemas in 2000, thirty eight were domestic or domestic–foreign co-productions (17 per cent), 54 per cent were from the United States and 23 per cent were from Western Europe. Between 25 per cent and 30 per cent of tickets sold are for Swedish films. On average, Swedes go to the cinema twice a year.

Home video recorders are available to 88 per cent of all individuals, DVD players to 16 per cent. The use of video recorders is divided fairly evenly between recording and subsequent replaying of television programmes and pre-recorded cassettes. The number of pre-recorded DVDs sold is increasing fast; they outnumber rental DVDs ten to one. Of VHS cassettes released, almost half are rented. The US share of VHS content is roughly the same as the origin of cinema films, a little more than 50 per cent, while DVD content is still predominantly US (73 per cent in 2000).

The average daily use of video is increasing slowly, mainly due to higher sales of cassettes and DVDs and more frequent use among the older generation. Most avid users are still younger teenagers, especially boys.

## The Internet and related on-line media

The Internet has spread quickly to Swedish homes, since a new law in 1997 allowed employers to lease home computers to their employees on favourable tax terms. In 2002 computers were found in more than 75 per cent of all private homes, Internet connection in 62 per cent. Using the Net is an established regular, and daily, activity among a growing number of Swedes of all ages. Only among those above sixty years of age does the rate fall to a (still) much lower level. About 90 per cent of Internet homes use a dial-up service, but fast Internet connection is found in a growing number of homes via cable television as well as via dedicated broadband services. Demand is high for fast Internet connections, but it is held back by high monthly fees.

The Internet is an area where established media companies are competing most visibly with new players, such as national and international telecom operators and specialized portal operators, national and international companies. Internet users are, however, reluctant to pay for their use, beyond the connection. For a few years, advertising revenue seemed to be the solution but it is clear that user fees must be part of the future financing of Internet services. Some specialized Web services introduced use fees in 2002. The dominant financial newspaper has made a regular print subscription a requirement for use of its Web service. The biggest portal in terms of unique users is Msn.se with a monthly reach of 50 per cent (October 2001). The biggest Web site, operated by the newspaper *Aftonbladet*, attracted 35 per cent of all surfers in one month.

Private use of the Internet is dominated by e-mail, searching for special information, banking, news and games. There is a great difference in Internet use according to age: games and chat among young people, news and banking among middle-aged people. E-mail is important among all. There is a trend among Internet users to use fewer sites and services over time. The Internet is finding its role among other established media and channels for personal communication in the pattern of daily activities. The average time spent on the Net in private homes is declining as people with more 'ordinary' needs and time budgets become users.

When asked where they find the time for Internet use, Swedes say they do it most often at weekends and in the evenings. Often the Internet and other media are used simultaneously. Of the media, radio and television seem to yield more time to Internet use than other media, at least in the minds of survey respondents. Asked about how different communication-related behaviours are affected by Internet, the most frequent answer found in one study was in replacing the use of the telephone.

Newspapers have so far not been hurt. People prefer to read the printed papers. News on the Web is a supplement for those most interested. Radio on the Internet has been predicted a bright future, but so far few listeners spend time on the growing number of Net-based radio stations. Maybe the number will increase as uninterrupted, always-on broadband connections are more common in Swedish homes. Ericsson, the telecom company, decided in 2001 not to introduce its wireless Internet radio receiver H100 on the market because of lack of demand.

# POLITICS, POLICY, LAW AND REGULATION

Media legislation in Sweden builds on a long tradition, in which the oldest part stems from 1766. That year the first law on freedom of information was introduced. Since then, citizens' right of access to public documents is guaranteed. Freedom of expression and freedom of information are embedded in the Swedish constitution, which gives a stronger protection than common law. All mass media covered by the constitution enjoy privileges such as no censorship (the only exception is publicly exhibited films, which require clearance by the State Film Board), protection of journalists' sources and the use of a special legal procedure in court cases concerning freedom of expression. Those affected by media coverage, individuals, authorities and private companies, on the other hand, discover that it is difficult to obtain redress.

## The Press

Sweden experienced a sharp decline in newspapers after the Second World War, and in the 1970s support measures were introduced for weak newspapers facing dominant rivals, in order to protect plurality in the press. Direct support for individual newspapers is still in place, on very specific conditions, support which is of declining importance to the press as a whole but is still critical to a number of individual publishers. A general support for distribution encourages local co-operation between competing papers. The Labour government tried for many years to propose a law against excessive ownership concentration in the press, but it failed. The constitution gives the press strong protection.

## The electronic media

Only broadcast media, using public airwaves, are subject to public policy limitations: a licence is needed in accordance with the Broadcasting Act. There are two kinds of licences: the government approves national terrestrial broadcasting (public service radio and television and TV-4), while local radio (commercial and public access) is licensed by the Swedish Radio and Television Authority (RTVV). In exchange for the broadcast licence, terrestrial broadcasters are subject to control by the RTVV and by the Broadcasting Complaints Commission (as far as content regulation is concerned). Satellite broadcasting as well as cable and other wired services to the general public require no licence.

There are limits on the amount of advertising that can be carried by licensed broadcasters and how adverts are inserted in the schedules. Public service broadcasting must not sell advertising but SVT may use sponsor money on certain live sports events. All viewers and listeners can submit personal complaints to the Broadcasting Complaints Commission. The content rules to be followed by public broadcasters and TV-4, primarily regarding news and information, are specified in their licence charter with the government.

Public service broadcasting is a matter of special political procedure and etiquette. The Swedish parliament and governments in power have, since the mid-1950s, respected the integrity and autonomy of programmes and editorial practices on public service channels. Gradually, public broadcasters have achieved greater freedom of operation in many areas, while in other respects more detailed conditions have been introduced. That is a consequence of market competition:

the role of public service broadcasting needs to be clearly defined. Such a remit is also required by EU regulation.

The present public service charter expires at the end of 2005. In preparation for the next one, a parliamentary committee will review the need for and resources for public service beyond 2006. Although there is still broad political support for the basic ideas of national public service, it is not universal and there are a number of issues that need to be determined. For example, the traditional licence fees collected from households owning a television set might not be a viable source of financing if viewers are watching television via other terminals or on demand. Another issue is to define the scope of operations (the width of the remit).

Sweden joined the European Union in 1995 and all national laws had to be harmonized with the European Union body of law. Media regulation is now dominated by the same agenda as in the European Union as a whole. In certain areas, however, Sweden's policy for domestic broadcasters still has a somewhat different character. One example is that public service broadcasters do not carry any advertising at all and all commercial activities on the Internet are banned under their current agreement with the government. Domestic terrestrial TV-4 has a lower limit on advertising volume (10 per cent) than satellite broadcasters are allowed by the European Union (15 per cent).

## The Internet-based media

The political priority in media and communications of the present government and parliament is to make Sweden an advanced IT economy. Broadband access to new digital services in every home is clearly an important goal. Broadband access is making progress at a moderately low pace, and the government is accused of not allocating enough public money to investment in infrastructure and to stimulate new services. EU regulation on free competition between different technologies and operators as well as strict interpretation of rules on state support force the Swedish government to act cautiously.

As part of the general IT vision, parliament approved building a digital terrestrial television (DTT) network, which was opened in April 1999. This has caused controversy. The political opposition sees no need of it, since satellite and cable already offer the whole population more than the terrestrial infrastructure does. The economics of digital television are not proven, and the need for state support of DTT was not part of the plan. Parliament is expected to review the DTT policy no later than early 2003 and also to decide on a date for switching off analogue transmissions. Policy on digital radio, DAB, might be headed for parliamentary review around the same time.

Conversion to digital services, dtt as well as DAB, much heralded by EU and member states alike, seems to be judged differently from the household perspective. Swedish television viewers, apart from those already subscribers to analogue pay-television, have been slow to invest in any form of digital reception, while they have accepted the cost of computers and Internet use at home. So far, there is little demand for advanced interactivity via television, at least at today's cost. One apparent 'problem', of course, with both FM and PAL (today's analogue technologies) is that they are good and trusted by the audiences.

## STATISTICS

| | |
|---|---|
| National population | 8,900,000 |
| Number of households | 4,200,000 |
| Number of households with television | 4,000,000 |
| Movie admissions, 2000 | 17,000,000 |
| Books published | |
| Total number of titles, all categories | 11,000 |
| *of which* fiction, children, non-fiction | |
| (commercially available non-fiction titles | |
| (excluding education), published by members | |
| of the Swedish Publishers' Association) | 3,600 |

(All figures are from MedieSverige 2001/2, Nordicom, 2002, unless otherwise noted)

**Print media** — Circulation of main daily newspapers (Tidningstatistik, March 2002)

| | |
|---|---|
| *Aftonbladet* (tabloid, national) | 411,000 |
| *Dagens Nyheter* (morning, Stockholm) | 368,000 |
| *Expressen* (tabloid, national) | 245,000 |
| *Göteborgs-Posten* (morning, Göteborg) | 258,000 |
| *Svenska Dagbladet* (morning, Stockholm) | 176,000 |
| *Sydsvenska Dagbladet* (morning, Malmö) | 141,000 |
| *Dagens Industri* (financial, national) | 125,000 |

**Broadcast media** — Electronic media (SVT, January 2002) (%)

| *Main television channels* | *Market penetration* | *Audience share, 2001* |
|---|---|---|
| *Public service* | | |
| SVT-1 and SVT-2 | 99.8 | 41.9 |
| *National terrestrial* | | |
| TV-4 | 99.8 | 27.5 |
| *Satellite/cable* | | |
| TV-3 | 64.0 | 11.3 |
| *Satellite/cable/terrestrial digital* | | |
| Kanal *5* | 58.0 | 6.5 |
| Eurosport | 52.0 | 1.6 |

Audience share of main radio channels (%)

*Public radio – SR national networks*

| | |
|---|---|
| P-1 | 8 |
| P-2 | 1 |

| | |
|---|---:|
| P-3 | 11 |
| P-4 | 45 |

*Public service – SR International*

| | |
|---|---:|
| P-6 (international) | 6 |
| P-7 (Finnish-language, also DAB) | 7 |
| All public service radio | 65 |

Source: SVT, January 2002

*Private radio networks*

| | |
|---|---:|
| NRJ | 9 |
| RIX FM | 9 |
| Mix Megapol | 7 |
| Fria Media | 6 |
| Local public access (180 transmitters) | 2 |

Percentage of households with:

| | |
|---|---:|
| Satellite | 22 |
| Cable | 46 |
| Pay-television subscriptions (2001) | 16 |
| Video-cassette recorder (2001) | 79 |
| Satellite receiver (2001) | 22 |
| DVD player | 12 |

Source: MMS, Basundersökning (2001: 2)

| | | |
|---|---|---:|
| **Electronic media** | Percentage of households with: | |
| | Digital television reception (2001) | 12 |
| | Internet connection (2002) | 52 |
| | Internet daily use in the home (2002) | 32 |
| | Mobile phone (2001) | 80 |

| | | |
|---|---|---:|
| **Advertising spend, 2001** | Shares of media advertising revenues (%) | |
| | Newspapers | 54 |
| | Magazines | 14.9 |
| | Television | 23.2 |
| | Radio | 3.2 |
| | Cinema | 0.5 |
| | Outdoor | 4.0 |
| | Source: Institutet för Mediestatistik, IRM, 2002. | |

| **Ownership** | | Revenue (SEK million) | Share of circulation (%) |
|---|---|---|---|
| | Daily press: | | |
| | Bonnier | 10,700 | 27.3 |
| | Schibsted | 3,700 | 14.6 |
| | SVT (public) | 3,600 | 41.9* |
| | MTG | 2,400 | 8.8 |
| | Egmont | 1,900 | † |

*Share of television audience.
†Not in press publishing.

# REFERENCES

Carlsson, Ulla and Harrie, Eva, eds (2001) *Media Trends 2001 in Denmark, Finland, Iceland, Norway and Sweden*. Göteborg: Nordicom.

Edin, Anna (1998) 'The well-organized competition: on the development of internal competition in Swedish television monopoly', *Nordicom Review* 1.

Ewertsson, Lena (2001) *The Triumph of Technology over Politics: Reconstructing Television Systems – the Example of Sweden*. Linköping: Department of Technology and Social Change, University of Linköping.

Hultén, Olof (1984) *Mass Media and State Support in Sweden*. 2nd edn. Stockholm: Swedish Institute.

Hultén, Olof (1995a) 'Sweden: broadcasting and the social project' in Marc Raboy (ed.) *Public Broadcasting for the Twenty-first Century*. Acamedia Monograph 17. Luton: University of Luton Press/John Libbey Media.

Hultén, Olof (1995b) 'Diversity or conformity? Television programming in competitive situations', *Nordicom Review* 1:000–00.

Hultén, Olof and Grondahl, Aulis (2001) 'Offentlicher Rundfunk und Internet in den nordischen Ländern', *Media Perspektiven* 7: 358–68.

Kleberg, Madeleine (1996) 'The history of Swedish television: three stages' in Ib Bondebjerg and Francesco Bono (eds) *Television in Scandinavia: History, Politics and Aesthetics*. Luton: John Libbey Media.

Swedish Radio and Television Authority (2001) *Developments in the Media Field*. Stockholm: Swedish Radio and Television Authority.

Weibull, Lennart (1994) 'Sweden' in Jeremy Mitchell and Jay G. Blumer (eds) *Television and the Viewer Interest: Explorations in the Responsiveness of European Broadcasters*. Luton: John Libbey Media.

# 22: Switzerland

WERNER A. MEIER

## NATIONAL PROFILE

Switzerland is a small, landlocked country in the heart of Europe. Neighbours of Switzerland are Germany, Austria, Liechtenstein, Italy, and France. Switzerland has a strategic location as a crossroads of Europe. In 1291 the three states Uri, Schwyz and Unterwalden united against the surrounding aggressors, the Habsburgs from Austria. In 1648 Switzerland became an independent nation and in 1812 the Swiss Federation declared its neutrality. After getting its final boundaries in 1848, the Swiss Federation changed from a union of states to a confederation.

One key feature of Switzerland is its cultural diversity. There are as many as four different official languages – German, spoken by 64 per cent of the population, French (19 per cent), Italian (8 per cent) and Romansh (less than 1 per cent) – which more or less define four different mentalities. The remaining 8 per cent consist of other languages, mainly among foreign inhabitants.

The Swiss political system is highly differentiated and therefore especially complex. It functions as a direct democracy on three different levels: the confederation, the regional provinces (twenty six cantons) and the local communities. This system is the result of Switzerland's socio-cultural and socio-political diversity and creates not only various opportunities for political articulation but also a variety of tensions among interest groups on these three levels.

The party scene is exceptionally stable. For more than fifty years the centre/right-wing parties (Democratic Union of the Centre, SVP, Liberal Democratic Party, FDP, and Christian Democratic Party, CVP) have shared 60–5 per cent of the voters among them, while the left-wing (socialist and green) parties have got support from 25–30 per cent of the voters.

Switzerland consists of twenty six cantons or states. Each canton consists of a number of districts. Each district consists of a number of municipalities. There are 2,929 municipalities. The duties of the municipalities include e.g. local services, electricity, water, fire brigade, police, local roads, schools, and taxes.

The parliament consists of two houses, the Ständerat ('small chamber') and the Nationalrat ('large chamber'). Two representatives of each canton, regardless of its size, form the Ständerat with forty six members. The Nationalrat has 200 members who come from all cantons in proportion to the size of the population of each canton. The Bundesrat ('federal council') is the highest executive authority and consists of seven members, elected by the federal assembly. The president of the Bundesrat, called the Bundespräsident, changes every year. Each of the seven Bundesräte heads a department: the Department of Transport, Energy and Communications is responsible for electronic media policies.

Switzerland is one of the last remaining European countries without EU membership. However, in May 2000 the Swiss people accepted the bilateral contracts with the European Union but the currency remains the Swiss franc. In March 2002 voters barely accepted a popular initiative which proposed Switzerland should become a member of the United Nations.

# STRUCTURE AND OWNERSHIP

The political opinion press developed in the nineteenth century. In the struggle between the absolutist state and the bourgeoisie the daily press contributed a great deal to establish a modern Swiss federal state.

After an enduring petit bourgeois phase eighteen party-oriented dailies with an admittedly small circulation were founded. They did that against the establishment and with the guarantee of freedom of the press (Article 45 of the federal constitution of 12 September 1848).

The *Neue Zürcher Zeitung*, founded in 1780, for example, sold only 4,000 copies per day. After this prime of a liberal and conservative political opinion press, the general newspapers (*General-Anzeiger*) appeared. Established by foreigners and mostly neutral or only loosely tied to parties, they could position themselves on the market as profit-making newspapers (*Anzeigeblätter*) (examples: *Tribune de Genève, Tribune de Lausanne, Tages-Anzeiger*). At the beginning of the twentieth century around 120 dailies appeared, most of them on a rather local and politically narrow market which gave the particularistic forces of Switzerland additional weight.

The social changes of the 1960s led to a first wave of concentration, decimating primarily the partisan press which operated in small areas and – on the other hand – fostering larger forum newspapers. The second wave of concentration started in the mid-1980s and can be seen as a result of a recessive economic situation and extrusive competition. It was responsible for an improving position of the leading regional papers – a trend that is still continuing: fewer titles from publishing houses with decreasing independence produce an increasing level of circulation.

The development of the Swiss broadcasting system goes back to 1911, when the first licences for radio reception were issued, and to 1921, when the first public radio station began transmissions. Local corporations in the bigger cities ran the first radio stations in the 1920s. Yet there was increasing demand for better co-ordination, to secure access rights for social minorities to the common good of a scarce radio spectrum and to guarantee sufficient output of non-partisan and culturally responsible programmes for all segments of the population. One of the main structural tensions in the Swiss broadcasting system is the struggle between federalist (particularistic) and centralist forces, ever since the Swiss Broadcasting Corporation (SBC) was founded in 1931. The fear of uncontrolled political influence and the resistance of the more influential publishers delayed the introduction of television until the late 1950s. The SBC did not go on air until 1958 with its programmes on a regular basis. Radio and television were 'public service monopolies' from 1931 to 1983.

This proved to be a type of institutionalization which served the interests not only of the political system but also of the printed press. While advertising has always been forbidden on radio and has been permitted on television in a restricted manner only since 1964, the revenue of the press was not jeopardized by the electronic media. The institutionalization of a public monopoly – financed mainly by licence fees – prevented economic competition between the print and electronic media and brought about a financially healthy private and a viable public system.

Pressure from pirate radio stations on the one hand, from the bourgeois parties and the advertising industry on the other, and the general trend towards demonopolized broadcasting in Western Europe forced the federal government in 1982 to issue provisional licences to thirty six private local radio stations in all parts of Switzerland. Furthermore, acceptance of the constitutional Article 55(b) in 1984 by the citizens provided the basis for the Federal Law on Radio and Television (RTVG), which became effective in 1992. These decisions opened up the broadcasting system to new private enterprises. A new era began for the Swiss media system as well as for Swiss media policy.

## The print media

### The newspaper press

The federal constitution which became effective on 1 January 2000 contains three legal regulations with regard to media. Article 16 stipulates the freedom of opinion and information; Article 17 expresses the freedom of the media, and Article 93 regulates radio and television. Explicitly, Article 16 allows anyone to build, express and spread her or his own opinion. Article 17 prohibits censorship and ensures the entrepreneurial freedom of the press, radio and television.

Article 93, which regulates radio and television, explicitly calls for the protection of the printed press. There is, however, no legal obligation on the press to fulfil any public service. Newspapers are private enterprises and depend on market mechanisms and on the rights of freedom of commerce and trade. Yet they are expected to be more than just businesses. Swiss media policy thus typifies the democratic paradox of autonomy and obligations that characterizes the mass media. The conflicting goals of the economy, the state apparatus and civil society lead to diffuse expectations concerning the public and social obligations of private enterprises.

*Ownership and financing of the newspaper press.* In Switzerland all daily newspapers with a circulation over 100,000 are owned by multimedia companies. Ringier, the largest publishing company, owns the tabloid *Blick* (309,444) and the tabloid Sunday edition *Sonntagsblick* (336,336), the leading Sunday newspaper. The second largest publishing company – on the basis of turnover – is Tamedia, the owner of the leading quality newspaper *Tages-Anzeiger* with a circulation of 250,000 copies. Tamedia publishes also the *Sonntags Zeitung*, a Sunday paper with a circulation of 221,100. In addition it has a minority share (49 per cent) in the leading newspaper in Berne, the *Berner Zeitung* (162,202), owned by the publishing company Espace Media Groupe. Both Ringier and Tamedia are located in Zurich and are financially controlled by one family each. The third salient media company is AG für die Neue Zürcher Zeitung, which publishes the *Neue Zürcher Zeitung* (170,113) and controls the *St Galler Tagblatt* (110,502), *Der Bund* in Berne (68,212) and – as 49 per cent minority shareholder – *Neue Luzerner Zeitung* (133,820). Other important multimedia companies with daily newspapers in the German-speaking part of Switzerland are *BaZ-Gruppe* with the *Basler Zeitung* (109,095), AZ-Gruppe with the *Aargauer Zeitung* (117,215) and Gasser Media with *Südostschweiz* (138,993).

Since March 2002 there has been a third Sunday paper, *NZZ am Sonntag,* on the market. In addition to the Sunday papers, five weekly newspapers are in fierce competition for readers and advertisers' money: *Weltwoche* (84,000), which changed its classical newspaper format to that of a news magazine in May 2002, *Cash* (68,088), *Finanz und Wirtschaft* (50,397), *HandelsZeitung* (35,571) and *Wochenzeitung* (15,000), an undogmatic left-wing paper without commercial advertising.

The leading publishing house in the French-speaking region is Groupe Edipresse, which controls two-thirds of the newspaper circulation with the four large dailies *Vingt-quatre heures* (88,467), *La Tribune de Genève* (77,420), *Le Matin* (65,121) and *Le Temps* (53,526).

The leading daily newspapers in the Italian-speaking part of the country are *Corriere del Ticino* (39,567), *La Regione Ticino* (32,556) and *Giornale del Popolo* (27,348).

Advertising provides 60–80 per cent of subscription newspaper revenue. In the last few years the indirect financing of newspapers by advertising has grown. Therefore the profitability of newspaper production depends more and more on the viability of the main advertisers and the state of the economy.

*Structure and organization.* Variety of choice cannot be measured by the number of different titles alone, but rather by the independence of the publishing house as well as by journalistic performance. The large publishing houses – all of them owned and controlled by Swiss capital and management – enjoy an increasing share of the market. The five most important newspapers with a daily circulation over 100,000 are read by almost as many people as the 235 smallest newspapers with a circulation of up to 25,000. More and more small and medium-size newspapers have been forced out of the market or have been taken over by large publishing companies. In 1995 the number of dailies amounted to 102, but the number of fully staffed newspapers fell from sixty seven to fifty two between 1990 and 1993 alone and in 2002 only forty fully staffed daily newspapers remained. Furthermore, hardly any new dailies are being launched. After the tabloid *Blick* was established in 1959, it took more than thirty years for a new daily to appear on the saturated market: the quality paper *Le Nouveau Quotidien*, which was relaunched as *Le Temps* in 2000.

In conclusion: all common forms of press concentration – publisher concentration (a declining number of publishing houses), journalistic concentration (a declining number of fully staffed papers) and concentration of circulation can be observed in Switzerland. The trend seems to be heading towards a two-tier newspaper landscape. Only a few high circulation papers will serve the economic centres and the conurbations; meanwhile many small newspapers have to fill the gaps, taking advantage of narrow local advertising and readership markets.

### The periodical and magazine press

Two consumer magazines are on the top of the magazine list. *K-Tipp* (337,486) and *Der Beobachter* (335,226), both fortnightly, devoted to consumer protection and practical advice, etc. In addition there are more consumer-oriented magazines: *Saldo* (161,277), the health magazines *Puls-Tipp* (139,409) and *Gesundheits-Sprechstunde* (78,416).

Ringier, the market leader of the magazine press, also publishes the weekly magazines *Schweizer Illustrierte* (254,657) and *L'Illustré* (84,290), as well as *Tele* (223,739) and *Glücks-post* (170,128). Tamedia is the publisher of *Facts* (103,363), the leading news magazine, of *Schweizer Familie* (155,724) and of *Annabelle* (100,015), a monthly women's magazine.

### Book publishing

Switzerland has no homogeneous book market, since it consists of three different independent markets of the corresponding markets from abroad of the same language. Switzerland has 500 publishing houses with a total of around 11,000 books getting on the market yearly. Most of them are small publishing houses fighting for survival. With the exception of Diogenes, none of the Swiss publishing houses plays any role abroad. The sales of all house reaches almost SFr1 billion yearly. About half of the books are exported (SFr 225 million) and four out of five books sold in Switzerland come from abroad (SFr 650 million), which makes a negative balance of trade.

In 2001 Switzerland could count about 600 bookstores. The biggest one – Orell Füssli in Zurich – has yearly sales of SFr 92 million. The publishing houses of German books set the prices for the books compulsory, while books from France and Italy are not bound officially to any prices.

Two-thirds of Swiss adults spend time on reading regularly. On average this amounts to ten to fifteen minutes daily only.

## The electronic (audio-visual) media

### Television

*Development patterns.* After World War II the introduction of television began with a debate on who should operate, be responsible for and cover the cost of this expensive medium: the state, private commercial owners or even foreign companies. There were also reservations about the 'seductive' and 'desensitizing' effects of the visual medium and fears about the loss of Swiss identity through mass consumption at the lowest common denominator. There was also concern about being swamped by foreign propaganda as a result of the anticipated exchange of programmes.

Because of the supposedly persuasive effects of television, the Federal Council was anxious to bring the new medium under its own control from the start, as it had done with radio. For that reason the national government's policy was to introduce television very carefully and sparingly. Its institutions were to be set up in the traditions of the cultural media of books, newspapers and radio, and based on the British model (the BBC). The Federal Council therefore decided to set up first of all an experimental operation. To this end it awarded a licence to the Swiss Broadcasting Corporation (SBC or SRG) in February 1952 for a three-year period, which was later extended to the end of 1957 to give enough time for a constitution for radio and television.

In spite of the absence of a constitutional basis the Federal Council awarded the SRG a definitive licence for television, so that on 1 January 1958 it could officially go into operation. Since the SRG intended to meet part of its costs through advertising, the newspaper publishers offered to make available an annual subsidy of SFr 2 million if the television institution would in exchange relinquish the broadcasting of advertisements. On 1 February 1965 the first commercials flickered across the screen. A maximum of twelve minutes per working day was permitted for advertising.

Contrary to pessimistic expectations, the number of new subscribers grew rapidly, and in 1968, after only ten years of official operation, the figure of 1 million licence payers could be celebrated. The strong growth of the SRG in the 1960s and 1970s demanded various consequential changes in the organizational structure which, however, were often in conflict with federal aspirations, and therefore subjected the SRG to almost permanent debate about reform. At all events, the SRG had to adapt to increased political control, because the federal government was inclined to give more weight in the future to complaints and involvement. The SRG nevertheless came under increasing pressure, also, from competition. It was primarily the trend towards the liberalization of broadcasting in large areas of Europe and the increase in the reception of channels from abroad thanks to the new transmission technology (satellite, cable) which were responsible for this. All the legal and illegal moves towards the liberalization of the broadcasting sector finally ended in a decision of the Federal Council, via a new regulation, to permit non-cable commercial broadcasting financed through advertising. Consequently the national government launched the regulation on local experimental broadcasting (RVO) on 7 June 1982, and allocated licences for a five-year experimental period to thirty six – mostly commercial – local radio and seven local television projects. This produced a transition from a national monopoly operation to a dual system, which scarcely tampered with existing structures. The situation of public and private broadcasting operating alongside and against each other finally achieved a basis in constitutional law in 1984.

*Structural and organizational patterns.* In 1992 Switzerland introduced at a legislative level the dual broadcasting system. In practice, however, public broadcast service has never ceased to dominate the electronic media landscape. In March 1999 the public broadcast service Schweizerische Radio- und Fernsehgesellschaft (SRG) changed its name to *SRG* SSR idée Suisse and indicated therewith its future effort to be dedicated to the public and to foster as a public institution social and cultural integration.

In 1993, to be well prepared for the increasing national and international competition, SRG SSR idée Suisse undertook a further structural reform. Under the motto 'From institution to enterprise', management committees were reduced in size, audience representation was reorganized and the divisions were given greater operational flexibility. As an enterprise SRG SSR idée Suisse now moves towards shareholding and forms a business grouping in the sense of a holding company. SRG SSR idée Suisse is still a non-profit-making enterprise, though, and commercial gains are channelled back into the public service.

SRG SSR idée Suisse is a company under private law and an association of societies but not a state institution. Such associations of societies still exist and form now a parent organization of SRG SSR idée Suisse, serving as a bridge between civil society and the

enterprise. It consists of four regional associations, each representing the federal element of the parent organization. All central and regional councils and committees have the – sometimes difficult – task of ensuring that the public interest is safeguarded in the programme production process. They also have to represent the concerns of the professionals towards the public. As representative of civil society, of the public and the professional institutions, the audience councils in particular, are constantly occupied with finding compromises for the different interests of all actors.

The Swiss Broadcasting Corporation holds two charters from the Swiss Federal Council: the SRG SSR charter to produce radio and television programming for Switzerland and the SRI charter to produce information programming for broadcast outside Switzerland. The charter defines the statuary framework of the SBC in greater detail, and lays down the number of radio and television stations that the SBC may operate in each language region and a programming mandate, which the SBC must fulfil across all radio and television schedules:

1. SBC has to promote understanding, cohesion, and exchange between the different parts of the country.
2. SBC has to consider the non-Swiss population and to support contact with Swiss residents abroad.
3. SBC has to promote Switzerland's international profile and foster understanding of its concerns.
4. SBC has to collaborate with the Swiss film industry and to commission work from the audio-visual sector.
5. SBC is not allowed to sell advertising air time on radio stations but may promote its own programmes on SRG SSR's stations and channels.

The seven operational departments of SRG SSR idée Suisse broadcast eighteen radio stations and seven television channels in various languages. They do so under the terms of the RTVG and the existing licence of 18 November 1992.

To improve its social cohesion and economic productivity the SRG SSR has formulated a medium-term business plan for operating departments and subsidiaries, which emphasizes its 'Swissness', its leading position in television, its diversity, its fair competition and last but not least its credo, that it 'needs money to make programmes and not programmes to make money'.

*Financing the public service.* The financing of the Swiss Broadcasting Corporation comes from various sources. It is primarily financed through the licence fee and advertising. Every household with a radio and/or television set is obliged by law to pay licence fees. In 2001 the SRG SSR received some SFr 1.06 billion through the licence fee (71 per cent of its income), while advertising (television only) and sponsorship (radio and television) brought in SFr 332 million (20 per cent). SFr 100 million or 9 per cent of its income derives from other sources, such as the sale of programming. The Federal Council sets the level of the fee as low as possible and does not index it, not least for political reasons. Private households will have a licence fee increase of 4.1 per cent in February 2003, paying SFr 165 for radio reception and SFr 275 for television reception per year.

The SRG allocates its funds internally in accordance with a financial equalization programme between the different sized language regions. In order that the French- and Italian-speaking parts of the country can produce and receive a similar number of programmes to the dominant German-speaking Switzerland, they receive a disproportionate amount of the total financial resources. While German Switzerland contributes some 71 per cent of licence fee income, it receives only 45 per cent of available resources. An equitable basic provision of programmes for all the linguistic cultures could not be achieved without this voluntary financial adjustment.

Not only the SRG SSR gets revenues from licence fees but also some commercial programme providers. Because of the small size of the markets the income of the commercial operators is modest overall, but there are very wide variables according to the size and economic value of their respective transmission areas. For this reason, according to the RTVG article, local and regional operators may receive a contribution from the licence fee ('fee splitting') if there are 'no adequate financing prospects available' in their area, and in so far as 'there is a particular public interest in their programmes'. Currently around two-thirds of all commercial radio

stations receive such adjustment payments, which can form up to a third of their annual incomes.

*Ownership patterns.* Also in television SRG SSR continues to enjoy its preferential position thanks to its statutorily guaranteed existence, even though internal competition has greatly increased at the linguistic-regional/national level. The market deregulation by the Swiss Federal Council together with its policy on licensing since the mid-1990s sparked off a battle for survival. With TV-3 and RTL/Pro 7 entering the market in autumn 1999 the competition for scarce resources has become even tougher and had notably implications. Demand in the Swiss television commercial market for new channels was less flexible than the optimistic business plans presumed. The Swiss 'programme windows' in RTL/Pro 7 in early 2000, the channel Tele 24 as well as TV-3 had to withdraw at the end of 2001 owing to sustained losses which reached around SFr 100 million all told.

Besides the SRG SSR channels, some commercial providers still operate on a small scale: Teleclub, which has had a licence as a pay-television channel since 1984 and provides some 85,000 households in German Switzerland with films; Star TV for film promotion; Swizz as a music channel with special emphasis on the Swiss musical scene, *Sat1 Schweiz*, a programme and advertising window from Germany and Presse-TV, a Swiss window channel on SF DRS-2, provided by some leading publishing houses (Ringier, NZZ group, Basler Media Group). Most of the private television providers operate at local/regional level. The annual budgets come to €2–8 million and the daily programme output – mainly news magazines and talk shows – amounts to two hours. Some of the country's leading media enterprises have significant shares in individual stations. However, it is still uncertain whether there is enough advertising money to keep the new stations alive. There are no Swiss enterprises operating television channels at an international level. In television only the SRG is active as a programme producer for the satellite channels 3-sat, TV-5 Europe, TV-5 Canada and RaiSat. The SRG acts as a programme supplier for Eurosport, arte, Euronews and CNN.

*Programming patterns.* Undoubtedly the starting point for the development of programme policies is the charge and mission of SRG SSR. However, it is confronted with some structural handicaps which have to be taken into account: the small, distinctively segmented Swiss market, steeply rising programme production costs in certain areas, mighty competitors from neighbouring countries and lately from emerging local television stations, limited financial and creative resources. Under such – partly new – circumstances the SRG SSR is developing programme policies which can be described under the headline 'helvetization, adaptation, commercialization': Swiss issues are focused, collaboration with major public service broadcasters in Europe is reinforced and new technologies will be used, and fourthly the SSR tries to be competitive in the transnational broadcasting markets with a more mass-audience-oriented programme schedule. In general, the SRG SSR – according to its latest charter – operates along entrepreneurial lines in order to optimize performance and enhance its position in a competitive environment. Success is measured in terms of audience ratings, market share and the reputation and viability of its programming.

The SRG broadcasts three television channels, one each in German (SF DRS), French (TSR) and Italian (TSI), as well as regular contributions in Romansch within the overall programme of SF DRS. Alongside the main channels a second, complementary channel has been provided since September 1997 in each of the main linguistic regions (SF-2/TSR-2/TS-2). These additional theme channels, concentrating on sport and films, are aimed primarily at a young audience, or endeavour to take account of the concerns of minorities.

In 2001 SRG SSR broadcast for a total of 45,308 hours (excluding Textvision, Euronews, weather maps and advertising): the category of 'films and television drama' was in the lead with a 26 per cent share, followed by current affairs (19 per cent), information (15 per cent), sport (13 per cent), culture and education (10 per cent), children's programmes (9 per cent) and entertainment (5 per cent). The shares of the remaining categories do not exceed 2 per cent, i.e. music (2 per cent), religion (0.6 per cent) and theatre (0.2 per cent).

The constant growth in air time and channels has led to a considerable increase in repeats, because of the stringent financial situation and owing to specific growth. From 1991 to 2001 the SRG SSR increased both its television services by a factor of

three in order to better withstand the intense competition. Moreover, the more popular programmes like 'films and television drama' and current affairs were extended at the expense of more highbrow programmes (see the example of SF DRS-1 in the Statistics section).

*Foreign media availability and audience patterns.* Geographically determined factors such as poor television reception in many regions have accelerated the installation of cable systems since the early 1960s. By 2002 more than 80 per cent of all households were either equipped with satellite receivers or linked to a broadband cable network. Since most of the cable systems are privately owned they show a strong interest in gearing the system to the consumer's preference with an array of appealing foreign television channels. These cable and satellite households receive around forty television channels in the German language. The high availability of foreign channels has a distinct effect on the total viewing time and the audience share.

In television the competition is primarily between the SRG SSR and foreign (private) broadcasters. The national broadcaster had to take losses in viewing figures particularly in the 1980s, but from the beginning of the 1990s has been able to maintain its market share – especially at prime time.

During prime time from 6.00 p.m. to 11.00 p.m., SF DRS-1 and SF DRS-2 achieved a market share of 41 per cent in 2001, followed by RTL, ARD, Pro 7 and ZDF by far. Daily television viewing in the German-speaking part of Switzerland, at 139 minutes per day, ranks low in national and international comparisons (all television statistics: Monday to Sunday).

Acceptance of the public television broadcasting programmes in the French-speaking part of Switzerland is similar. The market share of the public service in prime time amounts to 40 per cent, followed by TF-1 with 16 per cent, M-6 with 9 per cent, F-2 8 per cent and F-3 with 7 per cent (all French). Daily viewing time amounts to a total of 164 minutes, i.e. twenty five minutes more than in the German-speaking part of Switzerland.

In the Italian-speaking part of Switzerland the SRG SSR channels (TSI-1 and TSI-2) have a market share of 40 per cent at prime time, followed by Canale 5 with 14 per cent, Rai 1 with 11 per cent, Italia 1 with 7 per cent and Rai 2 with 6 per cent (all Italian). In southern Switzerland the television set is used 169 minutes per adult per day in average – five minutes longer even than in the French-speaking part.

### Radio

*Structural and organizational patterns.* The official start of Swiss radio was in 1922. In that year the town of Lausanne gave permission for the building of a public transmission facility. Even this pioneer station required a licence from the national government (Federal Council), which that same year had created the legal basis, with the coming into force of the Federal Act on the Telegraph and Telephone Service (TVG), by which to control the building and maintenance of radio stations. The rapid introduction of the TVG was influenced by the national strike of 1918 and the brief occupation of radio stations by workers' and soldiers' councils in Germany. To be able to intervene in similar situations in Switzerland, the national government gave the sole right in the TVG to the Supreme Telegraph Directorate (later the PTT) to erect and maintain radio installations (*Landessender*).

Four further radio companies were established in Zurich, Geneva, Berne and Basle by 1926. They were soon engaged in violent controversy over the distribution of the licence fee. Thus on 24 February 1931 the Schweizerische Rundspruchgesellschaft (SRG, Swiss Broadcasting Company) was formed. This development brought little pleasure to the mighty press associations, which nevertheless succeeded in influencing the competition conditions of the new medium in their favour. The publishers managed not only to restrict news programmes to two broadcasts per day, but also to ban advertising, which is still the situation for SRG Radio today.

After a federal start, the Federal Council strengthened its influence upon the SRG from the middle of the 1930s. Based on the revised licence of 1936 it determined for the first time the majority on the Central Board and took for itself the power to select the central Chairman and the Director General. Centralization gained added impetus from the growing threat on the international scene. From 1938 the Federal Council made radio a key instrument of psychological national defence and of national cultural propaganda. At the start of the war the SRG was finally released from its licence and placed under the control of the government and the army. Until this regulation was lifted on 20 March 1945 the Schweizerischer Rundspruchdienst, SR (the Government Swiss Broadcasting Service) and the 'Abteilung Presse und Rundfunk, APF (the Army's Department of Press and Broadcasting) determined the programming of the Swiss Broadcasting Company, which, thanks to it being a quasi-state institution, could be controlled far more directly than the press.

After the Second World War the environment of radio was radically changed as the PTT carried out the first experimental television broadcasts in 1947.

Currently the SRG broadcasts three radio programmes in each of the three main languages of the country and about twelve hours daily on FM in Romansh as well. Each of the three respective target channels contains each a 'majority programme', a 'culture programme' and an 'accompanying programme' for a younger, urban audience.

In 1983–84, in the first phase of commercial radio, around thirty licensed radio broadcasters went on the air, providing programmes and services for their relatively small local audiences in all three linguistic regions. At the end of the century, around forty commercial local/regional stations were in operation.

*Ownership patterns.* The strengthening of competition has become an increasingly centralized matter with the constant increase in the number of competitors both at home and abroad. Unlike television, competition for radio audiences is primarily between Swiss operators. The situation regarding the ownership of private stations has changed considerably since the start of the dual system. At the beginning most newspaper publishers took a sceptical attitude towards the development of local radio, but they have since participated increasingly in the stations and now control the majority of them. Thus in German Switzerland the SRG's market share for its radio channels dropped between 1984 and 2001 from 72 per cent to 63 per cent, while the Swiss private radio stations over the same period were able to show an increase from 18 per cent to 28 per cent.

In Suisse romande the relationships are somewhat different inasmuch as foreign radio stations have been able to maintain their considerable market share and reach. The private stations in Svizzera italiana were able to develop only a little. There they have only a 5 per cent market share, while the foreign stations have 15 per cent and the

SRG SSR channels clearly dominate the market with 80 per cent.

*Programming patterns.* Regarding programme categories, in 2001 SRG SSR gave 71 per cent of all air time (some 120,000 hours per year) to music, 11 per cent to news and current affairs, 11 per cent to entertainment through the spoken word and almost 6 per cent to culture through the spoken word.

In 2001 the most popular radio channel, SR DRS-1, broadcasted 60 per cent light music, 15 per cent e-music and 14 per cent current news. Almost 7 per cent goes to culture through the spoken word.

*Audience patterns.* With the introduction of dual broadcasting in Switzerland as in other German-speaking countries, the consumption pattern of the Swiss population has gradually changed. The once unchallenged market leader, the SRG, has been compelled to cede some of its market share to private competition.

In 1984, in the first phase of commercial radio in Switzerland, around thirty licensed radio broadcasters went on the air, providing programmes and services for their relatively small local audiences in all three linguistic regions. At the end of the century around forty five commercial and some non-commercial stations were in operation. The market share of local radio rose to 35 per cent (German-speaking), 19 per cent (French-speaking) and 11 per cent (Italian-speaking). Foreign stations are losing ground while the SRG SSR channels are still market leaders.

### Film and video

In 2001 the Swiss motion picture industry produced only fifteen fiction films with theatrical releases. Twenty seven old and new titles were distributed, in comparison with 110 American and ninety European movies. With 467,000 admissions the share of the market was almost 3 per cent, well below the very promising 5 per cent of 2000. Although the market share of Hollywood movies decreased from 76 per cent to 66 per cent, Swiss films were hardly able to benefit from the increased readiness of the public to go to the movies and to watch other than American movies. Beside American (66 per cent) and European (30 per cent) movies, only 4 per cent of production came from continents other than North America or Europe. The total admissions of 17.1 million are spread across 334 cinemas with 108,025 seats and generated gross box office takings of SFr 235 million. The market leader – way ahead of others – is Kitag, which owns thirty eight screens and generates 2.3 million admissions, or more than 20 per cent of all admissions in the German-speaking market, mainly by showing blockbusters from Hollywood.

The Swiss government subsidizes the national film industry in order to foster a certain diversity of supply. In the year 2002 the government was ready to spend some SFr 30 million: 48 per cent for the support of production, 13 per cent for the support of the film culture (festivals, etc.), 12 per cent for European collaboration (e.g. Eurimages, European co-production), 10 per cent for education and further development, 8 per cent for the promotion of movies at home and abroad, 5 per cent for film archives and 3 per cent for awards.

### The Internet and related on-line media

*Supply patterns.* Five years ago, around 10 per cent of Swiss, aged fourteen years and older had access to and used the Internet at least once a week. Based on representative Swiss surveys in 2001, 59 per cent of all persons have a personal computer at home and Internet use increased to 37 per cent of the population. Still, education and sex seem to be relevant factors. Only 28 per cent of all females – in comparison with 48 per cent of males – use the Internet on a fairly regularly basis. The typical Swiss user of the Internet is well educated, affluent, young and male. These obvious 'digital divides' do not seem to became smaller but rather larger. Moreover, besides gaps in access, additional gaps in content-related use of the Internet can be observed (see Bonfadelli, 2002). The greater the educational background a person has, the more she or he uses the Internet in a quite instrumental way. People with less education, on the other hand, seem to use the Internet almost exclusively for entertainment purposes.

## POLITICS, POLICY, LAW AND REGULATION

### The electronic media

*Current legislation and regulatory instruments.* Until 1984 all federal decisions were based upon the Federal Act on the Telegraph and Telephone Service (TVG) of 1922. Conditioned by its defeat in two referendums (1957 and 1976), it was not until 1984 that the Federal Council was able to have an article in the constitution for radio and television (55b) agreed by the people. This article – which was taken into the new federal constitution on 1 January 2000 as Article 93 – remains virtually unchanged and reads as follows:

1 Legislation on radio and television and on other forms of public telecommunication transmission of programmes and information is a federal government matter.
2 Radio and television should make a contribution to education and cultural development, to the free expression of opinion, and to entertainment. They must take the country's particular characteristics and the needs of the cantons into consideration, present events factually and reflect the full diversity of views.
3 The independence of radio and television from state influence and their autonomy in creating their programmes are guaranteed.
4 Attention should be paid to the position and the responsibilities of other media, particularly the press.
5 Complaints may be made to an independent complaints body.

*Main principles of regulation.* The competences *for* the allocation of licences are also subject to statutory regulation. The line of first competence is with the Federal Council, with, since 1992, the administrative support of the Federal Office *for* Communication (Bakom). This competence allows the Federal Council a comparatively great amount of flexibility in implementing the constitutional provisions and radio and television legislation. The Federal Council and the responsible Department *for* the Environment, Transport, Energy and Communication (UVEK), currently working on a revision of the radio and television law, is willing to liberalize the procedures for the commercial providers and tighten up the activities of the SRG SSR.

The Federal Council has shown a liberal attitude towards licence applicants, it has also indicated that it no longer sees itself as having responsibility for the financial survival of operators, although the Federal Council has declared that it is still willing to subsidize commercial channels so long as they are ready to make a contribution to the service public.

*Future trends.* Switzerland basically faces the same problems as every other 'information society' or 'media society'. The role of public service broadcasting in a digital media environment continues to elude clarity; its strong mission of integrating state and cultural policy is coming into ever greater conflict with the demands of business and the practical competitive situation of radio and television. This is why the SRG SSR is endeavouring to interpret and translate its legal contract from a more business-based perspective and tries to 'reconcile' the market and its public service mission.

Structural disadvantages in the form of inadequate market size, dependence on programmes from abroad, scarcity of resources (capital, know-how, creativity, talent, ability, etc.) can also produce 'solutions', which do not necessarily need to be a matter of low performance, even though many programmes have to be regarded as 'cheap television' and as 'provincial television'. The pragmatic, rather than ideological, maintenance of a viable public service sector provides society with a diversity of programming which continues to be appreciated by the majority of the population. Limited resources have also led to new forms of collaboration, which may in the long term prove superior to competition. Thus Presse TV, produced by the publishers, broadcasts its programmes at the weekends exclusively on the public service channel SF DRS-2.

The RTVG of 1991 is being revised by the Federal Council and the Federal Assembly. However, the amending legislation will not come into effect until 2004. The principal aims of the revised RTVG are to increase the financial viability of commercial providers (deregulation and liberalization) as well as to strengthen the public service providers through regulation or regulated self-regulation.

# STATISTICS

| | |
|---|---|
| National population | 7,300,000 |
| Number of households | 3,067,000 |
| Books published (titles) | approx. 11,000 |

**Print media**

Circulation of leading dailies in German-speaking Switzerland

| | | |
|---|---|---|
| *Blick* | (Zürich) | 309,444 |
| *Tagesanzeiger* | (Zürich) | 250,000 |
| *Neue Zürcher Zeitung* | (Zürich) | 170,113 |
| *Berner Zeitung* | (Berne) | 162,202 |
| *Südostschweiz* | (Chur) | 138,993 |
| *Neue Luzerner Zeitung* | (Lucerne) | 133,820 |
| *Aargauer Zeitung* | (Aarau) | 117,215 |
| *St. Galler Tagblatt* | (St Gall) | 110,502 |
| *Basler Zeitung* | (Basle) | 109,095 |

Circulation of leading dailies in French-speaking Switzerland

| | | |
|---|---|---|
| *Vingt-quatre Heures* | (Lausanne) | 88,467 |
| *La Tribune de Genève* | (Geneva) | 77,420 |
| *Le Matin* | (Lausanne) | 65,121 |
| *Le Temps* | (Genèva) | 53,526 |

Circulation of leading dailies in Italian-speaking Switzerland

| | | |
|---|---|---|
| *Corriere del Ticino* | (Lugano) | 39,567 |
| *La Regione Ticino* | (Bellinzona) | 32,556 |
| *Giornale del Popolo* | (Lugano) | 27,348 |

Sunday press

| | |
|---|---|
| *Sonntagsblick* | 336,336 |
| *Sonntagszeitung* | 221,100 |
| *NZZ am Sonntag* | 150,000 |

Financial and business press

| | |
|---|---|
| *Cash* | 68,088 |
| *Finanz und Wirtschaft* | 50,397 |
| *HandelsZeitung* | 35,571 |

Weekly press

| | |
|---|---|
| *Facts* | 103,363 |
| *Weltwoche* | 90,000 |
| *Wochenzeitung* | 15,000 |

General and special interest magazines

| | |
|---|---|
| *Schweizer Illustrierte* | 254,657 |
| *L'Illustré* | 84,290 |
| *Tele* | 223,739 |
| *Glückspost* | 170,128 |
| *Schweizer Familie* | 155,724 |
| *Annabelle* | 100,015 |
| *K-Tipp* | 337,486 |
| *Der Beobachter* | 335,226 |

| | |
|---|---|
| *Saldo* | 161,277 |
| *Puls-Tipp* | 139,409 |
| *Gesundheits-Sprechstunde* | 78,416 |

**Broadcast media**

*Television channels*
SRG SSR channels: (SF DRS, TSR) and Italian (TSI), (SF2/TSR2/TS/2). *Commercial (national) channels: Star TV, Presse-TV, Teleclub, SWIZZ, Sat1 Schweiz, plus around twenty regional television channels.*

Audience share of television channels, 2001 (%)

| *Market share* | *German-language* | *French-language* | *Italian-language* |
|---|---|---|---|
| SRG SSR42 | 40 | 40 | |
| Prime time | SF DRS-1 35 | TSR-1 32 | TSI-1 32 |
| SF DRS-2 6 | TSR-2 5 | TSI-2 5 | |
| All commercial Swiss channels | 9 | 0 | 1 |
| All foreign channels | 50 | 59 | 59 |
| Market leaders | RTL 7 | TF-1 16 | Canale 5 14 |
| ARD 6 | M6 9 | Rai1 11 | |
| Pro 7 5 | F2 8 | Italia 1 7 | |
| ZDF 4 | F3 7 | Rai 2 6 | |
| Daily use by person (minutes) | 139 | 164 | 169 |

Audience share of radio channels, 2001 (%)

| Market share | *German-language* | *French-language* | *Italian-language* |
|---|---|---|---|
| SRG SSR channels (24 hours) | 63 | 58 | 80 |
| National commercial stations | 28 | 25 | 5 |
| Foreign stations | 10 | 17 | 15 |

**Electronic media**

| | |
|---|---|
| Internet use, 2001 (% of population) | 57 |
| Source: Wemf. | |

**Advertising spend, 2001 (%)**

| | |
|---|---|
| Newspapers | 53 |
| Magazines | 18 |
| Television | 13 |
| Billboards | 13 |
| Radio | 3 |

**Ownership**

| *Media group* | | *Turnover (SFr million)* | *Work force* |
|---|---|---|---|
| PubliGroupe | (Lausanne) | 2,612 | 3,674 |
| SRG SSR | (Berne) | 1,549 | 5,454 |
| Ringier | (Zürich) | 1,063 | 6,079 |
| Tamedia | (Zürich) | 756 | 1,982 |
| Edipresse | (Lausanne) | 715 | 3,800 |
| NZZ | (Zürich) | 513 | 2,078 |
| Basler Medien | (Basel) | 512 | – |
| Publisuisse | (Berne) | 299 | 89 |
| Espace Media | (Berne) | 260 | 600 |
| AZ Medien | (Baden/Aarau) | 201 | 745 |

Source: *Handelszeitung*, June 2002.

# REFERENCES

Bonfadelli, Heinz (2002) 'Die Medien in der Informationsgesellschaft', in M. Huber *et al.*, *Informationsgesellschaft Schweiz. Standortbestimmung und Perspektiven*. Neuchâtel: Bundesamt für Statistik.

Bundesamt für Kommunikation, *Entwurf des neuen Radio- und Fernsehgesetzes*, http://www.bakom.ch/de/aktuell/revision_rtvg/index.html

Dumermuth, Martin (2001) 'Medienregulierung und öffentlicher Rundfunk. Unter Berücksichtigung der schweizerischen Verhältnisse', in Hanns Abele, Hermann Fünfgeld and Antonio Riva (eds) *Werte und Wert des öffentlich-rechtlichen Rundfunks in der digitalen Zukunft. FAR-Tagung 2000*. Potsdam: Verlag für Berlin-Brandenburg.

SRG SSR, ed. (2001) *Gesamtstrategie der SRG SSR idée suisse 2001–2006*. Berne.

SRG SSR, ed. (2002) *Geschäftsbericht 2001*. Berne.

Schanne, Michael (2001) *Bericht über den gesellschaftlichen Nutzen der SRG SSR idée suisse*. Bern: SRG.

# 23: The United Kingdom

JEREMY TUNSTALL

## NATIONAL PROFILE

In the United Kingdom, geography and population distribution, as well as language, all favour a highly centralized communications system. In 2002 the United Kingdom had a population of 59 million living in 24 million households. By European standards there is a negligible labour force engaged in farming. The population is 90 per cent urbanized and concentrated between London and Manchester. At least 95 per cent of the population speak English as a first language. Among other first languages are Urdu and Welsh.

The United Kingdom's increasingly centralized system of government changed direction after 1997, with Scotland (followed by Wales and Northern Ireland) leading a federalizing trend. In media terms, also, Scotland is the United Kingdom's most distinctive region.

## STRUCTURE AND OWNERSHIP

Gradualism – slow change, continuous evolution and policy consensus – characterized the media until the 1980s. This slow-change, gradualist tradition was in sharp contrast to what occurred in most other West European countries in the same century.

In media policy Britain was a tortoise. In British media history there were very few key dates or key events. A key date for television was 1955; the launch of a new ITV channel, entirely financed by advertising, marked the birth of Britain's BBC and ITV television duopoly. Another key date was

1990, when one of Margaret Thatcher's last exercises of prime ministerial power (like some medieval monarch) was to award Rupert Murdoch an effective monopoly of British satellite television. The setting up in 1955 of ITV as a second television channel established a pattern of gradualism and media policy consensus which lasted for the next three decades, until the mid-1980s. Gradualist policy ensured intervals of a decade or more between new national television channels. BBC television began in 1936 and relaunched in 1946; over the next half-century, new conventional television channels appeared in 1955 (ITV), 1964 (BBC-2), 1982 (Channel 4) and 1997 (Channel 5).

This duopolistic, public service, consensual system was slowly, and adroitly, modified between 1955 and 1982 to introduce another BBC channel and a second advertising-financed channel. BBC-2, launched in 1964, fitted very neatly into the duopoly and resulted in a roughly 40–10–50 audience split, between BBC-1, BBC-2, and ITV.

When Channel 4 was added to this system in 1982, considerable ingenuity was required in order to maintain both public service and financial duopoly. This was achieved, however, by giving Channel 4 a strong 'minority' mission and by sheltering its advertising sales under the wing of the ITV monopoly of television advertising. For several years after 1982, Channel 4's audience remained small, enabling ITV's big advertising revenue to be more than maintained.

A central element of the history of media developments between 1979 and 1990 cencerns Thatcher media problems and Thatcher–Murdoch solutions. Margaret Thatcher won three general elections (1979,

1983 and 1987) and was in power for nearly eleven years. Radical policies were, of course, pursued across a very broad range; media policy attracted only a small proportion of the Prime Minister's policy attention.

During each of her three administrations, when Mrs Thatcher did turn her attention to communications and media issues, the experience was often frustrating. Her policies took effect only slowly and often produced outcomes different from those intended. Mrs Thatcher (in this field as in others) tended to pursue one official Conservative policy line while privately she was trying to push a more radical policy. In this field a problem was that many of her Conservative politicians were torn between free-market conservatism and cultural conservatism; they wanted more competition, but they also wanted to preserve the BBC and public service broadcasting.

The third Thatcher administration (1987–90) saw the publication of a moderately radical 1988 Broadcasting White Paper. 1988 also saw the launch of a heavily regulated direct satellite broadcasting operation, British Satellite Broadcasting (BSB), which moved slowly. Consequently in 1989 (after ten years of Thatcher as Prime Minister) formal media policy had not greatly altered the media scene.

However, there had been some radical changes, associated in particular with Rupert Murdoch. There was a de facto policy of allowing exemptions to the normal anti-monopoly provisions in the case of most proposed newspaper take-overs. Margaret Thatcher took further the existing tendency to transform a press anti-monopoly policy into a newspaper preservation policy. The leading – but not the sole – beneficiary was Rupert Murdoch. The most notorious single case of this occurred in 1981, when Murdoch's British company News International was allowed to purchase *The Times* and the *Sunday Times* from the Thomson company. Margaret Thatcher's admiration for Murdoch increased in 1986 when he moved his two daily and two Sunday national papers to a massive new plant at Wapping in east London. The clash over the move to a high-technology plant marked the defeat of the previously powerful printing unions.

In late 1990 the moderately deregulatory Broadcasting Act was completing its legislative passage. The main target of this official policy was the 'comfortable duopoly' of BBC and ITV/Channel 4. The policy was against excessive trade union power and in favour of 'independent production' (on the existing Channel 4 model). In particular the Broadcasting Act 1990 targeted the ITV channel and its effective monopoly of all television advertising.

But, in addition to this public Conservative policy, there was the private Thatcher policy, which in late 1990 handed a monopoly of direct satellite broadcasting to Murdoch. This latter occurred in late 1990, shortly after the official Broadcasting Act became law and also just before Margaret Thatcher was removed as Prime Minister by the Conservative Party. In the summer of 1990 Britain had two rival direct-to-home satellite television offerings. One was the 'official' system, BSB, licensed by the official regulator and offering expensive programming with expensive technology. The other was Murdoch's Sky system, using a Luxembourg-regulated Astra satellite and offering cheap programming and cheap technology. Both BSB and Sky were losing money at an alarming rate and by October 1990 their plans to merge were being completed. Margaret Thatcher was informed of these plans during a visit by Rupert Murdoch (29 October 1990). She evidently did not object, even though the merged BSkyB was radically at odds with her current 'official' policy of the Broadcasting Act 1990.

The old commercial channel of ITV was the main victim of these combined 1990 public and private Thatcher policies. But Thatcher's public and private decisions - not only in broadcasting, but also in the press – combined to alter the entire UK media system. These continued changes were never articulated in any government document or Thatcher pronouncement.

While competition and deregulation were also the official policy for the press, Thatcher policies in practice favoured concentration. The Murdoch share of UK national newspaper circulation is sometimes exaggerated; if one combines national dailies and national Sundays, the Murdoch share of national newspaper sales per week was 24.7 per cent in 1975, 32.0 per cent in 1985 and 34.5 per cent in 2002.

But it was the combination of major press and television ownership which was so contrary to British tradition, contrary to Thatcher competition rhetoric, and contrary to the Thatcher 1990 Broadcasting Act. As a consequence of the 1990 decisions, Murdoch became not only the biggest owner of national newspapers, but the chief owner of the sole direct satellite television platform and also the dominant supplier of premium content to cable television across Britain.

## The Print media

### The newspaper press

Between 1975 and 2002 national daily newspapers roughly doubled their number of pages, while sales fell from 14 million to 13 million. This can be seen as either a near doubling of sales or as a modest decline. The main newspaper decline has been in local dailies. But in 2001 the United Kingdom had regional paid-for sales of 42 million copies a week; there was also a 30 million circulation of free local weekly papers; and a 5 million weekly circulation of free daily and Sunday papers.

Market leadership is especially rewarding in the newspaper business. The (Murdoch) *Sunday Times*, as the market leader in its sector, can charge premium advertising rates per thousand readers. Some single issues of this paper generate more than £3 million of gross revenue and over £1 million in profit.

There has been increased polarization between down-market tabloid newspapers financed by sales revenue and up-market broadsheet newspapers funded mainly by advertising. It has been the mid-market newspapers (such as the *Daily Express*) which have suffered the biggest sales losses since the 1950s. Competitive marketing expenditure reached new extremes in the early 1990s and led to aggressive price cutting during 1994–5. The price cutting was initiated by News International's *Sun* and *The Times* (down from £0.45 to £0.20). Selective price cutting has continued and has extended into numerous 'special offers' and 'bulk sales'.

The national press in the 1990s became more national, with few full-time staff journalists located outside London. All national dailies now use several printing centres.

Despite the polarization between more national national and more local local newspapers, the total circulation of paid-for and free newspapers remained at around 170 million copies per week in 1975, 1995 and 2002. By 2002 each household was consuming about seven newspapers per week, against the (slightly larger) household of a

decade earlier which had consumed eight papers per week. Less than one-third of national daily sales are subscribed for home delivery; many readers are 'promiscuous' (as the industry says) and buy different dailies on different weekdays.

The British press supposedly engages in 'self-regulation' via the Press Complaints Commission. The PCC is largely ineffectual, not least because it mainly represents the interests and inclinations of newspaper editors and owners. Probably most British politicians would support strong privacy legislation. But no incumbent Prime Minister is willing to risk the inevitably ferocious press resistance which would result. The weakness and frailty of the Press Complaints Commission mirrors (and results from) the strength and political muscle of the press.

### The periodical and magazine press

About half the top fifty consumer periodicals are foreign-owned; a full one-third are IPC magazines, now all owned by AOL Time Warner. German publishers own several others. Britain publishes over 5,000 business and professional magazines but the biggest of these publishers (and a big on-line publisher), *Reed-Elsevier*, is half Netherlands-owned.

### Book publishing

Britain is a significant book publisher and Pearson is the biggest educational book publisher in the United States. But Britain's huge annual book output, of over 110,000 new titles annually, reflects a closely integrated US–UK book business, with many titles published simultaneously in both London and New York. The majority of the larger 'British' book publishers are now American-owned.

## The electronic (audio-visual) media

### Television

As a result mainly of the 1990 decisions, British television grew steadily more competitive through the 1990s. Cable and satellite channels acquired about another 1.5 per cent of UK television audience each year. In seeking to contain the steady competitive growth, the conventional channels became more commercial. The two leading channels (ITV and BBC-1) together still had just over half the total audience in 2001 but both had become overwhelmingly commercial and competitive. The second tier of conventional channels (BBC-2, Channel 4 and, from 1997, Channel 5) were also much more commercially aggressive than either BBC-2 or Channel 4 had been in the 1980s, and attracted 24 per cent of viewers. By 2001 a third tier of cable and satellite channels existed. Each of the seven most successful cable and satellite channels (including Sky One, UK Gold, Sky Sports 1, Carlton Network, Nickelodeon, BBC Choice and Sky Premier) averaged about a 1 per cent share of total UK television viewing. A fourth tier of another eleven channels each had at least a 0.3 per cent share of the television market. These included Living, UK Style, Sky Sports 2, Sky Moviemax, Disney Channel, Discovery, E4, Granada Plus, S4C Wales, Sky News and the Sci-fiction Channel. There are over 150 other television channels, each with an audience share of, at most, 0.2 per cent.

The entire UK satellite and cable industry is foreign and US-controlled. The principal shareholder (and the management operator) of BSkyB has been the (Murdoch) News International company. The two remaining UK cable companies of the early 2000s were *Telewest* (US-controlled) and *NTL* (US-managed with major French and other foreign investment). Not surprisingly the bulk of all programming available on satellite and on cable was American movies, American series and scores of entire American niche channels.

ITV and BBC-1 entertainment programming in general – especially the early evening and now four-days-a-week super-British soap operas – dominated the UK ratings to an even greater degree than had the soaps in previous decades. Typically three early evening soaps (*EastEnders, Coronation Street, Emmerdale*) achieved about twelve of the top fifteen television ratings each week. On these major channels US imports were scheduled only at lower audience times. But BBC-2 and Channels 4 and 5 carried more US programming, including currently fashionable US comedies seen as part of the channel's 'brand image'. Channel 5 (with 6 per cent of the television audience in 2001–2) shows hundreds of Hollywood films (both theatrical and television) each year. The lower a channel's total audience, the more American programming it carried.

British television in the 1990s became more commercial in several other ways. There were more advertising minutes, more commercial sponsorship of programming and more promotional plugging of the channel's offerings. A larger proportion of

the money was paid out to star on-screen performers. Differentials between the high-paid and low-paid increased dramatically. The trade press (*Broadcast*) began to publish an annual 'Rich List'. Ever larger proportions of programming were produced by small independent companies, which lacked any professional security; most such companies had little chance of retaining the foreign rights in their own productions. The story of British digital television is told later in the chapter.

Regarding local television, the main providers have been the regional ITV companies. Some provide several different half-hour daily news shows in one region. These local offerings each average some 350 hours per year, with a total of 10,000 local ITV hours. The BBC does some 5,000 television hours in Scotland, Wales and Northern Ireland and in its three English regions. Meanwhile Channel 4 in Wales transmits another 1,650 hours of Welsh-language programming to a core audience of about 150,000 Welsh-speaking people, mainly in central inland Wales. This annual output of over 16,000 hours of non-national television is seen by audiences most of which number between 30,000 and 300,000 people; it is an important example of 'public service' in British television.

### Radio

In radio a compromise, or division of labour, has been arrived at by which the BBC specializes in national radio and has the cream of the national FM frequencies. Meanwhile, although there are three national commercial channels, only one (Classic FM) is on FM. The main local radio provision comes from 254 local commercial radio stations.

Four groups have become dominant in commercial radio: Capital, GWR, EMAP and Scottish Radio. These, along with six other groups, owned nearly all UK commercial radio. In audience terms, BBC radio held a 53 per cent share and commercial radio 45 per cent (see statistics section below).

### Film and video

Britain has a film industry which concentrates on two types of output. First Hollywood makes a few big budget 'movies' in Britain each year, often based on British books (including children's books) and using mainly British personnel; secondly there are low-budget British 'films', which often depend on television finance (Channel 4 and BBC). Overall Britain is a film importer, owing not least to BSkyB's heavy use of Hollywood product on its movie channels.

## The Internet and related on-line media

All of the major newspaper groups and the main television channels, especially the BBC, are active competitors in the Internet business. The proportion of UK homes with Internet access has increased rapidly, from 29 per cent at the end of 2000 to 45 per cent at the end of 2001. The BBC's Internet site, www.bbc.co.uk, claimed to be 'Europe's leading content site' (combined with the BBC World Service), had 614 million page impressions in the month of March 2002.

# POLITICS, POLICY, LAW AND REGULATION

Both before and since 1990 the United Kingdom's media successes have mostly been in sectors where there was little or no government policy involvement. The United Kingdom was successful in advertising, in music (although less so than before 1990) and in news agencies (Reuters). Video games were the main UK video export success (while the United Kingdom became a big net importer of television programming). The United Kingdom was also a European leader in the introduction of DVD (as it had been with VHS video equipment) and the Internet.

But in media sectors where government policy was active the story was mostly of failure. Britain became more dependent on the United States and also achieved little in Europe. The United Kingdom has failed to generate an adequately professional group of media regulators and policy specialists. In 1982–3, when this writer began to seek out UK media regulators and civil servants, there was much enthusiasm for, but almost no knowledge of, what the United States did. Senior people in London knew nothing about the FCC and had not heard of the MPAA (the Hollywood exporters) or John Malone (already the Denver-based King of Cable). Two decades later, regulator knowledge of US media policy had improved, but not enough.

The Independent Television Commission (ITC) was always chaired by educators or business people from non-media fields. Sir John Biggam, just appointed as ITC chairman in 1996, told a *Broadcast* journalist (6 December 1996) that his television viewing was restricted to news and documentaries: 'After that I fall asleep'.

Politicians also often have no previous media knowledge or experience before being put in charge of national media policy. Tessa Jowell was appointed Secretary of State for Culture, Media and Sport in 1999. Her professional and political background was in social work and health; she had had no previous involvement in culture, the media or sport. Unfortunately this somewhat amateurish approach is found also among the civil servants and some of the politicians on the relevant House of Commons select committee.

## The press

National newspapers dominate the UK media policy agenda. Eight separate companies own nationally distributed daily newspapers; these newspapers have enormous political power and they dominate not only the making of (or lack of) newspaper policy but also the making of broadcasting policy. This is not new. John Reith, who ran the BBC during 1922–38, was always acutely anxious about possible newspaper displeasure.

Newspaper power over media policy has, however, increased for two very simple reasons. Firstly, communications and media policy has become much more salient since the end of broadcasting and telecommunications monopoly. These policy areas are now much more commercially driven, more international and more political. Secondly, the newspaper press in recent decades has become less deferential, more aggressive, more tabloid, and more active in pursuing its own political and commercial agendas. British politicians go in fear of the press for very good reason; when the national press smells political blood, it can and does behave in a merciless manner. All politicians have seen other politicians' careers destroyed by the newspapers. Incumbent Prime Ministers (especially since the press-assisted political demise of Mrs Thatcher in 1990) have been especially sensitive to potential press displeasure. Tony Blair from 1997 onwards, for example, allowed anti-Europe newspapers to veto UK membership of the euro currency.

Of the eight national daily ownerships, Rupert Murdoch was the most salient.

Murdoch had career-long experience of 'persuading' anxious politicians. His UK properties included both *The Times* and *Sunday Times* and the two most Rottweiler tabloids (the daily *Sun* and Sunday *News of the World*). But three other ownerships were collectively probably even more politically potent than Murdoch. These were the *Daily Mail* mid-market group, the Hollinger/*Daily Telegraph* group (controlled by Canadian-born Conrad Black) and the Trinity Mirror group (*Daily Mirror* and a big slice of non-national newspapers).

Under British conditions, the Prime Minister often intervenes in media policy, and much of this intervention takes the form of face-to-face meetings between Prime Minister and press owner (meetings to which the Culture and Media Minister is often not invited). If all four of the leading newspaper groups want something, they will probably get it. All the other leading press groups supported Murdoch in the 1980s, especially in his anti-union struggles. When three of the four groups opposed UK euro entry in the 1990s, they also prevailed.

The four lesser newspaper groups are also not insignificant makers of media policy, and all by 2002 had their own wider media properties. The *Daily Express* ownership, in addition to owning the tabloid *Daily Star*, was financially dependent on a large collection of pornographic magazines. The *Independent* was part of a much bigger media group, controlled by the Dublin-based Tony O'Reilly (a former CEO of the Heinz food company). The *Financial Times* was part of the Pearson media company. Even *The Guardian* had substantial other print and commercial radio properties. Because newspaper editors now behave in a more entrepreneurial manner, they oversee and influence the news reporting of 'our media correspondent'. Consequently no national daily can convincingly claim neutrality or objectivity in its reporting of media business and policy issues.

The Internet has further increased newspaper involvement (and hence bias) in media business policy. As noted above, all the major newspaper groups and the main television channels (and especially the BBC) are active competitors in the Internet business. This media business involvement and commercial interest combine unhappily with the continuing inexperience and weakness of media regulators and government policy making.

## The electronic media

The Broadcasting Acts of 1990 and 1996 have allowed the big to get somewhat bigger. The 1996 Act covered 194 pages, and both the 1990 and 1996 Acts included much detail. But both Acts largely ignored the BBC (which is separately covered under a legislative oddity, a 'royal charter'). Both Acts also largely (but not entirely) ignored the Murdoch Sky operations. In 1990 this was because the Sky take-over of BSB had not yet (quite) happened. By 1996 BSkyB was subject only to super-light regulation from both Luxembourg and London. Mrs Thatcher's legal exemption developed into exemption for BSkyB from most regulation.

There was some gradual regulatory creep from 1990 until 2002–3. Some of the main 1990 and 1996 Acts' main provisions were as follows:

1  The Independent Television Commission in 1991 took over regulation of television (from the IBA) and also the regulation of cable and satellite. Radio went to a separate Radio Authority.
2  Previous to 1990 the single ITV channel was operated in fourteen areas by seventeen separate companies. This fragmented structure was allowed to merge into three main companies and then into just two (Granada and Carlton).
3  Newspaper groups with less than 20 per cent of national daily sales (and thus not News International or Trinity Mirror) could now own television companies.
4  Provincial newspaper groups were encouraged to merge, which eventually led to three main combines: Trinity-Mirror, Northcliffe/Daily Mail and Newsquest (later Gannett). Local newspapers were also encouraged to buy into local radio and television.
5  Each commercial radio group was in 1996 allowed to control up to 15 per cent of all radio advertising. As noted above, this allowed four groups to become dominant. These four plus another six groups owned nearly all of UK commercial radio.
6  Channel 4 was, in 1990, relieved of its requirement to share advertising profits

with ITV. Channel 4 subsequently increased its share of television advertising.

7 Channel 5 was eventually launched in 1997. When Pearson later withdrew from the consortium, Channel 5 was majority-controlled by the German Bertelsmann and its associate companies.

Recent governments have continued to proclaim the need to maintain 'Britain as a world media power'; but these same governments have also continued to exhibit a weak grasp of new technologies and commercial realities in general, and of the media in the United States in particular. The question to be asked is, is Britain a world media power or a US media dependency?

British media companies own few media properties in continental Europe, although the magazine publisher *EMAP* is strong in France. There is more French and German ownership in Britain than the other way around. French investors have been significant both in British cable and in BSkyB. The German Bertelsmann-CLT-UFA has a controlling interest in the UK's Channel 5.

Most UK international media activity, however, involves the United States. Britain's main world media presence is in news (Reuters, *Financial Times*, *The Economist* and the BBC). The WPP advertising group owns three of the largest US agencies (J. Walter Thompson, Ogilvy & Mather, Young & Rubicam). *Vodafone* also claims to be (with partners) the world's largest mobile phone operator. But all these activities (big in the world and big inside the United States) could come under US ownership in the future.

As noted above, in three media areas – film, periodicals and books – the British industry follows an almost Canadian pattern of being significantly incorporated into the US industry. Furthermore, the UK satellite and cable industry is foreign and US-controlled, and their programming is dominated by American movies and series. In commercial radio, by 2002 Clear Channel, the largest owner of American radio stations, was already a significant force in outdoor advertising and in the music business in Britain.

In the printed press North American influences were also extremely strong.

Companies controlled by Rupert Murdoch and (Canadian-born) Conrad Black had over 60 per cent of UK up-market daily newspaper sales (*The Times* and *Daily Telegraph*), which they used ruthlessly to support their Anglo-American interests and to oppose British involvement in Europe. The US-based Gannett newspaper giant also entered the UK market in 1999 and became the second largest owner of British regional newspapers, with some 14 per cent of non-national newspaper circulation.

The BBC remains Britain's only real media world leader – and this leadership is in the diminished field of 'public service broadcasting'. In the late 1990s and early 2000s the BBC did well, because its licence fee income was assured and inflation-proofed (until 2006). The BBC (unlike ITV) seemed quite well suited to the multi-channel era. The BBC in 2001–2 had two conventional television networks, four new niche BBC networks (such as BBC Choice and BBC News 24) and six 'UK' networks (such as UK Gold and UK Horizon) jointly owned with Flextech. The BBC had yet other partnerships (especially with Discovery); and BBC On-line also was vigorously developed. Including its five national radio networks, the BBC had some twenty separate television, on-line and radio national services; multiple cross-promotion between these twenty services could be aggressively pursued, not least because BBC output was not already cluttered up with commercial advertising.

Digital television attracted the usual British vague, warm feelings about exciting new technologies. Since BSkyB and cable were both heading for digital, the Labour government was attracted by the third option of DTT – digital terrestrial television. For a relatively modest extra household expenditure, DTT made possible reception of about thirty basic and premium television channels with a regular television set (and without a dish antenna). This might appeal to consumers as a slightly cheaper way of getting twenty-plus (but not 100-plus) extra channels. It appealed to the government as a 'platform' which could deliver the BBC's traditional channels and thus eventually free up the analogue spectrum for other uses (and government income).

But digital terrestrial television, launched in late 1998, lurched into financial disaster in 2001–2. DTT failed to navigate around the classic television start-up problems of unreliable new technology, costly programming, few customers and little revenue. By early 2002 the DTT offering (originally *ON-Digital*, later ITV *Digital*) was running third in a three-horse race. As so often with UK government media initiatives, responsibility and policy planning were hopelessly split, fragmented and lacking in commercial and technological realism.

The Independent Television Commission (ITC) once again made a disastrous key decision and demonstrated its traditional lack of commercial, technological and American insight. In the late 1990s it was the ITC which meekly accepted Brussels advice that BSkyB should withdraw from its early (one-third) involvement in the digital terrestrial enterprise. This insistence was self-defeating, because a digital terrestrial offering solely from ITV had no answer to a probable Murdoch all-out BSkyB *Blitzkrieg* attack. In seeking to persuade their existing satellite analogue customers to switch to digital, BSkyB (after some hesitation) made a big investment in an offer – a free set-top box – which customers could scarcely refuse. Fifteen months after the digital terrestrial launch, ITV Digital (as it became) in January 2000 had 550,000 subscribers, whereas BSkyB had 2 million digital satellite households. ITV Digital did struggle on for another two years, before collapsing into bankruptcy in April 2002; at this point of collapse, the three services were as follows:

1　The terrestrial service, ITV Digital, was in about 1 million homes with a basic tier of twelve channels and a total of thirty two channels, including premium film and sports channels. Both the transmitter system and the set-top boxes were inadequate; television pictures were unreliable and the 'churn' rate (de-subscribing) was high.

2　Digital cable was available from Telewest and NTL and was in 2 million homes. Telewest offered a basic tier of nineteen channels and a total (including pay-per-view) of ninety five channels; this included much of Sky's sport and film offerings. Both Telewest and NTL were thus beholden to Sky; both also obtained more revenue from their telephone, than from their cable television, services. Both developed a 'triple play' of television, telephone, and Internet/e-mail.

3　BSkyB's digital satellite service was now in nearly 6 million homes. It offered some 150 television channels (including fifteen movie channels, five sports, nine children's). Sky offered 'interactive' alternatives (for example, within major sports tournaments) and choices of start times. Sky's service offered much of the same range as contemporary US high-capacity systems, offering seven Discovery channels and seven separate MTV and VH1 Viacom channels. Compared with both cable and DTT, Sky offered more choices, better reliability and more efficient home service visits. Consequently it had a remarkably low 'churn' rate.

After the collapse of ITV Digital in April 2002, the responsibility for relaunching a digital terrestrial service was awarded to a BBC-led consortium.

A new Communications Bill was brought forward in 2002. The main provision of this Communications Act was to merge the ITC commercial television (and cable/satellite) regulator with the telecommunications regulator (OFTEL); the new grand regulator, OFCOM (Office of Communications) was also to swallow three other regulators – the Broadcasting Standards Commission, the Radio Authority and the Radio Communications Agency (the spectrum allocator).

The broad thrust of the 2002–3 policy was to take further the regulatory loosening of 1990 and 1996. The political thrust of the Blair government was both to protect the BBC (to satisfy Labour Party and educated elite fears) and also to calm Murdoch/News International/BSkyB anxieties. Cross-media ownership rules would be relaxed sufficiently to allow Murdoch/News International to (perhaps) buy Channel 5, but not sufficiently to buy ITV. Commercial television and radio could now be owned by US or any other foreign companies. 'Spectrum trading' would also be allowed.

The 2002 Bill outlined a complex structure for OFCOM's 'lighter' regulatory regime. There would still be quite different levels of regulation. The conventional commercial television channels (ITV, Channel 4, Channel 5) would be the most severely held to their remaining public service elements. The BBC would be left mainly to its traditional

BBC Governors' regime, with some OFCOM oversight. Satellite and cable would continue to be largely unregulated. Newspapers would continue to be almost completely unregulated.

Although the draft Communications Bill (and accompanying papers) ran to 500 pages, much of this focused on telecommunications regulation issues. On the bigger, and longer-term, media issues the three familiar weaknesses were still present: naive technological assumptions (such as analogue switch-off by 2006–10); lack of understanding of, or interest in, the future strategies of major US media players; lack of interest in major commercial trends and revenue sources.

The various media policy decisions of 2002 were widely seen as further assisting recent success at the BBC and BSkyB while further penalizing conventional advertising-funded television – ITV and Channels 4 and 5. The loose alliance between the BBC and BSkyB became especially noticeable in the reallocation of the digital terrestrial platform; DTT was to be BBC-led with the BBC providing the biggest batch of channels (nine out of twenty four). BSkyB was also a winner here, because it was in partnership with the BBC but was not contributing any of its (Sky's) more popular channels. The conventional commercial channels were the losers (their main DTT presence consisting merely of their main conventional channels). Clearly the digital terrestrial platform was not going to have much of an impact on future overall competition.

Regarding the future, it might be reasonably argued that, towards 2008–10, the television audience will be split into three roughly equal segments. Probably each of the three (BBC, satellite and cable, and ITV/Channel 4/Channel 5) will have an audience share of about 30–5 per cent. Satellite and cable had such a rapid growth in audience share before and after the year 2000 that their combined share by 2008 is unlikely to be below 30 per cent. Both cable and BSkyB will grow substantially, although both will focus on improving revenue and not just boosting subscriber numbers.

While ITV and Channels 4 and 5 were the clear losers in the early 2000s, this does not mean that they will shrivel away. On the contrary, they will certainly 'fight back' very aggressively indeed and they will continue to be funded by large (and growing) advertising

expenditure. These three will be fierce competitors both against each other and against the subscription and licence-financed players. Their increased competitive drive for advertising revenue will be a major contribution to an overall more commercially competitive system.

The BBC's audience share by 2008 could be between 30 per cent and 35 per cent. The BBC also will fight fiercely, although the conventional BBC-1 and BBC-2 will probably continue to account for nine-tenths of the BBC's television audience share.

Effectively the 2002–3 decisions confirmed new definitions of 'public service' and of the hierarchical 'brow levels' of British broadcasting. The new definition is as follows:

1 *Lowbrow/mass audience*: BBC-1, ITV, Channel 5, Sky One and most of the scores of themed satellite/cable offerings.
2 *Middlebrow/youth audience*: BBC-2, Channel 4 and a few basic (and pay) satellite/cable themed channels.
3 *Surviving public service*: digital terrestrial in general and the BBC (and 'UK') digital channels in particular.

Some other surviving public service elements will be found (such as the main evening news) on BBC-1. But a public/educational/serious factual service will mainly be found on the BBC digital channels and on a very few highbrow pay channels. This will loosely parallel the US pattern of PBS and a few up-market commercial cable channels.

The new (and supposedly more commercially minded) BBC is in fact highly risk-averse and will remain so. The BBC's idea of a big risk is a new digital channel costing £50 million; the BBC cannot behave like BSkyB, which invested some £2 billion in switching to digital and giving away set-top boxes. BBC television will focus on maintaining the early 2000s pattern, by which British programming dominated the evening peak hours on BBC-1 and BBC-2. ITV, Channel 4 and Channel 5 will do the same. But this British peak-time programming will become more expensive to produce as increased competition drives up the price of popular talent. (The BBC will, of course, endlessly repeat its more expensive programming on its small digital channels).

In late 2002 the BBC was awarded (by the dying ITC) the lead role in a relaunched digital terrestrial television service, now renamed Freeview; it's 'free' when you buy a cheap (£100) new set-top box. Freeview's thirty channels avoid entertainment, fiction and sport, but instead focus on twenty four-hour news channels, culture and history, new BBC children's channels and several of Sky's less popular offerings (BSkyB and Crown Castle are partners with the BBC). Freeview's lead offering is some ten BBC and 'UK' channels; this helps to solve the BBC's problem of making its new digital channels more widely available. People who want more news and factual channels will accept this cheap and non-commercial offer, but the national reach is less than 100 per cent of the United Kingdom. Freeview is unlikely

to add more than 1 per cent on 2 per cent to the BBC's total television audience share. Nearly all the BBC's total audience share will still be achieved by BBC-1 and BBC-2, which will still be accused of 'commercialism' funded by the licence fee.

The BBC will certainly survive beyond the year 2010. But both the BBC and British television will have absorbed additional doses of American material and influences. With so much cash going into peak-time British programming, there will be an irresistible urge to put yet more cheap US material into 'fringe' time (early evening and late night) and into daytime. Also by 2009–10 the BBC will be asking, yet again, whether it can survive solely on a licence fee which represents a still dwindling share of total broadcast expenditure.

It is also highly probable that American ownership will have spread from satellite and cable into one or more of ITV and Channels 4 and 5.

# STATISTICS

| National population, 2002 | 59,000,000 |
|---|---|
| Number of households | 24,000,000 |
| Overall movie admissions | |
| 1999 | 139,000,000 |
| 2001 | 156,000,000 |
| Books published, 2000 (new titles) | 116,415 |

**Print media**  Sales of national daily newspapers, February

| | 1997 | 2002 |
|---|---|---|
| Sun | 3,929,000 | 3,440,000 |
| Mirror/Record | 3,097,000 | 2,714,000 |
| Daily Star | 755,000 | 744,000 |
| Total down-market | 7,781,000 | 6,898,000 |
| Daily Mail | 2,156,000 | 2,403,000 |
| Daily Express | 1,234,000 | 924,000 |
| Total mid-market | 3,390,000 | 3,327,000 |
| Times | 768,000 | 714,000 |
| Daily Telegraph | 1,120,000 | 1,001,000 |
| Guardian | 400,000 | 400,000 |
| Independent | 258,000 | 225,000 |
| Financial Times | 306,000 | 488,000 |
| Total up-market | 2,852,000 | 2,828,000 |
| Overall total | 14,204,000 | 13,053,000 |

Circulation of larger regional daily newspapers, July–December 2001 (daily sale)

| | |
|---|---|
| London *Evening Standard* (p.m.) | 402,223 |
| *West Midlands Express and Star* (p.m.) | 172,476 |
| *Manchester Evening News* (p.m.) | 164,237 |
| *Liverpool Echo* (p.m.) | 146,656 |
| *Birmingham Evening Mail* (p.m.) | 121,159 |

**Broadcast media**

Audience share of television channels (%)

| | 2001 | 2002 (first half) |
|---|---|---|
| BBC-1 | 26.9 | 26.2 |
| BBC-2 | 11.1 | 11.2 |
| ITV | 26.8 | 24.6 |
| Channel 4 | 10.0 | 9.8 |
| Channel 5 | 5.7 | 6.4 |
| Other (Cable, Satellite, RTE) | 19.7 | 21.7 |

Audience share of main radio channels, January–March 2002 (%)

| | |
|---|---|
| BBC Radio 1 | 8.4 |
| BBC Radio 2 | 15.7 |
| BBC Radio 3 | 1.2 |
| BBC Radio 4 | 11.4 |
| BBC Radio 5 | 4.5 |
| BBC Local/regional | 11.4 |
| Total BBC | 52.6 |
| National commercial (three) | 7.7 |
| Local commercial (254) | 37.7 |
| Total commercial | 45.4 |
| Other listening | 1.9 |
| Overall total | 100 |

Source: Rajar.

Percentage of households (April 2002) with:

| | |
|---|---|
| Satellite television (BSkyB) | 25 |
| Terrestrial digital television | 4.2 |
| Cable television | 15.4 |
| Digital television by any means | 37 |

Percentage of households with:

| | 2000 | (late) 2001 |
|---|---|---|
| video-cassette recorder | 87 | 82 |
| DVD player | | 17 |
| Satellite receiver | 17 | 24 |

**Electronic media**

Percentage of homes with:

Internet access

| | |
|---|---|
| November 2000 | 29 |
| November 2001 | 45 |

Mobile telephones

By May 2001 70% of homes had at least one mobile telephone.

| | | |
|---|---|---|
| **Advertising spend, 2001** | National newspapers | 12.5 |
| | Regional newspapers | 17.1 |
| | Consumer magazines | 4.7 |
| | Business and professional magazines | 7.3 |
| | Directories | 5.8 |
| | Press production costs | 4.0 |
| | Total press | 51.5 |
| | Television | 25.1 |
| | Direct mail | 13.5 |
| | Outdoor and transport | 4.8 |
| | Radio | 3.3 |
| | Cinema | 1.0 |
| | Internet | 1.0 |
| | Total | 100.0 |
| | Total expenditure at current prices | £16.55 billion |
| | At constant (1995 = 100) prices | 129.2 |
| | Source: Advertising Association. | |

**Ownership**

Largest media companies, 2001–2 (%)

| | Share of national daily press circulation | Share of regional press circulation | Share of total television audience time |
|---|---|---|---|
| News International and BSkyB (Murdoch) | 34.5 | — | 6.1[a] |
| Trinity Mirror | 19.0 | 25 | — |
| Daily Mail | 19.0 | 21 | — |
| BBC | — | — | 39 |

[a]Arguably this figure is too high because News Corp owned only 36.3% of BSkyB.

273

# REFERENCES

BBC (annual) *Report and Accounts*.

Briggs, A. (1995) *The History of Broadcasting in the United Kingdom V, Competition, 1955–74*. Oxford: Oxford University Press.

Collins, R. and Murroni, C. (1996) *New Media, New Policies*. Oxford: Polity Press.

Compaine, B. and Gomery, D. (2002) *Who owns the Media? Competition and Concentration in the Mass Media Industry*. Mahwah NJ: Erlbaum.

Congdon, T., Graham, A., Green, D. and Robinson, B. (1995) *The Cross-media Revolution: Ownership and Control*. London: Libbey.

Franklin, B., ed. (2001) *British Television Policy: a Reader*. London: Routledge.

Goodwin, P. (1998), *Television under The Tories: Broadcasting Policy, 1979–1997*. London: British Film Institute.

Graham, A., ed. (1999) *Public Purposes in Broadcasting: Funding the* BBC. Luton: University of Luton Press.

Graham, A. and Davies, G. (1997), *Broadcasting, Society and Policy in the Multi-media Age*. Luton: University of Luton Press.

Hargreaves, I. (1992) 'A facelift for Auntie', *Financial Times*, 25 November.

Horsman, M. (1997) Sky *High: the Inside Story of* BSkyB. London: Orion.

Hughes, J. et al. (2000) *e-Britannia: the Communications Revolution*. Luton: University of Luton Press.

Independent Television Commission (annual) *Report and Accounts*.

Iosifides, P. (1999) 'Diversity versus concentration in the deregulated mass media domain', *Journalism and Mass Communication Quarterly* 76(5): 152–62.

O'Connor, A. (2002), 'Media Bill heralds TV free-for-all', *Financial Times*, 8 May.

Palmer, M. and Tunstall, J. (1990) *Liberating Communications: Policymaking in France and Britain*. Oxford: Blackwell.

Paterson, R. (2001) 'The television labour market in Britain', in J. Tunstall (ed.) *Media Occupations and Professions*. Oxford: Oxford University Press.

Peak, S. and Fisher, P. (annual) *The Guardian Media Guide*. London: The Guardian.

Tumber, H., ed. (2000) *Media Power, Professionals and Policies*. London: Routledge.

Tunstall, J. (1986) *Communications Deregulation: the Unleashing of America's Communications Industry*. Oxford: Blackwell.

Tunstall, J. (1996) *Newspaper Power*. Oxford: Oxford University Press.

Tunstall, J. and Machin, D. (1999) *The Anglo-American Media Connection*. Oxford: Oxford University Press.

Tunstall, J. and Palmer, M. (1991) *Media Moguls*. London: Routledge.

WPP (annual) *Report and Accounts*. London: WPP.

## Government publications

Davies, G., chairman (1999) *The Future Funding of the BBC*. London: Department of Culture, Media and Sport.

Department of Trade and Industry, and Department of Culture, Media and Sport (1998) *Regulating Communications: Approaching Convergence in the Digital Age*. London: HMSO.

Department of Trade and Industry, and Department of Culture, Media and Sport (2000) *A New Future for Communications*. London: HMSO.

Department of Trade and Industry, and Department of Culture, Media and Sport (2002) Draft Communications Bill.

Home Office (1981) *Direct Broadcasting by Satellite*. London: HMSO.

Hunt, Lord, chairman (1982) *Report of the Inquiry into Cable Expansion and Broadcasting Policy*. London: HMSO.

Peacock, A., chairman (1986) *Report of the Committee on Financing the* BBC. London: HMSO.